SOLUTIONS MANUAL

FINANCIAL ACCOUNTING
AN INTRODUCTION TO CONCEPTS, METHODS, AND USES

EIGHTH EDITION

CLYDE P. STICKNEY
Dartmouth College

ROMAN L. WEIL
University of Chicago

THE DRYDEN PRESS
Harcourt Brace College Publishers

Fort Worth Philadelphia San Diego New York Orlando Austin San Antonio
Toronto Montreal London Sydney Tokyo

Address for orders:
The Dryden Press
6277 Sea Harbor Drive
Orlando, FL 32887-6777
1-800-782-4479, or 1-800-433-0001 (in Florida)

Address for editorial correspondence:
The Dryden Press
301 Commerce Street, Suite 3700
Fort Worth, TX 76102

ISBN: 0-03-018274-3

Printed in the United States of America

7 8 9 0 1 2 3 4 5   0 2 3   9 8 7 6 5 4 3 2

The Dryden Press
Harcourt Brace College Publishers

CONTENTS

PREFACE

This book presents answers and solutions for the questions, exercises, problems and cases contained in each chapter of the textbook *Financial Accounting: An Introduction to Concepts, Methods and Uses* Eighth Edition.

If you have any suggestions as to how this book might be improved in subsequent editions, please feel free to bring them to our attention.

C.P.S.

R.L.W.

CHAPTER 1

INTRODUCTION TO BUSINESS ACTIVITIES AND OVERVIEW OF FINANCIAL STATEMENTS AND THE REPORTING PROCESS

Questions, Exercises, Problems, and Cases: Answers and Solutions

1.1   The first question at the end of each chapter requires the student to review the important concepts or terms discussed in the chapter. In addition to the definitions or descriptions in the chapter, a glossary appears at the end of the book.

1.2   *Setting Goals and Strategies*: A charitable organization would not pursue profit or increasing wealth as goals. Instead, it would direct its efforts at providing some type of service to particular constituencies.

   Financing: Charitable organizations generally obtain the majority of their financing from contributions, although they may engage in borrowing in some situations. Charitable organizations do not issue common stock or other forms of owners' equity. Because they do not operate for a profit, charitable organizations do not have retained earnings.

   Investing: Charitable organizations may acquire supplies, buildings, equipment and other assets to carry out their charitable activities.

   Operations: A charitable organization might prepare a financial statement each period that compares contributions received with operating expenses. Although such a financial statement might resemble an income statement, the organization would probably not label the difference between contributions received and operating expenses as net income or net loss.

1.3   A balance sheet reports the assets, liabilities, and shareholders' equity of a firm at a moment in time (similar to a snapshot), whereas the income statement and statement of cash flows report amounts for a period of time (similar to a motion picture).

1.4 Revenues measure the increase in net assets (assets minus liabilities) and expenses measure the decrease in net assets from selling goods and providing services. An asset such as inventory generally appears on the balance sheet at acquisition cost while it is held. Thus, the asset valuation remains the same and the firm recognizes no revenue. When the firm sells the inventory, the inventory item leaves the firm and cash or a receivable from a customer comes in. If more assets flow in than flow out, total assets increase and the firm recognizes income (revenue minus expense).

1.5 As Chapter 3 makes clear, firms do not necessarily recognize revenues when they receive cash or recognize expenses when they disburse cash. Thus, net income will not necessarily equal cash flow from operations each period. Furthermore, firms disburse cash to acquire property, plant and equipment, repay debt, and pay dividends. Thus, net income and cash flows usually differ. A profitable firm will likely borrow funds in order to remain in business, but eventually operations must generate cash to repay the borrowing.

1.6 No. The unqualified opinion of the CPA indicates that the presentation is a fair reflection of the financial position and operating results of the firm. Because the accountant bases this opinion on an audit of only a portion of the transactions occurring during the year, the CPA does not vouch for the absolute accuracy of every item in the financial statements. The unqualified opinion has evolved to mean, however, that the firm has made sufficient disclosures in the statements so they are not misleading. This interpretation of the unqualified opinion suggests that the statements are free of gross misrepresentations. In court suits against the independent accountants, where courts have found gross misrepresentation to exist, the principal issue is whether the CPA had reasonable grounds (based on audit tests) to believe that the statements were fairly presented at the time the accountant issued the unqualified opinion.

1.7 A wide range of individuals and entities (creditors, investors, security analysts, governmental agencies) use financial accounting reports for a broad range of purposes. If each firm selected whatever format and content of financial reports it deemed best, the resulting reporting process would probably be incomprehensible to many users. Accounting reports generated for internal management purposes, on the other hand, satisfy the information needs of a more limited set of users. Standardization is, therefore, not as necessary.

1.8 **Advantages**

   1. Government authorities can enforce their pronouncements by law.

   2. Firms need maintain only one set of accounting records that serves the needs of both financial and tax reporting.

1.8 continued.

3. Greater uniformity in accounting methods across firms likely results because firms either use the methods prescribed for tax purposes or, where there is a choice of several alternative methods for a particular item, use the method that minimizes the present value of tax payments.

Disadvantages

1. The objectives in setting accounting methods for tax purposes (raising tax revenues) may differ from the objectives for financial reporting (measuring financial position and result of operations).

2. Individuals in the government responsible for setting accounting methods may not have the necessary technical expertise or financial statement user perspective.

3. Political lobbying could dominate the standard-setting process.

1.9 The accounting method would be uniform but the resulting information in the financial statements may not provide uniform measures of financial position or results of operations. If the economic characteristics of firms' activities differ, then different accounting methods may be needed to reflect these differences.

1.10 Accounting standards set in the public sector (that is, by a government agency) become subject to political pressures inherent in a democratic system. Accounting standards set in the private sector become subject to political pressures of various preparer and user groups. Because accounting standards set in the private sector have no enforcement power on their own, private-sector standard-setting bodies must respond to these political pressures by gaining acceptance for their standards.

1.11 We would disagree. Within capital market settings, someone must analyze and interpret financial accounting reports if market prices are to incorporate information from those reports. The principal message of efficient market research is that digestion of such information occurs very quickly. In addition, there are many users and uses of financial accounting reports outside of a capital market setting (lending, antitrust regulation, competitor analysis).

1.12 (Preparing a personal balance sheet.)

There is no distinction between contributed capital and retained earnings, because an individual does not issue common stock. The excess of assets over liabilities is called an individual's *net worth*. The methods used in valuing an individual's assets and liabilities are critical variables in determining net worth. Possibilities include acquisition cost, current replacement cost, current selling price, and others.

 Solutions

1.13   (Classifying financial statement accounts.)

    a. NA.

    b. NI (revenue).

    c. CC.

    d. X.

    e. NA.

    f. CA.

    g. X (a footnote to the balance sheet would probably disclose the lawsuit).

    h. NI (expense).

    i. CA.

    j. CL.

    k. X (not recognized as a gain until the firm sells the land).

    l. X (firms report dividends on the statement of retained earnings).

    m. CL.

    n. NL.

1.14   (Georgia-Pacific Corporation; balance sheet relations.)

    a. The following equation characterizes the balance sheet:

$$\text{Current Assets} + \text{Noncurrent Assets} = \text{Current Liabilities} + \text{Noncurrent Liabilities} + \text{Shareholders' Equity}$$

$$\text{Total Assets} = \text{Total Liabilities} + \text{Shareholders' Equity}$$

The missing information is (amounts in millions):

Year 8

Shareholders' Equity	$2,635
Total Assets	7,115
Total Liabilities and Shareholders' Equity	7,115

1.14 a. continued.

Year 9

Total Assets	$7,056
Current Assets	1,829
Noncurrent Liabilities	3,415

Year 10

Current Liabilities	$2,535
Current Assets	1,766
Noncurrent Liabilities	6,550
Total Liabilities and Shareholders' Equity	12,060

Year 11

Noncurrent Assets	$9,060
Total Assets	10,622
Current Liabilities	2,722
Current Assets	1,562

b. Noncurrent assets increased as a proportion of total assets, suggesting major new investments in property, plant, and equipment or the acquisition of a firm with heavy investments in property, plant and equipment. The latter is the actual explanation in that Georgia-Pacific Corporation acquired Great Northern Nekoosa Corporation, a pulp and paper manufacturer.

c. The proportion of liabilities (both current and noncurrent) increased while the proportion of shareholders' equity decreased. Georgia-Pacific Corporation used debt to finance the acquisition of Great Northern Nekoosa.

d. The acquisition of Great Northern Nekoosa Corporation.

e. Possible explanations include:

(1) The sale of a portion of the assets acquired from Great Northern Nekoosa Corporation and the reduction in debt with the proceeds.

(2) Same as (*1*) above but common stock repurchased with the proceeds.

(3) The firm operated at a net loss for Year 11, so that net asset outflows for expenses exceeded net asset inflows from revenues.

 Solutions

1.15 (Mylan Laboratories; balance sheet relations.)

a. The following equation characterizes the balance sheet:

$$\begin{array}{c}\text{Current} \\ \text{Assets}\end{array} + \begin{array}{c}\text{Noncurrent} \\ \text{Assets}\end{array} = \begin{array}{c}\text{Current} \\ \text{Liabilities}\end{array} + \begin{array}{c}\text{Noncurrent} \\ \text{Liabilities}\end{array} + \begin{array}{c}\text{Shareholders'} \\ \text{Equity}\end{array}$$

$$\text{Total Assets} = \text{Total Liabilities} + \begin{array}{c}\text{Shareholders'} \\ \text{Equity}\end{array}$$

The missing information is (amounts in millions):

Year 8
Noncurrent Assets	$ 35
Total Liabilities and Shareholders' Equity	109
Shareholders' Equity	89

Year 9
Total Assets	$ 113
Current Liabilities	7
Current Assets	68

Year 10
Total Assets	$ 138
Noncurrent Liabilities	4
Total Liabilities and Shareholders' Equity	138

Year 11
Noncurrent Assets	$ 87
Total Liabilities and Shareholders' Equity	170
Shareholders' Equity	154

b. Noncurrent assets increased as a percentage of total assets, suggesting investments in property, plant and equipment to maintain the firm's rapid growth. Mylan Laboratories may have also acquired other firms which had higher proportions of noncurrent assets than Mylan.

c. Shareholders' equity increased as a percentage of total financing, suggesting either the issuance of additional common stock or the retention of earnings as the vehicles for financing the growth in noncurrent assets.

1.16 (Proctor & Gamble; balance sheet relations.)

a. The **given** (boldface) and missing items appear below (amounts in millions).

	Year 6	Year 7	Year 8	Year 9
Current Assets	**$ 8,435**	$ 9,366[a]	**$ 9,975**	$ 9,988
Noncurrent Assets............	12,033	14,659	**14,960**	15,547
Total Assets......................	$20,468	$24,025	$24,935	$25,535
Current Liabilities.............	**$ 6,733**	$ 7,642	**$ 8,287**	$ 8,040[c]
Noncurrent Liabilities	**5,999**	7,312	**9,207**	8,663
Contributed Capital...........	1,017	**1,149**	1,292	**1,399**
Retained Earnings	**6,719**	**7,922**	6,149[b]	7,433[d]
Total Liabilities and Shareholders' Equity...............	**$20,468**	$24,025	$24,935	**$25,535**

[a]$7,642 + $1,724 = $9,366.
[b]$7,922 − $656 − $1,117 = $6,149.
[c]$9,988 − $1,948 = $8,040.
[d]$6,149 + $2,524 − $1,240 = $7,433.

b. Proctor & Gamble likely acquired another firm. The acquired firm probably has a slightly higher percentage of noncurrent assets than Proctor & Gamble. Because the mix of short- versus long-term financing and debt versus equity financing did not change substantially between the two years, either Proctor & Gamble used a mix of these types of financing or the acquired firm has a capital structure similar to Proctor & Gamble's. The acquisition target in this case was the cosmetics and fragrance business of Revlon.

c. Noncurrent liabilities increased in an amount approximately equal to the decrease in retained earnings. Proctor & Gamble operated at a net loss during Year 10. One possible explanation is that the net loss reduced cash, requiring Proctor & Gamble to obtain additional financing. The actual explanation in this case is that Proctor & Gamble adopted the provisions of Financial Accounting Standards Board *Statement No. 106* and *Statement 109*. The adoptions resulted in a charge against earnings and an increase in noncurrent liabilities.

d. Proctor & Gamble was profitable during Year 9. It used a portion of the cash generated by profitable operations to repay short- and long-term financing.

 Solutions

1.17   (Nissan Motor Car Company; balance sheet relations.)

a. The **given** (boldface) and missing items appear below (amounts in millions).

	Year 6	Year 7	Year 8	Year 9
Current Assets	¥2,456	¥2,831	¥3,358	¥3,388
Noncurrent Assets	1,718	1,911	2,387	3,059
Total Assets	¥4,174	¥4,742	¥5,745	¥6,447
Current Liabilities	¥1,949	¥2,217	¥2,798	¥3,196
Noncurrent Liabilities	780	876	1,174	1,471
Contributed Capital	442	574	598	600
Retained Earnings	1,003	1,075	1,175	1,180
Total Liabilities and Share-holders' Equity	¥4,174	¥4,742	¥5,745	¥6,447
Net Income	¥ 65	¥ 105	¥ 135	¥ 40
Dividends	¥ 31	¥ 33	¥ 35	¥ 35
Current Assets/Current Liabilities	1.26	1.28	1.20	1.06

b. The structure of assets and the structure of liabilities and shareholders' equity were stable between Year 6 and Year 7. Between Year 7 and Year 8 and between Year 8 and Year 9, noncurrent assets became an increasing proportion of total assets, perhaps because Nissan added property, plant and equipment to build manufacturing capacity. Nissan financed these capital expenditures with a combination of short- and long-term borrowing (evidenced by the decreasing ratio of current assets to current liabilities and the increasing proportion of noncurrent liabilities in the financing structure). Shareholders' equity declined as a percentage of total liabilities and shareholders' equity primarily because of the increase in debt financing and, between Year 8 and Year 9, because of a drop in net income. Note that Nissan maintained its dividend in Year 9 despite the decrease in net income. The instructor may wish to point out the relatively high proportion of liabilities in the capital structure of Nissan, a practice typical of Japanese companies but not typical of companies in the United States.

1.18 (Texas Instruments; balance sheet relations.)

a. The **given** (boldface) and missing items appear below (amounts in millions).

	Year 5	Year 6	Year 7	Year 8
Current Assets	$2,381	$2,626	$3,314	$ 4,024
Noncurrent Assets	2,628	2,559	2,679	2,965
Total Assets	$5,009	$5,185	$5,993	$ 6,989
Current Liabilities	$1,568	$1,662	$2,001	$ 2,199
Noncurrent Liabilities	1,486	1,576	1,677	1,751
Contributed Capital	1,189	1,031	1,008	1,127
Retained Earnings	766	916	1,307[a]	1,912[b]
Total Liabilities and Shareholders' Equity	$5,009	$5,185	$5,993	$ 6,989
Current Assets/Current Liabilities	1.52	1.58	1.66	1.83

[a]$916 + $472 – $81 = $1,307.
[b]$1,307 + $691 – $86 = $1,912.

Δ RE = NI – D

b. Although current assets and noncurrent assets increased during the four years, current assets increased faster than noncurrent assets. One possible explanation is that Texas Instruments had unused manufacturing capacity at the beginning of Year 6 which it increasingly used in later years to manufacture inventory and to generate increased sales Thus, inventories and accounts receivable grew faster than property, plant and equipment. The proportion of noncurrent liabilities and contributed capital in the capital structure declined over the four years while the proportion from retained earnings increased. Texas Instruments experienced rapidly increased earnings during the three-year period. It used the assets generated by these earnings to finance the growth in assets. The growth in assets was also financed in part with additional noncurrent liabilities and contributed capital.

1.19 (Olin Corporation, retained earnings relations.)

a. The **given** (boldface) and missing items appear below (amounts in millions).

	Year 6	Year 7	Year 8	Year 9
Retained Earnings, Beginning of Year	$ 499	$ 435	$ 388	$ 238
Net Income	(13)	9	(92)	91
Dividends Declared and Paid	(51)	(56)	(58)	(60)
Retained Earnings, End of Year	$ 435	$ 388	$ 238	$ 269

 Solutions

1.19 continued.

b. The sales of Olin Corporation are cyclical. The economy was apparently in a recession during Year 6, Year 7 and Year 8 and began pulling out of the recession in Year 9.

c. A slowly growing but continuous dividend sends a signal to common shareholders that the firm expects to grow and return to profitable operations when the economy pulls out of the recession. Also, shareholders who rely on dividends for their living expenses will probably prefer steady dividends instead of distributions that vary with net income each year.

1.20 (Volvo Group; retained earnings relations.)

a. The changes in retained earnings appear below. **Given** amounts appear in boldface (amounts in millions of Swedish Kronor).

	Year 3	Year 4	Year 5	Year 6
Retained Earning, January 1...	**25,634**	30,484	**34,338**	**37,922**
Net Income............................	**5,665**	**4,940**	4,787	(1,020)*
Dividends.............................	**815**	1,086	**1,203**	**1,203**
Retained Earnings, December 31	30,484	**34,338**	**37,922**	**35,699**

*Net loss.

b. Volvo Group experienced decreasing amounts of net income over the four years, even operating at a net loss in Year 6. The firm, however, increased or at least maintained its dividends during this period of declining profitability. Thus, retained earnings grew at a declining rate (Year 3 to Year 5) or decreased (Year 6).

1.21 (LA Gear; relating net income to balance sheet changes.)

a.
(Amount in Millions)	Year 3	Year 4
Retained Earnings, Beginning of Year	$ 83	$ 115
Plus Net Income	32	(74)
Less Dividends Declared and Paid...................	0	(2)
Retained Earnings, End of Year......................	$ 115	$ 39

b.

$$\text{Net Income} = \text{Increase in Assets} - \text{Increase in Liabilities} - \text{Increase in Contributed Capital} + \text{Dividends}$$

Year 3
$32 = $98 – $60 – $6 + $0

Year 4
$(74) = $(–39) – $(–64) – $101 + $2

1.22 (Nestle Group; relating net income to balance sheet changes.)

a.

(Amount in Millions)	Year 5	Year 6
Retained Earnings, Beginning of Year	SF17,096	SF18,439
Plus Net Income	1,960	1,896
Less Dividends Declared and Paid................	(617)	(740)
Retained Earnings, End of Year..................	SF18,439	SF19,595

b.

$$\text{Net Income} = \text{Increase in Assets} - \text{Increase in Liabilities} - \text{Increase in Contributed Capital} + \text{Dividends}$$

Year 5

$$\text{SF1,960} = \text{SF1,996} - \text{SF635} - \text{SF18} + \text{SF617}$$

Year 6

$$\text{SF1,896} = \text{SF231} - \text{SF}(-925) - \text{SF0} + \text{SF740}$$

1.23 (Coca-Cola Company; income statement relations.)

a. The **given** (boldface) and missing items appear below (amounts are in millions).

	Year 4	Year 5	Year 6
Sales.....................................	**$11,828**	**$13,221**	**$14,208**
Cost of Goods Sold............................	**(4,649)**	**(5,055)**	(5,160)
Selling and Administrative Expenses..	**(4,604)**	**(5,249)**	**(5,695)**
Interest Expense.............................	**(192)**	**(171)**	**(168)**
Income Tax Expense	**(765)**	**(863)**	**(997)**
Net Income.....................................	$ 1,618	$ 1,883	$ 2,188

b. The common size income statement appears below:

	Year 4	Year 5	Year 6
Sales	100.0%	100.0%	100.0%
Cost of Goods Sold............................	(39.3)	(38.2)	(36.3)
Selling and Administrative Expenses....	(38.9)	(39.7)	(40.1)
Interest Expense.............................	(1.6)	(1.3)	(1.2)
Income Tax Expense........................	(6.5)	(6.5)	(7.0)
Net Income.....................................	13.7%	14.3%	15.4%

The ratio of net income to sales increased steadily during the three years. The cost of goods sold to sales percentage steadily decreased while the marketing and administrative expense to sales percentage steadily increased. Perhaps the Coca-Cola Company (Coke) increased its advertising expenditures and consumers responded by paying premium prices for Coke's products. Alternatively, Coke may have experienced reduced manufacturing costs as a result of higher volumes or decreased raw materials costs. The decreased

1.23 b. continued.

interest expense to sales percentage might relate to reduced debt or lower interest rates. The increased income tax expense to sales percentage results from a higher pre-tax profit margin. Income tax expense as a percentage of net income before taxes was 31.25 percent in Year 5 and Year 6.

1.24　(Wal-Mart Stores; income statement relations.)

a. The **given** (boldface) and missing items appear below (amounts in millions).

	Year 6	Year 7	Year 8
Sales	**$ 25,986**	**$ 32,864**	**$ 44,289**
Cost of Goods Sold	**(20,070)**	**(25,500)**	(34,786)
Marketing and Administrative Expense	**(4,070)**	**(5,152)**	**(6,684)**
Interest Expense	**(138)**	**(169)**	**(266)**
Income Tax Expense	**(632)**	**(752)**	**(945)**
Net Income	$ 1,076	$ 1,291	$ 1,608

b. The common size income statement appears below.

	Year 6	Year 7	Year 8
Sales	100.0%	100.0%	100.0%
Cost of Goods Sold	(77.3)	(77.6)	(78.6)
Marketing and Administrative Expenses	(15.7)	(15.7)	(15.1)
Interest Expense	(.5)	(.5)	(.6)
Income Tax Expense	(2.4)	(2.3)	(2.1)
Net Income	4.1%	3.9%	3.6%

Wal-Mart Stores experienced a declining net income to sales ratio during the three-year period. The primary contributing factor is an increase in the cost of goods sold to sales percentage. Although the problem does not give sufficient information for students to identify the reason for this increase, the explanation relates to a sales mix shift toward warehouse clubs that have higher cost of goods sold percentages than discount store chains. The shift to warehouse clubs, which carry lower overhead costs, reduced the marketing and administrative expense percentage in Year 8. The declining income tax expense to sales percentage occurs because of a lower income before income taxes to sales percentage.

1.25   (Delta Airlines; statement of cash flows relations.)

a.

DELTA AIRLINES
Statement of Cash Flows
(Amounts in Millions)

	Year 2	Year 3	Year 4
Operations:			
Revenues Increasing Cash	$10,519	$12,196	$12,528
Expenses Decreasing Cash	(10,369)	(11,519)	(11,204)
Cash Flow from Operations................	$ 150	$ 677	$ 1,324
Investing:			
Sale of Property and Equipment	$ 43	$ 87	$ 103
Acquisition of Property and Equipment................................	(3,082)	(1,414)	(1,613)
Cash Flow from Investing..................	$(3,039)	$(1,327)	$(1,510)
Financing:			
Increase (Decrease) in Short-term Debt	$ 746	$ (801)	$ 0
Increase in Long-term Debt.............	2,313	2,111	975
Increase in Common Stock	0	1,127	0
Decrease in Long-term Debt	(794)	(519)	(547)
Dividends......................................	(89)	(138)	(120)
Cash Flow from Financing.................	$ 2,176	$ 1,780	$ 308
Change in Cash..............................	$ (713)	$ 1,130	$ 122

b.   Although cash flow from operations increased during the three years, its amount was not sufficient to finance acquisition of property and equipment. Delta financed these acquisitions with long-term debt in all three years and with common stock in Year 3.

1-13

1.26   (Sun Microsystems; statement of cash flows relations.)

a.
SUN MICROSYSTEMS
Statement of Cash Flows
(Amounts in Millions)

	Year 8	Year 9	Year 10
Operations:			
Revenues Increasing Cash	$1,046	$1,258	$1,515
Expenses Decreasing Cash	(1,064)	(1,250)	(1,512)
Cash Flow from Operations.................	$ (18)	$ 8	$ 3
Investing:			
Acquisition of Property, Plant and			
Equipment..................................	$ (38)	$ (99)	$ (149)
Cash Flow from Investing...................	$ (38)	$ (99)	$ (149)
Financing:			
Proceeds of Bank Borrowings	$ 11	$ 21	$ --
Issue of Long-term Debt...................	4	121	--
Issue of Common Stock....................	47	96	63
Repayment of Bank Borrowing	--	--	(6)
Repayment of Long-term Debt...........	(2)	--	--
Cash Flow from Financing.................	$ 60	$ 238	$ 57
Change in Cash................................	$ 4	$ 147	$ (89)

b.   Sun Microsystems makes a larger amount of sales on account each
period than it collects from customers from sales on account of prior
periods (that is, accounts receivable increases). Likewise, Sun
Microsystems manufactures more computers each period than it
sells in order to meet growing demand. Thus, cash inflows are less
than sales revenues and cash outflows for operations exceed
expenses. The net result is that net income exceeds cash flow from
operations.

c.   A growing firm typically experiences an excess of net income over
cash flow from operations as the preceding answer explains. Also,
Sun Microsystems made significant expenditures on property, plant
and equipment to build production capacity. Because cash flow from
operations was not sufficient to finance these acquisitions, Sun
Microsystems relied on bank borrowing, long-term borrowing, and
common stock issues.

1.27   (Relations between financial statements.)

a. $630 + $3,290 − $2,780 = a; a = $1,140.

b. $1,240 + b − $8,290 = $1,410; b = $8,460.

c. $89,000 − c − $0 + $17,600 = $102,150; c = $4,450.

d. $76,200 + $14,200 − d = $83,300; d = $7,100.

1.28 (S, H & W Corporation; preparing a balance sheet and income statement.)

a.

S, H & W CORPORATION
Income Statement
For Year 2

Revenues:		
Revenues from Consulting Services...........	$400,000	
Rental Revenue	30,000	
Total Revenues		$430,000
Less Expenses:		
Salaries Expense....................................	$220,000	
Property Taxes and Insurance Expense.....	40,000	
Supplies Expense...................................	20,000	
Depreciation Expense............................	60,000	
Income Tax Expense..............................	30,000	
Total Expenses...................................		(370,000)
Net Income...		$ 60,000

b.

S, H & W CORPORATION
Comparative Balance Sheet
December 31, Year 1, and December 31, Year 2

	Dec. 31, Year 1	Dec. 31, Year 2
Assets		
Current Assets:		
Cash...	$750,000	$ 80,000
Accounts Receivable from Clients.............	0	195,000
Supplies Inventory.................................	0	5,000
Total Current Assets.........................	$750,000	$280,000
Noncurrent Assets:		
Office Equipment—Net of Depreciation......	$ 0	$ 85,000
Office Building—Net of Depreciation.........	0	480,000
Total Noncurrent Assets	$ 0	$565,000
Total Assets......................................	$750,000	$845,000
Liabilities and Shareholders' Equity		
Current Liabilities:		
Accounts Payable to Suppliers..................	$ 0	$ 20,000
Payroll Taxes Payable.............................	0	5,000
Income Taxes Payable.............................	0	20,000
Total Liabilities	$ 0	$ 45,000
Shareholders' Equity:		
Common Stock......................................	$750,000	$750,000
Retained Earnings	0	50,000
Total Shareholders' Equity...................	$750,000	$800,000
Total Liabilities and Shareholders' Equity	$750,000	$845,000

       Solutions

1.28 continued.

c.
Retained Earnings, December 31, Year 1	$ 0
Add Net Income for Year 2	60,000
Subtract Dividends Declared during Year 2	(10,000)
Retained Earnings, December 31, Year 2	$ 50,000

1.29   (Ben and Jerry's Homemade Ice Cream, Inc.: preparing a balance sheet and income statement.) (Amounts in Thousands)

a.   **BEN AND JERRY'S HOMEMADE ICE CREAM, INC.**
Balance Sheet
December 31, Year 6, and December 31, Year 7

	Dec. 31, Year 6	Dec. 31, Year 7
Assets		
Current Assets:		
Cash	$ 796	$ 6,704
Accounts Receivable	5,044	6,940
Inventories	10,083	9,000
Other Current Assets	518	1,091
Total Current Assets	$ 16,441	$ 23,735
Noncurrent Assets:		
Property, Plant and Equipment	$ 17,299	$ 19,300
Other Noncurrent Assets	559	21
Total Noncurrent Assets	$ 17,858	$ 19,321
Total Assets	$ 34,299	$ 43,056
Liabilities and Shareholders' Equity		
Current Liabilities:		
Accounts Payable	$ 5,219	$ 7,873
Salaries Payable	42	63
Other Current Liabilities	2,623	4,249
Total Current Liabilities	$ 7,884	$ 12,185
Noncurrent Liabilities:		
Bonds Payable (due Year 20)	10,313	4,602
Total Liabilities	$ 18,197	$ 16,787
Shareholders' Equity:		
Common Stock	$ 6,532	$ 12,959
Retained Earnings	9,570	13,310
Total Shareholders' Equity	$ 16,102	$ 26,269
Total Liabilities and Shareholders' Equity	$ 34,299	$ 43,056

1.29 continued.

b.   BEN AND JERRY'S HOMEMADE ICE CREAM, INC.
Income Statement
For Year 7

Revenues:
   Sales Revenue... $ 97,005
     Total Revenue.. $ 97,005

Expenses:
   Cost of Goods Sold.. $ 68,500
   Selling Expense... 16,466
   Administrative Expense.. 4,798
   Interest Expense.. 736
   Income Tax Expense 2,765
     Total Expenses .... $ 93,265
Net Income.. $ 3,740

c.   Retained Earnings, December 31, Year 6....................... $ 9,570
Plus Net Income for Year 7... 3,740
Less Dividends Declared and Paid................................... --
Retained Earnings, December 31, Year 7....................... $ 13,310

d.   Ben and Jerry's issued common stock and paid no dividends, despite positive net income for the year. It used cash flow from these activities to repay long-term debt, acquire property, plant and equipment, and increase the balance in the cash account.

                                        Solutions

1.30 (Wal-Mart Stores, Inc.; preparing a balance sheet and income statement.)

a.
WAL-MART STORES, INC.
Comparative Balance Sheet
December 31, Year 1 and Year 2
(Amounts in Millions)

	Dec. 31, Year 1	Dec. 31, Year 2
Assets		
Current Assets:		
Cash...	$ 20	$ 45
Accounts Receivable.................................	898	900
Merchandise Inventory	11,196	14,393
Total Current Assets.............................	$12,114	$15,338
Noncurrent Assets:		
Land...	$ 2,741	$ 3,036
Equipment (net of accumulated depreciation)..	4,307	4,675
Buildings (net of accumulated depreciation)....	6,128	8,163
Other Noncurrent Assets...........................	1,151	1,607
Total Noncurrent Assets	$14,327	$17,481
Total Assets...	$26,441	$32,819
Liabilities and Shareholders' Equity		
Current Liabilities:		
Bank Loan Payable (due Year 2 and Year 3)....	$ 1,646	$ 1,882
Accounts Payable	4,104	5,907
Income Taxes Payable	183	365
Other Current Liabilities	1,473	1,819
Total Current Liabilities.........................	$ 7,406	$ 9,973
Noncurrent Liabilities:		
Bonds Payable (due Year 16).......................	7,960	9,709
Total Liabilities	$15,366	$19,682
Shareholders' Equity:		
Common Stock..	$ 766	$ 769
Retained Earnings....................................	10,309	12,368
Total Shareholders' Equity......................	$11,075	$13,137
Total Liabilities and Shareholders' Equity ...	$26,441	$32,819

Solutions   1-18

1.30 continued.

b.   **WAL-MART STORES, INC.**
Income Statement
For Year 2
(Amounts in Millions)

Revenues:

Sales Revenue	$ 83,412
Expenses:	
Cost of Merchandise Sold	$ 65,586
Depreciation Expense	1,070
Interest Expense	706
Other Operating Expenses	11,788
Income Tax Expense	1,581
Total Expenses	$ 80,731
Net Income	$ 2,681

c.

Retained Earnings, December 31, Year 1	$ 10,309
Plus Net Income for Year 2	2,681
Less Dividends Declared and Paid during Year 2	(622)
Retained Earnings, December 31, Year 2	$ 12,368

1.31   (ABC Company; relation between net income and cash flows.)

a.

Month	Cash Balance at Beginning of Month	+ Cash Receipts from Customers	− Cash Disbursements for Production Costs	= Cash Balance at End of the Month
January	$ 875	$ 1,000	$ 750	$ 1,125
February	1,125	1,000	1,500	625
March	625	1,500	1,875	250
April	250	2,000	2,250	0

The cash flow problem arises because of a lag between cash expenditures incurred in producing goods and cash collections from customers once the firm sells those goods. For example, cash expenditures during February ($1,500) are for goods produced during February and sold during March. Cash is not collected from customers on these sales, however, until April ($2,000). A growing firm must generally produce more units than it sells during a period if it is to have sufficient quantities of inventory on hand for future sales. The cash needed for this higher level of production may well exceed the cash received from the prior period's sales. Thus, a cash shortage develops.

    1-19   **Solutions**

1.31 continued.

b. The difference between the selling price of goods sold and the cost of those goods equals net income for the period. As long as selling prices exceed the cost of the goods, a positive net income results. As the number of units sold increases, net income increases. A firm does not necessarily recognize revenues and expenses in the same period as the related cash receipts and expenditures. Thus, cash decreases, for reasons Part *a.* discusses, even though net income increases.

c. The income statement and statement of cash flows provide information about the profitability and liquidity respectively of a firm during a period. The fact that net income and cash flows can move in opposite directions highlights the need for information from both statements. A firm without sufficient cash will not survive, even if it operates profitably. The balance sheet indicates a firm's asset and equity position at a moment in time. The deteriorating cash position is evident from the listing of assets at the beginning of each month. Examining the cash receipts and disbursements during each month, however, identifies the reasons for the deterioration.

1.32 (Balance sheet and income statement relations.)

a. Bushels of wheat are the most convenient in this case with the given information. This question emphasizes the need for a common measuring unit.

b.
IVAN AND IGOR
Comparative Balance Sheets
(Amounts in Bushels of Wheat)

Assets	Beginning of Period	End of Period	Beginning of Period	End of Period
Wheat	20	223	10	105
Fertilizer	2	--	1	--
Ox	40	36	40	36
Plow	--	--	--	2
Land	100	100	50	50
Total Assets	162	359	101	193
Liabilities and Owners' Equity				
Accounts Payable	--	3	--	--
Owners' Equity	162	356	101	193
Total Liabilities and Owners' Equity	162	359	101	193

1.32 b. continued.

Questions will likely arise as to the accounting entity. One view is that there are two accounting entities (Ivan and Igor) to whom the Red Bearded Baron has entrusted assets and required a periodic reporting on stewardship. The "owner" in owners' equity in this case is the Red Bearded Baron. Another view is that the Red Bearded Baron is the accounting entity, in which case financial statements that combine the financial statements for Ivan and Igor are appropriate. Identifying the accounting entity depends on the intended use of the financial statements. For purposes of evaluating the performance of Ivan and Igor, the accounting entities are separate—Ivan and Igor. To assess the change in wealth of the Red Bearded Baron during the period, the combined financial statements reflect the accounting entity.

c.
IVAN AND IGOR
Comparative income Statement
(Amounts in Bushels of Wheat)

	IVAN	IGOR
Revenues	243	138
Expenses:		
Seed	20	10
Fertilizer	2	1
Depreciation on Ox	4	4
Plow	3	1
Total Expenses	29	16
Net Income	214	122

Chapter 1 does not expose students to the concept of depreciation. Most students, however, grasp the need to record some amount of expense for the ox and the plow.

d.

(Amounts in Bushels of Wheat)	IVAN	IGOR
Owners' Equity, Beginning of Period	162	101
Plus Net Income	214	122
Less Distributions to Owner	(20)	(30)
Owners' Equity, End of Period	356	193

1-21   **Solutions**

1.32 continued.

e. We cannot simply compare the amounts of net income for Ivan and Igor because the Red Bearded Baron entrusted them with different amounts of resources. We must relate the net income amounts to some base. Several possibilities include:

	IVAN	IGOR
Net Income/Average Total Assets	82.2%	83.0%
Net Income/Beginning Total Assets	132.1%	120.8%
Net Income/Average Noncurrent Assets	155.1%	137.1%
Net Income/Beginning Noncurrent Assets	152.9%	135.6%
Net Income/Average Owners' Equity	82.6%	82.0%
Net Income/Beginning Owners' Equity	132.1%	120.8%
Net Income/Acre	$10.70	$12.20

This question has no definitive answer. Its purpose is to get students to think about performance measurement. The instructor may or may not wish to devote class time at this point discussing which base is more appropriate.

CHAPTER 2

BALANCE SHEET: PRESENTING THE INVESTMENTS AND FINANCING OF A FIRM

Questions, Exercises, Problems, and Cases: Answers and Solutions

2.1   See the text or the glossary at the end of the book.

2.2   Based on the conservatively reported earnings, a shareholder might sell shares of stock based on the assessment that the firm is not performing well. If the economic or "true" earnings of the firm are larger, the shareholder's assessment would result in a poor decision. Or, shareholders might dismiss the management of a firm because they feel the firm is not performing well. It should be emphasized here that the principal objective of accounting reports as currently prepared is to present *fairly* the results of operations and the financial condition of the firm. When doubt exists as to the treatment of a particular item or transaction, accountants tend to select the procedure resulting in the more conservative measurement of earnings.

2.3   The justification relates to the need for a reasonably high degree of objectivity in the preparation of the financial statements. When there is an exchange between a firm and some other entity, there is market evidence of the economic effects of the transaction. The independent auditor verifies these economic effects by referring to contracts, cancelled checks and other documents underlying the transaction. If accounting recognized events without such a market exchange (for example, the increase in market value of a firm's assets), increased subjectivity would enter into the preparation of the financial statements.

2.4   The justification relates to the uncertainty as to the ultimate economic effects of the contracts. One party or the other may pull out of the contract. The accountant may not know the benefits and costs of the contract at the time of signing. Until one party or the other begins to perform under the contract, accounting gives no recognition. Accountants often disclose significant contracts of this nature in the notes to the financial statements.

2.5   Accountants record assets at acquisition cost. Cash discounts reduce acquisition cost and, therefore, the amount recorded for merchandise or equipment.

2.6   a. The contract between the investors and the construction company as well as cancelled checks provide evidence as to the acquisition cost.

        b. Adjusted acquisition cost differs from the amount in Part *a.* by the portion of acquisition cost applicable to the services of the asset consumed during the first five years. There are several generally accepted methods of computing this amount (discussed in Chapter 9). A review of the accounting records for the office building should indicate how this amount was calculated.

        c. There are at least two possibilities for ascertaining current replacement cost. One alternative is to consult a construction company to determine the cost of constructing a similar office building (that is, with respect to location, materials, size). The accountant would then adjust the current cost of constructing a new building downward to reflect the used condition of the five-year old office building. The current replacement cost amount could be reduced by 12.5 percent (= 5/40) if the asset's service potential decreases evenly with age. The actual economic decline in the value of the building during the first five years is likely to differ from 12.5 percent and, therefore, some other rate is probably appropriate. A second alternative for ascertaining current replacement cost is to consult a real estate dealer to determine the cost of acquiring a used office building providing services similar to the building that the investors own. The accountant might encounter difficulties in locating such a similar building.

        d. The accountant might consult a local real estate dealer to ascertain the current net realizable value of the office building. There is always the question as to whether an interested buyer could be found at the quoted price. The accountant might also use any recent offers to purchase the building received by the investors.

        e. The accountant measures the present value of the future net cash flows using estimated rental receipts and operating expenses (excluding depreciation) for the building's remaining 35-year life. These cash flows are then discounted to the present using an appropriate rate of interest.

2.7   a. Liability—Receivable from Supplier or Prepaid Merchandise Orders.

        b. Liability—Investment in Bonds.

        c. Asset—Interest Payable.

        d. Asset—Insurance Premiums Received in Advance.

        e. Liability—Prepaid Rent.

2.8   (Eli Lilly and Company; asset recognition and valuation.)

    a.   Prepaid Insurance, $12,000,000.

    b.   Deposit on Equipment, $500,000.

    c.   Investment in Securities, $325,000.

    d.   Raw Materials Inventory, $784,000.

    e.   Accounting does not recognize the employment contract, a mutually unexecuted contract, as an asset.

    f.   Marketable Securities, $3,200,000.

    g.   Accounting does not recognize the customer's order as an asset because no exchange between the buyer and the seller has occurred.

    h.   Raw Materials Inventory, $200,000. Legal rights to use the raw materials have passed to Eli Lilly, creating a legal obligation to make payment.

2.9   (IBM Corporation; asset recognition and valuation.)

    a.   Investment in Bond, $8,000,000.

    b.   Prepaid Rent, $600,000.

    c.   Deposit on Land, $1,000,000.

    d.   Accounting does not recognize the employment contract, a mutually unexecuted contract, as an asset.

    e.   Patent, $1,200,000.

    f.   Accounting does not recognize a patent developed from research and development expenditures by a firm as an asset because of the difficulties in ascertaining whether future benefits existed at the time the firm made the expenditures.

    g.   Accounting does not recognize an asset because an exchange has not yet occurred.

2.10   (General Mills, Inc.; asset recognition and valuation.)

    a. Accounting does not recognize as assets expenditures made internally to develop new products under generally accepted accounting principles.

    b. Contractual Rights to Food Products (or similar creative account title), $2,800,000. In contrast to Part a., the exchange between buyer and seller permits the identification and valuation of future benefits to justify recognition of an asset.

    c. Deposit on Land, $1,800,000.

    d. Accounting does not recognize an asset because of the difficulty of identifying and measuring any future benefits from these advertising expenditures.

    e. Investment in Securities, $3,500,000. The market value of the shares of General Mills given in exchange is probably a more reliable indicator of value than independent appraisals.

    f. Land, $2,188,000. Acquisition cost includes all expenditures made to prepare an asset for its intended use.

2.11   (Ford Motor company; asset recognition and valuation.)

    a. Raw Materials Inventory increases by $40,000,000.

    b. Because Ford has not paid the account, the return of the goods decreases Accounts Payable and Raw Materials Inventory by $2,500,000.

    c. The remaining liability from Parts a. and b. totals $37,500,000 (= $40,000,000 − $2,500,000). The cash payment of $36,750,000 (= .98 × $37,500,000) reduces Cash. Accounts Payable decreases by the invoice price of the goods ($37,500,000), and Raw Materials Inventory decreases by the amount of cash discount taken of $750,000 (= $37,500,000 − $36,750,000).

    d. Equipment increases by $330,000.

    e. Equipment increases by $4,900.

    f. Equipment increases by $1,800.

2.12   (Asset recognition and valuation.)

a.

Automobile, List Price	$20,000
Less Cash Discount	(1,600)
Dealer Preparation Charges	350
Sales Tax (.06 × $18,750)	1,125
Name Painted on Truck	190
Total Cost of Delivery Truck (a noncurrent asset)	$20,065
Prepaid Insurance (current asset)	$ 500
Prepaid License Fees (current asset)	$ 125

b.   This part and the next are designed to stimulate discussion. There is no right answer, although our reading of APB *Opinion No. 29* and the facts of the situation lead us to use $5,200,000, the apparent value of the Microsoft shares. (We recall once a student who answered this question in no uncertain terms that the appraiser's figure was correct. When pressed as to why he picked this answer and why he was so certain, he admitted that he was the son of a real estate appraiser and that appraisers never make mistakes!)

c.   Here we are more inclined to believe the appraiser rather than the stock market, but we are not unanimous in agreeing on the right answer. Historical cost accounting is not as objective and verifiable as is sometimes thought.

2.13   (Travelers Insurance Company; liability recognition and valuation.)

a.   Insurance Premiums Received in Advance or Advances from Customers, $6,500,000.

b.   Accounting normally does not recognize a liability for mutually unexecuted contracts. When the president renders services, a liability arises.

c.   Legal Fees Payable, $1,200,000.

d.   Common stock does not meet the definition of a liability because the firm need not repay the funds in a particular amount at a particular time.

e.   Salaries and Commissions Payable, $950,000; Payroll Taxes Payable, $76,000 (= .08 × $950,000).

f.   The treatment of this item depends on the probability of having to make a cash payment in the future, whose amount and timing of payment the Company can estimate with reasonable accuracy. Most firms do not recognize unsettled lawsuits as liabilities because it is not clear (1) that the firm received benefits in the past, and (2) that the lawsuit will require a future cash payment.

       Solutions

2.14   (Kansas City Royals, Inc.; liability recognition and valuation.)

    a. Accounting normally does not recognize a liability for mutually unexecuted contracts. When the player renders services, a liability arises.

    b. Advances from Customers, $2,700,000.

    c. Bonds Payable, $8,400,000.

    d. Utilities Payable, $3,400.

    e. The treatment of this item depends on the probability of having to make a cash payment in the future, whose amount and timing of payment the firm can estimate with reasonable accuracy. Most firms do not recognize unsettled lawsuits as liabilities because it is not clear (1) that the firm has received benefits in the past, and (2) that the lawsuit will require a future cash payment.

    f. The firm does not recognize a liability for the uniforms until the supplier makes delivery. The $10,000 deposit appears as a Deposit on Uniforms, an asset, on the firm's balance sheet and an Advance from Customers, a liability, on the balance sheet of the supplier.

2.15   (Dartmouth College; liability recognition and valuation.)

    a. Bonds Payable, $10,000,000.

    b. Accounting normally does not recognize a liability for unexecuted contracts. The $2,000,000 deposit appears as an asset, Deposit on Building, on the college's balance sheet and as a liability, Advance from Customers, on the balance sheet of the construction company.

    c. Advances from Customers, $1,800,000.

    d. Accounts Payable, $170,000.

    e. Compensation Payable, $280,000; Payroll Taxes Payable $16,800 (.06 × $280,000).

    f. The college does not recognize a liability for the grant. Although it receives the benefits of the funds, it incurs no obligation to repay the amount of the grant in the future.

2.16   (Liability recognition and valuation.)

   a. Accounting does not recognize a liability for the paving work, because there has merely been an exchange of promises for future performance.

   b. Fees Received in Advance, $400.

   c. Advances from Customers, $500,000.

   d. Common stock is not a liability because there is no fixed amount or repayment date.

   e. Note Payable, $30,000.

   f. Accounting does not recognize a liability for the reason in Part *a*. above.

   g. Accounting does not recognize a liability for the reason in Part *a*. above.

   h. Accounts Payable, $2,500.

2.17   (Balance sheet classification.)

a. 2	f. 2	k. 1	
b. 3	g. 1	l. 1 (if purchased from another firm)	
c. 1	h. 2	4 (if created by the firm)	
d. 4	i. 1	m. 4	
e. 1	j. 2	n. 3	

2.18   (Balance sheet classification.)

a. 3	h. 2
b. 1	i. 1
c. 4	j. 2
d. 1	k. 2
e. 3	l. 1
f. 1	m. 2
g. 1 (if purchased from another firm)	n. 3
4 (if created by the firm)	

2.19   (Jones Corporation; journal entries for various transactions.)

   (1) **October 2**

Cash..	8,000,000	
Common Stock....................................		2,500,000
Additional Paid-in Capital....................		5,500,000

Issue of 500,000 shares of $5 par value common stock at $16 per share.

       Solutions

2.19 continued.

(2) **October 3**

Building...	2,000,000	
Cash..		400,000
Note Payable...		1,600,000

Acquisition of building for cash and
issuance of a note.

(3) **October 8**

Equipment..	25,000	
Cash..		25,000

Acquisition of a machine for cash.

(4) **October 15**

Merchandise Inventory................................	90,000	
Accounts Payable.....................................		90,000

Acquisition of merchandise inventory on
account.

(5) **October 18**

Prepaid Insurance.......................................	700	
Cash..		700

Prepayment of insurance premium for coverage beginning November 1.

(6) **October 20**

Cash..	1,300	
Advances from Customers..........................		1,300

Advance from customers on merchandise to be
delivered on November 5.

(7) **October 26**

Accounts Payable.......................................	60,000	
Cash..		58,400
Merchandise Inventory		1,600

Payment of invoices totaling $80,000 but subject
to a 2 percent discount for prompt payment.

(8) **October 30**

Accounts Payable.......................................	30,000	
Cash..		30,000

Payment of invoices totaling $30,000.

Note: Some students treat the lost discounts of $600 (= .02 × $30,000) as an expense and reduce the book value of merchandise inventory accordingly. We allow this answer as well.

2.20 (Schneider Corporation; journal entries for various transactions.)

(1)	Cash	500,000	
	Common Stock		500,000
(2)	Land	40,000	
	Building	185,000	
	Cash		50,000
	Mortgage Payable		175,000
(3)	Equipment	13,200	
	Cash		13,200
(4)	Raw Materials Inventory	8,600	
	Accounts Payable		8,600
(5)	Accounts Payable	900	
	Raw Materials Inventory		900
(6)	Accounts Payable	7,700	
	Cash		7,546
	Raw Materials Inventory		154

.98($8,600 – $900) = $7,546.

(7)	Prepaid Insurance	4,950	
	Cash		4,950
(8)	Organization Costs	8,000	
	Cash		8,000
(9)	Prepaid Rent	1,800	
	Cash		1,800
(10)	Patent	90,000	
	Cash		90,000
(11)	Equipment	2,700	
	Cash		250
	Account Payable		2,450
(12)	Equipment	825	
	Cash		825

 Solutions

2.21   (Winkle Grocery Store; journal entries for various transactions.)

(1)	Cash	30,000	
	Common Stock		30,000

(2)	Cash	5,000	
	Notes Payable		5,000

(3)	Prepaid Rent	12,000	
	Cash		12,000

(4)	Equipment	8,000	
	Cash		8,000

(5)	Merchandise Inventory	25,000	
	Cash		12,000
	Accounts Payable		13,000

(6)	Cash	4,000	
	Advances from Customers		4,000

(7)	Prepaid Insurane	1,200	
	Cash		1,200

(8)	Prepaid Adertising	600	
	Cash		600

(9)   The placing of an order does not give rise to a journal entry because it represents a mutually unexecuted contract.

2.22   (Journal entries for various transactions.)

(1)	Investment in Bonds	82,500	
	Cash		82,500

(2)	Cash	3,240	
	Insurance Premiums Received in Advance		3,240

(3)	Land	10,000	
	Building	90,000	
	Equipment	40,000	
	Common Stock—Par Value		120,000
	Additional Paid-in Capital		20,000

(4)   Accounting makes no entry because an exchange between the buyer and seller has not yet occurred to warrant recognition of either an asset or a liability.

Solutions   2-10

2.22 continued.

 (5) Organizational Costs................................. 7,500
    Preferred Stock—Par Value......................   4,000
    Additional Paid-in Capital.........................   3,500

 (6) Cash... 80
    Admission Fees Received in Advance..........   80

 (7) No entry is made until accountants establish the amount and timing of payment.

 (8) Accounts Payable.................................... 3,000
    Merchandise Inventory............................   3,000

2.23 (Wendy's International, Inc.; journal entries for various transactions.)

 (1) The firm does not make an entry for the supplies until they are received.

 (2) Supplies Inventory 1,600,000
    Accounts Payable................................   1,600,000

 (3) Accounts Payable.................................... 40,000
    Supplies Inventory...............................   40,000

 (4) Accounts Payable.................................... 1,400,000
    Cash   1,372,000
    Supplies Inventory...............................   28,000

 (5) Accounts Payable.................................... 160,000
    Cash   160,000

 Note: Some students treat the lost discounts of $3,200 (= .02 × $160,000) as an expense and reduce Supplies Inventory accordingly. We allow this answer as well.

 (6) Deposit on Equipment............................... 200,000
    Cash   200,000

 (7) Equipment.. 900,000
    Deposit on Equipment...........................   200,000
    Cash   700,000

 (8) Equipment.. 27,000
    Cash   27,000

 (9) Receivable from Supplier........................... 22,000
    Equipment..   22,000

 (10) Cash... 22,000
    Receivable from Supplier.......................   22,000

         Solutions

2.24   (Effect of transactions on balance sheet equation.)

Transaction Number		Assets	=	Liabilities	+	Shareholders' Equity
(1)		+ $30,000				+ $30,000
	Subtotal	$30,000	=			$30,000
(2)		+ 18,900		+ $18,900		
	Subtotal	$48,900	=	$18,900	+	$30,000
(3)		+ 12,700				
		− 2,000		+ 10,700		
	Subtotal	$59,600	=	$29,600	+	$30,000
(4)		+ 1,800				
		− 1,800				
	Subtotal	$59,600	=	$29,600	+	$30,000
(5)				− 10,700		+ 10,700
	Subtotal	$59,600	=	$18,900	+	$40,700
(6)		− 18,900		− 18,900		
	Total	$40,700	=	-0-	+	$40,700

2.25   (T-account entries for various transactions.)

Cash (A)

(1)	240,000	80,000	(2)
(5)	20,000	3,000	(4)
(7)	600	22,000	(6)
	155,600		

Merchandise Inventory (A)

(3)	35,000	
	35,000	

Prepaid Insurance (A)

(4)	3,000	
	3,000	

Building (A)

(2)	500,000	
	500,000	

Equipment (A)

(3)	20,000	
	20,000	

Accounts Payable (L)

(6)	22,000	55,000	(3)
		33,000	

Note Payable (L)

	20,000	(5)
	20,000	

Advances from Customers

	600	(7)
	600	

Mortgage Payable (L)

	420,000	(2)
	420,000	

Common Stock— Par Value (SE)

	100,000	(1)
	100,000	

Additional Paid-in Capital (SE)

	140,000	(1)
	140,000	

2.26 (Patterson Manufacturing Corporation; T-account entries and balance sheet preparation.)

a.

Cash (A)			
(1) 210,000	5,400	(5)	
(11) 4,500	350	(6)	
	1,400	(8)	
	58,200	(9)	
	7,000	(12)	
	95,000	(14)	
47,150			

Marketable Securities (A)	
(14) 95,000	
95,000	

Receivable from Supplier (A)	
(13) 1,455	
1,455	

Raw Materials Inventory (A)			
(4) 75,000	800	(7)	
	1,800	(9)	
	1,455	(13)	
70,945			

Prepaid Rent (A)	
(8) 1,400	
1,400	

Land (A)	
(2) 80,000	
80,000	

Buildings (A)	
(2) 220,000	
(12) 60,000	
280,000	

Equipment (A)	
(2) 92,000	
(5) 5,400	
(6) 350	
97,750	

Organization Costs (A)	
(3) 28,000	
28,000	

? ok → MKt value of the share.

Accounts Payable (L)			
(7) 800	75,000	(4)	
(9) 60,000			
	14,200		

Advances from Customers (L)	
	4,500 (11)
	4,500

Mortgage Payable (L)	
	53,000 (12)
	53,000

Common Stock Par Value (SE)	
	150,000 (1)
	280,000 (2)
	20,000 (3)
	450,000

Additional Paid-in Capital (SE)	
	60,000 (1)
	112,000 (2)
	8,000 (3)
	180,000

(10) Because no insurance coverage has yet been provided and no cash has changed hands, the principle of mutual exchange suggests that no asset and no liability be recorded.

2.26 continued.

b.

PATTERSON MANUFACTURING CORPORATION
Balance Sheet
January 31

Assets

Current Assets:

Cash..	$ 47,150	
Marketable Securities.............................	95,000	
Receivable from Supplier	1,455	
Raw Materials Inventory.........................	70,945	
Prepaid Rent[a]..	1,400	
Total Current Assets.........................		$ 215,950

Property, Plant, and Equipment (at Acquisition Cost):

Land...	$ 80,000	
Buildings...	280,000	
Equipment	97,750	
Total Property, Plant, and Equipment...		457,750

Intangibles:

Organization Costs.................................		28,000
Total Assets		$ 701,700

Liabilities and Shareholders' Equity

Current Liabilities:

Accounts Payable[a]	$ 14,200	
Advances from Customers.......................	4,500	
Total Current Liabilities.......................		$ 18,700

Long-Term Debt:

Mortgage Payable..................................		53,000
Total Liabilities		$ 71,700

Shareholders' Equity:

Common Stock—$10 Par Value	$ 450,000	
Additional Paid-in Capital	180,000	
Total Shareholders' Equity....................		630,000
Total Liabilities and Shareholders' Equity		$ 701,700

[a]See discussion of transaction (10) on the preceding page. It is not wrong to show a current asset, Prepaid Insurance, of $400 and an additional $400 in the current liability, Accounts Payable. If that amount is shown, then, of course, the various subtotals and totals will increase by $400.

2.27 (Idaho Products Corporation; T-account entries and balance sheet preparation.)

a.

	Cash (A)		
(1)	240,000	40,000	(3)
(2)	50,000	8,000	(4)
(11)	12,000	1,200	(5)
		1,800	(6)
		1,300	(8)
		30,000	(10)
		39,200	(12)
	180,500		

	Merchandise Inventory (A)		
(7)	60,000	1,900	(9)
		800	(12)
	57,300		

	Prepaid License Fees (A)	
(8)	1,300	
	1,300	

	Land (A)	
(3)	25,000	
	25,000	

	Buildings (A)	
(3)	75,000	
	75,000	

	Equipment (A)	
(4)	46,000	
(5)	1,200	
(6)	1,800	
	49,000	

	Patent (A)	
(10)	30,000	
	30,000	

Note Payable (L)		
	38,000	(4)
	38,000	

	Accounts Payable (L)		
(9)	1,900	60,000	(7)
(12)	40,000		
		18,100	

Advances from Customers (L)		
	12,000	(11)
	12,000	

Preferred Stock (SE)		
	50,000	(2)
	50,000	

Common Stock (SE)		
	100,000	(1)
	25,000	(3)
	125,000	

Additional Paid-in Capital (SE)		
	140,000	(1)
	35,000	(3)
	175,000	

2.27 continued.

b.

IDAHO PRODUCTS CORPORATION
Balance Sheet
April 30

Assets

Current Assets:

Cash..	$ 180,500	
Merchandise Inventory	57,300	
Prepaid License Fees.............................	1,300	
Total Current Assets..........................		$ 239,100

Property, Plant, and Equipment:

Land...	$ 25,000	
Buildings..	75,000	
Equipment	49,000	
Total Property, Plant, and Equipment...		149,000

Intangibles:

Patent..		30,000
Total Assets......................................		$ 418,100

Liabilities and Shareholders' Equity

Current Liabilities:

Note Payable..	$ 38,000	
Accounts Payable..................................	18,100	
Advances from Customers......................	12,000	
Total Current Liabilities.....................		$ 68,100

Shareholders' Equity:

Preferred Stock—$100 Par Value	$ 50,000	
Common Stock—$5 Par Value................	125,000	
Additional Paid-in Capital	175,000	
Total Shareholders' Equity..................		350,000
Total Liabilities and Shareholders' Equity		$ 418,100

2.28   (Soybel Corporation; T-account entries and balance sheet preparation.)

a.

Cash (A)				Merchandise Inventory (A)				Prepaid Insurance (A)			
(1)	125,000	180,000	(3)	(5)	50,000	5,000	(6)	(7)	1,600		
(2)	200,000	78,400	(4)								
(8)	500	1,600	(7)								
		44,000	(9)								
	21,500				45,000				1,600		

Land (A)		Buildings (A)		Equipment (A)	
(3) 40,000		(3) 210,000		(4) 78,400	
40,000		210,000		78,400	

Accounts Payable (L)				Advances from Customers (L)		Mortgage Payable (L)	
(6)	5,000	50,000	(5)		500 (8)		70,000 (3)
(9)	44,000						
		1,000			500		70,000

Bonds Payable (L)		Common Stock (SE)		Additional Paid-in Capital (SE)	
	200,000 (2)		100,000 (1)		25,000 (1)
	200,000		100,000		25,000

b.

SOYBEL CORPORATION
Balance Sheet
January 31

Assets

Current Assets:
Cash..	$ 21,500	
Merchandise Inventory	45,000	
Prepaid Insurance.................................	1,600	
Total Current Assets...........................		$ 68,100

Property, Plant, and Equipment:
Land...	$ 40,000	
Buildings...	210,000	
Equipment	78,400	
Total Property, Plant, and Equipment ...		328,400
Total Assets.......................................		$ 396,500

2.28 b. continued.

Liabilities and Shareholders' Equity

Current Liabilities:
Accounts Payable	$ 1,000	
Advances from Customers	500	
Total Current Liabilities		$ 1,500

Long-Term Debt:
Mortgage Payable	$ 70,000	
Bonds Payable	200,000	
Total Long-Term Debt		270,000
Total Liabilities		$ 271,500

Shareholders' Equity:
Common Stock	$ 100,000	
Additional Paid-in Capital	25,000	
Total Shareholders' Equity		125,000
Total Liabilities and Shareholders' Equity		$ 396,500

2.29 (Computer Graphics, Inc.; T-account entries and balance sheet preparation.)

a.

Cash (A)				Supplies Inventory (A)				Prepaid Rent (A)		
(1) 150,000	18,000	(4)	(8)	4,900	98	(10)	(4)	18,000	
(7) 1,500	12,000	(5)	(9)	900					
	900	(9)							
	4,802	(10)							
115,798				5,702				18,000	

Equipment (A)			Computer Software (A)			Organization Costs (A)		
(5) 12,000		(2)	90,000		(3)	1,500	
12,000			90,000			1,500	

Accounts Payable (L)			Advances from Customers (L)			Common Stock (SE)	
(10) 4,900	4,900	(8)		1,500	(7)	100,000	(1)
						60,000	(2)
						1,000	(3)
--	--			1,500		161,000	

2.29 a. continued.

```
       Additional Paid-In
         Capital (SE)
    _____
              |  50,000  (1)
              |  30,000  (2)
              |     500  (3)
    _____|_____
              |  80,500
              |
```

b.

COMPUTER GRAPHICS, INC.
Balance Sheet
May 30

Assets

Current Assets:		
Cash..	$ 115,798	
Supplies Inventory.................................	5,702	
Prepaid Rent	18,000	
Total Current Assets..........................		$ 139,500
Noncurrent Assets:		
Equipment	$ 12,000	
Computer Software	90,000	
Organization Costs...............................	1,500	
Total Noncurrent Assets		103,500
Total Assets.......................................		$ 243,000

Liabilities and Shareholders' Equity

Current Liabilities:		
Advances from Customers		$ 1,500
Shareholders' Equity:		
Common Stock.......................................	$ 161,000	
Additional Paid-in Capital	80,500	
Total Shareholders' Equity...................		241,500
Total Liabilities and Shareholders' Equity		$ 243,000

2.30　(Blacksmith's Bakery, Inc.; T-account entries and balance sheet preparation.)

a.

Cash (A)				Supplies Inventory (A)			Prepayments (A)		
(1)	2,000	450	(4)	(7) 390			(6) 800		
(2)	220	580	(5)	(9) 240			(8) 120		
(3)	500	800	(6)						
		390	(7)						
		120	(8)						
	380			630			920		

Equipment (A)		Organization Costs (A)		Accounts Payable (L)	
(5) 580		(4) 450			240 (9)
		(10) 750			750 (10)
580		1,200			990

Advances from Customers (L)		Common Stock (SE)		Additional Paid-in Capital (SE)	
	220 (2)		2,000 (1)		500 (3)*
	220		2,000		500

Note: *The chapter does not discuss the correct credit entry for transaction (3). Students should realize that the absence of a repayment obligation precludes recognition of a liability. The principal issue is the appropriate shareholders' equity account. We tend to allow various account titles.

2.30 continued.

b.
BLACKSMITH'S BAKERY, INC.,
Balance Sheet
August 31

Assets

Current Assets:
Cash...	$ 380	
Supplies Inventory................................	630	
Prepaid Rent	920	
Total Current Assets........................		$ 1,930
Noncurrent Assets:................................		
Equipment	$ 580	
Organization Costs..............................	1,200	
Total Noncurrent Assets		$ 1,780
Total Assets......................................		$ 3,710

Liabilities and Shareholders' Equity

Current Liabilities:
Accounts Payable..................................	$ 990	
Advances from Customers......................	220	
Total Current Liabilities......................		$ 1,210
Shareholders' Equity:		
Common Stock.......................................	$ 2,000	
Additional Paid-in Capital	500	
Total Shareholders' Equity..................		2,500
Total Liabilities and Shareholders'		
Equity		$3,710

 2.31 (Effect of recording errors on balance sheet equation.)

Transaction Number	Assets	=	Liabilities	+	Shareholders' Equity
(1)	U/S $ 8,000		U/S $ 8,000		No
(2)	U/S $15,000		U/S $15,000		No
(3)	No		No		No
(4)	U/S $ 600		U/S $ 600		No
(5)	O/S $ 1,200[a]		No		No
	U/S $ 1,200[a]				
(6)	U/S $ 2,500		No		U/S $ 2,500
(7)	O/S $ 4,000		O/S $ 4,000		No
(8)	O/S $ 5,000[a]		No		No
	U/S $ 5,000[a]				

[a]The response "No" is also acceptable here.

     Solutions

2.32   (Effect of recording errors on balance sheet equation.)

Transaction Number	Assets	=	Liabilities	+	Shareholders' Equity
(1)	U/S $760,000		U/S $760,000		No
(2)	O/S $ 800[a]		No		No
	U/S $ 800[a]				No
(3)	No		No		No
(4)	No		O/S $10,000		U/S $10,000
(5)	U/S $ 900[a]		No		No
	O/S $ 900[a]				
(6)	No		No		No
(7)	O/S $ 2,000		No		O/S $2,000
(8)	O/S $ 3,000		O/S $ 3,000		No

[a]The response "No" is also acceptable here.

2.33   (Effect of recording errors on balance sheet equation.)

Transaction Number	Assets	=	Liabilities	+	Shareholders' Equity
(1)	U/S $8,000		U/S $ 8,000		No
(2)	O/S $3,000		O/S $ 3,000		No
(3)	U/S $ 800		U/S $ 800		No
(4)	O/S $1,000		O/S $ 1,000		No
(5)	U/S $2,500		No		U/S $2,500
(6)	O/S $4,900[a]		No		No
	U/S $4,900[a]				

[a]The response "No" is also acceptable here.

2.34 (Marks and Spenser; balance sheet format, terminology, and accounting methods.)

a.
MARKS AND SPENCER, PLC
Balance Sheet
(In Millions of Pounds)

	March 30 Year 4	March 30 Year 5
Assets		
Current Assets:		
Cash	£ 266	£ 293
Marketable Securities	28	29
Accounts Receivable	192	212
Inventories	374	351
Prepayments	134	142
Total Current Assets	£ 994	£ 1,027
Property, Plant and Equipment:		
Land and Buildings	£ 1,636	£ 1,733
Equipment	375	419
Total Property, Plant and Equipment	£ 2,011	£ 2,152
Other Assets	£ 212	£ 264
Total Assets	£ 3,217	£ 3,443
Liabilities and Shareholders' Equity		
Current Liabilities:		
Accounts Payable	£ 187	£ 168
Bank Loans	100	107
Other Current Liabilities	638	622
Total Current Liabilities	£ 925	£ 897
Noncurrent Liabilities:		
Bonds Payable	£ 565	£ 550
Other Noncurrent Liabilities	4	19
Total Noncurrent Liabilities	£ 569	£ 569
Total Liabilities	£ 1,494	£ 1,466
Shareholders' Equity:		
Common Stock	£ 675	£ 680
Additional Paid-in Capital	50	69
Retained Earnings	998	1,228
Total Shareholders' Equity	£ 1,723	£ 1,977
Total Liabilities and Shareholders' Equity	£ 3,217	£ 3,443

[a]£2,094 − £458 = £1,636.
[b]£2,193 − £460 = £1,733.

b. A close relation exists between the amount of current assets and current liabilities and between noncurrent assets and noncurrent liabilities plus shareholders' equity.

2.35 (United Breweries Group; balance sheet format, terminology, and accounting methods.)

a.

UNITED BREWERIES GROUP
Balance Sheet
(In Millions of Kronor)

	September 30 Year 8	September 30 Year 9
Assets		
Current Assets:		
Cash	Kr 810	Kr 1,224
Marketable Securities	3,018	3,460
Accounts Receivable	1,413	1,444
Inventories	1,290	1,393
Prepayments	317	285
Total Current Assets	Kr 6,848	Kr 7,806
Investments In Securities	422	573
Property, Plant and Equipment[a]	3,518	3,545
Total Assets	Kr 10,788	Kr 11,924
Liabilities and Shareholders' Equity		
Current Liabilities:		
Accounts Payable	Kr 913	Kr 902
Bank Debt	619	986
Other Current Liabilities	2,157	2,240
Total Current Liabilities	Kr 3,689	Kr 4,128
Bonds Payable	1,805	1,723
Other Noncurrent Liabilities	1,149	1,425
Total Liabilities	Kr 6,643	Kr 7,276
Shareholders' Equity:		
Common Stock	Kr 976	Kr 976
Retained Earnings	3,169	3,672
Total Shareholders' Equity	Kr 4,145	Kr 4,648
Total Liabilities and Shareholders' Equity	Kr 10,788	Kr 11,924

[a]The amounts for this account reflect historical costs instead of current market values as follows:

	As Reported By Company	Revaluation Reserve	As Restated
Property, Plant and Equipment:			
September 30, Year 8	Kr 3,934	Kr 416	Kr 3,518
September 30, Year 9	Kr 4,106	Kr 561	Kr 3,545

2.35 continued.

　　b.　Current assets significantly exceed current liabilities, primarily because of the high proportion of current assets that comprises cash and marketable securities. United Breweries has apparently generated substantial cash flow from operations which it has not reinvested in operating assets.

2.36　(Humana, Inc.; interpreting balance sheet changes.)

　　a.　The primary assets of a hospital are property, plant and equipment and accounts receivable from patients and reimbursement entities (insurance companies, Medicare). Hospitals finance a large portion of their fixed assets with long-term debt.

　　b.　Property, plant and equipment represent a decreasing percentage of total assets, suggesting either the absence or a decreasing rate of growth of additional investments in new facilities or equipment. Humana is probably continuing to use existing fixed assets. The decreasing percentage reflects depreciation on these facilities. The increasing percentages for cash and retained earnings suggest profitable operations that generated cash. Humana used some of the cash to increase long-term investments, perhaps in other health care-related businesses, and partially to reduce long-term debt.

　　c.　The percentages in the common size balance sheet are not independent of each other. A decrease in the dollar amount of property, plant and equipment may result in an increasing, decreasing, or stable proportion for this balance sheet item, depending on the changes in other assets.

2.37　(Kroger Company; interpreting balance sheet changes.)

　　a.　Inventories and property, plant and equipment dominate the asset side of the balance sheet. The mix of short-term financing matches the mix of short-term assets. Kroger Company finances its property, plant and equipment with a mixture of long-term debt and retained earnings. The large proportion for treasury stock suggests a buyback of stock perhaps to defend against an unfriendly takeover.

　　b.　Kroger Company increased the proportion of long-term debt in its capital structure and generated a negative balance in retained earnings. The most likely explanation for the negative retained earnings is the payment of a dividend to shareholders using the proceeds from the long-term borrowing. These transactions increased the proportion of debt in the capital structure and made Kroger Company a less attractive target for an unfriendly takeover.

　　　　　　　　　　　　　　　　Solutions

2.38   (Relating market value to book value of shareholders' equity.)

(1) **Coke**—One important asset missing from the balance sheet of Coke is the value of its brand names. Coke follows generally accepted accounting principles (GAAP) in expensing the cost of developing and maintaining its brand names each year (for example, product development, quality control, advertising). The future benefits of these expenditures are too difficult to identify and measure with sufficient precision to justify recognizing an asset. Coke also reports its property, plant and equipment at acquisition cost (adjusted downward for depreciation) instead of current market values. Acquisition cost valuations are more objective and easier to audit than current market valuations.

(2) **Pepsi**—Pepsi likewise does not report the full value of brand names on its balance sheet. Unlike Coke, however, Pepsi has acquired other companies in recent years. Part of the purchase prices of these companies (Taco Bell, KFC) is the value of their brand names. Pepsi includes the value of these brand names in goodwill, which appears on the Other Noncurrent Assets line in Exhibit 2.16. Thus, Pepsi's balance sheet reflects more of the value of brand names than Coke's and its market-to-book ratio is therefore smaller than the corresponding ratio for Coke. Also, the book value of property, plant and equipment for Pepsi more closely reflects market values as a result of recording these recent acquisitions.

(3) **Bristol**—Bristol engages in research and development to discover new drugs. GAAP requires firms to expense research and development expenditures immediately. The future benefits of these expenditures are too uncertain to justify recognizing an asset. Thus, the value of patents and technologies developed by Bristol, as well as the value of the research scientists employed by Bristol, do not appear on its balance sheet.

(4) **Bankers Trust**—The market-to-book ratio for Bankers is 1.0. Most of the assets and liabilities of Bankers are monetary items and turn over frequently. Thus, the market values and book values closely conform.

(5) **International Paper (IP)**—IP reports its forest lands on the balance sheet at acquisition cost. IP likely acquired the land many years ago. The acquisition cost of the land is considerably less than its current market value. Also, IP follows general industry practice and expenses the annual cost of maintaining its forest lands. Thus, the value of forest lands increases each year as trees grow. The market incorporates this value increase into its price of the common stock of IP even though GAAP does not reflect the value increase on the balance sheet. The value increase is too difficult to measure objectively to justify substituting market values for acquisition cost.

2.38 continued.

(6) **Disney**—Disney depreciates the cost of film inventory over its expected useful life. Fortunately for Disney and other film production companies, the value of old films has increased in recent years with the growth of cable networks. Thus, the market value of some of Disney's films exceeds their book values. The market-to-book ratio reflects this under valuation. Also, Disney reports its property, plant and equipment at acquisition cost (adjusted downward for depreciation) instead of current market values. The land underlying its theme parks has likely increased in value since the date of acquisition, but the accounting records do not reflect the value increase under GAAP.

Some instructors may also wish to use this problem to discuss the term structure of assets and the term structure of liabilities and shareholders' equity, even though the problem requirements do not ask students to discuss this factor.

(1) **Coke**—Coke's current assets are less than its current liabilities. This relation indicates short-term liquidity risk. The high market-to-book ratio suggests that the market value (selling price) of its inventory exceeds the book value, so current assets probably equal or exceed current liabilities at market value. Shareholders' equity represents a higher proportion of long-term financing than long-term debt. One explanation for the relatively low proportion of long-term debt is that Coke is very profitable (suggested by the high market-to-book ratio) and therefore generates most of its needed cash from operations. Further support for the internal generation of cash is the high proportion of retained earnings and significant treasury stock purchases. Another explanation for the relatively low proportion of long-term debt relates to the investments in its bottlers. Chapter 13 discusses the accounting for intercorporate investments. Because Coke owns less than 50 percent of the outstanding common stock of these bottlers, it does not consolidate them. Thus, the assets and the financing of the bottlers are "off balance sheet." These bottlers may carry significantly more long-term debt than Coke.

(2) **Pepsi**—Pepsi, like Coke, has a slight excess of current liabilities over current assets, but the market value of its inventory likewise probably exceeds the book value. Pepsi, however, has considerably more long-term debt in the capital structure. The major reason for Pepsi's higher proportion of long-debt is its need to finance recent acquisitions. Coke grew its operations internally as it generated cash flow from operations. Pepsi grew more from acquisitions and needed large sums of cash up front to pay the sellers of these businesses.

2.38 continued.

(3) **Bristol**—The interesting insight from studying Bristol's capital structure is the relatively small proportion of long-term debt. The products of Bristol are subject to technological obsolescence. Competitors could develop technologically superior drugs that would replace those of Bristol in the market. Given this product risk, Bristol probably does not want to add the financial risk that fixed interest and principal payments on debt create.

(4) **Bankers Trust**—Bankers relies heavily on short-term sources for financing, principally deposits and short-term borrowing. Customers can withdraw their funds on no, or very short, notice. Thus, Bankers must maintain a relatively liquid balance sheet. Most of its assets are in cash, short-term marketable securities, and loans. The loans are less liquid than cash and marketable securities but tend to have predictable cash flows. Note that shareholders' equity makes up approximately 5 percent of liabilities plus shareholders' equities. Such a low percentage is common for commercial banks. Banks carry high proportions of liabilities because of the high liquidity of their assets.

(5) **International Paper (IP)**—IP carries a high proportion of noncurrent assets and matches this with a high proportion of long-term financing. IP uses approximately equal proportions of long-term liabilities and shareholders' equity to finance its noncurrent assets. The sales of paper products vary with movements through economic cycles. During recessionary periods, demand slackens and firms reduce prices in order to utilize capital-intensive manufacturing facilities. Paper companies do not want too much debt in their capital structures that could force them into bankruptcy during these times. On the other hand, when the economy is booming, the profits and cash flows of paper companies increase significantly. Firms spread the cost of their capital-intensive plants over larger volumes of output. In these cases, shareholders benefit from debt in the capital structure (a phenomenon known as *financial leverage*, discussed in Chapter 6). Thus, the approximately equal proportions of long-term debt and shareholders' equity reflect these opposing considerations.

2.38 continued.

(6) **Disney**—Disney reports a significant excess of current assets over current liabilities. Interpreting this excess involves two opposing considerations. Some of Disney's films continue to generate revenues and cash flows, even though the films carry a zero book value on Disney's books. On the other hand, Disney accumulates the cost of films in process in the inventory account without knowing whether or not the films will be a commercial success. Disney uses a higher proportion of shareholders' equity than long-term debt in its long-term financing structure. Its property, plant and equipment can serve as collateral for long-term borrowing. Its predictable revenue and cash flows from theme parks also argues for a high proportion of long-term debt relative to shareholders' equity. Perhaps Disney did not want to use up its borrowing capacity in case it had the opportunity to make an acquisition (such as Capital Cities/ABC) and needed to borrow to finance the transaction.

CHAPTER 3

INCOME STATEMENT: REPORTING THE RESULTS OF OPERATING ACTIVITIES

Questions, Exercises, Problems, and Cases: Answers and Solutions

3.1   See the text or the glossary at the end of the book.

3.2   One factor considered in the accounting period decision is whether a firm has a natural business year upon which to base its accounting period. If a firm's activities are reasonably uniform throughout the year, it does not have a natural business year and, therefore, must choose an "artificial" one. In selecting such a period, a firm probably considers what other firms in its industry do. A large proportion of publicly held firms use the calendar year as their accounting period.

3.3   A natural business year is one beginning with a slack season, followed by a busy period, and ending with a slack season one year later. The ski resort and basketball team both have natural business years. The business of the grocery store is reasonably uniform throughout the year and, therefore, it does not have a natural business year.

3.4   Revenues measure the inflows of net assets from selling goods and providing services. Under the accrual basis of accounting, accountants recognize revenue in the period of sale rather than in the period when the firm receives cash. Under the cash basis of accounting, accountants recognize revenue at the time the firm receives cash.

       Under the accrual basis of accounting, revenue equals cash receipts in the case of cash sales (in contrast to sales on account). Under the cash basis of accounting, they are the same except for receipts from additional financing, such as borrowings from a bank or issuances of bonds or common stock on the market.

3.5   Expenses measure the outflows of net assets used up, or consumed, in the process of generating revenues. Under the accrual basis of accounting, accountants recognize expenses either in the period in which the firm recognizes associated revenues or in the period in which the firm consumes services. The timing of cash disbursements may precede (as in the case of purchasing a machine), coincide with (as in the case of weekly salespersons' salaries), or follow (as in the case of unpaid taxes at year-end) the expense recognition. Under the cash basis of accounting, accountants recognize expenses at the time of the cash expenditure.

3.5 continued.

Under the accrual basis of accounting, expenses equal cash expenditures in the case where goods or services are paid for at the time the firm consumes them. Under the cash basis of accounting, they will be the same except in cases where a firm repays bank loans or redeems long-term bonds or common stock.

3.6 The amount of revenue recognized equals the amount of cash the firm expects to collect from customers. The firm does not necessarily recognize the revenue, however, at the time it receives the cash. It typically recognizes revenue at the time of sale even though it has not yet collected cash from customers. Likewise, the amount of expense recognized equals the cash disbursement made for equipment, materials, labor, and so forth. However, the firm recognizes the expense when it consumes the services of these factor inputs, not when it makes the cash expenditure.

3.7 Accountants treat assets as expired costs, or expenses, when the firm consumes the services of the assets in generating revenues. The initial financing of the asset (for example, outright cash purchase, acquisition on account, acquisition by the issuance of common stock) is irrelevant to when the asset becomes an expense under the accrual basis of accounting. Likewise, the timing of the receipt of cash from customers is not relevant to when accountants recognize revenue under the accrual basis. Accounting recognizes revenue when a firm has performed all, or a substantial portion, of the services to be provided and has received cash, a receivable, or some other asset susceptible to reasonably precise measurement.

3.8 Depreciation on manufacturing equipment is a product cost (asset) until a firm sells the goods manufactured with the equipment. Depreciation on selling or administrative equipment is a period expense.

3.9 The accountant could record the revenue and expense aspects of transactions during the period and adjustments at the end of the period directly in the Retained Earnings or another shareholders' equity account.

3.10 Revenues and expenses measure the inflows and outflows of net assets from selling goods and providing services for a particular period of time. If the accountant did not close revenue and expense accounts at the end of each period, the revenue and expense amounts of one period would mingle with similar amounts of subsequent periods.

3.11   Before the books are closed, both balance sheet (permanent) and income statement (temporary) accounts have nonzero balances. After the closing of income statement accounts, only the balance sheet accounts have nonzero balances.

3.12   Some events occur that affect the net income and financial position of a firm but for which an external transaction does not occur by the end of a period that signals the need for an entry in the accounting records. For example, a firm uses depreciable assets during the year. Because no external exchange occurs, the use of such depreciable assets is not recorded until the accountant makes adjusting entries. Likewise, workers earn salaries during the last several days of the year but are not paid until early next year. Here, again, no external exchange occurs before year end to trigger recognition of the cost of the labor services in the accounts. The adjusting entry accomplishes this.

3.13   Contra accounts provide disaggregated information concerning the net amount of an asset, liability, or shareholders' equity item. For example, the account, Accounts Receivable Net of Estimated Uncollectible Accounts, does not indicate separately the gross amount of receivables from customers and the estimated amount of the gross receivables that the firm expects to collect. If the firm used a contra account, it would have such information. The alternative to using contra accounts is to debit or credit directly the principal account involved (for example, Accounts Receivable from Customers). This alternative procedure, however, does not permit computation of disaggregated information about the net balance in the account. Note that the use of contra accounts does not affect the total of assets, liabilities, shareholders' equity, revenues, or expenses.

3.14   (J. C. Penney; revenue recognition.)

a. None.

d. None.

b. $16,940,000.

e. $8,000.

c. $2,925,000.

f. $8,000.

3.15   (Revenue recognition.)

	April	May	June
a.	$6,500	--	--
b.	--	$28,600	--
c.	--	--	$2,200
d.	$ 150	$ 150	$ 150

3.15 continued.

e.	--	$ 150	$ 150
f.	--	--	$ 150

3.16   (Whirlpool Corporation; revenue recognition.)

a. 0.

b. 0.

c. $116,400 (could recognize revenue in *b.*, at time of shipment, if F.O.B. point is shipping point).

d. 0 (could recognize revenue here if F.O.B. point is destination).

e. 0.

f. Revenue reduction of $7,760 (= .97 × $8,000).

3.17   (Revenue recognition.)

a. No (Magnavox has not yet delivered the goods).

b. Yes.

c. No (this is a financing, not an operating, transaction).

d. No (NIKE has not identified a customer, set a price, or shipped the goods).

e. No (the concert will not take place for two weeks).

f. Yes (the agent has provided the services); the revenue amount is only the commission, however.

g. Yes (on an accrual basis, accounting recognizes interest as time passes).

h. No (accounting usually recognizes revenue when a firm sells goods or services).

i. Yes.

 3.18   (Computervision; expense recognition.)

a. 0 asset; 0 expense.

b. 0 asset; 0 expense.

3.18 continued.

    c.   0 asset; 0 expense.

    d. $406,000 asset; 0 expense.

    e.   0 asset; 0 expense.

    f.   Reduce assets by $14,000; 0 expense.

    g. $384,160 [= .98($406,000 – $14,000)] cash reduction + $7,840 [= .02($406,000 – $14,000)] inventory reduction.

    h. $115,840 (= $500,000 – $384,160) asset increase; $384,160 (= $406,000 – $14,000 – $7,840) expense.

3.19   (Expense recognition.)

    a. $1,500.   d. $5,500 (= $2,000 + $7,000 – $3,500).

    b. $4,600.   e. $4,000 (= $48,000/12).

    c. $6,500 (= $3,000 + $7,000 – $3,500).   f.   Zero (an expense of April).

3.20   (Expense recognition.)

	April	May	June
a.	$3,300	--	--
b.	--	$4,500	--
c.	--	--	$1,600
d.	--	$ 200	$ 200
e.	--	--	--
f.	$ 300	$ 300	$ 300

3.21   (Allocation of cost.)

    a.   The accountant allocates the cost less estimated salvage value over 30 years. The issue is whether the accountant allocates the cost of the building using a straight line, accelerating, or decelerating pattern.

    b.   The accountant should use the useful life of 5 years in this case, because obsolescence is more important than physical deterioration in measuring useful life.

 Solutions

3.21 continued.

    c.   The accountant should allocate rent over the two years of use of the warehouse.

    d.   The issue here is whether the accountant should substitute mileage for time in measuring service potential. The mileage basis is probably appropriate here because of the ease of measurement over time. There are questions, however, as to whether 90,000 miles is a reasonable estimate of total mileage.

    e.   The issue here is whether the accountant should assign all of the rent to the period from June 1 to September 1 when the firm generates revenues or whether to allocate the rent over the entire year.

    f.   The issue here is the difficulty in estimating the total amount of ore the firm is likely to extract from the mine.

3.22   (Demski Company; income recognition.)

    a.   Cash Equivalent Value of Consideration

Received at Time of Sale......................		$147,000
Less Expenses:		
Cost of Trucks....................................	$125,000	
Preparation Costs	8,000	
Delivery Costs....................................	6,000	
Total Expenses		139,000
Profit on Sale		$ 8,000

    b.   Same as *a.* above.

    c.   Same as *a.* above.

3.23   (Identifying missing half of journal entries.)

    a.   Merchandise Inventory or Finished Goods Inventory decreases because the firm has sold goods.

    b.   Sales Revenue increases because of sales.

    c.   Cash increases because of collections from customers.

    d.   Cash decreases because of payments to creditors.

    e.   Either an inventory account or an expense account increases because of receipts of goods or services.

3.23 continued.

f. Depreciation Expense increases because an adjusting entry recognizes the expense.

g. Dividends Payable increases because of the dividend; or closing entry for an expense or income summary account showing a loss.

h. Either Insurance Expense increases (period expense) or Work-in-Process Inventory increases (product cost) as a result of an adjusting entry.

i. Cash decreases because a firm pays property taxes.

j. Either Accounts Payable increases or Cash decreases because of acquisition of Inventory.

k. Revenue increases because a firm provides goods or services to customers.

l. Assets increase for the amount of the cash or goods received from supplier.

3.24 (Midland Grocery Stores; asset versus expense recognition.)

a. Supplies Inventory (A)..................................... 430
    Accounts Payable (L)..................................... 430

b. Accounting Expense (SE)............................... 1,500
    Accounts Payable (L)..................................... 1,500

c. Equipment (A)... 14,720
    Accounts Payable (L)..................................... 14,720

d. Supplies Inventory (A)..................................... 450
    Accounts Payable (L)..................................... 450

e. Equipment (A)... 790
    Accounts Payable (L)..................................... 790

f. Organization Costs (A)................................... 2,000
    Accounts Payable (L)..................................... 2,000

g. No entry.

h. Repair Expense (SE)...................................... 73
    Accounts Payable (L)..................................... 73

i. Utilities Expense (SE) 190
    Accounts Payable (L)..................................... 190

3.25   (Restaurant Supply Company/Wendy's; journal entries for notes receivable and notes payable.)

a.   **Year 6**
     Dec. 1
     Notes Receivable 40,000
          Accounts Receivable...................................   40,000

     Dec. 31
     Interest Receivable.. 200
          Interest Revenue   200
     $20,000 × .06 × 30/360.

     Dec. 31
     Interest Revenue... 200
          Retained Earnings (or Income Summary).....   200
     Entry assumes this note is the only one giving
     rise to interest revenue during the period.

     Year 7
     March 1
     Cash.. 40,600
          Interest Receivable....................................   200
          Interest Revenue   400
          Notes Receivable 40,000

b.   **Year 6**
     Dec. 1
     Accounts Payable... 40,000
          Notes Payable   40,000

     Dec. 31
     Interest Expense.. 200
          Interest Payable..   200

     Dec. 31
     Retained Earnings (or Income Summary)........ 200
          Interest Expense..   200
     Entry assumes this note is the only one giving
     rise to interest expense during the period.

     Year 7
     March 1
     Interest Payable.. 200
     Interest Expense.. 400
     Notes Payable 40,000
          Cash 40,600

3.26   (Rivera Company; journal entries for notes payable.)

      a.   **Jan. 15**

Accounts Payable..	12,000	
Notes Payable		12,000

         Jan. 31

Interest Expense..	30	
Interest Payable...		30
$12,000 × .06 × 15/360.		

         Feb. 28

Interest Expense..	60	
Interest Payable...		60
$12,000 × .06 × 30/360.		

      b.   **March 15**

Notes Payable	12,000	
Interest Payable...	90	
Interest Expense..	30	
Cash		12,120

      c.   **April 1**

Merchandise Inventory	3,000	
Notes Payable		3,000

         April 30

Interest Expense..	20	
Interest Payable...		20
3,000 × .08 × 30/360.		

         May 31
         Same entry as April 30.

         June 30
         Same entry as April 30.

      d.   **July 1**

Notes Payable	2,000	
Interest Payable...	60	
Cash		2,060

3.27   (Kelly Services; journal entries for office supply inventories.)

      a.   **1/1–3/31**

Office Supplies Inventory...............................	56,900	
Accounts Payable..		56,900

                       Solutions

3.27 a. continued.

March 31
Office Supplies Expense 62,200
    Office Supplies Inventory 62,200
$62,200 = $32,600 + $56,900 − $27,300.

b. **1/1–3/31**
Office Supplies Expense 56,900
    Accounts Payable 56,900

March 31
Office Supplies Expense 5,300
    Office Supplies Inventory 5,300
$5,300 = $32,600 − $27,300.

3.28   (Arizona Realty Company; journal entries for rental receipts and payments.)

(Arizona Realty Company)
May 1
Cash 900
    Advances from Tenant 900

May 30
Advances from Tenant 900
    Rent Revenue 900

May 30
Rent Revenue 900
    Income Summary 900

June 1
Cash 1,800
    Advances from Tenant 1,800

June 30
Advances from Tenant 900
    Rent Revenue 900

June 30
Rent Revenue 900
    Income Summary 900

July 31
Advances from Tenant 900
    Rent Revenue 900

3.28 continued.

July 31

Rent Revenue..	900	
Income Summary..		900

Aug. 1

Cash..	2,700	
Advances from Tenant....................................		2,700

Aug. 31

Advances from Tenant.......................................	900	
Rent Revenue..		900

Aug. 31

Rent Revenue..	900	
Income Summary..		900

Note: An alternative set of journal entries credits Rent Revenue instead of Advances from Tenant when the firm receives amounts on the first of any month covering rental fees for that month.

(Hagen Consultants)

May 1

Prepaid Rent	900	
Cash..		900

May 30

Rent Expense	900	
Prepaid Rent..		900

May 30

Income Summary..	900	
Rent Expense..		900

June 1

Prepaid Rent	1,800	
Cash..		1,800

June 30

Rent Expense	900	
Prepaid Rent..		900

June 30

Income Summary..	900	
Rent Expense..		900

July 31

Rent Expense	900	
Prepaid Rent..		900

 Solutions

3.28 continued.

July 31
Income Summary.. 900
    Rent Expense... 900

Aug. 1
Prepaid Rent 2,700
    Cash.. 2,700

Aug. 31
Rent Expense 900
    Prepaid Rent.. 900

Aug. 31
Income Summary.. 900
    Rent Expense... 900

Note: An alternative set of journal entries debits Rent Expense instead of Prepaid Rent when the firm pays amounts on the first of any month covering rental fees for that month.

3.29 (Using accumulated depreciation to estimate asset age.)

a. $\dfrac{\$9,000}{\$15,000} \times 10$ years = 6 years old.

b. $\dfrac{\$8,000}{\$4,000 \text{ per year}}$ = 2 years of accumulated depreciation, suggesting that the asset is two years old.

3.30 (Strength Corporation; effect of recording errors on financial statements.)

a. Current Assets—understated by $1,000 (= $3,200 – $2,000).

b. Property, Plant, and Equipment—understated by $20,000.

c. Current Liabilities—understated by $2,500.

d. Sales Revenue—overstated by $4,500 (= $2,500 + $2,000).

e. Marketing Expenses—overstated by $23,000 (= $20,000 + $3,000).

f. Net Income—understated by $18,500 (= $23,000 – $4,500).

g. Retained Earnings—understated by $18,500 (= $23,000 – $4,500).

3.31　(McDonalds Corporation; effect of recording errors on financial statements.)

    a.　Current Assets—overstated by $1,700 (= $4,000 – $2,300).

    b.　Property, Plant, and Equipment—overstated by $20,000.

    c.　Current Liabilities—understated by $1,800.

    d.　Selling and Administrative Expenses—understated by $24,000 (= $20,000 + $4,000).

    e.　Net Income—overstated by $23,500　(= $20,000 + $4,000 + $1,800 – $2,300).

    f.　Retained Earnings—overstated by $23,500 (same as *e.* above).

3.32　(Effect of recording errors on financial statements.)

	Assets	**Liabilities**	**Shareholders' Equity**
a.	O/S $300	NO	O/S $300
b.	U/S $7,500	NO	U/S $7,500
c.	NO	O/S $1,500	U/S $1,500
d.	U/S $300	NO	U/S $300
e.	NO	NO	NO
f.	U/S $270	NO	U/S $270

3.33　(K9 Supplies Company; reconstructing accounting records.)

    a.

K9 SUPPLIES COMPANY
Balance Sheet
October 31

Assets

Cash..	$ 3,995
Accounts Receivable.............................	1,510
Note Receivable	1,500
Interest Receivable................................	75
Merchandise Inventories........................	9,740
Prepaid Insurance.................................	1,100
Prepaid License Fee	500
Total Assets...	$18,420

　　　　Solutions

3.33 a. continued.

Liabilities and Shareholders' Equity

Liabilities:
Accounts Payable	$ 3,620	
Rent Payable	300	
Total Liabilities		$ 3,920

Shareholders' Equity:
Common Stock	$12,000	
Retained Earnings	2,500	
Total Shareholders' Equity		14,500
Total Liabilities and Shareholders' Equity		$18,420

b. The cash shortage is $705 (= $3,995 – $3,290).

3.34 (Argenti Corporation; cash versus accrual basis of accounting.)

a. and b.

	a. Accrual Basis	b. Cash Basis
Sales Revenue	$ 47,500	$ 40,800[a]
Less Expenses:		
Cost of Merchandise Sold	$ 32,100[b]	--
Payments on Merchandise Purchased	--	$ 34,900
Depreciation Expense	500[c]	--
Payments on Equipment Purchased	--	30,000
Utilities Expense	1,610[d]	850
Salaries Expense	4,840[e]	2,250
Rent Expense	2,500	5,000
Insurance Expense	200	2,400
Interest Expense	100[f]	--
Total Expenses	$(41,850)	$(75,400)
Net Income (Loss)	$ 5,650	$(34,600)

[a]$40,800 = $40,000 + $800.
[b]$32,100 = $34,900 + $4,400 – $7,200.
[c]$500 = ($30,000/5)/12.
[d]$1,610 = $850 + $760.
[e]$4,840 = $2,250 + $2,590.
[f]$100 = (.06 × $20,000) × 30/360.

c. The accrual basis of accounting provides superior measures of operating performance because it matches revenues generated from selling activities during January with the costs incurred in generating that revenue. Note that the capital contribution and bank loan do not give rise to revenue under either basis of accounting because they represent financing, not operating, activities.

3.35 (Management Consultants, Inc.; cash versus accrual basis of accounting.)

a. and b.

	a. Accrual Basis	b. Cash Basis
Consulting Revenue	$ 45,000	$ 39,000
Less Expenses:		
Rental Expense	$ 8,000	$ 8,000
Depreciation Expense	1,250[a]	--
Payments on Equipment Purchased	--	12,000
Utilities Expense	400[b]	350
Salaries Expense	30,000[c]	28,200
Supplies Expense	690[a]	650
Interest Expense	225[e]	--
Total Expenses	$ 40,565	$ 49,200
Net Income (Loss)	$ 4,435	$(10,200)

[a]$1,250 = ($12,000/4) \times 5/12$.
[b]$400 = $350 + 50.
[c]$30,000 = $28,200 + $1,800$.
[d]$690 = $650 + 40.
[e]$225 = ($6,000 \times .09) \times 5/12$.

c. See the answer for Problem 3.34, Part *c*. above.

3.36 (J. Hennessey; cash versus accrual basis of accounting.)

a. and b.

	a. Accrual Basis	b. Cash Basis
Sales Revenue	$100,000	$ 92,000
Less Expenses:		
Cost of Merchandise Sold	$ 72,000[a]	--
Payments on Merchandise Purchased	--	$ 76,000
Salaries Expense	21,200[b]	20,000
Utilities Expense	1,620[c]	1,500
Interest Expense	1,200[d]	--
Total Expenses	$ 96,020	$ 97,500
Net Income (Loss)	$ 3,980	$ (5,500)

[a]$72,000 = $84,000 - $12,000$.
[b]$21,200 = $20,000 + $1,200$.
[c]$1,620 = $1,500 + 120.
[d]$1,200 = $10,000 \times .12$.

c. See the answer for Problem 3.34, Part *c*.

 Solutions

3.37 (Miscellaneous transactions and adjusting entries.)

a. **Jan. 31**
Interest Receivable	45	
Interest Revenue		45

[$18,000 × .06 × (15/360)] = $45.

Feb. 28
Interest Receivable	90	
Interest Revenue		90

[$18,000 × .06 × (30/360)] = $90.

March 15
Cash	18,180	
Interest Receivable		135
Interest Revenue		45
Notes Receivable		18,000

b. **Dec. 31**
Cost of Goods Sold	570,000	
Merchandise Inventory		570,000

$620,000 − $50,000 = $570,000.

c. **Jan. 31**
Rent Receivable	1,200	
Rent Revenue		1,200

Feb. 1
Cash	3,600	
Advances from Tenants		2,400
Rent Receivable		1,200

Feb. 28
Advances from Tenants	1,200	
Rent Revenue		1,200

March 31
Advances from Tenants	1,200	
Rent Revenue		1,200

d. **July 1**
Prepaid Rent	12,000	
Cash		12,000

July 31
Rent Expense	2,000	
Prepaid Rent		2,000

If the payment on July 1 resulted in a debit to the expense account, the adjustment requires a credit to the expense account and a debit to the prepayment account for $10,000.

3.37 d. continued.

Aug. 31

Rent Expense...	2,000	
Prepaid Rent..		2,000

e. **Dec. 1**

Prepaid Insurance.....................................	11,700	
Cash		11,700

Dec. 31

Insurance Expense.....................................	925	
Prepaid Insurance.....................................		925

$600 for October and November plus $11,700/36 = $325 for December.

f. **Dec. 31**

Office Supplies on Hand...............................	20	
Office Supplies Expense............................		20

To reduce expense for office supplies purchased but not used: $420 − $400 = $20.

g. **Dec. 31**

Depreciation Expense....................................	3,000	
Accumulated Depreciation on Building.........		3,000

Two months depreciation expense = $1/480 \times 2 \times (\$820,000 - \$100,000)$.

3.38 (Miscellaneous transactions and adjusting entries.)

a. (1)

Accounts Payable (L)..............................	6,000	
Notes Payable (L).................................		6,000

(2)

Interest Expense (SE).............................	50	
Interest Payable (L)		50

$[\$6,000 \times .10 \times (30/360)] = \$50$.

b. (1)

Cash (A)...	18,000	
Advances from Customers (L)		18,000

(2)

Advances from Customers (L).................	3,000	
Insurance Revenue (SE).......................		3,000

$(\$18,000 \times 4/24) = \$3,000$.

c. (1)

Equipment (A).......................................	40,000	
Cash (A)...		40,000

       Solutions

3.38 c. continued.

    (2)   Depreciation Expense (SE).......................... 2,250
           Accumulated Depreciation (XA)............   2,250
          [.25($40,000 – $4,000)/4].

d. (1)   Automobile (A)....................................... 24,000
           Cash (A)   24,000

    (2)   Depreciation Expense (SE).......................... 3,500
           Accumulated Depreciation (XA)............   3,500
          .5 × [($24,000 – $3,000)/3] = $3,500.

e. (1)   Prepaid Rent (A) 12,000
           Cash (A)   12,000

    (2)   Rent Expense (SE) 4,000
           Prepaid Rent (A)   4,000

f. (1)   Office Supplies Inventory (A).................... 7,000
           Accounts Payable (L)...........................   7,000

    (2)   Accounts Payable (L) 5,000
           Cash (A)   5,000

    (3)   Office Supplies Expense (SE)..................... 5,500
           Office Supplies Inventory (A)................   5,500
          ($7,000 – $1,500) = $5,500.

3.39   (Miscellaneous transactions and adjusting entries.)

a. **Jan. 31**
    Rent Receivable.. 3,600
       Rent Revenue...   3,600

    Feb. 28
    Rent Receivable.. 3,600
       Rent Revenue...   3,600

    March 1
    Cash... 10,800
       Rent Receivable   7,200
       Rent Received in Advance..........................   3,600

    March 30
    Rent Received in Advance.............................. 3,600
       Rent Revenue...   3,600

3.39 continued.

b. **March 16**

Note Receivable...	10,000	
Accounts Receivable....................................		10,000

March 31

Interest Receivable.......................................	25	
Interest Revenue		25

$10,000 \times .06 \times 15/360 = \$25$.

April 30

Interest Receivable.......................................	50	
Interest Revenue		50

$10,000 \times .06 \times 30/360 = \$50$.

May 15

Cash..	10,100	
Interest Receivable......................................		75
Interest Revenue		25
Note Receivable..		10,000

c. **March 1**

Prepaid Insurance.......................................	6,600	
Cash		6,600

March 30

Insurance Expense.......................................	775	
Prepaid Insurance......................................		775

$500 + (\$6,600/24) = \$775$.

June 30

Insurance Expense.......................................	825	
Prepaid Insurance......................................		825

$3(\$6,600/24) = \$825$.

Sept. 30

Insurance Expense.......................................	825	
Prepaid Insurance......................................		825

Dec. 31

Insurance Expense.......................................	825	
Prepaid Insurance......................................		825

d. **Jan. 31**

Repair Expense..	200	
Repair Parts Inventory...............................		200

$4,000 - \$3,800 - \$200$. Alternatively, repair expense = $\$4,000 + \$14,900 - \$3,800 = \$15,100 = \$14,900 + \$200$.

3.39 continued.

e. **Dec. 31, Year 6**
Depreciation Expense 9,000
    Accumulated Depreciation   9,000
($200,000 − $20,000)/10 = $18,000; $18,000 × .50 = $9,000.

Dec. 31, Year 7
Depreciation Expense 18,000
    Accumulated Depreciation   18,000

f. **March 30**
Property Tax Expense 3,000
    Property Tax Payable   3,000

April 1
Property Tax Payable 3,000
Prepaid Property Taxes 9,000
    Cash   12,000

June 30
Property Tax Expense 3,000
    Prepaid Property Taxes   3,000

Sept. 30
Property Tax Expense 3,000
    Prepaid Property Taxes   3,000

Dec. 31
Property Tax Expense 3,000
    Prepaid Property Taxes   3,000

3.40 (Neslin Collection Agency; preparation of T-account entries and adjusted trial balance.)

a.

Office Supplies		Common Stock		Office Equipment	
(1) 2,500			10,000 (1)	(2) 4,000	
			8,000 (2)		
Bal. 2,500			18,000 Bal.	Bal. 4,000	

3.40 a. continued.

	Cash				Commissions Revenue		Office Salaries Expense	
(1)	7,500	800	(4)		300 (3)	(4)	800	
(2)	4,000	300	(6)					
(3)	600	800	(7)					
		2,500	(8)					
Bal.	7,700				300 Bal.	Bal.	800	

	Accounting System Installation		Accounts Payable, Lyband and Linn			Accounts Payable, Z-Mart Stores		
(5)	500			500 (5)	(6)	300	300	(3)
Bal.	500			500 Bal.			0	Bal.

	Prepaid Rent			Automobile		Installment Contract Payable	
(7)	800		(8)	9,000		6,500	(8)
Bal.	800		Bal.	9,000		6,500	Bal.

b.

NESLIN COLLECTION AGENCY
Trial Balance
January 31, Year 3

Office Supplies	$ 2,500	
Common Stock		$18,000
Office Equipment	4,000	
Cash	7,700	
Commissions Revenue (R)		300
Office Salaries Expense (E)	800	
Accounting System Installation	500	
Accounts Payable, Lyband and Linn		500
Prepaid Rent	800	
Automobile	9,000	
Installment Contract Payable		6,500
Totals	$25,300	$25,300

3.41 (Kleen Cleaners, Inc.; preparation of T-account entries, adjusted trial balance, income statement, and balance sheet.)

a., b., and d.

Cash				Accounts Receivable				Supplies on Hand			
Bal.	3,400	4,600	(5)	Bal.	15,200	11,200	(2)	Bal.	4,800	5,610	(8)
(1)	15,000	800	(6)	(1)	4,900			(4)	3,100		
(2)	11,200	10,930	(9)								
Bal.	13,270			Bal.	8,900			Bal.	2,290		

Prepaid Insurance				Equipment			Accumulated Depreciation		
Bal.	1,200	300	(11)	Bal.	65,000			9,680	Bal.
								2,560	(9)
Bal.	900			Bal.	65,000			12,240	Bal.

Accounts Payable				Common Stock		Retained Earnings		
(5)	4,600	7,900	Bal.		20,000 Bal.		40,000	Bal.
		700	(3)				10,220	(14)
		3,100	(4)					
		800	(10)					
		7,900	Bal.		20,000 Bal.		50,220	Bal.

Sales Revenue				Salaries and Wages Expense				Cost of Outside Work			
(12)	65,960	46,060	Bal.	Bal.	26,600	37,530	(13)	Bal.	2,040	2,740	(13)
		15,000	(1)	(9)	10,930			(3)	700		
		4,900	(1)								
	65,960	65,960			37,530	37,530			2,740	2,740	

Advertising Expense				Repairs Expense				Rent Expense			
Bal.	400	700	(13)	Bal.	500	580	(13)	Bal.	1,200	2,000	(13)
(10)	300			(10)	80			(6)	800		
	700	700			580	580			2,000	2,000	

Power, Gas, and Water Expense				Supplies Expense				Depreciation Expense			
Bal.	880	1,300	(13)	(7)	5,610	5,610	(13)	(8)	2,560	2,560	(13)
(10)	420										
	1,300	1,300			5,610	5,610			2,560	2,560	

3.41 a., b., and d. continued.

Insurance Expense		Miscellaneous Expense		Income Summary	
(11) 300	300 (13)	Bal. 2,420	2,420 (13)	(13) 55,740	65,960 (12)
				(14) 10,220	
300	300	2,420	2,420	65,960	65,960

Note: T-account entries (1) through (11) respond to Part *b.*, after which students can perform Part *c.* requirements. T-account entries (12) through (14) respond to Part *d.*, after which students can perform Part *e.* requirements.

c.

KLEEN CLEANERS, INC.
Adjusted Preclosing Trial Balance
March 31, Year 6

Cash	$ 13,270	
Accounts Receivable	8,900	
Supplies on Hand	2,290	
Prepaid Insurance	900	
Equipment	65,000	
Accumulated Depreciation		$ 12,240
Accounts Payable		7,900
Common Stock		20,000
Retained Earnings		40,000
Sales Revenue		65,960
Salaries and Wages Expense	37,530	
Cost of Outside Work	2,740	
Advertising Expense	700	
Repairs Expense	580	
Rent Expense	2,000	
Power, Gas, and Water Expense	1,300	
Supplies Expense	5,610	
Depreciation Expense	2,560	
Insurance Expense	300	
Miscellaneous Expense	2,420	
Totals	$ 146,100	$ 146,100

         Solutions

3.41 c. continued.

KLEEN CLEANERS, INC.
Income Statement
For the Three Months Ended March 31, Year 6

Sales Revenue		$65,960
Expenses:		
Salaries and Wages Expense	$37,530	
Cost of Outside Work	2,740	
Advertising Expense	700	
Repairs Expense	580	
Rent Expense	2,000	
Power, Gas, and Water Expense	1,300	
Supplies Expense	5,610	
Depreciation Expense	2,560	
Insurance Expense	300	
Miscellaneous Expense	2,420	
Total Expenses		55,740
Net Income for the Quarter		$10,220

e.
KLEEN CLEANERS, INC.
Balance Sheet
March 31, Year 6

Assets

Current Assets:		
Cash	$13,270	
Accounts Receivable	8,900	
Supplies on Hand	2,290	
Prepaid Insurance	900	
Total Current Assets		$25,360
Noncurrent Assets:		
Equipment	$65,000	
Less Accumulated Depreciation	(12,240)	
Total Noncurrent Assets		52,760
Total Assets		$78,120

Liabilities and Shareholders' Equity

Current Liabilities:		
Accounts Payable	$ 7,900	
Total Current Liabilities		$ 7,900
Shareholders' Equity:		
Common Stock	$20,000	
Retained Earnings	50,220	
Total Shareholders' Equity		70,220
Total Liabilities and Shareholders' Equity		$78,120

3.42   (Bosworth Computer Repair Services; preparation of T-account entries, adjusted trial balance, income statement, and balance sheet.)

a., b. and d.

Cash				Repair Parts Inventory				Office Supplies Inventory		
Bal.	4,800	1,000	(3)	Bal.	1,500	450	(11)	Bal.	200	100 (12)
(1)	2,250	240	(4)							
(8)	250	150	(5)							
		325	(6)							
		90	(7)							
		1,100	(9)							
Bal.	4,395			Bal.	1,050			Bal.	100	

Equipment			Accumulated Depreciation			Accounts Payable		
Bal.	5,500				750 Bal.	(3)	1,000	6,250 Bal.
					75 (13)			
Bal.	5,500				825 Bal.			5,250 Bal.

Common Stock		Retained Earnings		Repair Revenue			
	1,250 Bal.		3,750 Bal.	(14)	2,750	2,250	(1)
			440 (23)			500	(2)
	1,250 Bal.		4,190 Bal.		2,750		

Accounts Receivable				Prepaid Insurance				Advertising Expense			
(2)	500	250	(8)	(4)	240	20	(10)	(5)	150	150	(15)
Bal.	250			Bal.	220						

Rent Expense				Telephone Expense				Salary Expense			
(6)	325	325	(16)	(7)	90	90	(17)	(9)	1,100	1,100	(18)

Insurance Expense				Repair Parts Expense				Office Supplies Expense			
(10)	20	20	(19)	(11)	450	450	(20)	(12)	100	100	(21)

3.42 a., b., and d. continued.

Depreciation Expense			Income Summary			
(13)	75	75 (22)	(15)	150	2,750	(14)
			(16)	325		
			(17)	90		
			(18)	1,100		
			(19)	20		
			(20)	450		
			(21)	100		
			(22)	75		
			(23)	440		
				2,750		

Note: T-account entries (1) through (13) respond to Part *b.*, after which students can perform Part *c.* requirements. T-account entries (14) through (22) respond to Part *d.*, after which students can perform Part *e.* requirements.

c.
BOSWORTH COMPUTER REPAIR SERVICES
Adjusted Preclosing Trial Balance
July 31, Year 8

Cash	$ 4,395	
Repair Parts Inventory	1,050	
Office Supplies Inventory	100	
Equipment	5,500	
Accumulated Depreciation		$ 825
Accounts Payable		5,250
Common Stock		1,250
Retained Earnings		3,750
Repair Revenue		2,750
Accounts Receivable	250	
Prepaid Insurance	220	
Advertising Expense	150	
Rent Expense	325	
Telephone Expense	90	
Salary Expense	1,100	
Insurance Expense	20	
Repair Parts Expense	450	
Office Supplies Expense	100	
Depreciation Expense	75	
Totals	$13,825	$13,825

3.42 c. continued.

BOSWORTH COMPUTER REPAIR SERVICES
Income Statement
For the Month of July, Year 8

Repair Revenue..		$2,750
Expenses:		
Advertising Expense	$ 150	
Rent Expense.......................................	325	
Telephone Expense...............................	90	
Salary Expense	1,100	
Insurance Expense	20	
Repair Parts Expense	450	
Office Supplies Expense	100	
Depreciation Expense	75	
Total Expenses................................		2,310
Net Income		$ 440

e.

BOSWORTH COMPUTER REPAIR SERVICES
Balance Sheet
July 31, Year 8

Assets

Current Assets:		
Cash..	$4,395	
Accounts Receivable...........................	250	
Repair Parts Inventory	1,050	
Office Supplies Inventory	100	
Prepaid Insurance...............................	220	
Total Current Assets.......................		$ 6,015
Property, Plant, and Equipment:		
Equipment	$5,500	
Less Accumulated Depreciation	(825)	
Total Property, Plant, and Equip-ment...		4,675
Total Assets..................................		$10,690

Liabilities and Shareholders' Equity

Current Liabilities:		
Accounts Payable................................		$ 5,250
Shareholders' Equity:		
Common Stock....................................	$1,250	
Retained Earnings..............................	4,190	
Total Shareholders' Equity................		5,440
Total Liabilities and Shareholders' Equity		$10,690

3.43   (Jones Shoe Repair Shop, Inc.; preparation of T-account entries, adjusted trial balance, income statement, and balance sheet.)

a., b., and d.

Cash			
Bal. 6,060	5,800	(5)	
(1) 22,000	1,000	(6)	
(2) 18,200	11,900	(7)	
Bal. 27,560			

Accounts Receivable		
Bal. 15,200	18,200	(2)
(1) 14,900		
Bal. 11,900		

Supplies Inventory		
Bal. 4,800	6,820	(8)
(4) 3,700		
Bal. 1,680		

Prepaid Insurance		
Bal. 900	400	(11)
Bal. 500		

Equipment	
Bal. 65,000	
Bal. 65,000	

Accumulated Depreciation	
	11,460 Bal.
	2,820 (9)
	14,280 Bal.

Accounts Payable		
(5) 5,800	6,120	Bal.
	1,200	(3)
	3,700	(4)
	920	(10)
	6,140	Bal.

Common Stock	
	15,000 Bal.
	15,000 Bal.

Retained Earnings	
	47,360 Bal.
	23,860 (14)
	71,220 Bal.

Sales Revenue		
(12) 82,960	46,060	Bal.
	22,000	(1)
	14,900	(1)
82,960	82,960	

Salaries and Wages Expense		
Bal. 26,600	38,500	(13)
(7) 11,900		
38,500	38,500	

Cost of Outside Work		
Bal. 2,040	3,240	(13)
(3) 1,200		
3,240	3,240	

Advertising Expense		
Bal. 900	1,300	(13)
(10) 400		
1,300	1,300	

Rent Expense		
Bal. 1,200	2,200	(13)
(6) 1,000		
2,200	2,200	

Power, Gas, and Water Expense		
Bal. 880	1,400	(13)
(10) 520		
1,400	1,400	

Supplies Expense		
(8) 6,820	6,820	(13)
6,820	6,820	

Depreciation Expense		
(9) 2,820	2,820	(13)
2,820	2,820	

Insurance Expense		
(11) 400	400	(13)
400	400	

3.43 a., b., and d. continued.

Miscellaneous Expense			Income Summary		
Bal. 2,420	2,420 (13)		(13) 59,100	82,960 (12)	
			(14) 23,860		
2,420	2,420		82,960	82,960	

Note: T-account entries (1) through (11) respond to Part *b*., after which students can perform Part *c*. requirements. T-account entries (12) through (14) respond to Part *d*., after which students can perform Part *e*. requirements.

c.

JONES SHOE REPAIR SHOP, INC.
Adjusted Preclosing Trial Balance
March 31, Year 2

Cash	$ 27,560	
Accounts Receivable	11,900	
Supplies Inventory	1,680	
Prepaid Insurance	500	
Equipment	65,000	
Accumulated Depreciation		$ 14,280
Accounts Payable		6,140
Common Stock		15,000
Retained Earnings		47,360
Sales Revenue		82,960
Salaries and Wages Expense	38,500	
Cost of Outside Work	3,240	
Advertising Expense	1,300	
Rent Expense	2,200	
Power, Gas, and Water Expense	1,400	
Supplies Expense	6,820	
Depreciation Expense	2,820	
Insurance Expense	400	
Miscellaneous Expense	2,420	
Totals	$ 165,740	$ 165,740

3.43 c. continued.

JONES SHOE REPAIR SHOP, INC.
Income Statement
For the Three Months Ending March 31, Year 2

Sales Revenue...		$82,960
Expenses:		
Salaries and Wages Expense................	$38,500	
Cost of Outside Work	3,240	
Advertising Expense	1,300	
Rent Expense..	2,200	
Power, Gas, and Water Expense...........	1,400	
Supplies Expense	6,820	
Depreciation Expense...........................	2,820	
Insurance Expense...............................	400	
Miscellaneous Expense........................	2,420	
Total Expenses		59,100
Net Income for the Quarter		$23,860

e.

JONES SHOE REPAIR SHOP, INC.
Balance Sheet
March 31, Year 2

Assets

Current Assets:		
Cash...	$27,560	
Accounts Receivable...........................	11,900	
Supplies Inventory	1,680	
Prepaid Insurance..............................	500	
Total Current Assets.......................		$41,640
Property, Plant, and Equipment:		
Equipment	$65,000	
Less Accumulated Depreciation	(14,280)	
Total Property, Plant, and Equipment..		50,720
Total Assets.....................................		$92,360

Liabilities and Shareholders' Equity

Current Liabilities:		
Accounts Payable...............................	$ 6,140	
Total Current Liabilities...................		$ 6,140
Shareholders' Equity:		
Common Stock....................................	$15,000	
Retained Earnings..............................	71,220	
Total Shareholders' Equity...............		86,220
Total Liabilities and Shareholders' Equity		$92,360

3-44 (Rybowiak's Building Supplies; preparation of journal entries, T-accounts, adjusted trial balance, income statement, and balance sheet.)

a. (T): Transaction Entry   (A): Adjusting Entry

(1)	Accounts Receivable...............................	85,000	
(T)	Sales Revenue..		85,000
(2)	Merchandise Inventory...........................	46,300	
(T)	Accounts Payable...................................		46,300
(3)	Rent Expense...	11,750	
(T)	Cash..		11,750
(4)	Salaries Payable.....................................	1,250	
(T)	Salaries Expense....................................	19,350	
	Cash..		20,600
(5)	Cash..	34,150	
(T)	Accounts Receivable...............................		34,150
(6)	Accounts Payable...................................	38,950	
(T)	Cash..		38,950
(7)	Miscellaneous Expenses	3,200	
(T)	Cash..		3,200
(8)	Insurance Expense	50	
(A)	Prepaid Insurance..................................		50
	$400 / 8 months.		
(9)	Depreciation Expense	1,750	
(A)	Accumulated Depreciation......................		1,750
	1/12 × $210,000/10.		
(10)	Salaries Expense....................................	1,600	
(A)	Salaries Payable....................................		1,600
(11)	Interest Expense....................................	50	
(A)	Interest Payable.....................................		50
	$5,000 × .12 × 30/360.		
(12)	Cost of Goods Sold.................................	36,500	
(A)	Merchandise Inventory		36,500
	$68,150 + $46,300 − $77,950.		

Handwritten annotations:

Why not Prepaid Rent (A)?

OK! 1 month only.

← why include??

OK! expires on March 1st/9 = 8 months from today

6 months??

1/12 × $210,000/10. → Equipment cost!

3.44 continued.

b. and e.

Cash			
Bal.	44,200	11,750	(3)
(5)	34,150	20,600	(4)
		38,950	(6)
		3,200	(7)
Bal.	3,850		

Accounts Receivable			
Bal.	27,250	34,150	(5)
(1)	85,000		
Bal.	78,100		

Merchandise Inventory			
Bal.	68,150	36,500	(12)
(2)	46,300		
Bal.	77,950		

Prepaid Insurance			
Bal.	400	50	(8)
Bal.	350		

Equipment			
Bal.	210,000		
Bal.	210,000		

Accumulated Depreciation			
		84,000	Bal.
		1,750	(9)
		85,750	Bal.

Accounts Payable			
		33,100	Bal.
(6)	38,950	46,300	(2)
		40,450	Bal.

Note Payable			
		5,000	Bal.
		5,000	Bal.

Salaries Payable			
(4)	1,250	1,250	Bal.
		1,600	(10)
		1,600	Bal.

Common Stock			
		150,000	Bal.
		150,000	Bal.

Retained Earnings			
		76,650	Bal.
		10,750	(15)
		87,400	Bal.

Sales Revenue			
(13)	85,000	85,000	(1)

Rent Expense			
(3)	11,750	11,750	(14)

Salaries Expense			
(4)	19,350		
(10)	1,600	20,950	(14)
	20,950		

3.44 b. and e. continued.

Miscellaneous Expenses					Insurance Expense			
(7)	3,200	3,200	(14)	(8)	50	50	(14)

Depreciation Expense					Interest Expense			
(9)	1,750	1,750	(14)	(11)	50	50	(14)

Interest Payable				Cost of Goods Sold			
		50	(11)	(12)	36,500	36,500	(14)
		50	Bal.				

Income Summary			
(14)	74,250	85,000	(13)
(15)	10,750		
	85,000		

c.

RYBOWIAK'S BUILDING SUPPLIES
Adjusted Preclosing Trial Balance
July 31, Year 9

Cash	$ 3,850	
Accounts Receivable	78,100	
Merchandise Inventory	77,950	
Prepaid Insurance	350	
Equipment	210,000	
Accumulated Depreciation		$ 85,750
Accounts Payable		40,450
Note Payable		5,000
Salaries Payable		1,600
Common Stock		150,000
Retained Earnings (September 30)		76,650
Sales Revenue		85,000
Rent Expense	11,750	
Salaries Expense	20,950	
Miscellaneous Expenses	3,200	
Insurance Expense	50	
Depreciation Expense	1,750	
Interest Expense	50	
Interest Payable		50
Cost of Goods Sold	36,500	
Totals	$ 444,500	$ 444,500

continued.

d.

RYBOWIAK'S BUILDING SUPPLIES
Income Statement
For the Month of July, Year 9

Sales Revenue		$ 85,000
Less Expenses:		
Cost of Goods Sold	$ 36,500	
Salaries Expense	20,950	
Rent Expense	11,750	
Depreciation Expense	1,750	
Insurance Expense	50	
Interest Expense	50	
Miscellaneous Expenses	3,200	(74,250)
Net Income		$ 10,750

f.

RYBOWIAK'S BUILDING SUPPLIES
Balance Sheet
July 31, Year 9

Assets

Current Assets:		
Cash		$ 3,850
Accounts Receivable		78,100
Merchandise Inventory		77,950
Prepaid Insurance		350
Total Current Assets		$ 160,250
Noncurrent Assets:		
Equipment—At Cost	$ 210,000	
Less Accumulated Depreciation	(85,750)	
Total Noncurrent Assets		124,250
Total Assets		$ 284,500

Liabilities and Shareholders' Equity

Current Liabilities:		
Accounts Payable		$ 40,450
Note Payable		5,000
Salaries Payable		1,600
Interest Payable		50
Total Current Liabilities		$ 47,100
Shareholders' Equity:		
Common Stock		$ 150,000
Retained Earnings		87,400
Total Shareholders' Equity		$ 237,400
Equity		$ 284,500

3.45   (Reliance Appliance Company; preparation of adjusting entries.)

(1) Depreciation Expense   88
         Accumulated Depreciation   88
     1/12 X ($5,280/5).

(2) Depreciation Expense   500
         Accumulated Depreciation   500
     1/12 X ($24,000/4).

(3) Rent Expense 1,800
         Leasehold   1,800

(4) Accounts Payable   360
         Merchandise Inventory   360

(5) Salaries and Commissions Expense   210
         Salaries and Commissions Payable   210

(6) Advances by Customers   490
         Accounts Receivable   490

(7) Insurance Expense   50
         Prepaid Insurance   50
     $900/18 = $50.

(8) Retained Earnings 2,500
         Dividends Payable   2,500

(9) Merchandise Cost of Goods Sold 37,440
         Merchandise Inventory   37,440
     $99,000 − $360 − $61,200 = $37,440.

3.46 (Williamson Corporation; preparation of adjusting entries.)

(1) Depreciation Expense 6,250
      Accumulated Depreciation 6,250
      ($50,000/8) = $6,250.

(2) Advances from Customers............................ 290
      Sales Revenue 290

(3) Accounts Payable.. 860
      Accounts Receivable................................... 860

(4) Prepaid Rent 200
      Marketing and Administrative Expenses 200
      ($1,400 − $1,200) = $200.

(5) Salaries and Administrative Expenses 450
      Salaries Payable 450
      ($2,250 − $1,800) = $450.

(6) Merchandise Cost of Goods Sold....................... 94,800
      Merchandise Inventory 94,800
      ($110,000 − $15,200) = $94,800.

(7) Income Tax Expense 1,017
      Income Tax Payable................................... 1,017
      .30[($150,000 + $290) − ($94,800 + $45,600 + $6,250
      − $200 + $450)] = $1,017.

3.47   (Creative Photographers; preparation of closing entries.)

a. Revenue—Commercial Photography................   54,220
    Revenue—Printing Service   14,040
        Advertising Expense.................................   4,500
        Depreciation Expense—Cameras and Equip-
            ment...   540
        Depreciation Expense—Furniture and Fix-
            tures...   315
        Electricity Expense..................................   900
        Equipment Repairs Expense   540
        Insurance Expense...................................   990
        Photographic Supplies Expense...................   5,850
        Rent Expense   4,275
        Salaries Expense   32,400
        Telephone Expense   360
        Retained Earnings...................................   17,640

b.

Revenue—Commercial Photography		Revenue—Printing Service		Advertising Expense	
(1) 54,270	54,270 Bal.	(1) 14,040	14,040 Bal.	Bal. 4,500	4,500 (1)

Depreciation Expense—Cameras and Equipment		Depreciation Expense—Furniture and Fixtures		Electricity Expense	
Bal. 540	540 (1)	Bal. 315	315 (1)	Bal. 900	900 (1)

Equipment Repairs Expense		Insurance Expense		Photographic Supplies Expense	
Bal. 540	540 (1)	Bal. 990	990 (1)	Bal. 5,850	5,850 (1)

Rent Expense		Salaries Expense		Telephone Expense	
Bal. 4,275	4,275 (1)	Bal. 32,400	32,400 (1)	Bal. 360	360 (1)

Retained Earnings	
	42,414 Bal.
	17,640 (1)

3.48　(Prima Company; working backwards to balance sheet at beginning of period.)

PRIMA COMPANY
Balance Sheet
As of January 1, Year 2

Assets

Cash...		$ 11,700
Marketable Securities.......................................		12,000
Accounts Receivable...		22,000
Merchandise Inventory		33,000
Prepayments		1,700
Land, Buildings, and Equipment....................	$ 40,000	
Less Accumulated Depreciation	(12,000)	28,000
Total Assets...		$ 108,400

Equities

Accounts Payable..	$ 26,000
Interest Payable..	300
Taxes Payable...	3,500
Notes Payable (6 Percent)	20,000
Capital Stock	50,000
Retained Earnings.......................................	8,600
Total Equities......................................	$ 108,400

A T-account method for deriving the solution appears below and on the following page. The end-of-year balance appears at the bottom of the T-account. The derived starting balance appears at the top. "p" indicates plug; "c," closing entry.

	Cash					Marketable Securities	
(p)	11,700				(p)	12,000	
(1)	47,000	128,000	(3)		(8)	8,000	
(2)	150,000	49,000	(4)				
		7,500	(5)				
		1,200	(6)				
		5,000	(7)				
		8,000	(8)				
Bal.	10,000				Bal.	20,000	

	Accounts Receivable					Merchandise Inventory		
(p)	22,000				(p)	33,000		
(10)	153,000	150,000	(2)		(9)	127,000	130,000	(11)
Bal.	25,000				Bal.	30,000		

3.48 continued.

Prepayments for Miscellaneous Services

(p)	1,700		
(4)	49,000	47,700	(14)
Bal.	3,000		

Land, Buildings, and Equipment

(p)	40,000		
Bal.	40,000		

Accounts Payable (for Merchandise)

		26,000	(p)
(3)	128,000	127,000	(9)
		25,000	Bal.

Interest Payable

		300	(p)
(6)	1,200	1,200	(15)
		300	Bal.

Taxes Payable

		3,500	(p)
(5)	7,500	8,000	(13)
		4,000	Bal.

Notes Payable

		20,000	(p)
		20,000	Bal.

Accumulated Depreciation

		12,000	(p)
		4,000	(12)
		16,000	Bal.

Capital Stock

		50,000	(p)
		50,000	Bal.

Retained Earnings

		8,600	(p)
(7)	5,000	9,100	(22)
		12,700	Bal.

Sales

		47,000	(1)
(16c)	200,000	153,000	(10)

Cost of Goods Sold

(11)	130,000	130,000	(17c)

Depreciation Expense

(12)	4,000	4,000	(18c)

Taxes Expense

(13)	8,000	8,000	(19c)

Other Operating Expense

(14)	47,700	47,700	(20c)

Interest Expense

(15)	1,200	1,200	(21c)

Income Summary

(17)	130,000	200,000	(16)
(18)	4,000		
(19)	8,000		
(20)	47,700		
(21)	1,200		
(22c)	9,100		

3-39

3.49 (Secunda Company; working backwards to cash receipts and disbursements.)

SECUNDA COMPANY
Cash Receipts and Disbursements Schedule

Receipts:
Collections from Customers $85,000
Disbursements:
Suppliers of Merchandise and Other Services $81,000
Mortgage.. 3,000
Dividends... 10,000
Interest... 2,000
Total Disbursements 96,000
Decrease in Cash.. $11,000
Cash Balance, January 1............................. 20,000
Cash Balance, December 31......................... $ 9,000

A T-account method for deriving the solution appears below and on the following page. After Entry (6), we have explained all revenue and expense account changes. Plugging for the unknown amounts determines the remaining, unexplained changes in balance sheet accounts. A "p" next to the entry number designates these entries. Note that the revenue and expense accounts are not yet closed to retained earnings, so dividends account for the decrease in the Retained Earnings account during the year of $10,000.

Cash					Accounts Receivable			
Bal.	20,000				Bal.	36,000		
(7)	85,000				(1)	100,000	85,000	(7p)
		2,000	(9)					
		81,000	(10)					
		3,000	(11)					
		10,000	(12)					
Bal.	9,000				Bal.	51,000		

Merchandise Inventory					Prepayments			
Bal.	45,000				Bal.	2,000		
(8p)	65,000	50,000	(2)				1,000	(5)
Bal.	60,000				Bal.	1,000		

Land, Buildings and Equipment				Cost of Goods Sold		
Bal.	40,000			Bal.	0	
				(2)	50,000	
Bal.	40,000			Bal.	50,000	

3.49 continued.

Interest Expense		
Bal.	0	
(3)	3,000	
Bal.	3,000	

Other Operating Expenses		
Bal.	0	
(4)	2,000	
(5)	1,000	
(6p)	26,000	
Bal.	29,000	

Accumulated Depreciation		
	16,000	Bal.
	2,000	(4)
	18,000	Bal.

Interest Payable		
	1,000	Bal.
(9p)	2,000	3,000	(3)
	2,000	Bal.

Accounts Payable		
	30,000	Bal.
(10p)	81,000	26,000	(6)
	65,000	(8)
	40,000	Bal.

Mortgage Payable		
	20,000	Bal.
(11p)	3,000	
	17,000	Bal.

Capital Stock		
	50,000	Bal.
	50,000	Bal.

Retained Earnings		
	26,000	Bal.
(12p)	10,000	
	16,000	Bal.

Sales		
	0	Bal.
	100,000	(1)
	100,000	Bal.

3.50   (Tertia Company; working backwards to income statement.)

TERTIA COMPANY
Statement of Income and Retained Earnings

Revenues:
Sales..	$ 212,000	
Interest Revenue.....................................	700	
Total Revenues		$ 212,700

Expenses:
Cost of Goods Sold.................................	$ 126,500	
Property Tax Expense	1,700	
Depreciation Expense	2,000	
Interest Expense.....................................	500	
Miscellaneous Expenses	56,800	
Total Expenses....................................		187,500
Net Income		$ 25,200
Less Dividends.......................................		(2,000)
Increase in Retained Earnings...................		$ 23,200
Retained Earnings, Beginning of Year...........		76,000
Retained Earnings, End of Year		$ 99,200

A T-account method for deriving the solution appears below and on the following pages. Transactions (1) – (9) correspond to the numbered cash transactions information. In transactions (10) – (25), "p" indicates that the figure was derived by a "plug" and "c" indicates a closing entry. The final check is that the debit to close Income Summary in (25) matches the plug in the Retained Earnings account.

	Cash				Accounts and Notes Receivable		
Bal.	(a)			Bal.	36,000		
(1)	144,000	114,000	(4)	(10p)	149,000	144,000	(1)
(2)	63,000	5,000	(5)				
(3)	1,000	500	(6)				
		57,500	(7)				
		1,200	(8)				
		2,000	(9)				
Bal.	(b)			Bal.	41,000		

(a) Total debits, $183,000, less specific, known debits, $143,000, equal beginning balance in Cash account of $40,000.

(b) Beginning balance of $40,000 plus increase in cash balance for the year of $27,800 equals ending balance in Cash account of $67,800.

3.50 continued.

Merchandise Inventory			
Bal.	55,000		
(14)	121,000	126,500	(15p)
Bal.	49,500		

Interest Receivable			
Bal.	1,000		
(11p)	700	1,000	(3)
Bal.	700		

Prepaid Miscellaneous Services			
Bal.	4,000		
(7)	57,500	56,300	(12p)
Bal.	5,200		

Building, Machinery, and Equipment			
Bal.	47,000		
Bal.	47,000		

Accounts Payable (Miscellaneous Services)			
		2,000	Bal.
		500	(13p)
		2,500	Bal.

Accounts Payable (Merchandise)			
		34,000	Bal.
(4)	114,000	121,000	(14p)
		41,000	Bal.

Property Taxes Payable			
		1,000	Bal.
(8)	1,200	1,700	(16p)
		1,500	Bal.

Accumulated Depreciation			
		10,000	Bal.
		2,000	(17p)
		12,000	Bal.

Mortgage Payable			
		35,000	Bal.
(5)	5,000		
		30,000	Bal.

Capital Stock			
		25,000	Bal.
		25,000	Bal.

Retained Earnings			
		76,000	Bal.
(9)	2,000	25,200	(25p)
		99,200	Bal.

Sales			
		63,000	(2)
		149,000	(10)
(18c)	212,000	212,000	

Cost of Goods Sold			
(15)	126,500	126,500	(20c)

Interest Expense			
(6)	500	500	(21c)

3.50 continued.

	Interest Revenue		
(19c)	700	700	(11)

	Miscellaneous Expenses		
(12)	56,300		
(13)	500		
	56,800	56,800	(22c)

	Property Tax Expense		
(16)	1,700	1,700	(23c)

	Depreciation Expense		
(17)	2,000	2,000	(24c)

	Income Summary		
(20)	126,500	212,000	(18)
(21)	500	700	(19)
(22)	56,800		
(23)	1,700		
(24)	2,000		
(25c)	25,200		

CHAPTER 4

INCOME STATEMENT: EXTENDING
THE ACCRUAL CONCEPT

Questions, Exercises, Problems, and Cases: Answers and Solutions

4.1   See the text or the glossary at the end of the book.

4.2   Depreciation on manufacturing equipment is a product cost and remains in inventory accounts until the firm sells the manufactured goods. Depreciation on selling and administrative equipment is a period expense, because the use of such equipment does not create an asset with future service potential.

4.3   Both the Merchandise Inventory and Finished Goods Inventory accounts include the cost of completed units ready for sale. A merchandising firm acquires the units in finished form and debits Merchandise Inventory for their acquisition cost. A manufacturing firm incurs direct material, direct labor, and manufacturing overhead costs in transforming the units to a finished, salable condition. The Raw Materials Inventory and Work-in-Process Inventory accounts include such costs until the completion of manufacturing operations. Thus, the accountant debits the Finished Goods Inventory account for the cost of producing completed units. The accountant credits both the Merchandise Inventory and Finished Goods Inventory accounts for the cost of units sold and reports them as current assets on the balance sheet.

4.4   Manufacturing firms typically do not identify a customer or establish a firm selling price until they sell products. Thus, these firms do not satisfy the criteria for revenue recognition while production is taking place. In contrast, construction companies usually identify a customer and establish a contract price before construction begins. In addition, the production process for a manufacturing firm is usually much shorter than for a construction firm. The recognition of revenue at the time of production or at the time of sale does not result in a significantly different pattern of income for a manufacturing firm. For a construction company, the pattern of income could differ significantly.

4.5   Under the installment method, accountants recognize proportionate parts of the costs incurred as expenses each period as they recognize proportionate parts of the selling price as revenues. Under the cost-recovery-first method, costs match dollar-for-dollar with revenues until revenues equal total costs. Thus, the income patterns differ because of the *expense* recognition pattern, not the revenue recognition pattern.

4.6   Under both the installment method and the cash basis of accounting, accountants recognize revenue when the firm receives cash. The installment method recognizes expenses in the same period as the associated revenues. The cash basis recognizes expenses when the firm makes cash expenditures.

4.7   Application of the installment method requires a reasonably accurate estimate of the total amount of cash the firm expects to receive from customers. The cost-recovery-first method does not require such an estimate.

4.8   Accountants are more concerned with the objectivity or reliability of income data than are economists. Accountants are responsible for measuring and auditing income amounts and, therefore, require objective measures of wealth changes. Such evidence usually takes the form of market transactions.

4.9   Users of financial statements often predict future income amounts from the past trend of earnings. By separating income amounts expected to continue from those not expected to continue, more accurate earnings forecasts are likely to result.

4.10   The user of the financial statements must identify the reason for the decline in the quality of earnings. Does the measurement of revenues and expenses for a particular business require numerous estimates? Is there evidence that the firm has used the inherent flexibility in the measurement of revenues and expenses to its advantage? Is the declining quality of earnings due to unusual or nonrecurring items which the financial statement user can exclude when assessing operating profitability? In some cases the financial statement user can adjust net income to eliminate the source of the decreasing earnings quality; in other cases, such adjustments are not possible.

4.11   (Identifying product costs and period expenses.)

a. 1 (Product Cost)	g. 1	m. 2
b. 2 (Period Expense)	h. 1	n. 2
c. 1	i. 1	o. 1
d. 1	j. 1	p. 2
e. 1	k. 2	q. 2
f. 2	l. 2	

4.12   (Identifying product costs and period expenses.)

    a. 1 (Product Cost)   e. 2

    b. 2 (Period Expense)   f. 2

    c. 1   g. 1

    d. 1

4.13   (Identifying product costs, period expenses, and assets.)

    a. 1 (Period Expense)   g. 3

    b. 2 (Product Cost)   h. 2

    c. 3 (Other Balance Sheet) i. 1

    d. 1   j. 1

    e. 2   k. 2

    f. 1

4.14   (Raw materials inventory transactions.)

    a. The relationship among the four items is:

$$\begin{array}{c} \text{Beginning} \\ \text{Raw Materials} \\ \text{Inventory} \end{array} + \begin{array}{c} \text{Purchases} \\ \text{of Raw} \\ \text{Materials} \end{array} - \begin{array}{c} \text{Raw} \\ \text{Materials} \\ \text{Used} \end{array} = \begin{array}{c} \text{Ending} \\ \text{Raw Materials} \\ \text{Inventory} \end{array}$$

Year 2: $19,500 + $87,600 - $84,300 = a; a = $22,800$.

Year 3: $22,800 + $91,700 - b = $28,700; b = $85,800$.

Year 4: $28,700 + c - $87,600 = $36,000; c = $94,900$.

Year 5: $36,000 + $98,200 - $91,400 = d; d = $42,800$.

                      Solutions

4.14 continued.

b. Purchases exceeded usage each period, causing the amount in the Raw Materials Inventory account to increase each year. One possible explanation is that inventory quantities remained the same but purchase prices increased each year. The raw materials added to inventories cost more than those used. A second explanation is that inventory quantities increased while purchase prices remained the same. Perhaps the firm anticipated higher production levels than actually realized and purchased raw materials to support this higher level of production. Alternatively, the firm may have anticipated increased prices or shortages for raw materials and purchased sufficient quantities before these events occurred. Finally, the increase in the Raw Materials Inventory account may result from both price and quantity increases, a combination of the explanations above.

4.15 (Work-in-process inventory transactions.)

a. The relationship among the six items is:

Beginning Work-in-Process Inventory	+	Raw Materials Used	+	Direct Labor Costs Incurred	+	Mfg. Overhead Costs Incurred	−	Cost of Units Completed	=	Ending Work-in-Process Inventory

Year 4: $67,900 + $247,800 + $242,600 + $87,100 − $575,200 = a; a = $70,200.

Year 5: $70,200 + $260,190 + $254,730 + $91,455 − b = $72,615; b = $603,960.

Year 6: $72,615 + $156,115 + c + $87,600 − $426,670 = $42,500; c = $152,840.

Year 7: $42,500 + d + $275,110 + $96,100 − $607,340 = $76,970; d = $270,600.

b. This firm experienced a substantial decline in the level of its manufacturing operations during Year 6. An examination of the components of manufacturing costs (raw material, direct labor, and overhead) during Year 7 relative to Year 5 indicates a higher than proportional increase in direct labor costs. Perhaps a labor strike curtailed operations in Year 6. The final compensation settlement increased wage rates in Year 7.

4.16   (Finished goods inventory transactions.)

   a.   The relationship among the four items is:

Beginning Finished Goods Inventory	+	Cost of Units Completed	–	Cost of Goods Sold	=	Ending Finished Goods Inventory

   Year 6: $48,900 + $460,700 – $455,200 = a; a = $54,400.

   Year 7: $54,400 + $515,980 – b = $69,660; b = $500,720.

   Year 8: $69,660 + c – $560,800 = $91,920; c = $583,060.

   Year 9: $91,920 + $664,690 – $633,700 = d; d = $122,910.

   b.   The cost of units completed exceeded the cost of units sold each year, causing the Finished Goods Inventory account to increase. The cost of units sold increased at an increasing rate, suggesting growing sales levels. The firm likely continued to increase production each year to provide sufficient goods to satisfy these increasing sales levels. An alternative explanation is that manufacturing costs increased each year, but the firm experienced a lag between the incurrence of the cost in manufacturing and the recognition of this cost as an expense (that is, at the time of sale).

4.17   (The Proctor & Gamble Company; income computation for a manufacturing firm.)

Sales..	$ 33,434
Less Cost of Goods Sold	(19,623)
Less Marketing and Administrative Expenses....................	(9,632)
Income before Income Taxes...................................	$ 4,179
Income Tax Expense at 35%	(1,463)
Net Income..	$ 2,716

4.18   (Rockwell International Corporation; income computation for a manufacturing firm.)

Sales..	$ 11,123
Less Cost of Goods Sold	(8,675)
Less Marketing and Administrative Expenses....................	(1,412)
Less Interest Expense...	(97)
Income before Income Taxes...................................	$ 939
Income Tax Expense at 35%	(329)
Net Income..	$ 610
Work-in-Process Inventory, October 1	$ 850
Plus Manufacturing Costs Incurred during Year.................	8,771
Less Work-in-Process Inventory, September 30	(920)
Cost of Goods Completed during Year...........................	$ 8,701
Plus Finished Goods Inventory, October 1	330
Less Finished Goods Inventory, September 30....................	(356)
Cost of Goods Sold...	$ 8,675

4.19   (Bechtel Construction Company; percentage-of-completion and completed contract methods of income recognition.)

Percentage-of-Completion Method

Year	Degree of Completion		Revenue	Expense	Income
1	$ 800,000/$3,200,000	= 25.0%	$1,000,000	$ 800,000	$ 200,000
2	$2,000,000/$3,200,000	= 62.5%	2,500,000	2,000,000	500,000
3	$ 400,000/$3,200,000	= 12.5%	500,000	400,000	100,000
			$4,000,000	$3,200,000	$800,000

Completed Contract Method

Year	Revenue	Expense	Income
1	--	--	--
2	--	--	--
3	$ 4,000,000	$3,200,000	$ 800,000
	$ 4,000,000	$3,200,000	$ 800,000

4.20   (JMB Realty Partners; installment and cost-recovery-first methods of income recognition.)

Installment Method

Year	Revenue	Percentage of Selling Price	Expense	Income
1	$ 20,000	25%	$15,000	$ 5,000
2	20,000	25%	15,000	5,000
3	20,000	25%	15,000	5,000
4	20,000	25%	15,000	5,000
	$ 80,000		$60,000	$20,000

Cost-Recovery-First Method

Year	Revenue	Expense	Income
1	$ 20,000	$ 20,000	-0-
2	20,000	20,000	-0-
3	20,000	20,000	-0-
4	20,000	-0-	$20,000
	$ 80,000	$ 60,000	$20,000

 4.21   (Soft-Touch, Inc.; preparation of journal entries and income statement for a manufacturing firm.)

a.   (1)   Raw Materials Inventory 66,700

   Accounts Payable.................................. 66,700

   (2)   Work-in-Process Inventory....................... 63,900

   Raw Materials Inventory...................... 63,900

4.21 a. continued.

(3)	Work-in-Process Inventory	175,770	
	Selling Expenses	19,200	
	Administrative Expenses	22,500	
	Cash		217,470

(4)	Work-in-Process Inventory	16,200	
	Selling Expenses	3,100	
	Administrative Expenses	2,200	
	Accumulated Depreciation		21,500

(5)	Work-in-Process Inventory	18,300	
	Selling Expenses	5,600	
	Administrative Expenses	4,100	
	Cash		28,000

(6)	Finished Goods Inventory	270,870	
	Work-in-Process Inventory		270,870

(7)	Accounts Receivable	350,000	
	Sales		350,000

(8)	Cost of Goods Sold	273,670	
	Finished Goods Inventory		273,670

$38,000 + $270,870 − $35,200 = $273,670.

b.
SOFT-TOUCH, INC.
Income Statement
For the Month of January

Sales		$ 350,000
Less Expenses:		
Cost of Goods Sold	$ 273,670	
Selling	27,900	
Administrative	28,800	(330,370)
Net Income		$ 19,630 ✓

Note: Instead of using a functional classification of expenses (that is, selling, administrative), classification by their nature (salary, depreciation, other operating) is acceptable.

4.22 (Famous Horse Garment Factory; preparation of journal entries and income statement for a manufacturing firm.)

a.	(1)	Raw Materials Inventory	245,400	
		Accounts Payable		245,400

4.22 a. continued.

(2)	Work-in-Process Inventory		238,400	
	Raw Materials Inventory			238,400

(3)	Work-in-Process Inventory		175,200	
	Selling Expenses		37,800	
	Administrative Expenses		54,800	
	Cash			267,800

(4)	Work-in-Process Inventory		29,400	
	Selling Expenses		4,800	
	Administrative Expenses		5,800	
	Accumulated Depreciation			40,000

(5)	Work-in-Process Inventory		36,400	
	Selling Expenses		14,600	
	Administrative Expenses		8,800	
	Cash			59,800

(6)	Finished Goods Inventory		468,000	
	Work-in-Process Inventory			468,000

(7)	Accounts Receivable		650,000	
	Sales			650,000

(8)	Cost of Goods Sold		478,000	
	Finished Goods Inventory			478,000

$146,000 + $468,000 - $136,000 = $478,000.

b.
FAMOUS HORSE GARMENT FACTORY
Income Statement
For the Month of January
(In Hong Kong Dollars)

Sales		$ 650,000
Less Expenses:		
Cost of Goods Sold	$ 478,000	
Selling	57,200	
Administrative	69,400	(604,600)
Net Income		$ 45,400

Note: Instead of using a functional classification of expenses (that is, selling, administrative), classification by their nature (salary, depreciation, other operating) is acceptable.

4.23 (Parkhurst Company; flow of manufacturing costs through the accounts.)

a. The cost of raw materials used is $402,700. The cost of factory supplies used is $25,600.

b. The cost of units completed during July is $794,000. ⁊

c. The cost of units sold during July is $797,500. ⁊

The derivation of the amounts in Parts *a.*, *b.*, and *c.* above appear in the T-accounts below.

	Raw Materials Inventory		
Bal.	53,900		
(1)	397,400	402,700	(2)*
Bal.	48,600		

	Factory Supplies Inventory		
Bal.	8,700		
(3)	26,100	25,600	(4)*
Bal.	9,200		

(handwritten: ⁊ OK 402,700)

	Work-in-Process Inventory		
Bal.	73,200		
(2)	407,200		
(4)	25,600		
(5)	294,900	794,000	(10)*
(6)	12,200		
(7)	3,600		
(8)	47,300		
(9)	4,800		
Bal.	74,800		

	Finished Goods Inventory		
Bal.	49,200		
(10)	794,000		
		797,500	(11)*
Bal.	45,700		

	Cost of Goods Sold	
(11)	797,500	

	Cash or Various Liabilities	
	397,400	(1)
	26,100	(3)
	294,900	(5)
	12,200	(6)
	3,600	(7)

	Prepaid Rent	
	4,800	(9)

	Accumulated Depreciation	
	47,300	(8)

*Amount is calculated by plugging.

4.24 (Oak Ridge Industries; flow of manufacturing costs through the accounts.)

a. The cost of raw materials used is $89,400.

         Solutions

4.24 continued.

b. The cost of units completed and transferred to the finished goods storeroom is $183,700.

c. Net income is $16,300 (= $240,000 – $182,400 – $41,300).

The derivation of the amounts in Parts a., b., and c. above appear in the T-accounts below.

Raw Materials Inventory			
	25,300		
(1)	91,300	89,400	(2)*
	27,200		

Work-in-Process Inventory			
	78,100		
(2)	89,400		
(3)	72,400	183,700	(6)*
(4)	3,100		
(5)	17,600		
	76,900		

Finished Goods Inventory			
	38,400		
(6)	183,700	182,400	(7)*
	39,700		

Cost of Goods Sold	
(7)	182,400

Accumulated Depreciation	
17,600	(5)

Sales	
240,000	(8)

Selling and Administrative Expenses	
(9)	41,300

Other Accounts			
(8)	240,000	91,300	(1)
		72,400	(3)
		3,100	(4)
		41,300	(9)

*Amount derived by plugging.

4.25 (Quilt Manufacturing Company; flow of manufacturing costs through the accounts.)

a. The cost of raw materials used is $18,050. The cost of factory supplies used is $5,700.

b. The cost of units completed during July is $155,100.

c. The cost of goods sold during July is $153,850.

4.25 continued.

The derivation of the amounts in Parts *a.*, *b.*, and *c.*, above appear in the T-accounts below.

Raw Materials Inventory					Factory Supplies Inventory			
Bal.	28,150				Bal.	7,950		
(1)	21,350	18,050	(2)*		(3)	4,600	5,700	(4)*
Bal.	31,450				Bal.	6,850		

Work-in-Process Inventory					Finished Goods Inventory			
	148,600					41,850		
(2)	18,050				(10)	155,100	153,850	(11)*
(4)	5,700					43,100		
(5)	93,800							
(6)	6,050	155,100	(10)*		Cost of Goods Sold			
(7)	3,000				(11)	153,850		
(8)	7,500							
(9)	1,000							
	128,600							

Cash or Various Liabilities			Prepaid Rent			Accumulated Depreciation		
	21,350	(1)	1,000	(9)			7,500	(8)
	4,600	(3)						
	93,800	(5)						
	6,050	(6)						
	3,000	(7)						

*Amount derived by plugging.

4.26   (Orlando Manufacturing Company; preparing T-account entries, adjusted trial balance, income statement, and balance sheet for a manufacturing firm.)

a. and d.

Cash					Accounts Receivable			
Bal.	121,000	9,350	(3)		Bal.	242,000	368,500	(5)
(5)	368,500	118,800	(6)		(1)	341,000		
		86,350	(7)					
		8,800	(8)					
		44,000	(10)					
		11,000	(11)					
Bal.	211,200				Bal.	214,500		

4.26 a. and d. continued.

Raw Materials Inventory			
Bal.	88,000	126,500	(12)
(4)	110,000		
Bal.	71,500		

Work-in-Process Inventory			
Bal.	253,000	283,800	(14)
(2)	88,000		
(8)	8,800		
(9)	13,200		
(10)	44,000		
(12)	126,500		
(13)	8,800		
Bal.	258,500		

Finished Goods Inventory			
Bal.	187,000	287,650	(15)
(14)	283,800		
Bal.	183,150		

Factory Supplies Inventory			
Bal.	22,000	8,800	(13)
(3)	9,350		
Bal.	22,550		

Manufacturing Equipment		
Bal.	528,000	
Bal.	528,000	

Accumulated Depreciation		
	33,000	Bal.
	13,200	(9)
	46,200	Bal.

Accounts Payable			
(6)	118,800	61,600	Bal.
		110,000	(4)
		52,800	Bal.

Wages Payable			
(7)	86,350	26,400	Bal.
		88,000	(2)
		28,050	Bal.

Capital Stock		
	1,100,000	Bal.
	1,100,000	Bal.

Retained Earnings		
	220,000	Bal.
	42,350	(19)
	262,350	Bal.

Sales			
(16)	341,000	341,000	(1)

Selling and Administrative Expenses			
(11)	11,000	11,000	(17)

Cost of Goods Sold			
(15)	287,650	287,650	(18)

Income Summary			
(17)	11,000	341,000	(16)
(18)	287,650		
(19)	42,350		
	341,000	341,000	

4.26 continued.

b.

ORLANDO MANUFACTURING COMPANY
Adjusted Trial Balance
July 31

Cash	$ 211,200	
Accounts Receivable	214,500	
Raw Materials Inventory	71,500	
Work-in-Process Inventory	258,500	
Finished Goods Inventory	183,150	
Factory Supplies Inventory	22,550	
Manufacturing Equipment	528,000	
Accumulated Depreciation		$ 46,200
Accounts Payable		52,800
Wages Payable		28,050
Capital Stock		1,100,000
Retained Earnings (July 1)		220,000
Sales		341,000
Selling and Administrative Expenses	11,000	
Cost of Goods Sold	287,650	
Totals	$1,788,050	$1,788,050

c.

ORLANDO MANUFACTURING COMPANY
Statement of Income and Retained Earnings
For the Month of July

Sales		$ 341,000
Less Expenses:		
Cost of Goods Sold	$ 287,650	
Selling and Administrative Expenses	11,000	
Total Expenses		298,650
Net Income		$ 42,350
Retained Earnings, July 1		220,000
Retained Earnings, July 31		$ 262,350

4.26 continued.

e.
ORLANDO MANUFACTURING COMPANY
Balance Sheet
July 31

Assets

Current Assets:

Cash	$ 211,200	
Accounts Receivable	214,500	
Raw Materials Inventory	71,500	
Work-in-Process Inventory	258,500	
Finished Goods Inventory	183,150	
Factory Supplies Inventory	22,550	
Total Current Assets		$ 961,400

Property, Plant, and Equipment:

Manufacturing Equipment	$ 528,000	
Less Accumulated Depreciation	(46,200)	
Total Property, Plant, and Equipment		481,800
Total Assets		$1,443,200

Liabilities and Shareholders' Equity

Current Liabilities:

Accounts Payable	$ 52,800	
Wages Payable	28,050	
Total Current Liabilities		$ 80,850

Shareholders' Equity:

Capital Stock	$1,100,000	
Retained Earnings	262,350	
Total Shareholders' Equity		1,362,350
Total Liabilities and Shareholders' Equity		$1,443,200

4.27 (Wilmington Chemical Company; preparing T-account entries, income statement, and balance sheet for a manufacturing firm.)

a., b., and c.

Cash					Accounts Receivable		
Bal.	580,800	60,000	(4)	(10)	510,900	495,000	(11)
(11)	495,000	446,010	(5)				
		105,570	(13)				
Bal.	464,220			Bal.	15,900		

4.27 a., b., and c. continued.

Raw Materials Inventory			
Bal.	28,800	253,200	(3)
(1)	242,400		
Bal.	18,000		

Work-in-Process Inventory			
(2)	222,000	422,625	(9)
(3)	253,200		
(5)	9,000		
(5)	4,380		
(5)	39,600		
(6)	180		
(7)	1,800		
(8)	1,200		
Bal.	108,735		

Finished Goods Inventory			
(9)	422,625	334,125	(15)
Bal.	88,500		

Office Supplies Inventory			
(13)	2,400	1,200	(14)
Bal.	1,200		

Prepaid Insurance			
(5)	14,400	1,200	(8)
Bal.	13,200		

Factory Equipment			
Bal.	204,000		
(4)	168,000		
(6)	3,600		
Bal.	375,600		

Accumulated Depreciation			
		1,800	(7)
		1,800	Bal.

Accounts Payable			
(5)	210,000	33,600	Bal.
		242,400	(1)
		3,780	(6)
		69,780	Bal.

Equipment Contract Payable			
		108,000	(4)
		108,000	Bal.

Wages Payable			
(5)	168,630	222,000	(2)
(13)	41,445	93,000	(12)
(13)	41,325		
		63,600	Bal.

Capital Stock			
		780,000	Bal.
		780,000	Bal.

Retained Earnings			
		62,175	(18)
		62,175	Bal.

4.27 a., b., and c. continued.

	Sales Revenue					Cost of Goods Sold			
(17)	510,900	510,900	(10)		(15)	334,125	334,125	(16)

	Sales Salaries Expense					Office Salaries Expense			
(12)	46,200	46,200	(16)		(12)	46,800	46,800	(16)

	Advertising Expense					Office Rent Expense			
(13)	10,800	10,800	(16)		(13)	3,300	3,300	(16)

	Miscellaneous Office Expenses					Miscellaneous Selling Expenses			
(13)	2,100	2,100	(16)		(13)	4,200	4,200	(16)

	Office Supplies Expense					Income Summary			
(14)	1,200	1,200	(16)		(16)	448,725	510,900	(17)
					(18)	62,175		
						510,900		

d.

WILMINGTON CHEMICAL COMPANY
Statement of Income and Retained Earnings
For the Month of October

Sales..		$ 510,900
Less Operating Expenses:		
Cost of Goods Sold	$ 334,125	
Sales Salaries Expense	46,200	
Office Salaries Expense.......................	46,800	
Advertising Expense	10,800	
Office Rent Expense...........................	3,300	
Miscellaneous Office Expenses.............	2,100	
Miscellaneous Selling Expenses	4,200	
Office Supplies Expense.......................	1,200	
Total Operating Expenses................		(448,725)
Net Income...		$ 62,175
Retained Earnings, October 1...................		-0-
Retained Earnings, October 31		$ 62,175

4.27 continued.

e.

WILMINGTON CHEMICAL COMPANY
Balance Sheet
October 31

Assets

Current Assets:

Cash..	$ 464,220	
Accounts Receivable............................	15,900	
Raw Materials Inventory.....................	18,000	
Work-in-Process Inventory.................	108,735	
Finished Goods Inventory....................	88,500	
Office Supplies Inventory....................	1,200	
Prepaid Insurance.............................	13,200	
Total Current Assets........................		$ 709,755

Noncurrent Assets:

Factory Equipment.............................	$ 375,600	
Less Accumulated Depreciation	(1,800)	
Total Noncurrent Assets		373,800
Total Assets....................................		$1,083,555

Liabilities and Shareholders' Equity

Liabilities:

Accounts Payable...............................	$ 69,780	
Equipment Contract Payable	108,000	
Wages Payable.....................................	63,600	
Total Liabilities		$ 241,380

Shareholders' Equity:

Capital Stock	$ 780,000	
Retained Earnings..............................	62,175	
Total Shareholders' Equity................		842,175
Total Liabilities and Shareholders' Equity		$1,083,555

4.28 (General Electric Company; income recognition for nuclear generator manufacturer.)

a.1. Percentage-of-Completion Method

Year	Incremental Percentage Complete	Revenue Recognized	Expenses Recognized	Net Income
2	42/120 (.35)	$ 70,000,000	$ 42,000,000	$28,000,000
3	54/120 (.45)	90,000,000	54,000,000	36,000,000
4	24/120 (.20)	40,000,000	24,000,000	16,000,000
Total.....	120/120 (1.00)	$ 200,000,000	$ 120,000,000	$80,000,000

4.28 a. continued.

2. Completed Contract Method

Year	Revenue Recognized	Expenses Recognized	Net Income
2	-0-	-0-	-0-
3	-0-	-0-	-0-
4	$200,000,000	$120,000,000	$80,000,000
Total....	$200,000,000	$120,000,000	$80,000,000

3. Installment Method

Year	Cash Collected (= Revenue)	Fraction of Cash Collected	Expenses (= Fraction X Total Cost)	Net Income
2	$ 20,000,000	1/10	$ 12,000,000	$ 8,000,000
3	100,000,000	5/10	60,000,000	40,000,000
4	80,000,000	4/10	48,000,000	32,000,000
Total......	$ 200,000,000	1.00	$120,000,000	$80,000,000

4. Cost-Recovery-First Method

Year	Cash Collected (= Revenue)	Expenses Recognized	Net Income
2	$ 20,000,000	$ 20,000,000	-0-
3	100,000,000	100,000,000	-0-
4	80,000,000	-0-	$80,000,000
Total.....	$ 200,000,000	$120,000,000	$80,000,000

b. The percentage-of-completion method probably provides a better measure of performance over the life of the contract because each period receives a portion of the net income from the contract. General Electric's original estimates of the cost of the contract were correct. Also, the periodic payments from the Consolidated Edison suggest that General Electric will probably collect cash in the amount of the contract price.

4.29   (Clinton Construction Company; income recognition for construction company.)

a.1.   Percentage-of-Completion Method

Year	Incremental Percentage Complete	Revenue Recognized	Expenses Recognized	Net Income
1	20/100 (.20)	$ 24,000,000	$ 20,000,000	$ 4,000,000
2	30/100 (.30)	36,000,000	30,000,000	6,000,000
3	35/100 (.35)	42,000,000	35,000,000	7,000,000
4	15/100 (.15)	18,000,000	15,000,000	3,000,000
Total......	100/100 (1.00)	$120,000,000	$100,000,000	$20,000,000

2.   Completed Contract Method

Year	Revenue Recognized	Expenses Recognized	Net Income
1	-0-	-0-	-0-
2	-0-	-0-	-0-
3	-0-	-0-	-0-
4	$ 120,000,000	$100,000,000	$20,000,000
Total....	$ 120,000,000	$100,000,000	$20,000,000

3.   Installment Method

Year	Cash Collected (= Revenue)	Percentage of Cash Collected	Expenses (= Percentage × Total Cost)	Net Income
1	$ 24,000,000	.20	$ 20,000,000	$ 4,000,000
2	30,000,000	.25	25,000,000	5,000,000
3	30,000,000	.25	25,000,000	5,000,000
4	36,000,000	.30	30,000,000	6,000,000
Total......	$120,000,000	1.00	$100,000,000	$20,000,000

4.   Cost-Recovery-First Method

Year	Cash Collected (= Revenue)	Expense Recognized	Net Income
1	$ 24,000,000	$ 24,000,000	-0-
2	30,000,000	30,000,000	-0-
3	30,000,000	30,000,000	-0-
4	36,000,000	16,000,000	$20,000,000
Total.....	$ 120,000,000	$100,000,000	$20,000,000

b.   The percentage-of-completion method probably gives the best measure of Clinton's performance each year under the contract. The original estimates of costs on the contract turned out to be correct. Also, the periodic cash collections suggest that the firm will probably collect cash in the amount of the contract price.

4-19

4.30 (J. R. Spangle; point-of-sale versus installment method of income recognition.)

a.

	Year 8	Year 9
Sales	$ 200,000	$ 300,000
Expenses:		
Cost of Goods Sold*	$ 120,000	$ 186,000
All Other Expenses	32,000	44,000
Total Expenses	$ 152,000	$ 230,000
Net Income	$ 48,000	$ 70,000
*Beginning Inventory	$ 0	$ 60,000
Purchases	180,000	240,000
Goods Available	$ 180,000	$ 300,000
Ending Inventory	(60,000)	(114,000)
Cost of Goods Sold	$ 120,000	$ 186,000

Cost of Goods Sold/Sales:
Year 8--$120,000/$200,000 = 60 percent.
Year 9--$186,000/$300,000 = 62 percent.

b.

	Year 8	Year 9
Collections from Customers	$ 90,000	$ 230,000
Expenses:		
Merchandise Cost of Collections*	$ 54,000	$ 140,400
All Other Expenses	32,000	44,000
Total Expenses	$ 86,000	$ 184,400
Net Income	$ 4,000	$ 45,600

*Calculation:	Year 8	Year 9
Merchandise Cost of Collections:		
Of Goods Sold:		
In Year 8, 60 percent of $90,000	$ 54,000	
In Year 9, 60 percent of $110,000		$ 66,000
Of Goods Sold in Year 9:		
62 percent of $120,000		74,400
	$ 54,000	$ 140,400

An Alternative Presentation Would Be:	Year 8	Year 9
Realized Gross Margin	$ 36,000	$ 89,600
All Other Expenses	32,000	44,000
Net Income	$ 4,000	$ 45,600

4.31 (Revenue recognition for various types of businesses.)

We have found this question to be an excellent one for class discussion because it forces the student to think about both revenue *and* expense timing and measurement questions. It also generates active student interest. We have found it helpful to begin consideration of each item by drawing a time line similar to that in Figure 4.1 and appropriately labeling it. Some of the items are relatively obvious while others require more discussion.

a. Time of sale.

b. Probably as work progresses using the percentage-of-completion method. Students normally assume the sale is to the United States Government. We ask them if it would make any difference if the sale was to a relatively weak government in Africa or South America. This question gets at the issue of whether the amount of cash the firm will receive is subject to reasonably accurate estimation.

c. Probably as the firm collects cash using the installment method.

d. At the time of sale.

e. At the time the firm picks citrus products and delivers them to customers. We ask students if their response would change if the citrus farm had a five-year contract at a set price to supply a particular quantity of citrus products to a citrus processor. The issue here is whether, given uncertainties about future weather conditions, the citrus grower will be able to make delivery on the contract.

f. AICPA *Statement of Position 79-4* stipulates that the firm should not recognize revenue until it meets all of the following conditions:

1. The firm knows the sales price.

2. The firm knows the cost of the film or can reasonably estimate the loss.

3. The firm is reasonably assured as to the collectibility of the selling price.

4. A licensee has accepted the film in accordance with the license agreement.

5. The film is available (that is, the licensee can exercise the right to use the film and all conflicting licenses have expired).

 Solutions

Revenue recognition from the sale of rights to the television network is appropriate as soon as the firm meets these conditions even though the license period is three years. The firm cannot recognize revenues from the sale of subsequent rights to others until the three-year licensing period has expired. An important question in this example is when to recognize the production costs as an expense. Should the firm recognize all of the costs as an expense on the initial sale to the television network? Or, should it treat some portion of the costs as an asset, matched against future sales of license rights? Most accountants would probably match all of the costs against revenue from the television network license agreement, unless the firm has signed other license agreements for periods beginning after the initial three-year period at the same time as the television license agreement.

g. At the time of sale of each house to a specific buyer.

h. At the time of sale to a specific buyer at a set price. This will vary, depending on who owns the whiskey during the aging process. We pose the following situation: Suppose a particular whiskey producer has an on-going supplier relationship with a whiskey distributor. The quantity purchased by the distributor and the price set depend on supply and demand conditions at the time aged whiskey is brought to the market. The supplier always purchases some minimum quantity. When should the firm recognize revenue? This question gets at the issue of measuring revenue in a reasonably objective manner. You may also want to discuss the following other wrinkle. Suppose the whiskey producer doubles capacity. The firm cannot sell any of the whiskey produced from this new capacity for six years. What should the firm do with the costs of this new capacity?

i. As time passes and the firm lets borrowers use funds.

j. The alternatives here are (1) as customers make reservations, (2) as customers make some formal commitments to confirm their reservations, or (3) as the agency receives cash from commissions. The second alternative is probably best. However, past experience may provide sufficient evidence as to the proportion of reservations that customers ultimately confirm to justify earlier recognition.

k. At the completion of the printing activity.

4.31 continued.

l. The issue here is whether to recognize revenue when the firm sells stamps to food stores or when customers turn in the stamps for redemption. One might argue for revenue recognition at the time of sale of the stamps, since the seller must have some estimate of the redemption rate in setting the price for the sale of the stamps.

m. At the time the wholesaler delivers food products to stores.

n. The issue here is whether to recognize revenue while the livestock is growing. A grower of timber faces a similar issue. For the reasons Part *h*. above discusses, it is probably best to await the time of delivery to a specific customer at an agreed upon price.

o. Probably during each period in a manner similar to the percentage-of-completion method. In practice firms use several methods.

4.32 (Pickin Chicken; revenue recognition for franchise.)

a.
Year	Pickin Chicken, Inc.	Country Delight, Inc.
2	$400,000 (= $50,000 × 8)	$ 160,000 (= $20,000 × 8)
3	250,000 (= $50,000 × 5)	148,000 (= $20,000 × 5 + $6,000 × 8)
4	0	78,000 (= $6,000 × 13)
5	0	78,000 (= $6,000 × 13)
6	0	78,000 (= $6,000 × 13)
7	0	78,000 (= $6,000 × 13)
8	0	30,000 (= $6,000 × 5)
Total..	$650,000	$ 650,000

b. The issue here is whether sufficient uncertainty exists regarding the amount the firm will ultimately collect to justify postponing revenue recognition until the time of collection. The casualty rate among franchisees has been very high and has led some accountants to argue that the installment method is the appropriate basis for revenue recognition.

4.33 (Classifying items in income statement.)

a.	1		e.	1
b.	1		f.	3
c.	2		g.	1
d.	2		h.	3

 Solutions

4.34   (BMW; income statement format.)

a.	Year 6	Year 7
Sales	DM 15,493	DM 18,002
Operating Costs:		
Expenditures for Materials	DM 8,607	DM 10,260
Expenditures for Personnel	3,174	3,586
Depreciation	949	1,146
Other Operating Expenditures	2,064	2,461
Less Increase in Product Inventories	(75)	(91)
Total Operating Costs	DM 14,719	DM 17,362
Operating Income	DM 774	DM 640
Interest Income (net of interest expense)	270	286
Income before Income Taxes	DM 1,044	DM 926
Income Tax Expense	(707)	(551)
Net Income	DM 337	DM 375

b.		
Sales	100.0%	100.0%
Operating Costs:		
Expenditures for Material	55.6%	57.0%
Expenditures for Personnel	20.5	19.9
Depreciation	6.1	6.4
Other Operating Expenditures	13.3	13.7
Less Increase in Product Inventories	(.5)	(.5)
Total Operating Costs	95.0%	96.5%
Operating Income	5.0%	3.5%
Interest Income (net of interest expense)	1.7	1.6
Income before Income Taxes	6.7%	5.1%
Income Tax Expense	(4.5)	(3.0)
Net Income	2.2%	2.1%

c. The net income to sales percentage was relatively stable between Year 6 and Year 7. The ratio of operating income to sales decreased between the two years, however, largely as a result of an increase in the percentage for materials. The stable net income to sales percentage occurs because of a reduction in the income tax expense to sales percentage.

4.35   (Marks and Spencer; format and interpretation of income statement.)

MARKS AND SPENCER, PLC.
Income Statement

	a. Amounts		b. Common Size	
	Year 10	Year 11	Year 10	Year 11
Sales.....................................	£ 5,608.1	£5,774.8	100.0%	100.0%
Cost of Goods Sold	(3,768.5)	(3,864.1)	(67.2)	(66.9)
Selling and Adminis- tration Expenses.............	(1,219.2)[a]	(1,287.8)[b]	(21.7)	(22.3)
Operating Income..............	620.4	622.9	11.1%	10.8%
Interest Revenue................	33.6	47.5	.6	.8
Interest Expense................	(42.4)	(34.2)	(.8)	(.6)
Loss on Sale of Equipment...	(7.4)	(4.7)	(.1)	--
Restructuring Charge........	--	(16.0)	--	(.3)
Income before Taxes...........	604.2	615.5	10.8%	10.7%
Income Taxes	(214.5)	(215.8)	(3.8)	(3.7)
Net Income	£ 389.7	£ 399.7	7.0%	6.9%[c]

[a]£1,211.9 – £7.4 + £14.7 = £1,219.2.
[b]£1,277.2 – £4.7 + £15.3 = £1,287.8.
[c]Does not reconcile to the amounts above due to rounding.

c. The net income to sales percentage remained steady, suggesting no change in overall profitability. However, the common size percentages for Year 11 include a restructuring charge of .3 percent. If one views this change as nonrecurring, then the firm experienced a slight increase in its net income to sales percentage. Note that the operating income percentage declined between the two years. The decline results from a decreased cost of goods sold percentage and an increased selling and administrative expense percentage. The decreased cost of goods sold percentage may reflect a shift in sales mix towards products with a higher markup, quantity purchases to take advantage of discounts, or other factors. An examination of selling and administrative expenses relative to sales reveals the following:

	Amounts		Percentages	
	Year 10	Year 11	Year 10	Year 11
Compensation[a]............	£ 671.3	£ 731.7	12.0%	12.7%
Property[b]......................	333.3	355.3	5.9	6.1
Other	214.6	200.8	3.8	3.5
Total.......................	£1,219.2	£ 1,287.8	21.7%	22.3%

[a]Includes staff and profit sharing costs.
[b]Includes occupancy, repairs, and depreciation costs.

Thus, most of the increased selling and administrative expense percentage results from increased compensation cost.

4.36   (Merck, Inc.; interpreting a common-size income statement.)

a. A combination of near monopoly power as a result of patent protection and demand that is relatively price inelastic permits pharmaceutical companies to generate a high markup on their manufacturing cost. This markup must cover the multi-year cost of developing and gaining FDA approval of new drugs.

b. Merck experienced growth rates in sales in the low to mid-teens. Such growth permits Merck to spread the relatively fixed cost of its manufacturing facilities over a larger number of units sold and thereby reduce its cost of goods sold percentage. Another possibility is that Merck recently introduced new drugs that have lower cost of goods sold percentages (high markup potential) than the portfolio of its existing drugs. A third possibility is that prices for raw materials (basically chemicals) decreased.

c. Federal government efforts to contain price inflation in the medical sector have a dampening effect on sales revenues. Increased competition among pharmaceutical companies for the medical care dollar requires increased selling effort. The combination of these factors leads to the increasing selling and administrative expense percentage.

d. Merck has increased the dollar amount of its expenditure on research and development. Research and development expenditures have not grown as rapidly as sales, causing the R & D expense percentage to decline.

e. Merck earns more interest revenue on investment than it incurs interest expense on debt. Merck probably has substantially more interest-earning assets than it has interest-bearing debt. The interest-earning assets (marketable securities) result from Merck's relatively high level of profitability and the cash generated by the operating process. The low level of interest-bearing debt reflects Merck's lack of a need to borrow.
    The declining percentage for interest revenue indicates that either interest rates or the amount of interest-earning assets have not increased as fast as sales. The stable percentage for interest expense suggests that interest rates and/or the level of debt increased in line with increases in sales.

f. The income tax expense percentage remained the same. With an increase in the net income before tax percentage, Merck's income tax burden declined slightly. Chapter 11 discusses income tax disclosures in the notes to the financial statements that permit the financial statement user to gain additional insight into the reasons for the declining tax burden.

Solutions   4-26

4.37 (Texas Instruments; preparing and interpreting a common-size income statement.)

a.

	Year 5	Year 6	Year 7
Sales Revenue	100.0%	100.0%	100.0%
Cost of Goods Sold	(76.9)	(73.6)	(72.4)
Marketing and Administrative Expenses	(15.7)	(14.5)	(13.5)
Employees Retirement and Profit Sharing Plans	(1.8)	(3.2)	(3.6)
Operating Profit	5.6%	8.7%	10.5%
Interest Expense	(.7)	(.5)	(.4)
Income before Income Taxes	4.9%	8.2%	10.1%
Income Tax Expense	(1.6)	(2.6)	(3.4)
Net Income	3.3%	5.6%	6.7%

b. Sales increased 14.6 percent [= ($8,523/$7,440) – 1] between Year 5 and Year 6 and 21.0 percent [= ($10,315/$8,523) – 1] between Year 6 and Year 7. This rapid growth might indicate an excess of supply over demand, permitting Texas Instruments (TI) to raise selling prices and lower the cost of goods sold to sales percentage. Alternatively, the rapid growth might indicate substantial increases in the volume of products sold. The manufacture of semiconductors is capital intensive. TI spreads the relatively fixed cost of the manufacturing operations over a larger number of units, thereby lowering the cost of goods sold to sales percentage.

c. Increased selling prices for the reason given in the answer to Part b. above coupled with smaller increases in marketing and administrative expenses would account for the decreasing percentage. Also, increases in the volume of units sold coupled with fixed marketing and administrative expenses would result in a decreasing percentage. Finally, TI might have instituted cost controls or increased the efficiency of marketing or administrative activities, lowering the percentage.

d. Enhanced retirement benefits, increase in expected health care costs, and increased profitability could all increase this percentage.

e. Decreased interest rates and a lower proportion of debt in the capital structure would explain a decreasing percentage.

f. The income tax expense to sales percentage increased because the income before income taxes to sales percentage increased. Because governments impose income taxes on income before taxes, not on sales, the appropriate measure of a firm's tax position is income tax expense divided by income before income taxes. The calculations for TI are:

4.37 f. continued.

> Year 5: $122/$369 = 33.1%
> Year 6: $220/$696 = 31.6%
> Year 7: $351/$1,042 = 33.7%.

Thus, TI's income tax position has not changed significantly during the 3 year period.

4.38 (Income recognition for various types of businesses.)

a. **Amgen**—The principal income recognition issue for Amgen is the significant lag between the incurrence of research and development expenditures and the realization of sales from any resulting products. Biotechnology firms are a relatively new industry and therefore have few commercially feasible products. Thus, research and development expenditures will likely represent a significant percentage of revenues, as is the case for Amgen. More established technology firms, such as pharmaceuticals, have established products as well as products in the pipeline and therefore research and development expenditures represent both a smaller and a more stable percentage of revenues. GAAP requires biotechnology firms to expense research and development expenditures in the year incurred.

Brown Forman—The principal revenue recognition issue for Brown Forman is whether it should recognize the increase in value of hard liquors while they are aging (that is, revalue the liquors to market value each year) or wait until the liquors are sold at the end of the aging process. Most accountants would argue that the market values of aging liquors are too uncertain prior to sale to justify periodic revaluations and revenue recognition. Brown Forman should include in the cost of the liquor inventory not only the initial production costs but also the cost incurred during the aging process. In this way, the firm can match total incurred costs with revenues generated at the time of sale.

Deere—Deere faces issues of revenue recognition with respect to both the sale of farm equipment to dealers and the provision of financing services. The concern with respect to the sale of farm equipment to dealers is the right of dealers to return any unsold equipment. If dealers have no right of return, then recognition of revenue at the time of sale is appropriate. If dealers can return any equipment discovered to be faulty prior to sale and the amount of such returns is reasonably predictable, then Deere can reduce the amount of revenue recognized each year for estimated returns. If dealers can return any unsold equipment, then delaying recognition of revenue until the dealer sells the equipment is appropriate. Deere should match the cost of manufacturing the equipment against the sales revenue. Deere reports research and development expense in

4.38 a. continued.

its income statement. Given the farm equipment industry, one wonders about what proportions of these expenditures Deere makes to enhance existing products versus to develop new products. Although contrary to GAAP, one can make the case that Deere should capitalize and amortize expenditures on new products.

Deere should accrue revenue from financing (interest) and insurance (premiums) services over time. To achieve matching, Deere should capitalize and amortize any initial administrative costs to check customer credit quality and prepare legal documents.

Fluor—The appropriate timing of revenue recognition for Fluor depends on the basis for pricing its services. If the fee is fixed for any particular construction project, then Fluor should recognize the fee in relation to the degree of completion of the construction project. If the fee is a percentage of total construction costs incurred on the project, then Fluor should recognize revenue in relation to costs incurred. If the fee is a percentage of the costs incurred by Fluor (salaries of their employees working on the project), then it should recognize revenue in relation to the incurrence of these costs. It seems clear that a percentage of completion method of revenue recognition is more appropriate than the completed contract method.

Golden West—Golden West should recognize interest revenue from home mortgage loans as time passes. It should provide for estimated uncollectible accounts each year. The uncollectible amount should reflect the resale value of homes repossessed. The more difficult question relates to recognition of revenue from points. One possibility is to recognize the full amount in the initial year of the loan. The rationale for such a procedure is that the points cover administrative costs of setting up the loan. Both the points and the administrative costs would be recognized in full in the initial year of the loan. An alternative view is that the points effectively reduce the amount lent by the savings and loan company and increase its yield beyond the stated interest rate. This view suggests that Golden West amortize the points over the term of the loan and match against this revenue amortization of the initial administrative costs to set up the loan. Golden West should recognize interest expense on deposits as time passes. There is no direct relation between interest expense on deposits and interest revenue from loans so Golden West matches interest expense to the period it is incurred.

4.38 a. continued.

Merrill Lynch—The principal income recognition issue for Merrill Lynch is whether it should report financial instruments held as assets and liabilities at their acquisition cost or their current market value. These assets and liabilities generally have easily measured market values. They are typically held for short periods of time (days or weeks). Thus, one can argue that use of current market values is appropriate. However, we are still left with the question as to whether the unrealized gain or loss should flow through to the income statement immediately or wait until realization at the time of sale. The argument for immediate recognition is that Merrill Lynch takes short-term financing and investing positions for short-term returns. Its income statement should reflect its operating performance during this period. The case for not recognizing the unrealized gains and losses is that they could reverse prior to realization and, in any case, will be realized very soon. Merrill Lynch should recognize revenue from fee-based services as it provides the services.

Rockwell—The absence of research and development expense from the income statement suggests that Rockwell charges all such costs to specific contracts. These costs become expenses as Rockwell recognizes revenue from the contracts. The multi-year nature of its contracts and the credit quality of the U.S. government suggests use of the percentage-of-completion method of income recognition. One difficulty encountered in applying the percentage-of-completion method is that Rockwell's contracts for projects such as the space shuttle get continually renewed. This procedure makes it difficult to identify a single contract price and accumulate costs for a single contract, which the percentage-of-completion method envisions.

b. **Amgen**—Amgen realized the highest profit margin of the seven companies. Its biotechnology products are protected by patents. It therefore maintains a monopoly position. Note that the cost of manufacturing its products is a small percent of revenues. Amgen's major cost is for research and development. Sales of its existing products are not only sufficient to cover its high, on-going research work but to provide a substantial profit margin as well. Its relatively low revenue to assets percentage is somewhat unexpected, given that its major "assets" are patents and research scientists. The reason for this low percentage (reason not provided in the case) is that cash and marketable securities comprise approximately 25 percent of its assets. These assets generated a return of approximately 3 percent during the year. This rate of return decreased the overall ratio of revenues to assets for Amgen.

4.38 b. continued.

Brown Forman—Brown Forman realized the third highest profit margin among the seven companies. If one views the excise taxes as a reduction in revenues rather than as an expense, its profit margin is 10.4 percent [= 8.8%/(100.0% – 15.4%)]. Concerns about excess alcoholic drinking in recent years have resulted in some exodus of companies from the industry, leaving the remaining companies with a larger share of a smaller market. The products of Brown Forman carry brand name recognition, permitting the firm to obtain attractive prices.

Deere—Deere's relatively low profit margin reflects (1) weaknesses in the farming industry in recent years, which puts downward pressure on margins, and (2) decreased interest rates, which lowers profit margins. The revenue-to-assets percentage of Deere reflects its capital-intensive manufacturing operations and the low interest rate on outstanding loans to dealers and customers.

Fluor—The low profit margin of Fluor reflects the relatively low value added of construction services. It may also reflect recessionary conditions when construction activity is weak and profit margins are thin.

Golden West—The 12 percent profit margin seems high, relative to interest rates in recent years. Recall though that Golden West pays short-term interest rates on its deposits but obtains long-term interest rates on its loans. An upward-sloping yield curve provides a positive differential. Also, the existence of shareholders' equity funds in the capital structure means that Golden West has assets earning returns for which it recognizes no expense in its income statement (that is, firms do not recognize an expense for the implicit cost of shareholders' funds). Note also that the ratio of revenue to assets is only .1. Thus, the assets of Golden West earned a return of only 1.2 percent (= 12.0% X .1) during the year.

Merrill Lynch—The lower profit margin for Merrill Lynch relative to Golden West reflects in part the fact that both the investments and financing of Merrill Lynch are short term. Merrill Lynch, however, realizes revenue from fee-based services. Firms like Merrill Lynch can differentiate these services somewhat and realize attractive profit margins. However, such services have been quickly copied by competitors in recent years, reducing the profit margins accordingly.

4.38 b. continued.

Rockwell—Rockwell's profit margin is in the middle of the seven companies. Factors arguing for a high profit margin include Rockwell's technological know-how and its role in long-term contracts with the U.S. government. Factors arguing for a lower profit margin include cutbacks in defense expenditures and excess capacity in the aerospace industry.

CHAPTER 5

STATEMENT OF CASH FLOWS: REPORTING THE EFFECTS OF OPERATING, INVESTING, AND FINANCING ACTIVITIES ON CASH FLOWS

Questions, Exercises, Problems, and Cases: Answers and Solutions

5.1   See the text or the glossary at the end of the book.

5.2   One can criticize a single income statement using a cash basis of accounting from two standpoints: (1) it provides a poor measure of operating performance each period because of the inaccurate matching of revenues and expenses (see discussion in Chapter 3), and (2) it excludes important investing (acquisitions and sales of long-lived assets) activities and financing (issuance or redemption of bonds or capital stock) activities of a firm that affect cash flow.

5.3   Accrual accounting attempts to provide a measure of operating performance that relates inputs to output without regard to when a firm receives or disburses cash. Accrual accounting also attempts to portray the resources of a firm and the claims on those resources without regard to whether the firm holds the resource in the form of cash. Although accrual accounting may satisfy user's needs for information about operating performance and financial position, it does not provide sufficient information about the cash flow effects of a firm's operating, investing, and financing activities. The latter is the objective of the statement of cash flows.

5.4   The statement of cash flows reports changes in the investing and financing activities of a firm. Significant changes in property, plant, and equipment affect the maturity structure of assets on the balance sheet. Significant changes in long-term debt or capital stock affect both the maturity structure of equities as well as the mix of debt versus shareholder financing.

5.5   The indirect method reconciles net income, the primary measure of a firm's profitability, with cash flow from operations. Some would argue that the relation between net income and cash flow from operations is less evident when a firm reports using the direct method. The frequent use of the indirect method prior to the issuance of FASB *Statement No. 95* also probably explains its continuing popularity.

5-1

5.6   The classification in the statement of cash flows parallels that in the income statement, where interest on debt is an expense but payments on the principal amount of the debt are not an expense but a reduction in a liability.

5.7   The classification in the statement of cash flows parallels that in the income statement, where interest on debt is an expense but dividends are a distribution of earnings, not an expense.

5.8   Firms generally use accounts payable directly in financing purchases of inventory and other operating costs. Firms might use short-term bank financing indirectly in financing accounts receivable, inventories, or operating costs or use it to finance acquisitions of noncurrent assets or reductions in long-term financing. Thus, the link between short-term bank financing and operations is less direct and may not even relate to operating activities. To achieve consistency in classification, the FASB stipulates that changes in short-term bank loans are financing activities.

5.9   This is an investing and financing transaction whose disclosure helps the statement user understand why property, plant and equipment and long-term debt changed during the period. Because the transaction does not affect cash directly, however, firms must distinguish it from investing and financing transactions that do affect cash flow.

5.10   Both are correct, but the writer's point is not expressed clearly. Depreciation expense is a charge to operations, but does not require cash. If revenues precisely equal total expenses, there will be a retention of net funds in the business equal to the amount of the depreciation. As long as replacement of the depreciating assets is not necessary, it is possible to finance considerable expansion without resorting to borrowing or the issuance of additional stock.
        The "reader" is correct in saying that depreciation in itself is not a source of cash and that the total cash available would not have increased by adding larger amounts to the depreciation accounts. The source of cash is sales to customers.
        When one considers income tax effects, however, depreciation expenses do save cash because taxable income and, hence, income tax expense using cash are lower than they would be in the absence of depreciation charges.

5.11   The firm must have increased substantially its investment in accounts receivable or inventories or decreased substantially its current liabilities.

5.12   The firm might be capital intensive and, therefore, subtracted substantial amounts of depreciation expense in computing net income. This depreciation expense is added back to net income in computing cash flow from operations. In addition, the firm might have decreased significantly its investment in accounts receivable or inventories or increased its current liabilities.

Solutions   5-2

5.13   The accountant classifies the entire cash proceeds from the equipment sale as an investing activity. Because the calculation of cash flow from operations starts with net income (which includes the gain on sale of equipment), the accountant must subtract the gain to avoid counting cash flow equal to the gain twice, once as an operating activity and once as an investing activity.

5.14   (Stebbins Corporation; effect of various transactions on cash.)

a.

Transaction or Event	Cash	Other Current Assets	Noncurrent Assets	Current Liabilities	Noncurrent Liabilities	Share-holders' Equity
(1)		+$8,000		+$8,000		
(2)	−$3,000			− 3,000		
(3)		+ 6,000				+$6,000
		− 2,500				− 2,500
(4)	+ 5,000	− 5,000				
(5)			−$900			− 900
(6)				+ 1,500		− 1,500
(7)	− 1,400			− 1,400		
(8)	− 300	+ 300				
(9)				+ 700		− 700
(10)	− 500			− 500		
(11)	+ 1,200				+$1,200	
(12)	+ 200		− 200			
(13)	− 700		+ 700			
(14)			+ 300		+ 300	
(15)	− 200					− 200
Totals	+$ 300	+$6,800	−$ 100	+$5,300	+$1,500	+$ 200

b. (2) Operating   (8) Operating   (12) Investing
       (4) Operating   (10) Operating   (13) Investing
       (7) Operating   (11) Financing   (15) Financing

    5-3   **Solutions**

5.15 (Vertovec Corporation; effect of various transactions on cash.)

a.

Transaction or Event	Cash	Other Current Assets	Noncurrent Assets	Current Liabilities	Noncurrent Liabilities	Share-holders' Equity
(1)	−$5,000		+$5,000			
(2)	+$7,000		−$2,000			+$ 5,000
(3)		+$1,500		+$1,500		
(4)	−$1,200			−$1,200		
(5)	−$2,400	+$2,400				
(6)	+$8,000			+$8,000		
(7)	−$8,320			−$8,000		−$ 320
(8)				+$ 700		−$ 700
(9)	−$ 700			−$ 700		
(10)	+$4,000					+$ 4,000
(11)			+$6,000			+$ 6,000
(12)	−$1,400					−$ 1,400
(13)	−$5,000	+$5,000				
(14)	+$ 250					+$ 250
(15)	+$5,000	−$5,000				
Totals	+$ 230	+$3,900	+$9,000	+$ 300	---	+$ 12,830

b.

(1) Investing	(7) Financing, $8,000	(13) Investing
(2) Investing	Operating, $320	(14) Operating
(4) Operating	(9) Operating	(15) Investing
(5) Operating	(10) Financing	
(6) Financing	(12) Financing	

(3) ?

(8)?

(11)

5.16 (Upjohn; calculating and interpreting cash flow from operations.)

a.

Net Income	$ 489[a]
Additions:	
Depreciation Expense	163
Decrease in Accounts Receivable	3
Increase in Accounts Payable	58
Increase in Other Current Liabilities	62
Subtraction:	
Increase in Inventories	(46)
Increase in Prepayments	(195)
Cash Flow from Operations...	$ 534

[a]$489 = $3,275 − $163 − $154 − $2,469.

b. The production of pharmaceutical products is capital intensive. Upjohn reports a significant addback for depreciation, a noncash expense. Cash flow from operations was reduced during the year by a substantial increase in prepayments.

5.17 (Scott Paper Company; calculating and interpreting cash flow from operations.)

a. (Amounts in Millions)

	Year 10	Year 11
Net Income	$ 148	$ (70)
Depreciation Expense	346	353
(Inc.) Dec. in Accounts Receivable....................	(2)	110
(Inc.) Dec. in Inventories....................................	(72)	119
(Inc.) Dec. in Prepayments	1	(4)
Inc. (Dec.) in Accounts Payable	97	174
Inc. (Dec.) in Other Current Liabilities	(10)	(43)
Cash Flow from Operations.................................	$ 508	$639

[a]$5,356 − $346 − $8 − $4,854 = $148.
[b]$4,976 − $353 + $20 − $4,713 = $(70).

b. Cash flow from operations exceeds net income during Year 10 primarily because of the addback for depreciation expense. Changes in operating working capital accounts are largely offsetting. Cash flow from operations exceeds the net loss during Year 11 because of the addback for depreciation expense, decrease in accounts receivable and inventories (related to the decreased level of sales), and stretching of accounts payable.

5.18 (Kelly Services; calculating and interpreting cash flows.)

a.

KELLY SERVICES
Comparative Statement of Cash Flows
(Amounts in Thousands)

	Year 3	Year 4	Year 5
Operations			
Net Income	$ 39,225	$ 44,559	$ 61,057
Depreciation	13,977	16,614	17,309
(Inc.) Dec. in Accounts Receivable	(32,273)	(39,116)	(59,317)
(Inc.) Dec. in Prepayments	(2,340)	(2,656)	(9,137)
Inc. (Dec.) in Salaries Payable	14,793	14,465	34,460
Inc. (Dec.) in Other Current Liabilities	(21,203)	12,600	20,241
Cash Flow from Operations	$ 12,179	$ 46,466	$ 64,613
Investing			
Acquisition of Property, Plant and Equipment	$(32,449)	$(16,056)	$(18,433)
Decrease in Marketable Securities	31,571	9,614	2,265
Cash Flow from Investing	$ (878)	$ (6,442)	$(16,168)
Financing			
Common Stock Issued	$ 1,617	$ 1,031	$ 373
Dividends Paid	(21,999)	(23,846)	(26,570)
Cash Flow from Financing	$(20,382)	$(22,815)	$(26,197)
Change in Cash	$ (9,081)	$ 17,209	$ 22,248

b.   Net income and cash flow from operations both increased during the three-year period. Cash flow from operations was significantly less than net income during Year 3 but approximately the same in Year 4 and Year 5. Kelly Services repaid other current liabilities during Year 3, lowering cash flow from operations. The relation between Year 4 and Year 5 is typical of a service loan.

Expenditures for property, plant and equipment decreased in Year 4 and Year 5 relative to Year 3. Perhaps Kelly Services made significant expenditures on computer equipment during Year 3. Cash flow from operations was sufficient to finance capital expenditures in Year 4 and Year 5, but not in Year 3. Kelly Services sold marketable securities during Year 3 (as well as Year 4 and Year 5) to fund capital expenditures.

Kelly Services increased its dividends each year as net income increased, but dividends increased more slowly. The excess cash flow increased cash on the balance sheet.

5.19   (L.A. Gear; calculating and interpreting cash flow from operations.)

a. (Amounts in Millions)

	Year 4	Year 5	Year 6	Year 7
Net Income (Loss)	$ 22	$ 55	$ 31	$ (68)
Depreciation Expense	1	1	3	7
(Inc.) Dec. in Accounts Receivable	(35)	(51)	(56)	48
(Inc.) Dec. in Inventories	(51)	(73)	(21)	20
(Inc.) Dec. in Prepayments	(2)	(13)	(1)	(25)
Inc. (Dec.) in Accounts Payable	7	18	(4)	(15)
Inc. (Dec.) in Other Current Liabilities	12	13	7	7
Cash Flow from Operations	$ (46)	$ (50)	$ (41)	$ (26)

b.   Cash flow from operations is negative during Year 8, Year 9, and Year 10 despite positive earnings for each year because of the increases in accounts receivable and inventories. L.A. Gear, however, did not increase its accounts payable to finance the increased inventories. The negative cash flow from operations during Year 11 results primarily from the net loss from operations. Sales probably declined between Year 10 and Year 11, leading to decreased investment in accounts receivable and inventories and payment of accounts payable. Note that L.A. Gear is not capital intensive, so the depreciation addback is not significant.

5.20   (American Airlines; working backwards from changes in buildings and equipment account.)

Buildings and Equipment (Original Cost)		Accumulated Depreciation	
Balance, 12/31/Year 3	$16,825	Balance, 12/31/Year 3	$4,914
Outlays in Year 4	1,314	Depreciation in Year 4	1,253
	$18,139		$6,167
Balance, 12/31/Year 4	17,369	Balance, 12/31/Year 4	5,465
Retirements in Year 4	$ 770	Retirements in Year 4	$ 702

Proceeds = Book Value
          = $770 − $702
          = $68.

5.21 (Largay Corporation; effect of gains and losses from sales of equipment on cash flows.) (Amounts in Thousands)

Operations:			
Net Income	$ 100	$ 102	$ 98
Depreciation Expense	15	15	15
Gain on Sale of Equipment	--	(2)	--
Loss on Sale of Equipment	--	--	2
Changes in Working Capital Accounts	(40)	(40)	(40)
Cash Flow from Operations	$ 75	$ 75	$ 75
Investing:			
Sale of Equipment	$ 10	$ 12	$ 8
Acquisition of Buildings and Equipment	(30)	(30)	(30)
Cash Flow from Investing	$ (20)	$ (18)	$ (22)
Financing:			
Repayment of Long-term Debt	$ (40)	$ (40)	$ (40)
Change in Cash	$ 15	$ 17	$ 13
Cash, Beginning of Year	27	27	27
Cash, End of Year	$ 42	$ 44	$ 40

5.22 (Coca-Cola Company; preparing statement of cash flows from changes in balance sheet accounts.)

a.

THE COCA-COLA COMPANY
Statement of Cash Flows
For the Current Year
(Amounts in Millions)

Operations:	
Net Income ($1,755 Increase + $1,006 Dividend)............	$ 2,761
Additions:	
Depreciation Expense ($210 + $80).............................	290
Increase in Accounts Payable.......................................	347
Increase in Other Current Liabilities.........................	248
Decrease in Inventories	2
Subtractions:	
Increase in Accounts Receivable	(282)
Increase in Prepayments	(38)
Cash Flow from Operations...	$ 3,328
Investing:	
Sale of Equipment	$ 70
Acquisition of Property, Plant and Equipment	
($1,291 + $150)...	(1,441)
Cash Flow from Investing	$ (1,371)
Financing:	
Increase in Short-Term Borrowing	$ 411
Increase in Long-Term Borrowing ($195 + $150)............	345
Decrease in Long-Term Borrowing	(150)
Dividends...	(1,006)
Acquisition of Common Stock	(1,104)
Cash Flow from Financing...	$ (1,504)
Net Change in Cash...	$ 453
Cash, Beginning of Year	1,078
Cash, End of Year	$ 1,531

b. The Coca-Cola Company is a relatively mature and profitable firm. Its cash flow from operations was more than sufficient to fund capital expenditures. It used the excess to pay dividends and repurchase outstanding common stock.

5.23   (Delta Airlines; preparing statement of cash flows from changes in balance sheet accounts.)

a.

DELTA AIRLINES
Statement of Cash Flows
For the Year
(Amounts in Millions)

Operations:		
Net Income...	$	303
Additions:		
Depreciation Expense ($363 + $96)............................		459
Loss on Sale of Equipment [$30 – ($151 – $96)]..........		25
Decrease in Accounts Receivable		26
Increase in Accounts Payable....................................		14
Subtractions:		
Increase in Inventories		(11)
Increase in Prepayments		(19)
Decrease in Other Current Liabilities		(32)
Cash Flow from Operations...	$	765
Investing:		
Sale of Equipment	$	30
Acquisition of Property, Plant and Equipment		
($1,219 + $151)..		(1,370)
Acquisition of Securities		(345)
Cash Flow from Investing	$ (1,685)	
Financing:		
Increase in Notes Payable..	$	88
Increase in Long-term Debt		674
Decrease in Common Stock		(187)
Dividends Paid ($303 – $186)		(117)
Cash Flow from Financing...	$	458
Net Change in Cash	$	(462)
Cash, Beginning of Year		530
Cash, End of Year	$	68

b.   Cash flow from operations exceeds net income primarily because of the addback for depreciation expense. Cash flow from operations was insufficient to finance acquisitions of investments and plant and equipment so Delta Airlines relied on external borrowing, primarily long-term debt. Delta Airlines also repurchased shares of its common stock during the year, thereby increasing the proportion of debt in its capital structure.

5.24   (Jericho Steel Corporation; reformatting statement of cash flows.)

a.
                    JERICHO STEEL CORPORATION
                       Statement of Cash Flows
                            For the Year
                       (Amounts in Millions)

Operations:		
Net Income	$	245.7
Depreciation Expense		325.3
Decrease in Accounts Receivable		61.6
Increase in Accounts Payable		29.8
Increase in Inventories		(43.9)
Decrease in Other Current Liabilities		(14.9)
Cash Flow from Operations	$	603.6
Investing:		
Sale of Investments	$	72.1
Plant and Equipment Acquired		(421.3)
Cash Flow from Investing	$	(349.2)
Financing:		
Common Stock Issued	$	71.8
Long-term Debt Redeemed		(298.3)
Dividends Paid		(37.5)
Cash Flow from Financing	$	(264.0)
Change in Cash	$	(9.6)
Cash, Beginning of Year		530.5
Cash, End of Year	$	520.9

b. Cash flow from operations exceeded net income primarily because of the addback of depreciation expense for this capital-intensive business. Cash flow from operations was more than sufficient to finance capital expenditures, suggesting that this steel firm is in the mature phase of its life cycle. The firm used the excess cash flow to repay long-term debt.

5.25   (Effect of various transactions on statement of cash flows.)

If you use transparencies in class, it is effective to flash onto the screen the answer transparency for some problem showing a comprehensive statement of cash flows. Then you can point to the lines affected as the students attempt to answer the question. It helps them by letting them see the possibilities. We use this question for in-class discussion. We seldom assign it for actual homework. A favorite form of question for examinations is to present a schematic statement of cash flows and to ask which lines certain transactions affect and how much. When we use this problem in class, we invariably tell students that it makes a good examination question; this serves to strengthen their interest in the discussion.

5.25 continued.

    a. (1) Decreases by $600; reduces net income through amortization expense.
       (2) Increases by $600; amount of expense is added back to net income in deriving cash flow from operations.
    No effect on net cash flow from operations.

    b. (2) Increases $900; amount of amortization is an addition for amortization charge not using cash.
       (3) Increases $900; subtraction for the increase in inventory, an operating use of cash. The net effect of these two is no change in cash flow from operations. Noncurrent asset goes down; current asset inventory goes up.

    c. The transaction does not appear in the statement of cash flows because it does not affect cash. The firm must disclose information about the transaction in a supplemental schedule or note.

    d. (2) Increases by $7,500; operating increase in cash from increase in Accounts Payable.
       (3) Increases by $7,500; operating decrease in cash for increase in inventory.
    The net effect of these two transactions is to leave cash from operations unchanged, because the amounts added and subtracted change in such a way as to cancel out each other.

    e. (1) Decreases by $1,500; net income goes down.
       (2) Increases by $1,500; additions go up because inventory, not cash, was destroyed.

    f. (2) Increases by $1,450; operating increase in cash reflected by decrease in the amount of Accounts Receivable.
       (9) Increases by $1,450.

    g. (6) Increases by $10,000; increase in cash from security issue.
       (9) Increases by $10,000.

    h. (4) Increases by $4,500; increase in cash from sale of noncurrent asset.
       (9) Increases by $4,500.

5.26 (Swan Corporation; preparing statement of cash flows.)

a.
SWAN CORPORATION
Statement of Cash Flows
For the Current Year

Operations:		
Net Income	$50,000	
Additions:		
Depreciation Expense	79,000	
Increase in Income Taxes Payable..................	5,000	
Subtractions:		
Increase in Accounts Receivable	(12,000)	
Increase in Merchandise Inventories..............	(20,000)	
Decrease in Accounts Payable.........................	(25,000)	
Cash Flow from Operations....................................		$77,000
Investing:		
Acquisition of Property, Plant, and Equipment..		(75,000)
Financing:		
Issue of Common Stock......................................	$ 5,000	
Retirement of Bonds	(4,000)	
Cash Flow from Financing		1,000
Net Change in Cash		$ 3,000
Cash, January 1		12,000
Cash, December 31		$15,000

The amounts in the T-account work sheet below are in thousands.

		Cash			
	√	12			
		Operations			
Net Income	(1)	50	12	(3)	Increase in Accounts Receivable
Depreciation	(2)	79			
Increase in Income Taxes Payable	(7)	5	20	(4)	Increase in Merchandise Inventories
			25	(6)	Decrease in Accounts Payable
		Investing			
			75	(5)	Acquisition of Property, Plant, and Equipment
		Financing			
Issue of Common Stock	(9)	5	4	(8)	Retirement of Bond
	√	15			

5.26 a. continued.

Accounts Receivable		Merchandise Inventories		Property, Plant, and Equipment	
√ 144		√ 190		√ 700	
(3) 12		(4) 20		(5) 75	
√ 156		√ 210		√ 775	

Accumulated Depreciation		Accounts Payable		Income Taxes Payable	
	246 √		190 √		20 √
	79 (2)	(6) 25			5 (7)
	325 √		165 √		25 √

Bonds Payable		Common Stock		Retained Earnings	
	100 √		210 √		280 √
(8) 4			5 (9)		50 (1)
	96 √		215 √		330 √

b. Cash flow from operations was positive and sufficient to finance acquisitions of property, plant and equipment. The firm issued common stock to finance the retirement of long-term debt.

5.27 (Hale Company; preparing statement of cash flows.)

a.

HALE COMPANY
Statement of Cash Flows
For the Year

Operations:		
Net Income	$ 44,000	
Additions:		
Depreciation Expense	54,000	
Increase in Accounts Payable	4,000	
Subtractions:		
Increase in Accounts Receivable	(13,000)	
Increase in Inventory	(11,000)	
Decrease in Interest Payable	(2,000)	
Cash Flow from Operations		$76,000
Investing:		
Sale of Equipment	$ 6,000	
Acquisition of Equipment	(56,000)	
Cash Flow from Investing		(50,000)
Financing:		
Dividends	$(10,000)	
Retirement of Portion of Mortgage Payable	(10,000)	
Cash Flow from Financing		(20,000)
Net Change in Cash		$ 6,000
Cash, January 1		52,000
Cash, December 31		$58,000

5.27 a. continued.

The amounts in the T-account work sheet below are in thousands.

Cash

√	52				

Operations

Net Income	(1)	44	13	(5)	Increase in Accounts Receivable
Depreciation	(3)	54			
Increase in Accounts Payable	(8)	4	11	(6)	Increase in Inventory
			2	(9)	Decrease in Interest Payable

Investing

Sale of Equipment	(4)	6	56	(7)	Acquisition of Equipment

Financing

			10	(2)	Dividends
			10	(10)	Payment of Mortgage Payable

√	58		

Accounts Receivable			Inventory			Land		
√	93		√	151		√	30	
(5)	13		(6)	11				
√	106		√	162		√	30	

Buildings and Equipment (Cost)				Accumulated Depreciation				Accounts Payable			
√	790					460	√			136	√
(7)	56	16	(4)	(4)	10	54	(3)			4	(8)
√	830					504	√			140	√

Interest Payable				Mortgage Payable				Common Stock			
		10	√			120	√			250	√
(9)	2			(10)	10						
		8	√			110	√			250	√

 Solutions

5.27 a. continued.

Retained Earnings

		140	√
(2)	10	44	(1)
		174	√

b. Cash flow from operations was sufficient to finance acquisitions of equipment during the year. The firm used the excess cash flow to pay dividends and retire long-term debt.

 5.28 (Dickerson Manufacturing Company; preparing statement of cash flows.)

a.
DICKERSON MANUFACTURING COMPANY
Statement of Cash Flows
For the Year

Operations:		
Net Income	$ 568,000	
Additions:		
Depreciation	510,000	
Loss on Sale of Machinery	5,000	
Increase in Accounts Payable	146,000	
Increase in Taxes Payable	16,000	
Increase in Short-Term Payables	138,000	
Subtractions:		
Increase in Accounts Receivable	(106,000)	
Increase in Inventory	(204,000)	
Cash Flow from Operations		$ 1,073,000
Investing:		
Sale of Machinery	$ 25,000	
Acquisition of Land	(36,000)	
Acquisition of Buildings and Machinery	(1,018,000)	
Cash Flow from Investing		(1,029,000)
Financing:		
Issue of Common Stock	$ 32,000	
Dividends Paid	(60,000)	
Bonds Retired	(50,000)	
Cash Flow from Financing		(78,000)
Net Change in Cash		$ (34,000)
Cash, January 1		358,000
Cash, December 31		$ 324,000

5.28 a. continued.

The amounts in the T-account work sheet below are in thousands.

Cash

√		358			

Operations

Net Income	(1)	568	106	(5)	Increase in Accounts Receivable
Depreciation Expense	(3)	510			
Loss on Sale of Equipment	(4)	5	204	(6)	Increase in Inventory
Increase in Accounts Payable	(9)	146			
Increase in Taxes Payable	(10)	16			
Increase in Other Short-Term Payables	(11)	138			

Investing

Sale of Machinery	(4)	25	1,018	(7)	Acquisition of Buildings and Machinery
			36	(8)	Acquisition of Land

Financing

Issue of Common Stock	(13)	32	60	(2)	Dividends
			50	(12)	Retirement of Bonds

√		324	

Accounts Receivable			Inventory	
√	946		√	1,004
(5)	106		(6)	204
√	1,052		√	1,208

Buildings and Machinery				Accumulated Depreciation—Buildings and Machinery			
√	8,678					3,974	√
(7)	1,018	150	(4)	(4)	120	510	(3)
√	9,546					4,364	√

5.28 a. continued.

	Land				Accounts Payable	
√	594				412	√
(8)	36				146	(9)
√	630				558	√

	Taxes Payable				Other Short-Term Payables	
	274	√			588	√
	16	(10)			138	(11)
	290	√			726	√

	Bonds Payable				Common Stock	
	1,984	√			1,672	√
(12)	50				32	(13)
	1,934	√			1,704	√

	Retained Earnings		
	2,676	√	
(2)	60	568	(1)
	3,184	√	

b. Dickerson Manufacturing Company is heavily capital intensive. Its cash flow from operations exceeds net income because of the depreciation expense addback. Cash flow from operations appears substantial, but so are its expenditures for building and equipment. The firm's relatively low dividend payout rate suggests that it expects large capital expenditures to continue.

5.29 (Vincent Company; preparing income statement and statement of cash flows.)

a.

VINCENT COMPANY
Statement of Income and Retained Earnings
for the Year

Sales		$ 1,300,000
Gain on Sale of Equipment		6,000
Total Revenues		$ 1,306,000
Expenses:		
Cost of Goods Sold	$ 910,000	
Selling and Administrative Expenses	428,000	
Depreciation Expense	85,000	
Interest Expense	24,000	
Total Expenses		(1,447,000)
Net Loss for Year		$ (141,000)
Retained Earnings, January 1		176,000
Retained Earnings, December 31		$ 35,000

5.29 continued.

b.

VINCENT COMPANY
Statement of Cash Flows
For the Year

Operations:		
Net Loss..	$(141,000)	
Additions:		
Depreciation	85,000	
Decrease in Accounts Receivable...............	17,000	
Decrease in Inventories............................	14,000	
Subtractions:		
Gain on Sale of Equipment	(6,000)	
Decrease in Accounts Payable	(8,000)	
Cash Flow from Operations		$(39,000)
Investing:		
Sale of Equipment..	$ 70,000	
Acquisition of Plant and Equipment	(60,000)	
Cash Flow from Investing		10,000
Financing:		
Issue of Long-Term Debt............................		25,000
Net Change in Cash...		$ (4,000)
Cash, January 1...		42,000
Cash, December 31		$ 38,000

The amounts in the T-account work sheet below are in thousands.

5.29 b. continued.

	Accounts Receivable			Merchandise Inventory			Plant and Equipment	
√	130		√	216		√	872	
		17 (5)			14 (6)	(3)	60	82 (4)a
√	113		√	202		√	850	

	Accumulated Depreciation			Accounts Payable			Long-Term Debt	
		473 √			61 √			250 √
(4)a	18	85 (2)	(7)	8				25 (8)
		540 √			53 √			275 √

	Common Stock			Retained Earnings	
		300 √			176 √
			(1)	141	
		300 √			35 √

a(4)   Journal entry made at time of sale:

Cash...	70,000	
Accumulated Depreciation	18,000	
Plant and Equipment (Cost).........		82,000
Gain on Sale of Equipment...........		6,000

Plug for Cash in this journal entry; plug for $82,000 amount in T-account for Plant and Equipment and for $18,000 amount in T-account for Accumulated Depreciation.

c.   Although Vincent Company's heavy capital intensity resulted in a large addback for depreciation expense, its net loss from operations led to negative cash flow from operations. Sales of equipment and the issue of long-term debt provided the cash needed to cover the negative operating cash flow and fund capital expenditures.

5.30 (Clark Corporation; preparing statement of cash flows.)

a.

CLARK CORPORATION
Statement of Cash Flows
For the Current Year

Operations:		
Net Income	$60,000	
Additions:		
Depreciation Expense	22,000	
Increase in Accounts Payable	17,000	
Increase in Income Taxes Payable	5,000	
Subtractions:		
Increase in Accounts Receivable	(20,000)	
Increase in Merchandise Inventories	(16,000)	
Cash Flow from Operations....................................		$68,000
Investing:		
Sale of Property, Plant, and Equipment..............	$ 8,000	
Acquisition of Property, Plant, and Equipment..	(80,000)	
Cash Flow from Investing		(72,000)
Financing:		
Issue of Bonds	$10,000	
Dividends Paid	(10,000)	
Cash Flow from Financing		0
Net Change in Cash		$ (4,000)
Cash, January 1		42,000
Cash, December 31		$ 38,000

    Solutions

a. continued.

The amounts in the T-account work sheet below are in thousands.

Cash

| | | √ | 42 | | | |

Operations

Net Income	(1)	60		20	(7)	Increase in Accounts Receivable
Depreciation	(6)	22				
Increase in Accounts Payable	(9)	17		16	(8)	Increase in Merchandise Inventories
Increase in Income Taxes Payable	(10)	5				

Investing

Sale of Property, Plant, and Equipment	(5)	8		80	(3)	Property, Plant, and Equipment Acquired for Cash

Financing

Issue of Long-Term Debt for Cash	(11)	10		10	(2)	Dividends

| | | √ | 38 | | | |

Accounts Receivable		
√	146	
(7)	20	
√	166	

Merchandise Inventories		
√	162	
(8)	16	
√	178	

Property, Plant, and Equipment			
√	180		
(3)	80		
(4)	20	14	(5)
√	266		

Accumulated Depreciation			
		62	√
(5)	6	22	(6)
		78	√

Accounts Payable		
	182	√
	17	(9)
	199	√

Income Taxes Payable		
	20	√
	5	(10)
	25	√

5.30 a. continued.

Bonds Payable		Common Stock		Retained Earnings		
	20 √		50 √			196 √
	20 (4)			(2)	10	60 (1)
	10 (11)					
	50 √		50 √			246 √

b. Clark Company generated cash flow from operations slightly in excess of net income. It used the operating cash flow to finance capital expenditures.

5.31 (Quebec Company; preparing statement of cash flows over 2-year period.)

a.
QUEBEC COMPANY
Statement of Cash Flows
For Year 2

Operations:		
Net Income	$166,000	
Additions:		
Depreciation Expense	174,000	
Decrease in Merchandise		
Inventories	20,000	
Subtractions:		
Increase in Accounts Receivable	(20,000)	
Decrease in Accounts Payable	(2,000)	
Cash Flow from Operations		$338,000
Investing:		
Sale of Property, Plant, and Equipment	$ 88,000	
Acquisition of Property, Plant, and		
Equipment	(342,000)	
Cash Flow from Investing		(254,000)
Financing:		
Issue of Common Stock	$ 92,000	
Dividends Paid	(80,000)	
Retirement of Bonds	(32,000)	
Cash Flow from Financing		(20,000)
Net Change in Cash		$ 64,000
Cash, January 1, Year 2		110,000
Cash, December 31, Year 2		$174,000

 Solutions

5.31 a. continued.

		Cash			
√		110			
		Operations			
Net Income	(1)	166[a]	20	(6)	Increase in Accounts Receivable
Depreciation	(3)	174			
Decrease in Merchandise Inventories	(7)	20	2	(8)	Decrease in Accounts Payable
		Investing			
Sale of Property, Plant, and Equipment	(4)	88[b]	342	(5)	Acquisition of Property, Plant, and Equipment
		Financing			
Issue of Common Stock	(10)	92	80	(2)	Dividends
			32	(9)	Retirement of Bonds
√		174			

[a]See footnote *a* on following page.
[b]See footnote *b* on following page.

	Accounts Receivable			Merchandise Inventories			Property, Plant, and Equipment	
√	220		√	250		√	3,232	
(6)	20				20 (7)	(5)	342	216[b](4)
√	240		√	230		√	3,358	

	Accounts Payable			Accumulated Depreciation			Bonds Payable	
		162 √			1,394 √			212 √
(8)	2		(4)	128	174 (3)	(9)	32	
		160 √			1,440 √			180 √

5.31 a. continued.

Common Stock		Retained Earnings	
	754 √		1,290 √
92 (10)	(2) 80		166[a] (1)
	846 √		1,376 √

[a]$166 = $1,820 + $10 − $740 − $640 − $174 − $110.

[b]Journal entry made at time of sale:

Cash (Plug)	88	
Accumulated Depreciation	128	
Property, Plant, and Equipment		216

b.

QUEBEC COMPANY
Statement of Cash Flows
For Year 3

Operations:		
Net Income	$ 198,000	
Additions:		
Depreciation Expense	192,000	
Loss on Sale of Equipment	4,000	
Decrease in Accounts Receivable	30,000	
Increase in Accounts Payable	6,000	
Subtractions:		
Increase in Merchandise Inventories	(50,000)	
Cash Flow from Operations		$ 380,000
Investing:		
Sale of Property, Plant, and Equipment	$ 98,000	
Acquisition of Property, Plant, and Equipment	(636,000)	
Cash Flow from Investing		(538,000)
Financing:		
Issue of Bonds	$ 90,000	
Issue of Common Stock	182,000	
Dividends Paid	(94,000)	
Cash Flow from Financing		178,000
Net Change in Cash		$ 20,000
Cash, January 1, Year 3		174,000
Cash, December 31, Year 3		$ 194,000

         Solutions

5.31 b. continued.

The amounts in the T-account work sheet below are in thousands.

Cash

√		174				

Operations

Net Income	(1)	198[a]	50	(7)	Increase in Merchandise Inventories	
Depreciation	(3)	192				
Loss on Sale of in Equipment	(5)	4				
Decrease in Accounts Receivable	(6)	30				
Increase in Accounts Payable	(8)	6				

Investing

Sale of Property, Plant, and Equipment	(5)	98[b]	636	(4)	Acquisition of Property, Plant, and Equipment

Financing

Issue of Bonds Payable	(9)	90	94	(2)	Dividends
Issue of Common Stock	(10)	182			
√		194			

[a]See footnote *a* on following page.
[b]See footnote *b* on following page.

Accounts Receivable				Merchandise Inventories				Property, Plant, and Equipment			
√	240			√	230			√	3,358		
		30	(6)	(7)	50			(4)	636	244[b]	(5)
√	210			√	280			√	3,750		

Accounts Payable				Accumulated Depreciation				Bonds Payable			
		160	√			1,440	√			180	√
		6	(8)	(5)	142[b]	192	(3)			90	(9)
		166	√			1,490	√			270	√

Solutions　　　　　5-26

5.31 b. continued.

Common Stock				Retained Earnings	
	846 √				1,376 √
	182(10)	(2)	94		198[a](1)
	1,028 √				1,480 √

[a]$198 = $1,940 + $14 − $826 − $602 − $192 − $4 − $132.

[b]Journal entry made at time of sale:

Cash (Plug)..	98	
Accumulated Depreciation	142	
Loss on Sale of Equipment	4	
Property, Plant, and Equipment..................		244

c.   During Year 2, cash flow from operations was more than sufficient to fund capital expenditures and pay dividends. The firm issued common stock and used the proceeds to retire debt and increase the amount of cash on hand. During Year 3, expenditures on property, plant and equipment increased significantly. Operating cash flows were insufficient to fund these capital expenditures and pay dividends, so the firm issued additional bonds and common stock.

5.32   (Quinta Company; working backwards through statement of cash flows.)

QUINTA COMPANY
Balance Sheet
January 1, Year 5
($ in 000's)

Assets

Current Assets:

Cash..	$ 20	
Accounts Receivable	190	
Merchandise Inventories......................................	280	
Total Current Assets......................................		$490
Land..		50
Buildings and Equipment......................................	$ 405	
Less Accumulated Depreciation......................	(160)	245
Investments		140
Total Assets...		$925

                                            Solutions

Liabilities and Shareholders' Equity

Current Liabilities:		
Accounts Payable	$ 255	
Other Current Liabilities	130	
Total Current Liabilities		$385
Bonds Payable		60
Common Stock		140
Retained Earnings		340
Total Liabilities and Shareholders' Equity		$925

Shown below are T-accounts for deriving the solution. Entries (1)—(13) are reconstructed from the statement of cash flows. Changes for the year are appropriately debited or credited to end-of-year balances to get beginning-of-year balances. T-account amounts are shown in thousands.

Cash

	20		
(1)	200	30	(4)
(2)	60	40	(5)
(3)	25	45	(6)
(7)	40	130	(10)
(8)	15	200	(13)
(9)	10		
(11)	60		
(12)	40		
√	25		

Accounts Receivable

	190	
(4)	30	
√	220	

Merchandise Inventories

	280	
(5)	40	
√	320	

Land

50			
		10	(9)
√	40		

Buildings and Equipment

	405		
(10)	130	35	(8)
√	500		

Investments

140			
		40	(7)
√	100		

Accumulated Depreciation

		160	
(8)	20	60	(2)
		200	√

Accounts Payable

		255	
		25	(3)
		280	√

Other Current Liabilities

		130	
(6)	45		
		85	√

Bonds Payable

	60	
	40	(12)
	100	√

Common Stock

	140	
	60	(11)
	200	√

Retained Earnings

		340	
(13)	200	200	(1)
		340	√

5.33   (RV Suppliers, Incorporated; interpretative case using statement of cash flows.)

This problem was adapted from financial statement data of Winnebago Industries for its 1973 and 1974 fiscal years. A statement of cash flows, and T-account work sheets for Year 5 and Year 6, follow.

The Year 5 period for RV Suppliers, Incorporated, shows results that are typical of those for a growing firm. Although net income is $34,600, cash flow from operations is only $4,000, due primarily to an increase in accounts receivable and inventories. To finance acquisitions of property, plant, and equipment, the firm relied on short-term bank borrowing. Sound financial policy usually dictates the financing of noncurrent assets with long-term debt or capital stock. The market prospects for recreational vehicles were sufficiently poor during this period that the firm was probably unable to tap the long-term credit and equity markets and had to use short-term bank financing.

The Year 6 period shows results that are typical of those for a firm experiencing a business contraction. Because of decreased sales, accounts receivable decreased and the level of inventories decreased. Cash flow generated from the decrease in receivables and inventories was used to pay off accounts payable. Operations was a net user of cash. The firm again financed acquisitions of property, plant, and equipment with short-term bank borrowing. The firm reduced drastically its rate of capital expenditures, however, during Year 6.

5.33 continued.

RV SUPPLIERS, INCORPORATED
Statement of Cash Flows
For Year 5 and Year 6

	Year 5	Year 6
Operations:		
Net Income (Loss)	$ 34.6	$ (13.4)
Plus Additions:		
Depreciation Expense	4.8	7.6
Decrease in Accounts Receivable	--	31.4
Decrease in Inventories	--	4.6
Decrease in Prepayments	--	1.8
Increase in Accounts Payable	21.8	--
Increase in Income Taxes Payable	1.2	--
Increase in Other Current Liabilities	2.6	--
Less Subtractions:		
Increase in Accounts Receivable	(26.8)	--
Increase in Inventories	(31.6)	--
Increase in Tax Refund Receivable	--	(5.0)
Increase in Prepayments	(2.6)	--
Decrease in Accounts Payable	--	(36.0)
Decrease in Income Taxes Payable	--	(7.0)
Decrease in Other Current Liabilities	--	(2.4)
Cash Flow from Operations	$ 4.0	$ (18.4)
Investing:		
Sale of Property, Plant, and Equipment	$ .4	$ 5.4
Acquisition of Property, Plant, and Equipment	(48.4)	(11.8)
Cash Flow from Investing	$ (48.0)	$ (6.4)
Financing:		
Bank Borrowing (Net)	$ 42.0	$ 18.0
Net Change in Cash	$ (2.0)	$ (6.8)

5.33 continued.

RV SUPPLIERS, INCORPORATED—YEAR 5

Cash

√	14.0		

Operations

(1)	34.6	26.8	(5)
(2)	4.8	31.6	(6)
(9)	21.8	2.6	(7)
(10)	1.2		
(11)	2.6		

Investing

(4)	.4	48.4	(3)

Financing

(8)	42.0		
√	12.0		

Accounts Receivable

√	28.8	
(5)	26.8	
√	55.6	

Inventories

√	54.0	
(6)	31.6	
√	85.6	

Prepayments

√	4.8	
(7)	2.6	
√	7.4	

Property, Plant, and Equipment (Net)

√	30.2			
(3)	48.4	4.8	(2)	
		.4	(4)	
√	73.4			

Bank Note Payable

	10.0	√
	42.0	(8)
	52.0	√

Accounts Payable

	31.6	√
	21.8	(9)
	53.4	√

Income Taxes Payable

	5.8	√
	1.2	(10)
	7.0	√

Other Current Liabilities

	4.2	√
	2.6	(11)
	6.8	√

Capital Stock

	44.6	√
	44.6	√

Retained Earnings

	35.6	√
	34.6	(1)
	70.2	√

5-31

5.33 continued.

RV SUPPLIERS, INCORPORATED—YEAR 6

Cash

√	12.0		

Operations

(2)	7.6	13.4	(1)
(5)	31.4	5.0	(7)
(6)	4.6	36.0	(10)
(8)	1.8	7.0	(11)
		2.4	(12)

Investing

(4)	5.4	11.8	(3)

Financing

(9)	18.0		
√	5.2		

Accounts Receivable				Inventories				Tax Refund Receivable		
√	55.6			√	85.6			√	.0	
		31.4	(5)			4.6	(6)	(7)	5.0	
√	24.2			√	81.0			√	5.0	

Prepayments				Property, Plant, and Equipment (Net)				Bank Note Payable		
√	7.4			√	73.4					52.0	√
		1.8	(8)	(3)	11.8	7.6	(2)			18.0	(9)
						5.4	(4)				
√	5.6			√	72.2					70.0	√

Accounts Payable				Income Taxes Payable				Other Current Liabilities		
		53.4	√			7.0	√			6.8	√
(10)	36.0			(11)	7.0			(12)	2.4		
		17.4	√			0.0	√			4.4	√

Capital Stock				Retained Earnings		
		44.6	√			70.2	√
				(1)	13.4		
		44.6	√			56.8	√

5.34   (Electrobel; formatting and interpreting the statement of cash flows.)

a.   ELECTROBEL
                          Statement of Cash Flows
                               For Year 7
                        (In Millions of Belgian Francs)

Operations:
    Net Income.. BEF   23,842
    Depreciation   23,070
    (Inc.) Dec. in Accounts Receivable...............................   (941)
    (Inc.) Dec. in Inventories...   154
    (Inc.) Dec. in Prepayments   364
    Inc. (Dec.) in Accounts Payable   160
    Inc. (Dec.) in Other Current Liabilities.......................   3,045
       Cash Flow from Operations.................................... BEF   49,694
Investing:
    Sale of Property, Plant and Equipment .... BEF   2,739
    Acquisition of Property, Plant and Equipment ....   (31,796)
    Sale of Marketable Securities....................................   6,387
    Acquisition of Investments in Securities ....   (9,285)
       Cash Flow from Investing .... BEF (31,955)
Financing:
    Decrease in Bank Loans Payable .... BEF   (4,576)
    Increase in Long-Term Debt.......................................   13,482
    Decrease in Long-Term Debt......................................   (17,505)
    Dividends Paid ....   (8,076)
       Cash Flow from Financing .... BEF (16,675)
Change in Cash .... BEF   1,064

b.   Cash flow from operations exceeds net income because of the addback
      from depreciation in this capital-intensive business. Cash flow from
      operations was more than sufficient to fund capital expenditures. The
      firm used the excess cash flow to reduce short- and long-term
      borrowing and to pay dividends.

5.35   (Rolls-Royce PLC; formatting and interpreting the statement of cash flows.)

a.
ROLLS-ROYCE, PLC.
Statement of Cash Flows
For Years 8 and 9

	Year 8	Year 9
Operations:		
Net Income	£ 142[a]	£ 13[b]
Depreciation Expense	69	64
(Gain) Loss on Sale of Equipment	9	(15)
Increase in Accounts Payable	133	101
Increase in Inventories	(134)	(36)
Increase in Accounts Receivable	(67)	(115)
Cash Flow from Operations	£ 152	£ 12
Investing:		
Disposals of Fixed Assets and Investments	£ 19	£ 15
Acquisition of Fixed Assets	(112)	(119)
Acquisition of Investments	(19)	(17)
Cash Flow from Investing	£ (112)	£ (121)
Financing:		
Increase in Short-term Borrowing	£ 24	£ 97
Increase in Long-term Borrowing	59	33
Issue of Common Stock	1	4
Dividends	(69)	(45)
Cash Flow from Financing	£ 15	£ 89
Change in Cash	£ 55	£ (20)
Cash, Beginning of Year	376	431
Cash, End of Year	£ 431	£ 411

[a]£142 = £176 – £34.
[b]£13 = £51 – £38.

b. Cash flow from operations during Year 8 was more than sufficient to pay dividends and almost finance capital expenditures. Rolls-Royce assumed additional short- and long-term borrowing, with most of the proceeds increasing the cash account at year end. Rolls-Royce experienced a significant decrease in net income in Year 9 and an associated decrease in cash flow from operations. The firm maintained its capital expenditures, requiring additional financing to fund the expenditures and pay dividends.

5.36   (NIKE, Inc.; interpreting the statement of cash flows.)

    a.   NIKE's growth in sales and net income led to increases of account receivable and inventories. NIKE, however, did not increase its accounts payable and other current operating liabilities to help finance the buildup in current assets. Thus, its cash flow from operations decreased.

    b.   NIKE increased its acquisitions of property, plant and equipment to provide the firm with operating capacity to sustain its rapid growth. NIKE also acquired investments in securities of other firms. It is not clear from the statement of cash flows whether the investments represented short-term investments of temporarily excess cash (a current asset) or long-term investments made to develop an operating relation with another firm (noncurrent asset).

    c.   NIKE used cash flow from operations during Year 7 and Year 8 to finance its investing activities. The excess cash flow after investing activities served to repay short- and long-term debt and pay dividends. Cash flow from operations during Year 9 was insufficient to finance investing activities. NIKE engaged in short-term borrowing to make up the shortfall and finance the payment of dividends.

    d.   Operating cash flows should generally finance the payment of dividends. Either operating cash flows or long-term sources of capital should generally finance acquisitions of property, plant and equipment. Thus, NIKE's use of short-term borrowing seems inappropriate. One might justify such an action if NIKE (1) expected cash flow from operations during Year 10 to return to its historical levels, (2) expected cash outflows for property, plant and equipment to decrease during Year 10, or (3) took advantage of comparatively low short-term borrowing rates during Year 9 and planned to refinance this debt with long-term borrowing during Year 10.

5.37   (Boise Cascade; interpreting the statement of cash flows.)

    a.   Forest products companies are capital intensive. Depreciation is therefore a substantial non-cash expense each year. The addback for depreciation converts a net loss each year into positive cash flow from operations. Note that cash flow from operations increased each year as the net loss decreased.

    b.   Boise Cascade had substantial changes in its property, plant and equipment during the three years. It likely built new, more efficient production facilities and sold off older, less efficient facilities.

5.37 continued.

c.   For the three years combined, Boise Cascade reduced its long-term debt and replaced it with preferred stock. The sales of forest products are cyclical. When the economy is in a recession, as apparently occurred during the three years, the high fixed cost of capital-intensive manufacturing facilities can result in net losses. If Boise Cascade is unable to repay debt on schedule during such years, it causes expensive financial distress or even bankruptcy. Firms have more latitude with respect to dividends on preferred stock than interest on debt. Thus, a shift toward preferred stock and away from long-term debt reduces the bankruptcy risk of Boise Cascade. Note that Boise Cascade continued to pay, and even increase, dividends despite operating at a net loss. Most shareholders prefer less rather than more fluctuation in their dividends over the business cycle.

5.38   (Interpreting statement of cash flows relations.)

American Airlines—Property, plant and equipment comprises a large proportion of the total assets of American Airlines. Depreciation expense is a major expense for the airline. The firm operated at a net loss for the year, but the addback for depreciation resulted in a positive cash flow from operations. Cash flow from operations was not sufficient to fund capital expenditures on new property, plant and equipment. American Airlines is apparently growing since its capital expenditures exceed depreciation expense for the year. The firm financed its capital expenditures in part with cash flow from operations and in part with the issuance of additional long-term debt and capital stock. The net effect of the cash flow from financing is a reduction in liabilities and an increase in capital stock (actually preferred stock). Operating at a net loss increases the risk of bankruptcy. Perhaps American Airlines reduced the amount of debt in its capital structure to reduce fixed payment claims and substituted preferred stock that generally requires dividend payments only when declared by the board of directors.

American Home Products—Because of patent protection, pharmaceutical companies tend to generate relatively high profit margins and significant cash flows from operations. Although the manufacturing process for pharmaceutical products is capital intensive, cash flow from operations is usually sufficient to fund capital expenditures. American Home Products used the excess cash flow to pay dividends and repurchase capital stock. The firm also borrowed short-term funds and invested the proceeds in the acquisition of another business. Borrowing short term to finance investments in long-term assets is usually undesirable, because the firm must repay the debt before the long-term assets generate sufficient cash flow. Perhaps American Home Products needed to borrow short term to consummate the acquisition, with the expectation of refinancing the short-term debt with long-term borrowing soon after the acquisition. Alternatively, American Home Products might have anticipated a decline in long-term rates in the near future and borrowed short term until long-term rates actually declined.

5.38 continued.

Interpublic Group—An advertising agency serves as a link between clients desiring advertising time and space and various media with advertising time and space to sell. Thus, the principal asset of an advertising agency is accounts receivable from clients and the principal liability is accounts payable to various media. Interpublic Group reports an increase in accounts receivable of $66 million and an increase in accounts payable of $59 million. Thus, the firm appeared to manage its receivables/payables position well. Advertising agencies lease most of the physical facilities used in their operations. They purchase equipment for use in designing and producing advertising copy. Thus, they must make some capital expenditures. Cash flow from operations, however, is more than sufficient to finance acquisitions of equipment. Interpublic Group used the excess cash flow plus the proceeds of additional short- and long-term borrowing to pay dividends, repurchase capital stock, and increase cash on the balance sheet.

Proctor & Gamble—Proctor & Gamble's brand names create high profit margins and cash flows from operations. Cash flow from operations is more than adequate to finance capital expenditures. Note that capital expenditures significantly exceed depreciation, suggesting that the firm is still in a growth mode. The firm used the excess cash flow to repay short- and long-term debt and to pay dividends.

Reebok—Cash flow from operations for Reebok is less than net income plus depreciation, a somewhat unusual relationship for a seasoned firm. Reebok increased its accounts receivable and inventories during the year but did not stretch its accounts payable commensurably. The financing section of the statement of cash flows suggests that Reebok might have e used short-term debt to finance some of its working capital needs. Cash flow from operations was still more than sufficient to fund capital expenditures. One explanation for the sufficiency of cash flow from operations to cover capital expenditures is that Reebok is not very capital intensive. The relation between depreciation expense and net income supports this explanation. Reebok outsources virtually all of its manufacturing. Reebok used the excess cash flows from operating and investing activities to pay dividends and repurchase its capital stock.

Texas Instruments—Like American Home Products and Upjohn (discussed later), Texas Instruments invests heavily in technology to create a competitive advantage. Patents and copyrights on computer hardware, software, and other products serve as a barrier to entry by competitors and provide Texas Instruments with an attractive profit margin. Texas Instruments differs from the two pharmaceutical companies with respect to the amount of depreciation relative to net income. Despite generating less than one-half of the net income of American Home Products, Texas Instruments has more than twice the amount of depreciation expense and capital expenditures. Thus, Texas Instruments is likely more capital intensive than the other two technology-

5.38 continued.

based companies. Note that the changes in individual working capital accounts are relatively large, compared to the amount of net income. These relations suggest, although do not prove, that the operations of Texas Instruments grew significantly during the year. Cash flow from operations was sufficient to fund capital expenditures and increase the balance of cash on the balance sheet. Note that Texas Instruments issued capital stock during the year and repaid long-term debt. The amounts involved, however, are small.

The Limited—Current assets and current liabilities dominate the balance sheets of retailers. Thus, working capital management is of particular importance. The Limited increased its current liabilities in line with increases in accounts receivable and inventories. Thus, cash flow from operations approximately equals net income plus depreciation. The Limited invested most of the cash flow from operations in additional property, plant and equipment, the acquisition of other businesses, the repayment of short-term debt, and the payment of dividends.

Upjohn—This problem includes Upjohn primarily to compare and contrast it with American Home Products, also a pharmaceutical company. Both companies generated sufficient cash flow from operations to fund capital expenditures and pay dividends. Upjohn sold a portion of its business during the year and invested the proceeds in marketable securities.

CHAPTER 6

INTRODUCTION TO FINANCIAL STATEMENT ANALYSIS

Questions, Exercises, Problems, and Cases: Answers and Solutions

6.1   See the text or the glossary at the end of the book.

6.2   1.   The firm may have changed its methods of accounting over time.

2.   The firm may have changed its product lines, production techniques, investment or financing strategies, or even its managerial personnel.

6.3   1.   The firms may use different methods of accounting.

2.   The firms may pursue different operating, investing, or financing strategies, so that they have different technologies, production techniques, and selling strategies.

6.4   The adjustment in the numerator of rate of return on assets is for the *incremental* effect on *net* income of having versus not having interest expense.   Because interest expense reduces taxable income and, therefore, income taxes otherwise payable, the tax savings from interest expense incrementally affect net income.   The computation of the numerator must, therefore, incorporate this tax effect.

6.5   The first company apparently has a relatively small profit margin and must rely on turnover to generate a satisfactory rate of return.   A discount department store is an example.   The second company, on the other hand, has a larger profit margin and does not need as much turnover as the first company to generate a satisfactory rate of return.

6.6   Management strives to keep its inventories at a level that is neither too low so that it loses sales nor too high so that it incurs high storage costs.   Thus, there is an optimal level of inventory for a particular firm in a particular period and an optimal inventory turnover ratio.

6.7   The rate of return on common shareholders' equity exceeds the rate of return on assets when the latter rate exceeds the return required by creditors and preferred shareholders (net of tax effects).   In this situation, leverage is working to the benefit of the common shareholders.   The rate of return on common shareholders' equity will be less than the return on assets when the latter rate is less than the return required by creditors and preferred shareholders.   This situation generally occurs during periods of very poor earnings performance.

6-1

6.8　This statement suggests that the difference between the rate of return on assets and the aftertax cost of debt is positive but small. Increasing the amount of debt will require a higher interest rate that will eliminate this positive difference and leverage will work to the disadvantage of the common shareholders.

6.9　Financial leverage involves using debt capital that has a smaller aftertax cost than the return a firm can generate from investing the capital in various assets. The excess return belongs to the common shareholders. A firm cannot continually increase the amount of debt in the capital structure without limit. Increasing the debt level increases the risk to the common shareholders. These shareholders will not tolerate risk levels that they consider too high. Also, the cost of borrowing increases as a firm assumes larger proportions of debt. Sooner or later, the excess of the rate of return on assets over the aftertax cost of borrowing approaches zero or even becomes negative. Leverage then works to the disadvantage of the common shareholders.

6.10

	Dec. 31, Year 1	Dec. 31, Year 2
Current Assets	$ 800,000	$ 600,000
Current Liabilities	(400,000)	(240,000)
Working Capital	$ 400,000	$ 360,000
Current Ratio	2:1	2.5:1

6.11　(Coca-Cola Co. and PepsiCo, Inc.; calculating and disaggregating rate of return on assets.)

a.　**Coca-Cola Co.:**　$\dfrac{\$2,554 + (1 - .35)(\$199)}{\$12,947}$ = 20.7 percent.

　　PepsiCo Inc.:　$\dfrac{\$1,784 + (1 - .35)(\$645)}{\$24,249}$ = 9.1 percent.

b.

Rate of Return on Assets	=	Profit Margin Ratio	X	Total Asset Turnover Ratio

Coca-Cola Co.:

$$\dfrac{\$2,554 + (1 - .35)(\$199)}{\$12,947} = \dfrac{\$2,554 + (1 - .35)(\$199)}{\$16,172} \times \dfrac{\$16,172}{\$12,947}$$

20.7 percent　=　16.6 percent　X　1.25

PepsiCo Inc.:

$$\dfrac{\$1,784 + (1 - .35)(\$645)}{\$24,249} = \dfrac{\$1,784 + (1 - .35)(\$645)}{\$28,472} \times \dfrac{\$28,472}{\$24,249}$$

9.1 percent　=　7.7 percent　X　1.17

6.11 continued.

    c.   The Coca-Cola Company was the more profitable firm during the year analyzed. It had a significantly higher profit margin than PepsiCo, Inc., and a slightly higher total assets turnover. Coca-Cola's lack of involvement in the highly competitive restaurant market, in contrast to that of PepsiCo (Pizza Hut, KFC, Taco Bell), may account for the higher profit margin. It may also account for Coke's higher assets turnover, because restaurants are more capital intensive than soft drink manufacturing.

6.12   (Wal-Mart and The Limited; profitability analysis for two types of retailers.)

Company A is the specialty retailer (The Limited) because of its higher profit margin and lower total assets turnover, relative to Company B (Wal-Mart).

	Rate of Return On Assets	=	Profit Margin Ratio	X	Total Assets Turnover Ratio
Company A:	$\dfrac{\$448 + (1-.35)(\$65)}{\$4,353}$	=	$\dfrac{\$448 + (1-.35)(\$65)}{\$7,321}$	X	$\dfrac{\$7,321}{\$4,353}$
	11.3 percent	=	6.7 percent	X	1.68
Company B:	$\dfrac{\$2,681 + (1-.35)(\$706)}{\$29,630}$	=	$\dfrac{\$2,681 + (1-.35)(\$706)}{\$83,412}$	X	$\dfrac{\$83,412}{\$29,630}$
	10.6 percent	=	3.8 percent	X	2.82

6.13   (Campbell Soup Company and Heinz; analyzing accounts receivable for two companies.)

    a.

Campbell Soup	**Heinz**
$\dfrac{\$6,690}{.5(\$646 + \$578)}$	$\dfrac{\$7,047}{.5(\$979 + \$813)}$
= 10.9 Times per Year.	= 7.9 Times per Year.

    b. $\dfrac{365}{10.9} = 33.5$ days. $\dfrac{365}{7.9} = 46.2$ days.

        Solutions

6.13 continued.

c. Campbell Soup collected its accounts receivable more quickly than did Heinz. However, Heinz may have more liberal credit and collection policies than Campbell in an effort to stimulate sales. For example, Campbell Soup may require collection in 30 days and Heinz in 45 days. Also, both companies reported significant decreases in their accounts receivable during the year. Perhaps sales declined during the current year relative to the preceding one so that the accounts receivable turnovers calculated in Part *a.* are not representative of other years.

6.14 (Bristol-Myers Squibb; analyzing inventories over 4 years.)

a.

Year	Numerator	Denominator	Inventory Turnover
5	$2,717	$ 1,409	1.93
6	2,857	1,471	1.94
7	3,029	1,408	2.15
8	3,122	1,360	2.30

b.

Year	Numerator	Denominator	Days Inventory Held
5	365	1.93	189
6	365	1.94	188
7	365	2.15	170
8	365	2.30	159

c.

Year	Numerator	Denominator	Cost of Goods Sold Percentage
5	$2,717	$ 10,571	25.7%
6	2,857	11,156	25.6%
7	3,029	11,413	26.5%
8	3,122	11,984	26.1%

d. The increasing inventory turnover coupled with the increased cost of goods sold percentage suggests a shift in product mix toward faster-moving, lower-margin products. A shift in sales mix toward nonprescription health products and toiletries is consistent with faster inventory turnover and lower gross margin.

6.15   (Boise Cascade; analyzing plant asset turnover over 4 years.)

a.

Year	Numerator	Denominator	Plant Asset Turnover
2	$3,950	$3,550	1.11
3	3,716	3,503	1.06
4	3,958	3,232	1.22
5	4,142	2,951	1.40

b.   Boise Cascade is capital intensive. It experienced decreased sales between Year 2 and Year 3. Although it reduced its capital expenditures slightly, the decrease in sales caused its plant asset turnover to decline. Sales increased during the next two years while capital expenditures declined, causing the plant asset turnover to increase significantly. Given the capital intensity of the forest products industry, one must wonder whether Boise Cascade has sufficient plant capacity to support continuing sales increases.

6.16   (Glaxo; calculating and disaggregating rate of return on common shareholders' equity.)

a.

Year	Numerator	Denominator	Rate of Return on Common Shareholders' Equity
4	£1,033	£3,461	29.8%
5	1,207	4,148	29.1%
6	1,303	4,850	26.9%

b.   **Profit margin**

Year	Numerator	Denominator	Profit Margin
4	£1,033	£4,096	25.2%
5	1,207	4,930	24.5%
6	1,303	5,656	23.0%

Total Asset Turnover

Year	Numerator	Denominator	Total Asset Turnover
4	£4,096	£5,713	.72
5	4,930	6,570	.75
6	5,656	7,673	.74

Leverage Ratio

Year	Numerator	Denominator	Leverage Ratio
4	£5,713	£3,461	1.65
5	6,570	4,148	1.58
6	7,673	4,850	1.58

     Solutions

6.16 continued.

c. The rate of return on common shareholders' equity declined during the three years. The decline between Year 4 and Year 5 results from a decrease in capital structure leverage. The decline in the profit margin between Year 4 and Year 5 is offset by an increase in the total assets turnover, so that Glaxo's operating profitability improved between these two years. The decline in the rate of return on common shareholders' equity between Year 5 and Year 6 is due to decreased operating profitability, given that the leverage ratio remained constant. Both the profit margin and total assets turnover declined. Sales increased 20.4 percent [= (£4,930/£4,096) − 1] between Year 4 and Year 5 and 14.7 percent [= (£5,656/£4,930) − 1] between Year 5 and Year 6. The decrease in the rate of sales growth might have squeezed the profit margin and resulted in some diseconomies of scale with Glaxo's manufacturing, selling, or administrative facilities.

6.17 (Profitability analysis for three companies.)

a.

	Rate of Return on Assets	=	Profit Margin	X	Total Asset Turnover
Company A:	$\frac{\$932}{\$13,493}$	=	$\frac{\$932}{\$6,373}$	X	$\frac{\$6,373}{\$13,493}$
	6.9 percent	=	14.6 percent	X	.47
Company B:	$\frac{\$735}{\$4,352}$	=	$\frac{\$735}{\$6,562}$	X	$\frac{\$6,562}{\$4,352}$
	16.9 percent	=	11.2 percent	X	1.51
Company C:	$\frac{\$934}{\$9,136}$	=	$\frac{\$934}{\$12,223}$	X	$\frac{\$12,223}{\$9,136}$
	10.2 percent	=	7.6 percent	X	1.34

6.17 continued.

b.

	Rate of Return on Common Shareholders Equity	=	Profit Margin	X	Total Assets Turnover	X	Leverage Ratio
Company A:	$\dfrac{\$699}{\$5,192}$	=	$\dfrac{\$699}{\$6,373}$	X	$\dfrac{\$6,373}{\$13,493}$	X	$\dfrac{\$13,493}{\$5,192}$
	13.5 percent	= 11.0 percent	X	.47	X	2.60	
Company B:	$\dfrac{\$705}{\$1,760}$	=	$\dfrac{\$705}{\$6,562}$	X	$\dfrac{\$6,562}{\$4,352}$	X	$\dfrac{\$4,352}{\$1,760}$
	40.1 percent	= 10.7 percent	X	1.51	X	2.47	
Company C:	$\dfrac{\$782}{\$3,887}$	=	$\dfrac{\$782}{\$12,223}$	X	$\dfrac{\$12,223}{\$9,136}$	X	$\dfrac{\$9,136}{\$3,887}$
	20.1 percent	= 6.4 percent	X	1.34	X	2.35	

c. Company A is Consolidated Edison, Company B is Kellogg's, and Company C is May Department Stores. The principal clues that Company A is Consolidated Edison are the slow total assets turnover (capital-intensive plant facilities), low rate of return on assets and relatively high financial leverage (low risk due to regulation and guaranteed returns). The principal clue that Company B is Kellogg's is its higher profit margin, relative to Company C. Kellogg's has substantial brand names and realizes higher profit margins than May Department Store. May's relatively low profit margin reflects heavy competition in this sector of the retail industry from discount stores on the low end and specialty retailers on the high end. It carries short-term debt to finance accounts receivable and inventories and long-term debt to finance its stores.

6.18   (Relating profitability to financial leverage.)

a.

Case	Net Income Plus Aftertax Interest Expense[a]	Aftertax Interest Expense[b]	Net Income[c]	Rate of Return on Common Shareholders' Equity
A	$12	$6.0	$ 6	$ 6/$100 = 6%
B	$16	$6.0	$10	$10/$100 = 10%
C	$16	$7.2	$ 8.8	$8.8/$80 = 11%
D	$ 8	$6.0	$ 2	$ 2/$100 = 2%
E	$12	$3.0	$ 9	$ 9/$100 = 9%
F	$10	$3.0	$ 7	$ 7/$100 = 7%

[a]Numerator of the rate of return on assets. In Case A, 12 = .06 × $200.

[b]After tax cost of borrowing times interest-bearing debt. In Case A, $6.0 = .06 × $100.

[c]Net income plus after tax interest expense minus after tax interest expense. In Case A, $6 = $12 – $6.

b. Leverage works successfully in Cases B, C, E, and F with respect to total debt. With respect to interest-bearing debt, leverage works successfully in Cases B and C.

6.19   (Borrowing Company; analyzing financial leverage.)

a. Let Y represent net income. Then,

$$\frac{Y + .70(.10 \times \$20{,}000)}{\$100{,}000} = \frac{Y}{\$80{,}000}$$

$$\$100{,}000Y = \$80{,}000(Y + \$1{,}400)$$

$$20Y = \$112{,}000$$

$$Y = \$5{,}600 \text{ net income.}$$

b. $\dfrac{\$5{,}600}{\$80{,}000}$ = 7 percent rate of return on common shareholders' equity.

c. Let X represent pretax income. Then .7X = $5,600; X = $8,000 and income before interest and taxes is $8,000 + $2,000 = $10,000.

6.19 continued.

d.
$$\frac{Y + .70(.10 \times \$80,000)}{\$100,000} = \frac{Y}{\$20,000}$$

$$\$100,000Y = \$20,000(Y + \$5,600)$$

$$80Y = \$112,000$$

$$Y = \$1,400; \frac{\$1,400}{\$20,000} = 7 \text{ percent.}$$

.7X = \$1,400; X = \$2,000; income before interest and taxes must be $2,000 + $8,000 = $10,000.

e. The breakeven rates of return are identical, 7 percent, although the net incomes differ. The required incomes before interest and taxes are the same. Breakeven occurs when the rate of return on common shareholders' equity equals the aftertax interest rate for borrowing: $(1 - .30) \times 10$ percent equals 7 percent, in this example.

6.20 (Company A/Company B; interpreting changes in earnings per share.)

a. **Company A Earnings per Share:**

Year 1.................. $\frac{\$100,000}{100,000 \text{ Shares}} = \$1$ per Share.

Year 2.................. $\frac{\$100,000}{100,000 \text{ Shares}} = \$1$ per Share.

Company B Earnings per Share:

Year 1.................. $\frac{\$100,000}{100,000 \text{ Shares}} = \$1$ per Share.

Year 2.................. $\frac{.10 \times (\$1,000,000 + \$100,000)}{100,000 \text{ Shares}} = \$1.10$ per Share.

b. Company A: No growth.
Company B: 10 percent annual growth.

c. Company B: This result is misleading. Comparisons of growth in earnings per share are valid only if firms employ equal amounts of assets in the business. Both the rate of return on assets and on shareholders' equity are better measures of growth performance. Earnings per share results do not, in general (as in this problem), take earnings retention into account.

 Solutions

6.21   (Sun Microsystems; calculating and interpreting short-term liquidity ratios.)

a. **Current Ratio**

Year End	Numerator	Denominator	Current Ratio
5	$1,801	$ 713	2.53
6	2,148	839	2.56
7	2,272	947	2.40
8	2,305	1,148	2.01

Quick Ratio

Year End	Numerator	Denominator	Quick Ratio
5	$1,349	$ 713	1.89
6	1,724	839	2.05
7	1,766	947	1.86
8	1,736	1,148	1.51

b. **Cash Flow from Operations to Current Liabilities Ratio**

Year	Numerator	Denominator	Cash Flow from Operations to Current Liabilities Ratio
6	$508	$ 776.0[a]	65.5%
7	336	893.0[b]	37.6%
8	355	1,047.5[c]	33.9%

[a].5($713 + $839) = $776.0.
[b].5($839 + $947) = $893.0.
[c].5($947 + $1,148) = $1,047.5.

Accounts Receivable Turnover Ratio

Year	Numerator	Denominator	Accounts Receivable Turnover Ratio
6	$ 3,589	$ 509.5[a]	7.04
7	4,309	565.5[b]	7.62
8	4,690	740.0[c]	6.34

[a].5($515 + $504) = $509.5.
[b].5($504 + $627) = $565.5.
[c].5($627 + $853) = $740.0.

6.21 b. continued.

Inventory Turnover Ratio

Year	Numerator	Denominator	Inventory Turnover Ratio
6	$1,963	$201.5[a]	9.74
7	2,518	217.5[b]	11.58
8	2,753	275.5[c]	9.99

[a].5($224 + $179) = $201.5.
[b].5($179 + $256) = $217.5.
[c].5($256 + $295) = $275.5.

Accounts Payable Turnover Ratio

Year	Numerator	Denominator	Accounts Payable Turnover Ratio
6	$1,918[a]	$224.0[d]	8.56
7	2,595[b]	253.5[e]	10.24
8	2,792[c]	317.5[f]	8.79

[a]$1,963 + $179 − $224 = $1,918. [d].5($212 + $236) = $224.0.
[b]$2,518 + $256 − $179 = $2,595. [e].5($236 + $271) = $253.5.
[c]$2,753 + $295 − $256 = $2,792. [f].5($271 + $364) = $317.5.

c. The current, quick, and cash flow from operations to average current liabilities ratios all decreased during the three-year period, suggesting increased short-term liquidity risk. Sales increased 20.0 percent [= ($4,309/$3,589) − 1] between Year 6 and Year 7 but only 8.8 percent [= ($4,690/$4,309) − 1] between Year 7 and Year 8. The rapid growth in sales between Year 6 and Year 7 caused the accounts receivable, inventory, and accounts payable turnover ratios to increase. The slower rate of growth in sales between Year 7 and Year 8 caused these turnover ratios to decline. Thus, the changes in the turnover ratios do not seem to explain the consistently declining current, quick, and cash flow ratios. The profit margin declined steadily over the three years, resulting in part from an increase in the cost of goods sold to sales percentage. As computer products have become more commodity-like, their profit margins have declined. Thus, the declining short-term liquidity ratios reflect in part decreased profitability. The declining ratios also reflect a rapid increase in other current liabilities. In addition to examining the trend in the short-term liquidity ratios, the analyst should also look at the levels of these ratios. Sun Microsystems had sufficient cash and marketable securities to pay all current liabilities in Year 5, Year 6, and Year 7. These liquid assets were not quite sufficient to cover current liabilities at the end of Year 8. Thus, it is unlikely that Sun Microsystems would experience difficulty paying its short-term commitments on time. The cash flow from operations to average

 Solutions

6.21 c. continued.

current liabilities ratios for Year 7 and Year 8 are somewhat below the 40 percent level typically found for a financially-healthy firm, but are not alarmingly low.

6.22 (International Paper Company; calculating and interpreting short-term liquidity ratios.)

a. **Current Ratio**

Year End	Numerator	Denominator	Current Ratio
2	$4,131	$3,727	1.11
3	4,366	4,531	.96
4	4,401	4,009	1.10
5	4,830	4,034	1.20

Quick Ratio

Year End	Numerator	Denominator	Quick Ratio
2	$2,079	$3,727	.56
3	2,086	4,531	.46
4	2,098	4,009	.52
5	2,511	4,034	.62

b. **Cash Flow from Operations to Current Liabilities Ratio**

Year	Numerator	Denominator	Cash Flow from Operations to Current Liabilities Ratio
3	$1,078	$4,129.0[a]	26.1%
4	929	4,270.0[b]	21.8%
5	1,275	4,021.5[c]	31.7%

[a].5($3,727 + $4,531) = $4,129.0.
[b].5($4,531 + $4,009) = $4,270.0.
[c].5($4,009 + $4,034) = $4,021.5.

6.22 b. continued.

Accounts Receivable Turnover Ratio

Year	Numerator	Denominator	Accounts Receivable Turnover Ratio
3	$13,598	$1,851.0[a]	7.35
4	13,685	1,858.5[b]	7.36
5	14,966	2,048.5[c]	7.31

[a].5($1,841 + $1,861) = $1,851.0.
[b].5($1,861 + $1,856) = $1,858.5.
[c].5($1,856 + $2,241) = $2,048.5.

Inventory Turnover Ratio

Year	Numerator	Denominator	Inventory Turnover Ratio
3	$10,987	$1,859.0[a]	5.91
4	11,089	1,981.0[b]	5.60
5	12,028	2,049.5[c]	5.87

[a].5($1,780 + $1,938) = $1,859.0.
[b].5($1,938 + $2,024) = $1,981.0.
[c].5($2,024 + $2,075) = $2,049.5.

Accounts Payable Turnover Ratio

Year	Numerator	Denominator	Accounts Payable Turnover Ratio
3	$11,145[a]	$1,184.5[d]	9.41
4	11,175[b]	1,174.0[e]	9.52
5	12,079[c]	1,146.5[f]	10.54

[a]$10,987 + $1,938 − $1,780 = $11,145.
[b]$11,089 + $2,024 − $1,938 = $11,175.
[c]$12,028 + $2,075 − $2,024 = $12,079.
[d].5($1,110 + $1,259) = $1,184.5.
[e].5($1,259 + $1,089) = $1,174.0.
[f].5($1,089 + $1,204) = $1,146.5.

         Solutions

6.22 continued.

c. The short-term liquidity risk of International Paper declined slightly over the three year period. The current and quick ratios showed steady improvement. The accounts receivable and inventory turnover ratios changed relatively little, so one must look at current liabilities to understand the reasons for the improvements in the current and quick ratios. The accounts payable turnover ratio increased, indicating that International Paper paid its suppliers more quickly. Also, International Paper reduced its short-term borrowing. The cash flow from operations to average current liabilities ratio decreased between Year 3 and Year 4 but increased between Year 4 and Year 5. The decline between Year 3 and Year 4 is due primarily to reduced profitability in Year 4. Sales were relatively flat between these two years and the profit margin declined. Improved profitability in Year 5 resulted in increased cash flow from operations. The levels of these short-term liquidity ratios suggest that International Paper still has considerable short-term liquidity risk. Its quick ratio is considerably less than 1.0 and its cash flow from operations to average current liabilities ratio is less than the 40 percent commonly found for a financially-healthy firm.

6.23   (Hasbro; calculating and interpreting long-term liquidity ratios.)

a. **Long-Term Debt Ratio**

Year End	Numerator	Denominator	Long-Term Debt Ratio
1	$ 57	$ 57 + $ 867	6.2%
2	380	380 + 955	28.5%
3	206	206 + 1,106	15.7%
4	200	200 + 1,277	13.5%

Debt-Equity Ratio

Year End	Numerator	Denominator	Debt-Equity Ratio
1	$ 418	$ 418 + $ 867	32.5%
2	995	995 + 955	51.0%
3	977	977 + 1,106	46.9%
4	1,016	1,016 + 1,277	44.3%

6.23 continued.

b. **Cash Flow from Operations to Total Liabilities Ratio**

Year	Numerator	Denominator	Cash Flow from Operations to Total Liabilities Ratio
2	$ 120	.5($418 + $ 995)	17.0%
3	230	.5($995 + $ 977)	23.3%
4	217	.5($977 + $1,016)	21.8%

Interest Coverage Ratio

Year	Numerator	Denominator	Times Interest Charges Earned
2	$ 248	$ 43	5.8
3	328	36	9.1
4	370	30	12.3

c. Hasbro's debt ratios increased as a result of the acquisition of Tonka in Year 2. Hasbro has reduced its debt levels since Year 2. Its cash flow and interest average ratios are at healthy levels, suggesting low long-term solvency risk.

6.24 (Delta Airlines; calculating and interpreting long-term liquidity ratios.)

a. **Long-Term Debt Ratio**

Year End	Numerator	Denominator	Long-Term Debt Ratio
4	$ 2,059	$2,059 + $2,506	45.1%
5	2,833	2,833 + 1,965	59.0%
6	3,716	3,716 + 1,996	65.1%
7	3,228	3,228 + 1,569	67.3%

Debt-Equity Ratio

Year End	Numerator	Denominator	Debt-Equity Ratio
4	$ 5,905	$ 5,905 + $2,506	70.2%
5	8,197	8,197 + 1,965	80.7%
6	9,875	9,875 + 1,996	83.2%
7	10,327	10,327 + 1,569	86.8%

6.24 continued.

b. **Cash Flow from Operations to Total Liabilities Ratio**

Year	Numerator	Denominator	Cash Flow from Operations to Total Liabilities Ratio
2	$ 150	.5($5,905 + $ 8,197)	2.1%
3	677	.5($8,197 + $ 9,875)	7.5%
4	1,324	.5($9,875 + $10,327)	13.1%

Interest Coverage Ratio

Year	Numerator	Denominator	Times Interest Charges Earned
2	$(635)	$ 151	Neg.
3	(474)	177	Neg.
4	(389)	271	Neg.

c. The debt ratios increased during the three-year period, suggesting increased long-term solvency risk. The cash flow from operations to average total liabilities increased during the three years, but its level is less than that usually encountered for a healthy firm. Delta's interest coverage ratio is negative. Thus, Delta evidences significant long-term solvency risk.

6.25   (Effect of various transactions on financial statement ratios.)

Transaction	Rate of Return on Common Shareholders' Equity	Current Ratio	Debt-Equity Ratio
a.	No Effect	(1)	Increase
b.	Increase	Increase	Decrease
c.	No Effect	No Effect	No Effect
d.	No Effect	(1)	Decrease
e.	No Effect	Increase	No Effect
f.	Increase	Decrease	Increase
g.	Decrease	Increase	Decrease
h.	No Effect	Decrease	Increase

(1) The current ratio remains the same if it was one to one prior to the transaction, decreases if it was greater than one, and increases if it was less than one.

6.26   (Effect of various transactions on financial statement ratios.)

Transaction	Earnings per Common Share	Working Capital	Quick Ratio
a.	Increase	Increase	Increase
b.	No Effect	Decrease	Decrease
c.	No Effect	No Effect	Decrease
d.	No Effect	Increase	Increase
e.	No Effect	No Effect	Increase
f.	Decrease	Increase	Decrease

6-17

6.27 (Wal-Mart Stores, Inc.; calculating and interpreting profitability and risk ratios.)

a. 1. Rate of Return on Assets

$$= \frac{\$2,681 + (1 - .35)(\$706)}{.5(\$26,441 + \$32,819)} = 10.6 \text{ percent.}$$

2. Profit Margin for Rate of Return on Assets

$$= \frac{\$2,681 + (1 - .35)(\$706)}{\$83,412} = 3.8 \text{ percent.}$$

3. Total Assets Turnover

$$= \frac{\$83,412}{.5(\$26,441 + \$32,819)} = 2.8 \text{ times.}$$

4. Cost of Goods Sold/Sales

$$= \frac{\$65,586}{\$83,412} = 78.6 \text{ percent.}$$

5. Selling Administrative Expense/Sales

$$= \frac{\$12,858}{\$83,412} = 15.4 \text{ percent.}$$

6. Interest Expense/Sales

$$= \frac{\$706}{\$83,412} = .8 \text{ percent.}$$

7. Income Tax Expense/Sales

$$= \frac{\$1,581}{\$83,412} = 1.9 \text{ percent.}$$

8. Accounts Receivable Turnover Ratio

$$= \frac{\$83,412}{.5(\$690 + \$700)} = 120.0 \text{ times.}$$

9. Inventory Turnover Ratio

$$= \frac{\$65,586}{.5(\$11,014 + \$14,064)} = 5.2 \text{ times.}$$

10. Plant Asset Turnover

$$= \frac{\$83,412}{.5(\$13,175 + \$15,874)} = 5.7 \text{ times.}$$

11. Rate of Return on Common Shareholders' Equity

$$= \frac{\$2,681}{.5(\$10,753 + \$12,726)} = 22.8 \text{ percent.}$$

12. Profit Margin for Return on Common Shareholders' Equity

$$= \frac{\$2,681}{\$83,412} = 3.2 \text{ percent.}$$

6.27 a. continued.

13.   Leverage Ratio $= \dfrac{.5(\$26,441 + \$32,819)}{.5(\$10,753 + \$12,726)} = 2.5.$

14.   Current Ratio $= \dfrac{\$15,338}{\$9,973} = 1.5.$

15.   Quick Ratio $= \dfrac{\$45 + 700}{\$9,973} = .1.$

16.   Cash Flow from Operations to Current Liabilities Ratio $= \dfrac{\$2,906}{.5(\$7,406 + \$9,973)} = 33.4$ percent.

17.   Accounts Payable Turnover $= \dfrac{(\$65,586 + \$14,064 - \$11,014)}{.5(\$4,104 + \$5,907)} = 13.7$ times.

18.   Long-Term Debt Ratio $= \dfrac{\$9,709}{(\$9,709 + \$12,726)} = 43.3$ percent.

19.   Debt-Equity Ratio $= \dfrac{\$20,093}{\$32,819} = 61.2$ percent.

20.   Cash Flow from Operations to Total Liabilities Ratio $= \dfrac{\$2,906}{.5(\$15,688 + \$20,093)} = 16.2$ percent.

21.   Interest Coverage Ratio $= \dfrac{(\$2,681 + \$1,581 + \$706)}{\$706} = 7.0$ times.

          Solutions

6.27 continued.

b. The rate of return on assets steadily declined during the 3-year period, the result of a slightly decreased profit margin and a steadily decreased assets turnover. The decreased assets turnover results from a decreased plant asset turnover. Wal-Mart increased its capital expenditures to construct new stores faster than sales increased. Sales normally lag capital expenditures for a growing company, so the decline in the plant assets turnover is not a concern. Note in this regard that sales increased 21.4 percent between Year 3 and Year 4 and 22.7 percent between Year 4 and Year 5. Note also that accounts receivable turn over very quickly (every three days). The inventory turnover declined slightly in Year 5, consistent with the stocking of new stores. The surprising thing is that the turnover did not decline even more. Wal-Mart probably awaits the near opening of a new store before it stocks it with inventory. The common size income statement indicates that the cost of goods sold to sales percentage declined slightly and the selling and administrative expense to sales percentage increased slightly during the last three years. One would expect the movement to warehouse clubs and food stores to have just the opposite effect on these two expense percentages. The decline between Year 3 and Year 4 in the cost of goods sold percentage might reflect the movement out of the recession and the ability to obtain a higher margin. The increase in the selling and administrative expense percentage might relate to the rapid expansion in new stores. Wal-Mart probably experienced increased costs of obtaining approval of its new stores because of concerns about the effect of Wal-Mart on smaller local stores. It probably incurred additional costs to promote its movement in warehouse clubs and grocery stores.

c. The rate of return on common shareholders' equity steadily declined during the 3-year period as well, the result of declines in the profit margin for the rate of return on common shareholders' equity and the assets turnover but offset by an increase in the leverage ratio. The decline in the profit margin and the increase in the leverage ratio are the result of increased interest expense from additional borrowing to finance the expansion of stores. The decline in the assets turnover as discussed in Part b. is a result of a decline in the plant asset turnover, also related to store expansion. Thus, the decline in the rate of return on common shareholders' equity is not of particular concern.

6.27 continued.

d. The levels of the quick ratio and the cash flow from operations to average current liabilities ratio suggest short-term liquidity risk. The values of these ratios, however, are not major concerns for Wal-Mart. The low quick ratio occurs in part because Wal-Mart sells for cash or customers use third-party credit cars. In either case, Wal-Mart receives cash quickly. Wal-Mart also maintains a relatively small amount of cash on its balance sheet each year. Wal-Mart generates about $228 million (= $83,412/365) of sales each day and thus does not need to maintain a very large balance in its cash account. The low cash flow from operations to current liabilities ratio occurs primarily because of Wal-Mart growth and the need to invest in inventories. Wal-Mart chooses not to stretch its suppliers (accounts payable) to the full extent of its inventory holding period. Perhaps Wal-Mart receives discounts for paying suppliers within thirty days.

Wal-Mart could probably stretch its suppliers or borrow for the short term if liquidity problems arose.

e. Wal-Mart's debt levels increased during the 3-year period to finance its growth in the number of stores. The cash flow from operations to average total liabilities ratio is somewhat low. However, its interest coverage ratio is very healthy and its ability to cover capital expenditures with cash flow from operations improved during the 3-year period. Thus, long-term solvency risk is not a major concern.

6.28 (NIKE and Reebok; calculating and interpreting profitability and risk ratios.)

The financial statement ratios on pages 6-23, 6-24, and 6-25 form the basis for the responses to the questions raised.

a. Reebok was more profitable than NIKE in Year 11 as judged by both the rate of return on assets (ROA) and the rate of return on common shareholders' equity (ROCE). NIKE has a higher profit margin for ROA but Reebok has a higher assets turnover. The two firms have similar cost of goods sold to sales percentages. When we compare income tax expense to net income before taxes, the two firms have similar effective tax rates. Thus, the differences in the profit margin for ROA relate to selling and administrative expenses. Perhaps Reebok's greater emphasis on fashion relative to NIKE's greater emphasis on performance caused Reebok to spend more heavily on advertising. Also, Reebok's number two position in industry sales could also have led to proportionally greater advertising and promotion expenditures.

Reebok, however, has a higher total assets turnover. The asset turnover amounts for NIKE for Year 11 are affected by an acquisition made during the year in which NIKE recognized signifi-

 Solutions

6.28 a. continued.

cant goodwill (included in other assets). The acquisition affects each of NIKE's assets and therefore its asset turnovers. Reebok has a slightly higher accounts receivable turnover (55 days versus 68 days for NIKE). The problem gives no clues as to the reason for this difference. The receivables are from distributors and retailers of each firm's products. Perhaps NIKE gives more generous terms as an inducement for attractive shelf space allocations. NIKE has a significantly higher inventory turnover ratio. The problem again does not provide information to interpret the reason for the difference in the inventory turnover ratio. NIKE has an arrangement with its manufacturers and customers whereby merchandise is made to order as needed. Thus, NIKE has a higher inventory turnover. Reebok's plant asset turnover is significantly higher than that of NIKE's. Neither company is capital intensive, both subcontracting manufacturing to suppliers in East Asia. Thus, their plant assets relate primarily to administrative facilities. NIKE built a new company headquarters building in the equivalent of Year 9. In addition, NIKE engages more heavily than Reebok in research to improve its performance-driven athletic shoes. The research facilities are included in plant assets.

Reebok also has a higher ROCE than NIKE. Reebok's advantage on ROA is augmented by a larger leverage ratio. Reebok carries higher levels of both long-term debt and total liabilities in its capital structure than NIKE.

b. Neither of these companies carries much short-term liquidity risk. NIKE's short-term liquidity risk increased during Year 11 as a result of borrowing short-term to help finance its acquisition. NIKE's short-term liquidity ratios are less than those of Reebok at the end of Year 11 (except for a slightly faster accounts payable turnover for NIKE). Thus, NIKE appears to carry somewhat more short-term liquidity risk.

c. Neither of these companies carries much long-term solvency risk. The debt ratios are at reasonable levels and the cash flow and interest coverage ratios are quite healthy. Reebok carries a higher proportion of debt in its capital structure and would thus be viewed as having slightly more long-term solvency risk than NIKE.

6-23 continued.

		NIKE	Reebok
1.	Rate of Return on Assets	$= \dfrac{\$400 + (1 - .35)(\$24)}{.5(\$2,374 + \$3,143)} = 15.1$ percent.	$\dfrac{\$254 + (1 - .35)(\$17)}{.5(\$1,392 + \$1,649)} = 17.4$ percent.
2.	Profit Margin for Return on Assets	$= \dfrac{\$400 + (1 - .35)(\$24)}{\$4,761} = 8.7$ percent.	$\dfrac{\$254 + (1 - .35)(\$17)}{\$3,280} = 8.1$ percent.
3.	Total Assets Turnover	$= \dfrac{\$4,761}{.5(\$2,374 + \$3,143)} = 1.7$ times per year.	$\dfrac{\$3,280}{.5(\$1,392 + \$1,649)} = 2.2$ times per year.
4.	Cost of Goods Sold to Sales	$= \dfrac{\$2,865}{\$4,761} = 60.2$ percent.	$\dfrac{\$1,966}{\$3,280} = 59.9$ percent.
5.	Selling and Administration Expenses to Sales	$= \dfrac{\$1,222}{\$4,761} = 25.7$ percent.	$\dfrac{\$889}{\$3,280} = 27.1$ percent.
6.	Interest Expenses to Sales	$= \dfrac{\$24}{\$4,761} = .5$ percent.	$\dfrac{\$17}{\$3,280} = .5$ percent.
7.	Income Tax Expenses to Sales	$= \dfrac{\$250}{\$4,761} = 5.3$ percent.	$\dfrac{\$154}{\$3,280} = 4.7$ percent.
8.	Accounts Receivable Turnover	$= \dfrac{\$4,761}{.5(\$703 + \$1,053)} = 5.4$ times per year.	$\dfrac{\$3,280}{.5(\$457 + \$532)} = 6.6$ times per year.
9.	Inventory Turnover	$= \dfrac{\$2,865}{.5(\$470 + \$630)} = 5.2$ times per year.	$\dfrac{\$1,966}{.5(\$514 + \$625)} = 3.5$ times per year.
10.	Plant Asset Turnover	$= \dfrac{\$4,761}{.5(\$406 + \$555)} = 9.9$ times per year.	$\dfrac{\$3,280}{.5(\$131 + \$165)} = 22.2$ times per year.

 Solutions

6.28 continued.

11. Rate of Return on Common Shareholders' Equity

$$= \frac{\$400}{.5(\$1,741 + \$1,965)} = 21.6 \text{ percent.} \qquad \frac{\$254}{.5(\$847 + \$990)} = 27.7 \text{ percent.}$$

12. Profit Margin for Return on Common Shareholders' Equity

$$= \frac{\$400}{\$4,761} = 8.4 \text{ percent.} \qquad \frac{\$254}{\$3,280} = 7.7 \text{ percent.}$$

13. Leverage Ratio

$$= \frac{.5(\$2,374 + \$3,143)}{.5(\$1,741 + \$1,965)} = 1.5. \qquad \frac{.5(\$1,392 + \$1,649)}{.5(\$847 + \$990)} = 1.7.$$

14. Current Ratio: Beginning of Year

$$= \frac{\$1,770}{\$562} = 3.1. \qquad \frac{\$1,127}{\$396} = 2.8.$$

End of Year

$$= \frac{\$2,046}{\$1,108} = 1.8. \qquad \frac{\$1,337}{\$506} = 2.6.$$

15. Quick Ratio: Beginning of Year

$$= \frac{(\$519 + \$703)}{\$562} = 2.2. \qquad \frac{(\$79 + \$457)}{\$396} = 1.4.$$

End of Year

$$= \frac{(\$216 + \$1,053)}{\$1,108} = 1.1. \qquad \frac{(\$84 + \$532)}{\$506} = 1.2.$$

16. Cash Flow from Operations to Current Liabilities

$$= \frac{\$255}{.5(\$562 + \$1,108)} = 30.5 \text{ percent.} \qquad \frac{\$173}{.5(\$396 + \$506)} = 38.4 \text{ percent.}$$

17. Accounts Payable Turnover

$$= \frac{\$2,865 + \$630 - \$470}{.5(\$211 + \$298)} = 11.9 \text{ times per year.} \qquad \frac{\$1,966 + \$625 - \$514}{.5(\$282 + \$171)} = 9.2 \text{ times per year.}$$

6-24

6.28 continued.

18. Long-Term Debt Ratio:

Beginning of Year $= \dfrac{\$12}{(\$12 + \$1,741)} = .7$ percent.

End of Year $= \dfrac{\$10}{(\$10 + \$1,965)} = .5$ percent.

19. Debt-Equity Ratio:

Beginning of Year $= \dfrac{\$633}{\$2,374} = 26.7$ percent.

End of Year $= \dfrac{\$1,178}{\$3,143} = 37.5$ percent.

20. Cash Flow from Operations to Total Liabilities $= \dfrac{\$255}{.5(\$633 + \$1,178)} = 28.2$ percent.

21. Interest Coverage Ratio $= \dfrac{\$400 + \$250 + \$24}{\$24} = 28.1$ times.

$\dfrac{\$134}{(\$134 + \$847)} = 13.7$ percent.

$\dfrac{\$132}{(\$132 + \$990)} = 11.8$ percent.

$\dfrac{\$545}{\$1,392} = 39.2$ percent.

$\dfrac{\$659}{\$1,649} = 40.0$ percent.

$\dfrac{\$173}{.5(\$545 + \$659)} = 28.7$ percent.

$\dfrac{\$254 + \$154 + \$17}{\$17} = 25.0$ times.

6-25   **Solutions**

6.29 (Layton Ball Corporation; case introducing earnings-per-share calculations for a complex capital structure.)

a. $\dfrac{\$9,500}{2,500} = \$3.80$ per share.

b. 1,000 options $\times$ $15 = $15,000 cash raised.

$$\dfrac{\$15,000 \text{ new cash}}{\$25 \text{ per share}} = 600 \text{ shares.}$$

Total number of shares increases by 400 (= 1,000 − 600).

$$\dfrac{\$9,500}{2,500 + 400} = \$3.276 \text{ per share.}$$

c. 2,000 warrants $\times$ $30 = $60,000 cash raised.

$$\dfrac{\$60,000 \text{ new cash}}{\$25 \text{ per share}} = 2,400 \text{ shares purchased.}$$

Total number of shares decreases by 400 (= 2,000 − 2,400).

$$\dfrac{\$9,500}{2,500 - 400} = \$4.524 \text{ per share.}$$

d. Before taxes, each converted bond saves $41.66 2/3 in annual interest expense. After taxes, the savings in expense and increase in income is only $25 [= (1 − .40) $\times$ $41.66 2/3].

There are 100 bonds outstanding; each is convertible into 10 shares. Thus, the new earnings per share figure is:

$$\dfrac{\$9,500 + \$25 \text{ savings per bond} \times 100 \text{ bonds}}{2,500 + 10 \text{ shares/bond} \times 100 \text{ bonds}} = \dfrac{\$12,000}{3,500 \text{ shares}} =$$

$3.429 per share.

e. The warrants are antidilutive and should be ignored if we seek the maximum possible dilution of earnings per share.

$$\dfrac{\$9,500 + \$2,500 \text{ (Increase from interest savings)}}{2,500 + 1,000 \text{ (bond conversion)} + 400 \text{ (option exercise)}} = \dfrac{\$12,000}{3,900} =$$

$3.077 per share.

6.29 continued.

    f.   Probably the *Wall Street Journal* should use the earnings per share that results in the maximum possible dilution. It should clearly ignore antidilutive securities. Do not conclude from the presentation in this problem that one can check the dilution characteristics of potentially dilutive securities one by one and know for sure which combination of assumed exercise and conversions lead to the minimum earnings per share figure. See S. Davidson and R. L. Weil, "A Shortcut in Computing Earnings per Share," *Journal of Accountancy*, December 1975, page 45.

6.30   (Detective analysis—identify company.)

The names of the thirteen companies appear below.

Company Number	Industry	Company Name
1	Grocery Store Chain	Winn-Dixie Stores
2	Public Accounting Partnership	Arthur Andersen & Company
3	Computer Manufacturer	Sun Microsystems
4	Distiller of Hard Liquor	Brown Forman Distillers
5	Department Store Chain	May Department Stores
6	Tobacco Products Company	Philip Morris, Incorporated
7	Soft Drink Company	Coca-Cola Company
8	Steel Manufacturer	Bethlehem Steel Corporation
9	Pharmaceutical Company	Eli Lilly & Company
10	Electric Utility	Consolidated Edison Company of New York
11	Advertising Agency	Interpublic Group of Companies
12	Insurance Company	St. Pauls, Inc.
13	Finance Company	C. I. T. Group Holdings, Inc.

Authors' Clues

1.   The problem includes only one partnership. Only partnerships have no federal income tax burden. Company (2) has essentially no income taxes, but otherwise high profits. This suggests that *(2) is the public accounting firm*. The relatively small size of plant and total assets required to do business confirms this reasoning.

         Solutions

6.30 continued.

2. Utilities, finance companies, and insurance companies have a large investment in assets per dollar of revenue. For the utility, most of those assets are plant; for the insurance company most assets are investments, and for the finance company most assets are receivables. This aids in identifying *(10) as the utility, (13) as the finance company*, and *(12) as the insurance company*. See also Clue 3 below.

3. Steel companies have relatively old plants. We can estimate the age of plant by dividing accumulated depreciation at the end of the year by depreciation charge for the year. Company (8) has accumulated depreciation of about 91 (= 147 – 56). The average age of its assets is about 14.7 years (= 91/6.20). Note how much older this plant is than that of the electric utility whose plant age is only about (208 – 153)/5.97 = 9.2 years old. *Company (8) is the steel company*.

4. The drug company and the computer company have relatively high R & D expenses. Patents and relatively long product life cycles permit pharmaceutical companies to earn a higher profit margin than computer companies. *Company (9) is the drug company* and *Company (3) is the computer company*.

5. The advertising agency acts as an agent between media sellers and media buyers. Thus, it should have significant accounts receivable and accounts payable. *Company (11) is the advertising agency*.

6. The grocery chain has relatively large turnover of inventory, and relatively small investment in assets other than inventory relative to the size of sales. Note the low rate of return on sales, but the high rate of return on assets (and shareholders' equity) and the lack of receivables of (1). This points to *Company (1) as the grocery store chain*.

7. The department store chain has relatively large inventories, large inventory turnover (which the manufacturers of products that must age do not), and high receivables. *Company (5) is the department store chain*.

8. This leaves the manufacturers of soft drinks, tobacco products, and hard liquor. The clue we have in mind using here is the amount of aging required by the inventories. Note that the inventory turnover of companies (4), (6), and (7) are as follows:

Company Number	Inventory Turnover per Year
(4)	33.99/23.19 = 1.47 times
(6)	45.37/14.02 = 3.24 times
(7)	40.17/8.54 = 4.70 times

6.30 continued.

This suggests that (4) has the most aging to do, the hard liquor distiller, (6) shows the next slowest inventory turnover and is the tobacco manufacturer (the somewhat higher inventory turnover than expected occurs because Philip Morris also sells consumer food products). Soft drinks require no aging, therefore, *Company (7) is the soft drink company*.

Note that all of these three companies have relatively high advertising expenses as appropriate for nondurable consumer goods companies.

Analysis of Successful Strategies (Compiled by Ellen K. Hochman.)

The students might use one of two strategies to solve this problem. In the first, study the balance sheets and income statements looking for unusual items such as zero or a relatively high balance in an account. Then try to match these "abnormalities" with the type of firm that would exhibit such characteristics. Alternatively, for each industry, begin by determining distinguishing characteristics in terms of account balances that are unusually high or low. Then scan the data for statements with corresponding "unusual" balances.

A. Following the first strategy, it is noted that four firms, (2), (11), (12), and (13), have zero inventory amounts. These probably correspond to the firms which have operating expenses instead of Cost of Goods Sold: the advertising firm, the finance company, the insurance company, and the accounting firm.

Company (13) also has a large amount of current receivables—it is the *finance company*.

Company (12) has large Other Assets, probably investments, and high current liabilities—it is the *insurance company*.

Company (2) pays almost no income taxes—it is a partnership instead of a corporation—it is the *CPA firm*.

Company (11) is, therefore, the *advertising company*.

B. Two companies, (8) and (10), have large plant and equipment accounts. These are the steel manufacturer and the utility.

Company (10) has low inventories and a large amount of debt and, therefore, high interest expense—it is the *utility*.

Company (8) has substantial inventories—it is the *steel manufacturer*.

                                  Solutions

6.30 continued.

C. Two companies (3) and (9) have a very large amount of R & D expense. These are the *computer company* and the *pharmaceutical company*. Company (3) has a lower profit margin and faster inventory turnover—it is the *computer company*. Company (9) has a higher profit margin (patent protection and long product life cycle—it is the *pharmaceutical company*.

D. There are five industries remaining: the distiller, the grocery store, the tobacco manufacturer, the department store, and the soft drink bottler.

Company (1) has very low receivables. Of the industries left, this must be the *grocery store chain* (very few sales on account).

From the data on the remaining companies, (4), (5), (6), and (7), note that Company (5) has the largest current receivables. This is the *department store*, since it carries its own receivables.

It is very difficult to identify the remaining three companies. Tobacco products and distilled products require aging. Thus, the inventories for these firms are larger and turn over more slowly than for the soft drink company. This suggests Company (7) as the *soft drink company*. Distilled liquor turns over more slowly than tobacco products. This suggests Company (4) as the *distiller* and Company (6) as the *tobacco products company*.

Following the second strategy, the following list was compiled. [An asterisk (*) designates characteristics which were particularly useful in identifying the companies.]

6.30 continued.

Industry	Expected Characteristics	Company Number
Finance Company	*High receivables No inventory High other assets (investments) No (low?) plant and equipment	13
Public Accounting Firm	*No (low?) income taxes (a partnership) No inventory No advertising Low (no?) R & D	2
Insurance Company	*High current liabilities (to pay claims) *High assets—other (investment of premiums) No inventory Substantial current receivables (insurance premiums)	12
Electric Utility	*High plant and equipment *Large debt (financed with bonds) Low inventory (fuel)	10
Steel Manufacturer	*Large plant—but not as large as the utility No advertising	8
Advertising Agency	*Large accounts receivable and accounts payable No inventory Low plant and equipment No advertising No R & D	11
Pharmaceutical Company	*High R & D *Highest Profit Margin Medium plant and equipment Medium advertising	9
Computer Company	*High R & D *Lower profit margin than Company (9)	3
Grocery Store	*Low net income as a percentage of sales *Low receivables (few credit sales) Low advertising Low plant and equipment	1
Department Store	*High receivables No R & D Substantial inventory	5

The logic to identify the remaining three companies, the distiller, the soft drink company, and the tobacco manufacturer, is the same as used in the first strategy.

 Solutions

6.31   (Texas Instruments; interpreting profitability and risk ratios.)

a. The decreasing profit margin for the rate of return on assets for Texas Instruments (TI) occurs primarily because of a decrease in the cost of goods sold to sales percentage. The manufacture of semiconductors and other electronics products is capital intensive. The rapid sales growth over the three-year period permitted TI to spread its fixed manufacturing cost over a larger volume and thereby reduce its unit cost. In addition, the excess demand might have permitted TI to increase its selling prices. Both of these factors would have led to a lower cost of goods sold to sales percentage. The outsourcing of production would have raised the cost of goods sold percentage because TI would have had to share some of its margin with its suppliers (unless the excess demand permitted TI to pass along its higher costs). The net effect of these three factors was a decrease in the cost of goods sold to sales percentage.

b. Excess demand for semiconductors permitted TI to ship to customers soon after it completed manufacturing, causing the inventory turnover to decrease. The full utilization of fixed manufacturing facilities caused the plant asset turnover to increase. The outsourcing of production permitted both the inventory and plant asset turnovers to increase because amounts appear in sales and cost of goods sold (the numerators of these turnover ratios) without corresponding increases in the denominators.

c. One possible explanation for the decreasing leverage is that the increasing profitability and associated cash flows permitted TI to reduce its outstanding debt. Another possible explanation is that retained earnings increased because of the increased profitability, permitting the leverage ratio to decrease.

d. The most likely explanation is increased profitability and increases in the inventory turnover ratio. Both of these factors caused cash flow from operations to increase. The proportion of debt in the capital structure declined, another possible explanation for the increased cash flow ratios.

Solutions   6-32

6.31 continued.

    e. The accounts receivable and accounts payable turnovers are relatively stable and the inventory turnover increased. Thus, the explanation lies in other working capital accounts. TI probably reduced any short-term borrowing. Equal reductions in the numerator and denominator when the current ratio exceeds 1.0 results in an increase in the ratio. The most likely explanation is a buildup of cash and marketable securities on the balance sheet. Note that the total assets turnover did not increase very much despite significant increases in the inventory and plant asset turnovers and a relatively stable accounts receivable turnover, consistent with a buildup of cash on the balance sheet.

6.32   (The Limited; interpreting profitability and risk ratios.)

    a. The Limited experienced significantly decreased operating profitability in the women's apparel segment but increased profitability in its other three business segments. One cannot determine for sure whether the reduced profitability in the women's apparel segment results from an increased cost of goods sold to sales percentage, to an increased selling and administrative expense to sales percentage, or to a combination of the two. Given the increased operating profitability in the other three segments, the increased cost of goods sold to sales percentage probably relates to the decreased profitability in women's apparel. The shift in sales mix from women's apparel to men's apparel and personal care could have also increased the cost of goods sold percentage but the shift toward lingerie from women's apparel would likely have the opposite effect.

    b. Sales increased but sales per employee decreased, indicating the hiring of additional employees and the increase in the selling and administrative expense to sales percentage. Sales per square foot declined but capital expenditures decreased and the fixed asset turnover increased, suggesting ambiguous signals about whether depreciation to sales might have increased or decreased.

    c. Sales increased while capital expenditure decreased, leading to a declining plant asset turnover.

    d. Financial leverage worked to the advantage of the common shareholders in each year since the rate of return on assets exceeded the rate of return on common shareholders' equity. This occurs because ROA exceeded the after-tax cost of debt financing.

    e. The current ratio increased because of a slow down in the inventory turnover ratio, suggesting a buildup of inventories. The quick ratio probably declined because of less cash on the balance sheet. Note

         Solutions

6.32 continued.

> that the cash flow from operations ratios declined, supporting this explanation. Note that the accounts receivable turnover declined, which should lead to an increase in the current ratio.

> f. The decline in the accounts receivable and inventory turnovers should reduce cash flow from operations. Note that the debt equity ratio did not change much between Year 4 and Year 5, indicating that the explanation is in the numerator rather than the denominator of the ratios.

6.33   (W. T. Grant Company; case analysis of bankruptcy.)

We begin discussion of this case by placing the following headings on the board:

Major Contributing Factors	Relevant Ratios or Measures	Questionable Policies

We then have the students list all of the contributing factors they found in preparing their solutions. Their list tends to be lengthy, particularly if they consulted other sources in preparing their solutions. We then have the student that suggested each factor indicate which ratios or other measures he or she used in forming the conclusions. We finish the discussion by listing questionable policies in light of Grant's worsening financial condition in the few years before bankruptcy.

The following ratios are used in various parts of this case:

January 31	1972	1973	1974	1975
Current Ratio	1.75:1	1.55:1	1.60:1	1.23:1
Quick Ratio	1.11:1	.91:1	.93:1	.68:1
Long-Term Debt Ratio	28.3%	27.5%	40.5%	65.5%
Debt/Equity Ratio	65.5%	70.0%	74.2%	89.5%

Year Ended January 31	1972	1973	1974	1975
Rate of Return on Assets	5.0%	4.7%	3.0%	(6.3)%
Net Income/Total Revenues	2.6%	2.3%	.5%	(10.1)%
Accounts Receivable Turnover	3.1	3.2	3.2	3.4
Inventory Turnover	3.3	3.2	3.0	3.0
Plant Assets Turnover	19.8	19.5	19.3	17.4
Total Assets Turnover	1.6	1.6	1.6	1.5
Rate of Return on Common Shareholders' Equity	11.2%	11.4%	2.6%	(81.1)%
W. T. Grant Sales/Industry Sales	19.7%	21.9%	22.5%	20.2%
Sales per Square Foot	30.74	32.49	34.43	32.17
Average Size of Stores (in Thousand Square Feet)	38.29	41.90	45.18	47.54

6.33 continued.

Contributing Factors

1. Operations were a net user of cash in each of the years analyzed. In only two of the years during Grant's last decade did operations provide (net) cash. Grant simply lost its ability to generate cash internally. Students should be pushed as to the reason for Grant's inability to generate cash from operations. Possibilities include:

    a. A decreasing profit margin, resulting in smaller amounts of potential cash flow from each sales transaction. The decreasing profit margin percentage between 1972 and 1975 supports this explanation.

    b. A buildup of accounts receivable. The data do not support this explanation because the accounts receivable turnover increased during the period under study. However, data from 1965 to 1971 show a dramatic *decrease* in the accounts receivable turnover. Grant instituted a credit card system during this period. Extremely liberal credit extension and collection policies resulted in a significant buildup of receivables during the late 1960s and a drain on cash.

    c. A buildup of inventories. The decreasing inventory turnover supports this explanation. Since 1965, the inventory turnover decreased from 4 times to 3 times a year. The decrease is largely due to a change in product mix to furniture and appliances.

2. Financing Strategies—Grant relied heavily on short-term bank loans for much of its needed cash during the period under study. It used this financing to carry receivables and inventories. As these assets built up, the firm required more and more bank loans. The significant increases in interest rates that occurred in the early 1970s made such financing more difficult. The two long-term bond issues were used primarily to obtain funds for store equipment. Grant leased most of its store space (which was not required to be shown on the balance sheet at that time).

Questionable Policies

1. Liberal extension and collection policies on credit sales.

2. Switch to furniture and large appliances.

3. Switch to larger stores.

4. Continued payment of dividends.

5. Continued purchases of Grant's own common stock.

6. Continued investments in securities.

6.34   (Wal-Mart Stores, Inc.; preparing pro forma financial statements.)

a. See attached pro forma financial statements and related financial ratios.

b. Fixing the cash flow problem requires the analyst to identify the reason for the cash shortfall. One view is that the cash flow problem results from the rapid growth in the number of stores. Cash flow from operations is not sufficient to finance capital expenditures and Wal-Mart has relied on long-term debt financing. If the cash flow problem is long-term in nature, then a long-term financing solution seems appropriate. Wal-Mart can either grow its long-term debt at a faster rate than now assumed or issue common stock. Wal-Mart's rate of return on assets exceeds its after cost of borrowing, so additional financial leverage helps the common shareholders. Also, the interest coverage ratio more than adequately covers current interest payments. These observations suggest the issue of long-term debt instead of additional common stock.

We assume, however, that long-term debt will grow at the growth rate in property, plant, and equipment. Thus, the cash shortfall does not appear to result from growth in capital expenditures. Rather, the cash shortfall is more of a working capital problem. We assume that working capital accounts except cash and short-term borrowing (notes payable) will grow directly or indirectly with the growth rate in sales. Thus, the cash shortfall occurs because sales are assumed to grow faster than the growth in short-term borrowing. Wal-Mart has relied on short-term borrowing to finance a portion of its purchases of inventory (note that the days accounts payable is shorter than the days inventory). Thus, we can grow short-term borrowing at a rate closer to the growth rate in sales and eliminate the cash flow problem. Alternatively, we might accelerate the inventory turnover or stretch accounts payable to obtain needed cash. One must consider Wal-Mart's relations with its suppliers. Wal-Mart's inventory control system provides for immediate ordering of merchandise when stock reaches certain levels. Thus, suppliers provide inventory on an on-going basis throughout each month. As an inducement for suppliers to maintain information systems that permit on-going replacement of inventories, Wal-Mart may have agreed to pay suppliers regularly. Thus, it is unclear how much latitude Wal-Mart has to increase its inventory or stretch its payables.

6.34 continued.

WAL-MART STORES
PRO FORMA INCOME STATEMENT
YEAR ENDED JANUARY 31

	Year 5	Year 6	Year 7	Year 8	Year 9
Sales Revenue:	$ 83,412	$ 101,763	$ 124,150	$ 151,464	$ 184,786
Expenses:					
Cost of Goods Sold...	$ 65,586	$ 79,985	$ 97,582	$ 119,050	$ 145,241
Marketing and Administration....	12,858	15,773	19,243	23,477	28,642
Interest................	706	880	1,028	1,202	1,408
Income Taxes........	1,581	1,896	2,330	2,862	3,513
Total Expense......	$ 80,731	$ 98,534	$ 120,183	$ 146,591	$ 178,804
Net Income..............	$ 2,681	$ 3,229	$ 3,967	$ 4,873	$ 5,982
Dividends................	(391)	(489)	(611)	(764)	(955)
Increase in Retained Earnings..............	$ 2,290	$ 2,740	$ 3,356	$ 4,109	$ 5,027

Assumptions:

Growth Rate of Sales..	22.0%	
Cost of Goods Sold......	78.6%	of sales
Marketing and Administration..........	15.5%	of sales
Interest Expense........	7.0%	of interest bearing debt
Income Tax Rate	37.0%	of income before income taxes
Dividends.................	25.0%	growth rate

 Solutions

6.34 continued.

WAL-MART STORES
PRO FORMA BALANCE SHEET
JANUARY 31

	Year 5	Year 6	Year 7	Year 8	Year 9
Cash	$ 45	$ (54)	$ (140)	$ (521)	$ (349)
Accounts Receivable	700	854	1,042	1,271	1,551
Inventories	14,064	16,700	20,832	24,957	30,905
Prepayments	529	645	787	960	1,172
Total Current Assets	$ 15,338	$ 18,145	$ 22,521	$ 26,667	$ 33,279
Property, Plant and Equipment	15,874	18,874	22,441	26,683	31,726
Other Assets	1,607	1,960	2,392	2,918	3,560
Total Assets	$ 32,819	$ 38,979	$ 47,354	$ 56,268	$ 68,565
Accounts Payable	$ 5,907	$ 6,804	$ 8,844	$ 10,106	$ 13,155
Notes Payable	1,882	2,000	2,100	2,200	2,300
Other Current Liabilities	2,184	2,664	3,251	3,966	4,838
Total Current Liabilities	$ 9,973	$ 11,468	$ 14,195	$ 16,272	$ 20,293
Long-Term Debt	9,709	11,544	13,726	16,320	19,404
Other Noncurrent Liabilities	411	501	611	745	910
Total Liabilities	$ 20,093	$ 23,513	$ 28,532	$ 33,337	$ 40,607
Common Stock	$ 230	$ 230	$ 230	$ 230	$ 230
Additional Paid-in Capital	539	539	539	539	539
Retained Earnings	11,957	14,697	18,053	22,162	27,189
Total Shareholders' Equity	$ 12,726	$ 15,466	$ 18,822	$ 22,931	$ 27,958
Total Liabilities and Shareholders' Equity	$ 32,819	$ 38,979	$ 47,354	$ 56,268	$ 68,565

(See Following Page for Assumptions)

6.34 continued.

(Assumptions for Pro Forma Balance Sheet)

Assumptions:

Cash	PLUG			
Accounts Receivable...	Sales Growth Rate			
Inventory Turnover....	5.2			
Average Inventory	15,382	18,766	22,894	27,931
Prepayments.............	Sales Growth Rate			
Property, Plant and Equipment.............	18.9% Growth Rate			
Other Assets	Sales Growth Rate			
Accounts Payable Turnover..............	13.0			
Merchandise Purchases..................	82,621	101,715	123,175	151,190
Average Payables.......	6,355	7,824	9,475	11,630
Notes Payable............	2,000	2,100	2,200	2,300
Other Current Liabilities..............	Sales Growth Rate			
Long-Term Debt.........	Property, Plant and Equipment Growth Rate			
Other Noncurrent Liabilities..............	Sales Growth Rate			
Common Stock, APIC....................	0.0% Growth Rate			

6.34 continued.

WAL-MART STORES
PRO FORMA CASH FLOW STATEMENT
FOR THE YEAR ENDED JANUARY 31

Cash Flow Statement	Year 5	Year 6	Year 7	Year 8	Year 9
Operations:					
Net Income.............	$ 2,681	$ 3,229	$ 3,967	$ 4,873	$ 5,982
Depreciation...........	1,070	1,272	1,513	1,799	2,139
Other....................	21	90	110	134	165
(Inc.)/Dec. in Accounts Receivable..................	(84)	(154)	(188)	(229)	(280)
(Inc.)/Dec. in Inventory....................	(3,053)	(2,636)	(4,132)	(4,125)	(5,948)
(Inc.)/Dec. in Prepayments...........	(139)	(116)	(142)	(173)	(212)
Inc./(Dec.) in Accounts Payable.....	1,914	897	2,040	1,262	3,049
Inc./(Dec.) in Other Current Liabilities....................	496	480	587	715	872
Cash Flow from Operations.............	$ 2,906	$ 3,062	$ 3,755	$ 4,256	$ 5,767
Investing:					
Acquisition of Property, Plant and Equipment....	$ (3,734)	$ (4,272)	$ (5,080)	$ (6,041)	$ (7,182)
Other Investing.......	(58)	(353)	(432)	(526)	(642)
Cash Flow from Investing...............	$ (3,792)	$ (4,625)	$ (5,512)	$ (6,567)	$ (7,824)
Financing:					
Inc./(Dec.) in Short-Term Borrowing..	$ 220	$ 118	$ 100	$ 100	$ 100
Inc./(Dec.) in Long-Term Borrowing..	1,143	1,835	2,182	2,594	3,084
Inc./(Dec.) in Common Stock...........	0	0	0	0	0
Dividends...............	(391)	(489)	(611)	(764)	(955)
Other Financing.....	(61)	0	0	0	0
Cash Flow from Financing..............	$ 911	$ 1,464	$ 1,671	$ 1,930	$ 2,229
Change in Cash........	$ 25	$ (99)	$ (86)	$ (381)	$ 172
Cash, Beginning of Year.....................	20	45	(54)	(140)	(521)
Cash, End of Year......	$ 45	$ (54)	$ (140)	$ (521)	$ (349)

(See Following Page for Assumptions)

6-40

6.34 continued.

(Assumptions for Pro Forma Cash Flow Statement)

Assumptions:

Depreciation Growth
Rate...................... Same as Property, Plant, and Equipment
Other Operating Add-
backs .... Change in Noncurrent Liabilities
Other Investing Cash
Flows................... Change in Other Noncurrent Assets

WAL-MART STORES
PRO FORMA FINANCIAL RATIOS

	Year 6	Year 7	Year 8	Year 9
Rate of Return on Assets........	10.5%	10.7%	10.9%	11.0%
Profit Margin for ROA...........	3.7%	3.7%	3.7%	3.7%
Total Assets Turnover	2.8	2.9	2.9	3.0
Cost of Goods Sold/Sales.........	78.6%	78.6%	78.6%	78.6%
Marketing and Administra-tive Expenses/Sales............	15.5%	15.5%	15.5%	15.5%
Interest Expense/Sales	0.9%	0.8%	0.8%	0.8%
Income Tax Expense/Sales.....	1.9%	1.9%	1.9%	1.9%
Accounts Receivable Turnover Ratio.............................	131.0	131.0	131.0	131.0
Inventory Turnover Ratio.......	5.2	5.2	5.2	5.2
Plant Assets Turnover Ratio...	5.9	6.0	6.2	6.3
Rate of Return on Common Equity.............................	22.9%	23.1%	23.3%	23.5%
Profit Margin for ROCE.........	3.2%	3.2%	3.2%	3.2%
Leverage Ratio......................	2.5	2.5	2.5	2.5
Current Ratio.......................	1.58	1.59	1.64	1.64
Quick Ratio	0.07	0.06	0.05	0.06
Cash Flow from Operations/ Current Liabilities.............	28.6%	29.3%	27.9%	31.5%
Accounts Payable Turnover Ratio..............................	13.0	13.0	13.0	13.0
Long-Term Debt Ratio...........	42.7%	42.2%	41.6%	41.0%
Debt-Equity Ratio..................	60.3%	60.3%	59.2%	59.2%
Cash Flow from Operations/ Total Liabilities	14.0%	14.4%	13.8%	15.6%
Interest Coverage Ratio	6.8	7.1	7.4	7.7

CHAPTER 7

THE LIQUID ASSETS:
CASH, MARKETABLE SECURITIES, AND RECEIVABLES

Questions, Exercises, Problems, and Cases: Answers and Solutions

7.1   See the text or the glossary at the end of the book.

7.2   Current assets do not include cash that is not readily available for the general use of a firm. For example, cash in a sinking fund to be used for the retirement of bonds in the future appears among Investments rather than Current Assets. Cash held by a foreign unit in a country that severely restricts the outflow of cash also might not appear as a current asset.

7.3   The compensating balance effectively increases the cost of any borrowing because the firm cannot access all of the cash in its bank account.   The increased cost negatively influences the firm's profitability. Also, the reported amount for cash on the balance sheet may overstate the amount of liquid resources freely available to a firm to satisfy creditors, negatively influencing assessments of risk.

7.4   **Cafeteria:** There are two registers; one at the end of the counter turns out a ticket which the cashier retrieves when the patron leaves. The total in the register of the checker should correspond to the total of the register of the cashier, excluding sales of candy and other items sold by the cashier.

Department Store: A cash register rings cash sales, prints a receipt for the customer, and records the amount of the sale in the register. A store verifies charge accounts by use of charge plates or keys, or initials of floor walker, or telephone to credit department computer. Cash refunds require approval of a floor walker before a special cashier makes the refunds.

Theater: A locked mechanism stores unused tickets. The cashier has to account for the number of tickets sold; tickets are numbered serially. An employee picks up tickets at the door and deposits them in a mangling machine.

Gasoline Station: A device on the gasoline pump records dollars and cents. There is a perpetual inventory of oil in cans and a recording device for quarts of bulk oil pumped.

                                                        Solutions

7.5   Typically, the sales clerks in such enterprises are not owners. The owners want to make sure that cash receipts stay in the cash register and that clerks do not transfer them into the clerks' pockets. Tastee Delight's policy gives the clerk an incentive to present a receipt. If a customer makes a claim for a free purchase because a receipt was not presented, then the owner will probably dock the clerk's pay. The Oakland's Original policy gives the customer an incentive to ask for a receipt. Each time the cash register prints a receipt, it records the amount of the sale in the cash register. All the owner or manager does each day is check the cash in the register with the amounts the tapes show should be in the register.

7.6   Securities that a firm intends to sell within approximately one year of the date of the balance sheet appear as current assets. All other securities appear as noncurrent assets.

7.7   a.   Debt securities that a firm intends to hold to maturity (for example, to lock in the yield at acquisition for the full period to maturity) and has the ability to hold to maturity (for example, the firm has adequate liquid assets and borrowing capacity such that it need not sell the debt securities prior to maturity to obtain cash) appear as "debt held to maturity." All other debt securities appear in the "available for sale" category. The latter includes short-term investments in government debt securities that serve as a liquid investment of excess cash and short-and long-term investments in government and corporate debt securities that serve either as hedges of interest rate, exchange rate, or similar risks or as sources of cash at a later date to pay debt coming due.

         b.   The classification as "trading securities" implies a firm's active involvement in buying and selling securities for profit. The holding period of trading securities is typically measured in minutes or hours instead of days. The classification as "available for sale" implies less frequent trading and usually relates to an operating purpose other than profit alone (for example, to generate income while a firm haws temporarily excess cash, to invest in a firm with potential new technologies). The holding period of securities available for sale is typically measured in days, months, or years.

         c.   Amortized acquisition cost equals the purchase price of debt securities plus or minus amortization of any difference between acquisition cost and maturity value. Amortized acquisition cost bears no necessary relation to the market value of the debt security during the periods subsequent to acquisition. The market value of a debt security depends on the risk characteristics of the issuer, the provisions of the debt security with respect to interest rate, term to maturity, and similar factors, and the general level of interest rates in the economy.

7.7 continued.

  d. Unrealized holding gains and losses occur when the market value of a security changes while the firm holds the security. The unrealized holding gain or loss on trading securities appears in the income statement each period, whereas it appears in a separate shareholders' equity account each period for securities available for sale.

  e. Realized gains and losses appear in the income statement when a firm sells a security. The realized gain or loss on trading securities equals the selling price minus the market value of the security on the most recent balance sheet. The realized gain or loss on securities available for sale equals the selling price minus the acquisition cost of the security.

7.8 Firms acquire trading securities primarily for their short-term profit potential. Including the unrealized holding gain or loss in income provides the financial statement user with relevant information for assessing the performance of the trading activity. Firms acquire securities available for sale to support an operating activity (for example, investment of temporarily excess cash) instead of primarily for their profit potential. Deferring recognition of any gain or loss until sale treats securities available for sale the same as inventories, equipment and other assets. Excluding the unrealized gain or loss from earnings also reduces earnings volatility.

7.9 The realized gain or loss for a security classified as available for sale equals the selling price minus the acquisition cost of the security. The realized gain or loss for a trading security equals the selling price minus the market value on the date of the most recent balance sheet. GAAP allocate all of the income from a security classified as available for sale to the period of sale, whereas GAAP allocate this same amount of income on a trading security to all periods between purchase and sale.

7.10 The required accounting does appear to contain a degree of inconsistency. One might explain this seeming inconsistency by arguing that the balance sheet and income statement serve different purposes. The balance sheet attempts to portray the resources of a firm and the claims on those users by creditors and owners. Market values for securities are more relevant than acquisition cost or lower-of-cost-or-market for assessing the adequacy of resources to satisfy claims. The income statement reports the results of operating performance. One might argue that operating performance from investing in marketable securities available for sale is not complete until the firm sells the securities. Another argument for excluding at least unrealized gains on marketable securities from earnings is that it achieves consistency with the delayed recognition of unrealized gains on inventories, equipment, and other assets.

7.11   The allowance method, because it reports bad debt expense during the period of the sale, not during the later period(s) when the specific accounts become uncollectible.

7.12   The direct write-off method matches the loss from an uncollectible account with revenue of the period when a particular account becomes uncollectible.   The allowance method matches the loss from an uncollectible account with revenue of the period of the sale that later gave rise to an uncollectible account.

7.13   a. A firm with stable sales (both volume and price) and a constant proportion of uncollectible accounts will likely report similar amounts for bad debt expense each period.

        b. The direct write-off method should always result in larger amounts for accounts receivable-net on the balance sheet than the allowance method.

7.14   a. This statement is valid. Most businesses ought not to set credit policies so stringent that they have no uncollectible accounts. To do so would require extremely careful screening of customers, which is costly, and the probable loss of many customers who will take their business elsewhere. So long as the revenues collected from credit sales exceed the sum of both selling costs and the cost of goods sold on credit, then the firm should not be concerned if some percentage of its accounts receivable are uncollectible.

        b. If a business liberalizes its credit policy by granting to a group of customers, who were not previously granted this privilege, the right to buy on account, it can find that its net revenues from the new credit customers exceed the cost of goods sold to them and the selling expenses of executing the sales. The extension of credit to new customers can increase net income even though it results in more uncollectible accounts.

        c. When the net present value of the receipts from selling to new customers is larger than the net present value of the costs of putting goods into their hands.

7.15   If a firm computes the Bad Debt Expense figure at the end of the accounting period but writes off specific accounts receivable during the period as information about uncollectible accounts becomes available, then the Allowance for Uncollectibles will have a debit balance whenever the amount of accounts written off during the period exceeds the opening credit balance in the Allowance account. Firms prepare balance sheets only after making adjusting entries. Both the Bad Debt Expense and the Allowance for Uncollectibles accounts must be made current with appropriate adjusting entries before preparing the balance sheet. Because the Allowance for Uncollectibles account is an asset contra, it will always show a credit (or perhaps a zero) balance after making adjusting entries.

7.16   Transferring a note with recourse requires footnote disclosure of the contingent obligation which might arise if the note is not paid by the maker at maturity. Transferring a note without recourse does not lead to a contingent obligation and, therefore, need not be disclosed.

7.17   (O'Brien Company; inclusions in Cash account.)

"Cash" should include the following:

Checking Account ($97,400 – $150 – $240 – $20,000)...............	$ 77,010
Cash Fund ($500 – $125 – $15)...	360
Certificates of Deposit [$20,000 + ($20,000 × .06 × 4/12)]	20,400
Canadian Bank Account ($1.22 × C39,700)	48,434
Total	$ 146,204

The outstanding checks do not represent cash. Because the company's books have already subtracted these checks, no additional adjustment is required. Cash excludes deposits on the land purchase because the company cannot access this amount for its general cash needs.

7.18   (Sprohl Company; inclusions in Cash account.)

"Cash" should include the following:

Undeposited Coins, Currency, and Checks..........................	$ 3,970
Cash in Petty Cash Fund ($1,000 – $132).............................	868
Cash in Checking Account ($49,700 – $270 + $2,500)..............	51,930
Certificate of Deposit [$50,000 + ($50,000 × .08 × 6/12)]	52,000
Japanese Yen (¥100,000/100)	1,000
Total	$ 109,768

Cash does not include postage because it is not accepted as a medium of exchange.

7.19   (Cristoff Corporation; effect of compensating balances on effective interest rate.)

a.   (.08 × $2,000,000)/$1,900,000 = 8.42 percent.

b.   The bank is implicitly telling Cristoff Corporation that its credit standing is insufficient to justify lending at the prime interest rate of 8 percent. The compensating balance arrangement is a mechanism for increasing the interest rate charged on the loan to 8.42 percent.

 7.20   (Classifying securities.)

a.   Securities available for sale; current asset.

b.   Debt securities held to maturity; noncurrent asset.

     Solutions

7.20 continued.

    c.   Securities available for sale; current asset.

    d.   Securities available for sale; noncurrent asset.

    e.   Trading securities; current asset.

    f.   Securities available for sale; noncurrent asset (although a portion of these bonds might appear as a current asset).

7.21   (Vermont Company; journal entries for holdings of marketable equity securities.)

8/21

Marketable Securities	45,000	
Cash		45,000

To record the cost of purchases in asset account: (1,000 X $45) = $45,000.

9/13

No entry because September 13 is not the end of an accounting period.

9/30

Dividends Receivable	500	
Dividend Revenue		500

To record declaration of dividend as revenue.

10/25

Cash	500	
Dividends Receivable		500

To record receipt of dividend in cash.

12/31

Marketable Securities	6,000	
Unrealized Holding Gain on Securities Available for Sale (SE)		6,000

To record increase in market price: 1,000 X ($51 – $45) = $6,000.

1/20

Cash (600 X $55)	33,000	
Marketable Securities (600 X $45)		27,000
Realized Gain on Sale of Securities Available for Sale (IncSt) [600 X ($55 – $45)]		6,000

To record sale of 600 shares of Texas Instruments.

Unrealized Holding Gain on Securities Available for Sale (SE) [600 X ($51– $45)]	3,600	
Marketable Securities		3,600

To eliminate changes previously recorded in the market value of Texas Instruments.

7.22   (Elson Corporation; journal entries for holdings of marketable equity securities.)

10/15/Year 4
Marketable Securities (Security A)........................ 28,000
    Cash.. 28,000
To record acquisition of shares of Security A.

11/02/Year 4
Marketable Securities (Security B)........................ 49,000
    Cash.. 49,000
To record acquisition of shares of Security B.

12/31/Year 4
Cash... 1,000
    Dividend Revenue... 1,000
To record dividend received from Security B.

12/31/Year 4
Unrealized Holding Loss on Security A Available
    for Sale (SE)... 3,000
        Marketable Securities (Security A)............... 3,000
To record unrealized holding loss on Security A.

12/31/Year 4
Marketable Securities (Security B)........................ 6,000
    Unrealized Holding Gain on Security B Avail-
        able for Sale (SE)...................................... 6,000
To record unrealized holding gain on Security B.

2/10/Year 5
Cash... 24,000
Realized Loss on Sale of Securities Available for
    Sale ($24,000 − $28,000) (IncSt)........................ 4,000
        Marketable Securities (Security A)............... 28,000
To record sale of Security A.

Marketable Securities (Security A)........................ 3,000
    Unrealized Holding Loss on Security A Avail-
        able for Sale (SE)...................................... 3,000
To eliminate the effects of changes previously re-
corded in the market value of Security A.

12/31/Year 5
Cash... 1,200
    Dividend Revenue... 1,200
To record dividend received from Security B.

         Solutions

7.22 continued.

12/31/Year 5

Unrealized Holding Gain on Security B Available for Sale (SE)	2,000	
Marketable Securities (Security B) ($53,000 – $55,000)		2,000

To revalue Security B to market value.

7/15/Year 6

Cash	57,000	
Marketable Securities (Security B)		49,000
Realized Gain on Sale of Securities Available for Sale ($57,000 – $49,000) (IncSt)		8,000

To record sale of Security B.

Unrealized Holding Gain on Security B Available for Sale ($6,000 – $2,000) (SE)	4,000	
Marketable Securities (Security B)		4,000

To eliminate the effects of changes previously recorded in the market value of Security B.

7.23 (Simmons Corporation; journal entries for holdings of marketable equity securities.)

6/13/Year 6

Marketable Securities (Security S)	12,000	
Marketable Securities (Security T)	29,000	
Marketable Securities (Security U)	43,000	
Cash		84,000

To record acquisition of marketable equity securities as a temporary investment.

10/11/Year 6

Cash	39,000	
Realized Loss on Sale of Security U Available for Sale (IncSt)	4,000	
Marketable Securities (Security U)		43,000

To record sale of Security U.

12/31/Year 6

Marketable Securities (Security S) ($13,500 – $12,000)	1,500	
Unrealized Holding Gain on Security S Available for Sale (SE)		1,500

To revalue Security S to market value.

7.23 continued.

12/31/Year 6

Unrealized Holding Loss on Security T Available for Sale (SE)	2,800	
Marketable Securities (Security T) ($26,200 – $29,000)..		2,800
To revalue Security T to market value.		

12/31/Year 7

Marketable Securities (Security S) ($15,200 – $13,500)...	1,700	
Unrealized Holding Gain on Security S Available for Sale (SE)		1,700
To revalue Security S to market value.		

12/31/Year 7

Marketable Securities (Security T) ($31,700 – $26,200)...	5,500	
Unrealized Holding Loss on Security T Available for Sale (from 12/31/Year 6 Entry) (SE)...		2,800
Unrealized Holding Gain on Security T Available for Sale (SE)		2,700
To revalue Security T to market value.		

2/15/Year 8

Cash...	14,900	
Marketable Securities (Security S)		12,000
Realized Gain on Sale of Security S Available for Sale ($14,900 – $12,000) (IncSt)....................		2,900
To record sale of Security S.		

Unrealized Holding Gain on Security S Available for Sale ($1,500 + $1,700) (SE)............................	3,200	
Marketable Securities (Security S).................		3,200
To eliminate the effects of changes previously recorded in the market value of Security S.		

8/22/Year 8

Cash...	28,500	
Realized Loss on Sale of Securities Available for Sale (Security T) ($28,500 – $29,000) (IncSt).........	500	
Marketable Securities (Security T)................		29,000
To record sale of Security T.		

Unrealized Holding Gain on Security T Available for Sale (SE)	2,700	
Marketable Securities (Security T)................		2,700
To eliminate the effects of changes previously recorded in the market value of Security T.		

 Solutions

7.24   (Kesler Company; journal entries for the allowance method.)

a. **Year 6**

Bad Debt Expense..	8,400	
Allowance for Uncollectible Accounts...........		8,400

.02 × $420,000 = $8,400.

Allowance for Uncollectible Accounts..............	1,200	
Accounts Receivable...................................		1,200

Year 7

Bad Debt Expense..	9,600	
Allowance for Uncollectible Accounts...........		9,600

.02 × $480,000 = $9,600.

Allowance for Uncollectible Accounts..............	7,000	
Accounts Receivable...................................		7,000

Year 8

Bad Debt Expense..	11,000	
Allowance for Uncollectible Accounts...........		11,000

.02 × $550,000 = $11,000.

Allowance for Uncollectible Accounts..............	9,800	
Accounts Receivable...................................		9,800

b. Yes. Uncollectible accounts arising from sales of Years 6, 7 and 8 total $28,900, which equals 1.99 percent (= $28,900/$1,450,000) of total sales on account during the three year period.

7.25   (Emmons Company; journal entries for the allowance method.)

a. **Dec. 31**

Bad Debt Expense..	37,500	
Allowance for Uncollectible Accounts...........		37,500

.025 × $1,500,000 = $37,500.

Allowance for Uncollectible Accounts..............	2,300	
Accounts Receivable...................................		2,300

Year 2

Bad Debt Expense..	45,000	
Allowance for Uncollectible Accounts...........		45,000

.025 × $1,800,000 = $45,000.

Allowance for Uncollectible Accounts..............	22,100	
Accounts Receivable...................................		22,100

Year 3

Bad Debt Expense.....................................	60,000	
Allowance for Uncollectible Accounts...........		60,000
.025 × $2,400,000 = $60,000.		

Allowance for Uncollectible Accounts.............	38,000	
Accounts Receivable.................................		38,000

b. No. The actual loss experience is 2 percent (= $113,800/$5,700,000) of sales on account for sales during Years 1 through 3.

7.26 (Milton Corporation; reconstructing events when using the allowance method.)

Accounts Receivable		Allowance for Uncollectible Accounts	
√ 15,200,000			1,400,000 √
(see below)			(see below)
√ 17,900,000			1,550,000 √

Accounts Receivable	75,000,000	
Sales..		75,000,000
$750,000 is 1 percent of sales; sales = $750,000/.01.		

Bad Debt Expense	750,000	
Allowance for Uncollectible Accounts.............		750,000

Allowance for Uncollectible Accounts..................	600,000	
Accounts Receivable.....................................		600,000
$1,400,000 + $750,000 − $1,550,000 = $600,000.		

Cash...	71,700,000	
Accounts Receivable.....................................		71,700,000
$15,200,000 + $75,000,000 − $600,000 − $17,900,000 = $71,700,000.		

7.27 (Seward Corporation; reconstructing events when using the allowance method.)

Cash		Accounts Receivable		Allowance for Uncollectible Accounts	
		√ 82,900			8,700 √
(4) 231,200		(1) 240,000	4,400 (3)	(3) 4,400	4,800 (2)
			231,200 (4)		
		√ 87,300			9,100 √

 Solutions

7.27 continued.

Bad Debt Expense			Sales	
--				--
(2) 4,800				240,000 (1)
√ 4,800				240,000

(1) Sales on account.
(2) Provision for estimated uncollectible accounts.
(3) Write off of actual uncollectible accounts.
(4) Collection of cash from customers for sales on account.

7.28   (Logue Corporation; reconstructing events when using the allowance method.)

Cash		Accounts Receivable		Allowance for Uncollectible Accounts	
		√ 115,900			18,200
(4) 422,000		(1) 450,000	21,100 (2)	(2) 21,100	
			422,100 (3)		
		√ 122,700		√ 2,900	
					22,500 (4)
					19,600 √

Bad Debt Expense			Sales	
--				--
(4) 22,500				450,000 (1)
				450,000 √

(1) Sales on account.
(2) Write off of actual uncollectible accounts during year.
(3) Collection of cash from customers for sales on account.
(4) Provision for estimated uncollectible accounts on December 31.

7.29   (Dove Company; aging accounts receivable.)

Bad Debt Expense	1,700	
Allowance for Uncollectible Accounts..............		1,700

To adopt auditor's suggestion that total allowance now be $18,900 [(= .005 × $400,000) + (.01 × $90,000) + (.10 × $40,000) + (.60 × $20,000)]. $18,900 − $17,200 = $1,700.

7.30 (Rorke Company; aging accounts receivable.)

Allowance for Uncollectible Accounts 1,250
    Bad Debt Expense   1,250

The Allowance account requires a balance of $34,750 = (.005 × $700,000) + (.01 × $225,000) + (.10 × $90,000) + (.40 × $50,000). The adjusting entry *reduces* the Allowance account by $1,250 (= $36,000 − $34,750) and reduces Bad Debt Expense for the period by the same amount.

7.31 (Simple interest computations.)

a. $\dfrac{60}{360}$ × .09 × $10,000 = $150.

b. $\dfrac{90}{360}$ × .06 × $10,000 = $150.

c. $\dfrac{60}{360}$ × .10 × $10,000 = $166.67.

d. $\dfrac{15}{360}$ × .12 × $10,000 = $50.

e. $\dfrac{(8 \times 30) + 15}{360}$ × .12 × $10,000 = $850.

7.32 (Dukes/Beaver; journal entries for notes.)

a. **Dukes**

5/21
Notes Receivable 20,000
    Accounts Receivable—Salk Builders, Inc.   20,000

6/30
Interest Receivable 200
    Interest Revenue   200
$20,000 × .09 × 40/360 = $200.

7/21
Accounts Payable—Beaver Company 20,300
    Notes Receivable   20,000
    Interest Receivable   200
    Interest Revenue   100
.09 × $20,000 × 2/12 = $300; $300 − $200 = $100.

Also make a memorandum notation about the contingent obligation for the note transferred with recourse.

         Solutions

7.32 a. continued.

2/21 Next Year
Contingent obligation is canceled; make a memorandum notation.

b. **Beaver**

7/21

Notes Receivable......................................	20,000	
Interest Receivable...................................	300	
Accounts Receivable—Dukes Company........		20,300

9/30

Interest Receivable......................................	350	
Interest Revenue....................................		350

$$\frac{(2 \times 30) + 10}{360} \times .09 \times \$20,000 = \$350.$$

12/31

Interest Receivable......................................	450	
Interest Revenue....................................		450

$.09 \times \$20,000 \times 3/12 = \$450.$

2/21

Cash..	21,350	
Notes Receivable		20,000
Interest Receivable................................		1,100
Interest Revenue..................................		250

$.09 \times \$20,000 \times 50/360 = \$250.$

7.33   (Sharp Company; journal entries for notes.)

October 15

Notes Receivable	2,000	
Accounts Receivable		2,000

December 31

Interest Receivable......................................	25	
Interest Revenue..................................		25

$\$2,000 \times .06 \times 2.5/12 = \$25.$

March 30

Interest Receivable......................................	30	
Interest Revenue..................................		30

$\$2,000 \times .06 \times 3/12 = \$30.$

7.33 continued.

April 15

Cash...	2,060	
Notes Receivable...		2,000
Interest Receivable		55
Interest Revenue...		5

$2,000 × .06 × 15/360 = $5.

7.34   (Reconstructing events from journal entries.)

a.   A firm receives a note from a customer in settlement of an account receivable of $300.

b.   A firm acquires marketable securities costing $10,000 for cash.

c.   Estimated bad debt expense for the period is $2,300 using the allowance method.

d.   The market value of a marketable security is $4,000 less than its book value and the firm increases the Unrealized Holding Loss account on the balance sheet. Alternatively, the firm sold a security with a cumulative unrealized loss recorded on the books and must now eliminate the effects of changes previously recorded in the market values of the security sold.

e.   A firm either collects a note from a customer or discounts it at a bank or other financial institution.

f.   A firm sells marketable securities for an amount that is $100 (= $1,200 – $1,300) less than was originally paid for them.

g.   A firm writes off specific customers' accounts totaling $450 as uncollectible under the allowance method.

h.   A firm writes off specific customers' accounts totaling $495 as uncollectible under the direct write-off method.

i.   The market value of marketable securities is $750 more than its book value and the firm increases the unrealized holding gain account on the balance sheet.

j.   A firm sells marketable securities for an amount that is $100 (= $1,800 – $1,700) more than was originally paid for them.

7.35   (Effects on statement of cash flows.)

a. The journal entry to record this transaction is as follows:

Marketable Securities.................................	59,700	
Cash..		59,700

Because this entry involves a credit to the Cash account, Line (9) decreases by $59,700. The purchase of marketable securities is an Investing activity, so Line (5) increases by $59,700. Note that Line (5) carries a negative sign, so increasing it reduces cash.

b. The journal entries to record this transaction are as follows:

Cash...	47,900	
Marketable Securities..........................		42,200
Realized Gain on Sale of Securities Avail- able for Sale (IncSt)...................		5,700
Unrealized Holding Gain on Securities Avail- able for Sale (SE)	1,800	
Marketable Securities ($44,000 – $42,200)...		1,800

Because the first entry involves a debit to the Cash account, Line (9) increases by $47,900. The sale of marketable securities is an Investing activity, so Line (4) increases by $47,900. Because the Realized Gain on Sale of Securities Available for Sale account is an income statement account, Line (1) increases by $5,700. We show all of the cash proceeds of sale ($47,900) on Line (4). We double count cash in the amount of the gain if we do not eliminate $5,700 from the Operations section of the statement of cash flows. Thus, Line (3) increases by $5,700 to offset the realized gain. The net effect of the entries on Line (1) and Line (3) is zero. The second entry does not involve an income statement account or the Cash account and therefore would not appear on the statement of cash flows.

c. The journal entries to record this transaction are as follows:

Cash...	18,700	
Realized Loss on Sale of Securities Available for Sale (IncSt)...............................	6,400	
Marketable Securities		25,100
Marketable Securities ($25,100 – $19,600)..........	5,500	
Unrealized Holding Loss on Securities Available for Sale (SE).................		5,500

7.35 c. continued.

> Because the first entry involves a debit to the Cash account, Line (9) increases by $47,900. The sale of marketable securities is an Investing activity, so Line (4) increases by $47,900. Because the Realized Gain on Sale of Securities Available for Sale account is an income statement account, Line (1) increases by $5,700. We show all of the cash proceeds of sale ($47,900) on Line (4). We double count cash in the amount of the gain if we do not eliminate $5,700 from the Operations section of the statement of cash flows. Thus, Line (3) increases by $5,700 to offset the realized gain. The net effect of the entries on Line (1) and Line (3) is zero. The second entry does not involve an income statement account or the Cash account and therefore would not appear on the statement of cash flows.

d. The journal entry is as follows:

Unrealized Holding Loss on Securities Available for Sale (SE)	19,000	
Marketable Securities ($220,500 – $201,500)		19,000

> This entry does not involve a debit or credit to the Cash account, so Line (9) is not affected. This entry also does not affect an income statement account (the Unrealized Holding Loss on Securities Available for Sale account is a shareholders' equity account), so Line (1) is not affected. Thus, this entry does not appear on the statement of cash flows.

e. The journal entry is as follows:

Marketable Securities	6,400	
Unrealized Holding Gain on Securities Available for Sale (SE)		6,400

> For the same reasons given in Part d. above, this entry does not appear on the statement of cash flows.

f. The journal entry is as follows:

Bad Debt Expense	79,300	
Allowance for Uncollectible Accounts...........		79,300

> Because this entry does not involve a debit or credit to the Cash account, Line (9) is not affected. Because the Bad Debt Expense account is an income statement account, Line (1) decreases by $79,300. This expense does not use cash, so Line (2) increases by $79,300 to offset the amount on Line (1). The net effect of the entries on Line (1) and Line (2) is zero.

 Solutions

7.35 continued.

g. The journal entry is as follows:

Allowance for Uncollectible Accounts.............. 67,200
    Accounts Receivable................................... 67,200

Because this entry does not involve a debit or credit to the Cash account, Line (9) is not affected. Because this entry does not involve a debit or credit to an income statement account, Line (1) is not affected. Thus, this entry does not appear on the statement of cash flows.

h. The journal entry is as follows:

Interest Receivable....................................... 8,000
    Interest Revenue....................................... 8,000

This entry does not involve a debit or credit to the Cash account, so Line (9) is not affected. Interest Revenue is an income statement account, so Line (1) increases by $8,000. Because the accrual of interest revenue does not increase cash, Line (3) must increase for the increase in Interest Receivable. The net effect of the entries on Line (1) and Line (3) is zero.

i. The journal entry is as follows:

Cash.. 18,000
    Interest Receivable.................................... 12,000
    Interest Revenue....................................... 6,000

Because this entry involves a debit to the Cash account, Line (9) increases by $18,000. The receipt of cash from interest is an operating activity. The Interest Revenue account is an income statement account, so Line (1) increases by $6,000. Because the firm received cash at the time of recognizing the interest revenue, no adjustment for it is required on the statement of cash flows. However, we must show an additional $12,000 in the Operating section of the statement of cash flows if we are to account for the full $18,000 received in cash. Line (2) must increase by $12,000 for the decrease in the Interest Receivable account.

7.35 continued.

j. The journal entry is as follows:

Cash..	500	
Note Receivable...		500

This entry involves a debit to the Cash account, so Line (9) increases by $500. Collection of a customer's note appears as an Operating transaction in the statement of cash flows. Thus, Line (2) increases by $500 for the decrease in the Note Receivable account.

7.36 (Postal Corporation; journal entries and financial statement presentation of marketable equity securities.)

a. **2/05/Year 1**

Marketable Securities (Security A)	60,000	
Cash..		60,000

8/12/Year 1

Marketable Securities (Security B)..................	25,000	
Cash..		25,000

12/31/Year 1

Marketable Securities (Security A) ($66,000 – $60,000)...	6,000	
Unrealized Holding Gain on Security A Available for Sale (SE).........................		6,000

Unrealized Holding Loss on Security B Available for Sale (SE)	5,000	
Marketable Securities (Security B) ($20,000 – $25,000)		5,000

Note: The two entries on December 31, Year 1 could be combined into a single entry.

1/22/Year 2

Marketable Securities (Security C)...................	82,000	
Cash..		82,000

2/25/Year 2

Marketable Securities (Security D)...................	42,000	
Cash..		42,000

3/25/Year 2

Marketable Securities (Security E)...................	75,000	
Cash..		75,000

 Solutions

7.36 a. continued.

6/05/Year 2

Cash..	72,000	
Marketable Securities (Security A)...............		60,000
Realized Gain on Sale of Securities Available for Sale (IncSt)................................		12,000

Unrealized Holding Gain on Security A Available for Sale (SE).....................................	6,000	
Marketable Securities (Security A)...........		6,000

6/05/Year 2

Cash..	39,000	
Realized Loss on Sale of Securities Available for Sale (IncSt)...	3,000	
Marketable Securities (Security D)...........		42,000

12/31/Year 2

Marketable Securities (Security B) ($23,000 – $20,000)...	3,000	
Unrealized Holding Loss on Security B Available for Sale (SE).........................		3,000

12/31/Year 2

Unrealized Holding Loss on Security C Available for Sale (SE).....................................	3,000	
Marketable Securities (Security C) ($79,000 – $82,000)...		3,000

12/31/Year 2

Marketable Securities (Security E) ($80,000 – $75,000)...	5,000	
Unrealized Holding Gain on Security E Available for Sale (SE).........................		5,000

Note: The three entries on December 31, Year 2 could be combined into a single entry.

b. **Balance Sheet on December 31, Year 1**

Marketable Securities at Market Value.........................	$ 86,000
Net Unrealized Holding Gain on Securities Available for Sale ($6,000 – $5,000)	$ 1,000

Footnote

Marketable Securities on December 31, Year 1 had an acquisition cost of $85,000 and a market value of $86,000. Gross unrealized gains total $6,000 and gross unrealized losses total $5,000.

7.36 continued.

c. **Balance Sheet on December 31, Year 2**
Marketable Securities at Market Value .... $ 182,000
Net Unrealized Holding Loss on Securities Available for
Sale .... $ 182,000

Footnote

Marketable Securities on December 31, Year 2 had an acquisition
cost of $182,000 and a market value of $182,000. Gross unrealized
gains total $5,000 and gross unrealized losses total $5,000. Proceeds
from sales of marketable securities totaled $111,000 during Year 2.
These sales resulted in gross realized gains of $12,000 and gross
realized losses of $3,000. The net unrealized holding loss on
securities available for sale changed as follows during Year 2:

Balance, December 31, Year 1	$ 1,000	Cr.
Unrealized Gain on Securities Sold	(6,000)	Dr.
Change in Net Unrealized Loss on Securities Held at		
Year End ($3,000 – $3,000 + $5,000)	5,000	Cr.
Balance, December 31, Year 2	$ --	

7.37 (Rice Corporation; journal entries and financial statement presentation
of marketable equity securities.)

a. **3/05/Year 1**

Marketable Securities (Security A)	40,000	
Cash		40,000

5/12/Year 1

Marketable Securities (Security B)	80,000	
Cash		80,000

12/31/Year 1

Marketable Securities (Security A) ($45,000 –		
$40,000)	5,000	
Unrealized Holding Gain on Security A		
Available for Sale (SE)		5,000

12/31/Year 1

Unrealized Holding Loss on Security B Avail-		
able for Sale (SE)	10,000	
Marketable Securities (Security B) ($70,000		
– $80,000)		10,000

Note: The two entries on December 31, Year 1 could be combined into a
single entry.

     Solutions

7.37 a. continued.

3/22/Year 2

Marketable Securities (Security C).................	32,000	
Cash...		32,000

5/25/Year 2

Marketable Securities (Security D).................	17,000	
Cash...		17,000

5/25/Year 2

Marketable Securities (Security E).................	63,000	
Cash...		63,000

10/05/Year 2

Cash..	52,000	
Marketable Securities (Security A)...............		40,000
Realized Gain on Sale of Securities Available for Sale (IncSt)................................		12,000
Unrealized Holding ~~Gain~~ on Security A Available for Sale (SE).....................................	5,000	
Marketable Securities (Security A)............		5,000

10/05/Year 2

Cash..	15,000	
Realized Loss on Sale of Securities Available for Sale (IncSt)................................	2,000	
Marketable Securities (Security D)............		17,000

12/31/Year 2

Marketable Securities (Security B) ($83,000 – $70,000)..	13,000	
Unrealized Holding ~~Loss~~ GAIN on Security B Available for Sale (SE).........................		13,000

12/31/Year 2

Unrealized Holding Loss on Security C Available for Sale (SE) ($27,000 – $32,000)..............	5,000	
Marketable Securities (Security C)............		5,000

12/31/Year 2

Marketable Securities (Security E) ($67,000 – $63,000)...	4,000	
Unrealized Holding Gain on Security E Available for Sale (SE).........................		4,000

Note: The three entries on December 31, Year 2 could be combined into a single entry.

7.37 continued.

b. **Balance Sheet on December 31, Year 1**

Marketable Securities at Market Value.......................... $ 115,000
Net Unrealized Holding Loss on Securities Available for
   Sale ($5,000 – $10,000) .... $ (5,000)

Footnote

Marketable Securities on December 31, Year 1 had an acquisition cost of $120,000 and a market value of $115,000. Gross unrealized gains total $5,000 and gross unrealized losses total $10,000.

c. **Balance Sheet on December 31, Year 2**

Marketable Securities at Market Value........................ $ 177,000
Net Unrealized Holding Gain on Securities Available for
   Sale .... $ 2,000

Footnote

Marketable Securities on December 31, Year 2 had an acquisition cost of $175,000 and a market value of $177,000. Gross unrealized gains total $7,000 (= $3,000 + $4,000) and gross unrealized losses total $5,000. Proceeds from sales of marketable securities totaled $67,000 during Year 2. These sales resulted in gross realized gains of $12,000 and gross realized losses of $2,000. The net unrealized holding loss on securities available for sale changed as follows during Year 2:

Balance, December 31, Year 1 .... $ (5,000) Dr.
Unrealized Gain on Securities Sold .... (5,000) Dr.
Change in Net Unrealized Loss on Securities Held at
   Year End ($13,000 – $5,000 + $4,000).................... 12,000 Cr.
Balance, December 31, Year 2 .... $ 2,000 Cr.

 Solutions

7.38   (Zeff Corporation; reconstructing transactions involving marketable securities.)

Cash			Marketable Securities		
√ 14,000			√ 187,000		
					10,000 (1)
			(2) 1,000		3,000 (1)
		20,000 (3)	(3) 20,000		
			√ 195,000		

Net Unrealized Holding Gain on Securities Available for Sale			Realized Gain on Sale of Securities Available for Sale	
		12,000 √		
(1) 3,000				4,000 (1)
		1,000 (2)		
		10,000 √		4,000 √

(1) Sale of marketable securities during Year 2.
(2) Revaluation of marketable securities on December 31, Year 2.
(3) Purchase of marketable securities during Year 2.

7.39   (Sunshine Mining Company; analysis of financial statement disclosures for marketable equity securities.) (Amounts in Thousands)

a. $10,267 loss = $11,418 – $21,685.

b. $2,649 gain = $8,807 – $6,158.

c. $12,459 gain = $21,685 – $6,158 – $3,068.

d.   None. The unrealized holding loss on current marketable securities of $2,466 (= $4,601 – $7,067) and the unrealized holding gain on noncurrent marketable securities of $2,649 (= $8,807 – $6,158) appear in the shareholders' equity section of the balance sheet.

7.40 (Sprouse Company; financial statement presentation of marketable equity securities.)

	December 31	
	Year 1	Year 2
Current Assets:		
Marketable Securities at Market Value.........	$ 925,000	$ 850,000
Noncurrent Assets:		
Investments in Securities at Market Value....	700,000	540,000
Shareholders' Equity:		
Net Unrealized Holding Gain (Loss) on Securities Available for Sale Held as A:		
Current Asset..................................	25,000	(50,000)
Noncurrent Asset............................	50,000	(110,000)

Note

Marketable securities held as a current asset had an acquisition cost of $900,000 and a market value of $925,000 on December 31, Year 1. Marketable securities held as a current asset had an acquisition cost of $900,000 and a market value of $850,000 on December 31, Year 2. Gross unrealized holding gains totaled $125,000 and gross unrealized holding losses totaled $100,000 on December 31, Year 1. Gross unrealized holding gains total $75,000 and gross unrealized holding losses total $125,000 on December 31, Year 2. Proceeds from the sale of marketable securities classified as a current asset totaled $190,000 during Year 2. These sales resulted in gross realized gains of $25,000 and gross realized losses of $35,000 during Year 2. The net unrealized holding gain (loss) on securities classified as a current asset changed as follows during Year 2:

Balance, December 31, Year 1	$ 25,000 Cr.
Net Unrealized Gain on Securities Sold ($205,000 – $200,000)..	(5,000) Dr.
Change in Net Unrealized Gain (Loss) on Securities Held at Year End (–$25,000 – $10,000 + $15,000 – $100,000 + $25,000 + $25,000)..	(70,000) Dr.
Balance, December 31, Year 2	$(50,000) Dr.

7.40 continued.

Note

Marketable securities held as a noncurrent asset had an acquisition cost of $650,000 and a market value of $700,000 on December 31, Year 1. Marketable securities held as a noncurrent asset had an acquisition cost of $650,000 and a market value of $540,000 on December 31, Year 2. Gross unrealized holding gains totaled $150,000 and gross unrealized holding losses totaled $100,000 on December 31, Year 1. Gross unrealized holding gains totaled $90,000 and gross unrealized holding losses totaled $200,000 on December 31, Year 2. The firm neither purchased nor sold marketable securities classified as a noncurrent asset during Year 2. The net unrealized holding gain (loss) changed as follows during Year 2:

Balance, December 31, Year 1	$ 50,000 Cr.
Change in Net Unrealized Gain (Loss) on Securities Held at Year End (–$60,000 – $100,000)....................	(160,000) Dr.
Balance, December 31, Year 2	$(110,000) Dr.

7.41   (Callahan Corporation; effect of various methods of accounting for marketable equity securities.)

a. **Trading Securities**

	Year 1	Year 2
Income Statement:		
Dividend Revenue......................................	$ 3,300	$ 2,200
Unrealized Holding Gain (Loss):		
($54,000 − $55,000)................................	(1,000)	--
($15,000 − $14,000)................................	--	1,000
Realized Holding Gain (Loss) ($14,500 + $26,000) − ($16,000 + $24,000).................	--	500
Total...	$ 2,300	$ 3,700
Balance Sheet:		
Current Assets:		
Marketable Securities at Market Value...	$ 54,000	$ 15,000

7.41 continued.

b. **Securities Available for Sale (Current Asset)**

	Year 1	Year 2
Income Statement:		
Dividend Revenue....................................	$ 3,300	$ 2,200
Realized Holding Gain (Loss): [$40,500 – ($18,000 + $25,000)]...............................	--	(2,500)
Total...	$ 3,300	$ (300)
Balance Sheet:		
Current Assets:		
Marketable Securities at Market Value...	$ 54,000	$ 15,000
Shareholders' Equity:		
Net Unrealized Holding Gain (Loss) on Securities Available for Sale:		
($54,000 – $55,000).............................	(1,000)	--
($15,000 – $12,000).............................	--	3,000

c. Same as Part *b*. except that the securities appear in the noncurrent assets section of the balance sheet.

d.

	Trading Securities	Securities Available for Sale	
		Current Assets	Noncurrent Assets
Year 1.........................	$2,300	$3,300	$3,300
Year 2.........................	3,700	(300)	(300)
Total	$6,000	$3,000	$3,000

The unrealized gain on Security I of $3,000 (= $15,000 – $12,000) at the end of Year 2 appears in income if these securities are trading securities but in a separate shareholders' equity account if these securities are securities available for sale (either a current asset or a noncurrent asset). Total shareholders' equity is the same. Retained earnings (pretax) are $3,000 larger if these securities are trading securities and the unrealized holding gain account is $3,000 larger if these securities are classified as securities available for sale.

7.42 (Whirlpool Corporation; analyzing changes in accounts receivable.)

a.

	Year 5	Year 6	Year 7
(1) Sales on Account			
Accounts Receivable..	4,008.7	4,179.0	4,314.5
Sales Revenue	4,008.7	4,179.0	4,314.5
(2) Provision for Estimated Uncollectible Accounts			
Bad Debt Expense......	6.0	17.7	11.5
Allowance for Uncollectible Accounts............	6.0	17.7	11.5
(3) Write Off of Actual Bad Debts			
Allowance for Uncollectible Accounts..	5.8[a]	17.0[b]	10.4[c]
Accounts Receivable..............	5.8	17.0	10.4

[a]$2.4 + $6.0 − $2.6 = $5.8.
[b]$2.6 + $17.7 − $3.3 = $17.0.
[c]$3.3 + $11.5 − $4.4 = $10.4.

	Year 5	Year 6	Year 7
(4) Collection of Cash from Customers			
Cash.....................	3,988.8[d]	4,098.8[e]	4,206.9[f]
Accounts Receivable.................	3,988.8	4,098.8	4,206.9

[d]$249.4 + $4,008.7 − $5.8 − $263.5 = $3,988.8.
[e]$263.5 + $4,179.0 − $17.0 − $326.7 = $4,098.8.
[f]$326.7 + $4,314.5 − $10.4 − $423.9 = $4,206.9.

b.

	Year 5	Year 6	Year 7

(1)

$$\frac{\text{Bad Debt Expense}}{\text{Sales on Account}} \qquad \frac{\$6.0}{\$4,008.7} = .15\% \qquad \frac{\$17.7}{\$4,179.0} = .42\% \qquad \frac{\$11.5}{\$4,314.5} = .27\%$$

(2)

$$\frac{\text{Allowance for Uncollectible Accounts}}{\text{Accounts Receivable Gross}} \qquad \frac{\$2.6}{\$263.5} = .99\% \qquad \frac{\$3.3}{\$326.7} = 1.01\% \qquad \frac{\$4.4}{\$423.9} = 1.04\%$$

7.42 continued.

c. It does not appear that Whirlpool Corporation uses the percentage-of-sales method to provide for estimated uncollectibles because the ratio of bad debt expense to sales on account varies significantly over the three-year period. The firm appears to maintain a relatively constant ratio of allowance for uncollectible accounts as a percentage of accounts receivable. This suggests that Whirlpool Corporation increases its provision in years when charge offs increase (such as Year 6) and vice versa.

7.43 (May Department Stores; analyzing changes in accounts receivable.)

a.

(Amounts in Millions)	Year 9	Year 10	Year 11	Year 12
Allowance for Uncollectable Accounts, Beginning of Year.......	$ 47	$ 61	$ 66	$ 84
Plus Bad Debt Expense...................	57	64	82	96
Less Accounts Written Off (Plug)....	(43)	(59)	(64)	(81)
Allowance for Uncollectable Accounts, End of Year...............	$ 61	$ 66	$ 84	$ 99

b.

	Year 9	Year 10	Year 11	Year 12
Accounts Receivable, Gross at Beginning of Year.....................	$1,592	$2,099	$2,223	$2,456
Plus Sales on Account[a].................	5,181	6,137	6,713	7,293
Less Accounts Written Off..............	(43)	(59)	(64)	(81)
Less Cash Collections from Credit Customers (Plug).....................	(4,631)	(5,954)	(6,416)	(7,061)
Accounts Receivable, Gross at End of Year...................................	$2,099	$2,223	$2,456	$2,607

[a]Total Sales X (Credit Sales ÷ Total Sales Percentage).

c.

Total Sales/Average Accounts Receivable, Net:	Year 9	Year 10	Year 11	Year 12
$8,330/.5($1,545 + $2,038)..........	4.65			
$9,456/.5($2,038 + $2,157)..........		4.51		
$10,035/.5($2,157 + $2,372).........			4.43	
$10,615/.5($2,372 + $2,508).........				4.35

d.

Credit Sales/Average Accounts Receivable, Net:	Year 9	Year 10	Year 11	Year 12
$5,181/.5($1,545 + $2,038)..........	2.89			
$6,137/.5($2,038 + $2,157)..........		2.93		
$6,713/.5($2,157 + $2,372)..........			2.96	
$7,293/.5($2,372 + $2,508)..........				2.99

 Solutions

7.43 continued.

　　e.　The accounts receivable turnover ratio based on total sales decreases because of the increasing proportion of credit sales in total sales. The increasing accounts receivable turnover ratio based on credit sales results from actions that cause customers to pay more quickly. Examples include increased finance charges on unpaid balances, reduced repayment period on credit sales, and more stringent controls on the granting of credit.

7.44　(Pins Company; reconstructing transactions affecting accounts receivable and uncollectible accounts.)

　　a.　$192,000 Dr. = $700,000 − $500,000 − $8,000.

　　b.　$6,000 Cr. = (.02 × $700,000) − $8,000.

　　c.　$19,000 = $10,000 + $9,000.

　　d.　$16,000 = $6,000 + $10,000.

　　e.　$676,000 = $192,000 + $800,000 − $16,000 − $300,000.

　　f.　$291,000 = $300,000 − $9,000.

7.45　(Nordstrom; decision to extend credit to a new class of customers.)

Gross Margin on New Sales:	**a.**	**b.**
a. .30 × $10,000;　b. .30 × $7,000	$3,000	$2,100
Less: Uncollectibles (.08 × $10,000).....................	(800)	(800)
Selling Expenses	(1,000)	(1,000)
Contribution to Profits	$1,200	$ 300

　　a.　Nordstrom will be $1,200 better off.

　　b.　Nordstrom will be $300 better off.

7.46　(Hanrahan Company; decision to extend credit: working backwards to uncollectible rate.)

Gross Margin on New Sales (.20 × $20,000)...........		$ 4,000
Less: Uncollectibles on Total Sales (.03 × $270,000)	$ 8,100	
Previous Amount of Uncollectibles (.02 × $250,000)	(5,000)	
Increase in Uncollectibles		(3,100)
Less Selling Expenses		(300)
Incremental Contribution to Profits...................		$ 600

Percentage Uncollectible: $3,100/$20,000 = 15.5 percent.

7.47 (Citibank; analysis of financial statement disclosures related to marketable securities.) (Amounts in Millions.)

a.

Cash..	37,600	
Realized Loss on Sale of Securities Available for Sale..	113	
Realized Gain on Securities Available for Sale..		443
Marketable Securities...........................		37,270[a]

    [a]$14,075 + $37,163 − $13,968 = $37,270.

Marketable Securities................................	262	
Unrealized Holding Loss on Securities Available for Sale ($37,270 − $37,008).........		262

b.

Balance, December 31, Year 10	$	447 Cr.
Net Unrealized Holding Loss on Securities Sold (from Part *a*.)..		262 Cr.
Increase in Net Unrealized Holding Gain on Securities Held on December 31, Year 11 (Plug)		518 Cr.
Balance, December 31, Year 11	$	1,227 Cr.

c.

Interest and Dividend Revenue	$	1,081
Net Realized Gain on Securities Sold from Market Price Changes Occurring During Year 11: ($37,600 − $37,008)...		592
Net Unrealized Holding Gain on Securities Held on December 31, Year 11 (from Part *b*.)		518
Total Income	$	2,191

d. Citibank sold marketable securities during Year 11 which had net unrealized holding losses of $262 million as of December 31, Year 10. The sale of these securities at a gain suggests that market prices increased substantially ($592 million) during Year 11. The substantial increase in the net unrealized holding gain of $518 lends support to this conclusion about market price increases. Citibank could have increased its income still further by selecting securities for sale that had unrealized holding *gains* as of December 31, Year 10. If prices continued to increase on such securities during Year 11 prior to sale, the realized gain would have been even larger than the reported realized gain of $330 million (= $443 − $113).

 Solutions

7.48 (Effect of errors involving marketable securities and accounts receivable on financial statement polices.)

		Rate of Return on Assets	CFO/ Average Current Liabilities	Debt Equity Ratio
a.	Unrealized Holding Loss on Securities Available for Sale (Shareholders Equity)...... Marketable securities......	X X	NO/O/S = U/S	NO/NO = NO	NO/O/S = U/S
b.	Bad Debt Expense...... Allowance for Uncollectible Accounts......	X X	O/S/O/S = O/S	NO/NO = NO	NO/O/S = U/S
c.	Allowance for Uncollectible Accounts...... Accounts Receivable......	X X	NO/NO = NO	NO/NO = NO	NO/NO = NO
d.	Advances from Customers...... Accounts Receivable......	X X	NO/O/S = U/S	NO/O/S = U/S	O/S/O/S = O/S
e.	Interest Receivable...... Interest Revenue......	X X	U/S/U/S = U/S	NO/NO = NO	NO/U/S = O/S

Note: This problem asks only for the net effect of each error on the three financial ratios. The journal entries and the numerator and denominator effects appear to show the reason for the net effect.

7.49   (Agee Electronics; preparing statement of cash flows.) A T-account worksheet appears on the page following the statement of cash flows.

AGEE ELECTRONICS
Statement of Cash Flows
For Year 5

Operations:

Net Income	$ 320
Depreciation Expense	350
Bad Debt Expense	45
Loss on Sale of Investments in Securities	40
Gain on Sale of Marketable Securities	(30)
Gain on Sale of Equipment	(40)
Decrease in Investments	50
Increase in Other Current Liabilities	110
Increase in Accounts Receivable	(235)
Increase in Prepayments	(50)
Decrease in Accounts Payable	(30)
Cash Flow from Operations	$ 530

Investing:

Sale of Marketable Securities	$ 145
Sale of Investments in Securities	70
Sale of Equipment	80
Acquisition of Marketable Securities	(125)
Acquisition of Property, Plant and Equipment	(480)
Cash Flow from Investing	$ (310)

Financing:

Income in Bank Borrowing	$ 60
Issue of Common Stock	60
Payment of Dividends	(285)
Cash Flow from Financing	$ (165)
Change in Cash	$ 55
Cash, December 31, Year 4	130
Cash, December 31, Year 5	$ 185

                         Solutions

7.49 continued.

Cash

√	130				

Operations

Net Income	(1)	320	30	(4)	Gain on Sale of Marketable Securities
Bad Debt Expense	(7)	45			
Loss on Investment in Securities	(8)	40	40	(11)	Gain on Sale of Equipment
Decrease in Inventories	(15)	50	235	(14)	Increase in Accounts Receivable
Depreciation	(19)	350			
Increase of Current Liabilities	(22)	110	50	(16)	Increase in Prepayments
			30	(20)	Decrease in Accounts Payable

Investing

Sale of Marketable Securities	(4)	145	125	(13)	Purchase or Marketable Securities
Sale of Investments	(8)	70			
Sale of Equipment	(11)	80	480	(18)	Purchase of PP&E

Financing

Bank Loan	(21)	60	285	(3)	Dividend Paid
Issue Common Stock	(23)	60			
√		185			

Marketable Securities				Accounts Receivable				Allowance for Uncollectible Accounts			
√	270			√	770					40	√
		115	(4)			35	(6)	(6)	35	45	(7)
(12)	15	5	(5)	(14)	235						
(13)	125										
√	290			√	970					50	√

7.49 continued.

Inventories			
√	620		
		50	(15)
√	570		

Prepayments			
√	120		
(16)	50		
√	170		

Investments in Securities			
√	460		
(9)	40	110	(8)
		10	(17)
√	380		

Property, Plant and Equipment			
√	2,840		
(10)	140	150	(11)
(18)	480		
√	3,310		

Accumulated Depreciation			
		1,210	√
(11)	110		
		350	(19)
		1,450	√

Accounts Payable			
		490	√
(20)	30		
		460	√

Bank Loans Payable			
		820	√
		60	(21)
		880	√

Dividends Payable			
		60	√
(3)	285	305	(2)
		80	√

Other Current Liabilities			
		90	√
		110	(22)
		200	√

Long-Term Debt			
		510	√
		140	(10)
		650	√

Common Stock			
		100	√
		50	(23)
		150	√

Additional Paid-In Capital			
		460	√
		10	(23)
		470	√

Unrealized Holding Gain—Marketable Securities			
		40	√
(5)	5		
		15	(12)
		50	√

Unrealized Holding Loss—Investment in Securities			
√	120		
		40	(9)
(17)	10		
√	90		

Retained Earnings			
		1,510	√
(2)	305	320	(1)
		1,525	√

Solutions

CHAPTER 8

INVENTORIES: THE SOURCE OF OPERATING PROFITS

Questions, Exercises, Problems, and Cases: Answers and Solutions

8.1　See the text or the glossary at the end of the book.

8.2　The underlying principle is that acquisition cost includes all costs required to prepare an asset for its intended use. Assets provide future services. Costs that a firm must incur to obtain those expected services add value to the asset. Accountants therefore include such costs in the acquisition cost valuation of the asset.

8.3　The accountant allocates the total income (cash inflow minus cash outflow) over the periods between purchase and sale. The inventory valuation method dictates this allocation. The acquisition cost valuation method allocates all of the income to the period of sale. A current cost valuation method allocates holding gains and losses to the periods when a firm holds inventory and an operating margin (sales minus replacement cost of goods sold) to the period of sale. A lower-of-cost-or-market valuation allocates holding losses to the periods when a firm holds inventory and holding gains plus operating margins to the period of sale.

8.4　Income increases in the year of change because of the recognition of the unrealized holding gains. Cost of goods sold in the next year will increase by the same amount, so that income in the second year will be less by the same amount as it was greater in the year of change. Over long enough time spans, accounting income equals cash inflows minus cash outflows; the valuation method affects the timing of income recognition, not its amount.

8.5　a.　A periodic inventory system assumes that the difference between (1) units in beginning inventory plus units purchased during the period and (2) units in the ending inventory count were either sold or lost to shrinkage. The periodic inventory system cannot identify the portion sold versus the portion lost to shrinkage.

8.5 continued.

b. A perpetual inventory system maintains records to indicate the number of units that should be in ending inventory. Firms using a perpetual system must take a physical count, as in a periodic system, to verify that the expected number is actually on hand. Any difference between expected and actual amounts represents a loss from shrinkage.

c. Perpetual inventory systems are cost effective when a firm has a small number of large-value items because accounting can easily trace and record individual inventory purchases and sales. When a firm has a large number of small-value items, such individual tracing of inventory flows is costly; periodic inventory systems are usually more cost effective in this case.

d. Customer goodwill and loyalty are more critical for some businesses than others. Customers who find a firm "out of stock" of a needed item may never return to give the firm another chance. For such businesses, being out-of-stock is costly. The firm's inventory system should provide the necessary information to ensure adequate levels of inventory at all times. Perpetual inventory systems provide such information. The cost of an "out of stock" condition is less costly for other firms, so that the extra cost of a perpetual system may exceed the expected benefits.

8.6   **Periodic**:   *a., e., f.* (but this is changing), *g., i.* You can tell the story of the salad oil scandal, see below, in *e.* if you choose. With product bar codes and automatic scanners, use of perpetual methods increases.

    Perpetual: *b., c., d., h.* If, however, the automated production line need not close down in case of stockouts (an unusual case), then periodic for Part *c*.

The salad oil scandal was recounted by Earl K. Littrell in *Management Accounting*, July 1980, page 61, and August 1980, page 63, as follows:

Those unfamiliar with field warehousing can quickly grasp the basic ideas involved. A company surrenders control of its inventory storage facility to an independent warehousing company. Based on its count, the warehousing company issues receipts representing the quantity of goods in storage at that facility. By carefully checking inventory movement and by frequent audits, the warehousing company keeps the receipts in line with the goods on hand. Meanwhile, since the receipt may be pledged as collateral or sold, it passes through many hands and eventually is sold to a company wishing to take possession of the goods. The holder presents the receipt at the warehouse and hauls away the goods.

8.6 continued.

Creating Oil from Air

In the late 1950s, Allied Crude Vegetable Oil Refining Corp. had vegetable oil stored in its tanks. It entered into field warehousing agreements with several warehousing companies. By late 1963, warehouse receipts for almost two billion pounds of vegetable oil were outstanding, even though the tanks contained only 130 million pounds of vegetable oil. The nonexistent 1.8 billion pounds of oil were worth about $175 million, thus making this case the first nine-figure swindle in decades.

The various warehousing companies kept pads of their blank warehouse receipts on Allied's premises in an unlocked cabinet in the office of an Allied employee. It was simple to steal and forge these blank warehouse receipts. By November 1963, about $40 million in forged warehouse receipts were outstanding.

Most of the other 1.4 billion pound overstatement involved deceiving auditors about just how much oil was actually in the tanks. Tank contents were customarily measured by climbing the 42-foot tank and measuring the distance between the tank top and the liquid surface with a tape measure. If the tape read 15 feet, that meant there were 27 vertical feet of liquid in the tank. It was customary for an employee to operate the tape and call out the tape measure to a warehouse company employee. It was also customary for employees to short the measure by 10 to 20 feet, creating between a fourth to a half tank of oil out of air, and apparently this went undiscovered by the auditors prior to November 1963.

One device for overstating quantity of oil on hand was simply to add water to the tanks. The oil floated on top of the water, and an observer looking through the observation port at the top of the tank would see oil. The fact that there might only be two feet of oil on top of 35 feet of water could not be discerned readily. Curiously, as early as 1959, the warehousing companies had strong evidence from an anonymous informer and from the U.S. Department of Agriculture that the tanks contained an unusually large amount of water. Inexplicably, the warehousing companies did not follow through on this information.

One of the more ingenious devices employed by Allied Crude Vegetable Oil Refining Corp. was to weld a vertical pipe a few feet in diameter directly underneath the observation port in a tank. This pipe then could be filled with oil or with water with oil floated on top, and an observer could have no idea that the rest of the tank was actually empty. This device is in the same class as the nail manufacturing company that nailed empty nail barrels to the floor of its warehouse. For several years, auditors recorded the barrels as full since they were unable to lift them.

         Solutions

8.6 continued.

Allied's tank farm had a capacity that was much less than two billion pounds of oil, and it was only natural that some nonexistent tanks were on Allied's books. This meant that the tank numbers on the tanks were repainted often, depending on just which tanks the auditors wished to see. In addition to these phantom tanks, Allied was counting at least seven tanks that were in unusable condition and at least 24 tanks leased to petroleum companies that had contained gasoline throughout the period Allied was in business.

These devices apparently were sufficient to take care of the weekly audit performed by the warehousing company. Occasionally, a more thorough audit would be done by an independent accounting firm or some other independent agency. Since these outside audits were done at a more leisurely pace, usually taking at least two weeks, they permitted an additional inventory trick. That is, the auditors apparently failed to station anyone to observe the pumps, and Allied was able to keep pumping the oil from tank to tank, just ahead of the auditors.

While there were some other fraudulent activities involved, such as a blatant check-kiting scheme for some $3 million, this caper basically was an inventory fraud of the first magnitude. Considering the financial losses and other fallout from the salad oil swindle, this incident served as a very expensive lesson in inventory accounting and auditing.

8.7 Accounting reports cost flows, not flows of physical quantities. Cost flow assumptions trace costs, not physical flows of goods. With specific identification, management manipulates cost flows by controlling goods flows.

8.8 Rising Purchase Prices:
Higher Inventory Amount: FIFO
Lower Inventory Amount: LIFO

Falling Purchase Prices:
Higher Inventory Amount: LIFO; LIFO results in a constant inventory amount so long as quantities do not change.
Lower Inventory Amount: FIFO; FIFO results in an even lower inventory than does the weighted-average assumption.

8.9 a. Higher cost of goods sold amount: LIFO
Lower cost of goods sold amount: FIFO

b. Higher cost of goods sold amount: FIFO
Lower cost of goods sold amount: LIFO

8.10   LIFO provides cost of goods sold closer to current costs than does FIFO so long as inventory quantities do not decrease and a firm does not liquidate old LIFO layers. Some would say, then, that LIFO does provide more meaningful income data when quantities do not decrease. The LIFO balance sheet always reflects older costs than does the FIFO balance sheet.

8.11   a.   FIFO typically uses older acquisition costs for cost of goods sold than LIFO (except during a period of dipping into a LIFO layer), whereas LIFO uses older acquisition costs for ending inventory than FIFO. The larger the rate of change in the acquisition cost of inventory items, the more the older costs will differ from current costs and the larger will be the difference in cost of goods sold and ending inventory values between FIFO and LIFO.

        b.   As the rate of inventory turnover increases, purchases during a period comprise an increasing proportion of cost of goods sold for that period under both FIFO and LIFO and differences in the beginning or ending inventory values under FIFO and LIFO play a decreasing role. Because purchases are the same regardless of the cost flow assumption, cost of goods sold under FIFO and LIFO should not differ significantly (unless the firm experienced dips into old LIFO layers).

        c.   The inventory turnover ratio relates cost of goods sold to average inventories. A faster inventory turnover means a smaller level of inventories in the denominator relative to cost of goods sold in the numerator. The difference between FIFO and LIFO amounts in the denominator depends on the age of a firm's LIFO layers and the rate of change in the cost of inventory items since the firm adapted LIFO. These latter items relate to the passage of time rather than to the rate of turnover within a period of time.

8.12   The steel company, as long as equal rates of price increase occur for both firms' purchases. (If prices decline or increase at differing rates, then a different answer could result.) The larger the inventory turnover, the smaller the ratio of ending inventory to cost of goods sold. The smaller the percentage variation in ending inventory, the smaller the percentage variation in cost of goods sold, because the sum of the two must equal the cost of goods available (= beginning inventory + purchases). Because the retailer has the larger inventory turnover, it will have the smaller percentage variation in cost of goods sold by switching.

8.13   Dipping into an old LIFO layer may not be within a firm's control, such as when shortages prevent the firm from replacing a particular raw material. A dip may be partially within a firm's control, such as when a labor strike by employees forces the firm to reduce its finished goods inventory. A dip may be fully within a firm's control, such as when it delays purchases toward the end of the period in an effort to decrease cost of goods sold and increase net income.

8.14   Firms that maintain a relatively constant relation between the replacement cost of inventory items and selling prices will show a constant operating margin percentage (that is, operating margin/sales) each period. The operating margin will be the same under FIFO and LIFO. Both firms also include a realized holding gain or loss in their gross margins. The realized holding gain or loss reflects the change in the replacement cost of inventory items between the time of acquisition and the time of sale. The assumed holding period for FIFO is longer than for LIFO. Thus, FIFO likely includes more price changes (both increases and decreases) in the realized holding gain or loss than LIFO. If prices change at a constant rate and in a constant direction, then both FIFO and LIFO produce a smooth gross margin trend over time. If either the rate or direction of price change varies over time, FIFO more fully reflects these variations in the gross margin than LIFO.

8.15   Assuming a period of rising purchase prices, the firm might prefer to report higher earnings to shareholders and give up the tax savings that LIFO provides. Management's compensation often uses reported earnings as a base in its computation. Management obtains higher compensation by reporting higher earnings under FIFO. The firm might be experiencing operating difficulties and need to report higher earnings to keep shareholders happy. We question the rationality of such thinking but don't doubt that such reasoning occurs.

The firm might be experiencing decreasing prices (costs) for its inventory items and obtain the maximum tax benefits by using FIFO. Note, however, that the Internal Revenue Code does not preclude a firm from using FIFO for tax purposes and LIFO for financial reporting. This combination minimizes taxes but maximizes earning reported to shareholders.

If prices are not changing much or if inventory turns over rapidly, then FIFO and LIFO do not differ significantly in terms of their effects on earnings or balance sheet amounts. The record keeping costs and fears of dipping into very old LIFO layers might lead a firm to use FIFO under these circumstances.

8.16   The firm saved taxes in earlier years when it created its LIFO layers and must pay the taxes in the year that it dips. It has at least delayed paying the taxes relative to FIFO, even if it must pay the same amount of taxes over time under both cost flow assumptions. Thus, the present value of the taxes saved under LIFO exceeds the present value under FIFO.

8.17   (Trembly Department Store; identifying inventory cost inclusions.)

Purchase Price	$ 300,000
Freight Cost	13,600
Salary of Purchasing Manager	3,200
Depreciation, taxes, Insurance and Utilities on Warehouse	27,300
Salary of Warehouse Manager	2,600
Merchandise Returns	(18,900)
Cash Discounts Taken	(4,900)
Acquisition Cost	$ 322,900

The underlying principle is that inventories should include all costs required to get the inventory ready for sale. The purchase of the inventory items (items a., c., f., and g.) provides the physical goods to be sold, the freight cost (item b.) puts the inventory items in the place most convenient for sale, and the storage costs (items d. and e.) keep the inventory items until the time of sale. Economists characterize these costs as providing form, place, and time utility, or benefits. Although accounting theory suggests the inclusion of each of these items in the valuation of inventory, some firms might exclude items c., d., e., and g. on the basis of lack of materiality.

8.18   (Colt Real Estate Development Corporation; effect of inventory valuation basis on net income.)

a.

	Parcel A	Parcel B
(1) Acquisition Cost		
Year 6:	--	--
Year 7: ($24,600 – $10,000)	$ 14,600	--
Year 8: ($19,700 – $10,000)	--	$ 9,700
Total	$ 14,600	$ 9,700
(2) Current Cost		
Year 6: ($16,700 – $10,000);		
($8,500 – $10,000)	$ 6,700	$ (1,500)
Year 7: ($24,600 – $16,700);		
($14,400 – $8,500)	7,900	5,900
Year 8: ($19,700 – $14,400)	--	5,300
Total	$ 14,600	$ 9,700
(3) Lower of Cost or Market		
Year 6: ($8,500 – $10,000)	--	$ (1,500)
Year 7: ($24,600 – $10,000)	$ 14,600	--
Year 8: ($19,700 – $18,500)	--	$ 11,200
Total	$ 14,600	$ 9,700

       Solutions

8.18 continued.

b. The three inventory valuation methods report the same total income for the three years combined, equal to cash inflows minus cash outflows for each parcel. The acquisition cost basis allocates all of the income to the year of sale. The current cost basis allocates a portion of the income to each period while the firm holds the land. The lower-of-cost-or-market method allocates holding gains to the period of sale but unrealized holding losses to the period when inventory values decline.

 8.19 (Duggan Company; over sufficiently long spans, income is cash in less cash out; cost basis for inventory.)

a. **Lower of Cost or Market:**

	Year 1	Year 2	Year 3
Sales.................................	$ 200,000	$ 300,000	$ 400,000
Inventories, January 1	--	$ 50,000	$ 75,000
Purchases.........................	$ 210,000	271,000	352,000
Goods Available for Sale......	$ 210,000	$ 321,000	$ 427,000
Less Inventories, December 31.....................................	(50,000)	(75,000)	(115,000)
Cost of Goods Sold	$ 160,000	$ 246,000	$ 312,000
Gross Profit on Sales	$ 40,000 ✓	$ 54,000 ✓	$ 88,000 ✓

b. **Acquisition Cost:**

	Year 1	Year 2	Year 3
Sales.................................	$ 200,000	$ 300,000	$ 400,000
Inventory, January 1..........	--	$ 60,000	$ 80,000
Purchases.........................	$ 210,000	271,000	352,000
Gain Available from Sale....	$ 210,000	$ 331,000	$ 432,000
Less Inventory, December 31.....................................	(60,000)	(80,000)	(115,000)
Cost of Goods Sold	$ 150,000	$ 251,000	$ 317,000
Gross Profit on Sales	$ 50,000 ✓	$ 49,000 ✓	$ 83,000 ✓

c. The lower-of-cost-or-market basis recognizes lower income in years when prices are falling. However, when that trend is reversed, it produces higher reported income figures than the cost basis. Over long enough time periods, income is constant, equal to cash inflows minus cash outflows. Compare the total gross profit over all three years, a constant $182,000.

8.20 (Cypres; When goods available for sale exceed sales, firms can manipulate income even when they use specific identification.)

	Revenue	– Cost of Goods Sold =	Gross Margin
a. FIFO Cost Flow:	200 × $700 = $140,000	100 × $300 + 100 × $400 = $70,000	$70,000
b. Minimum Income:	200 × $700 = $140,000	100 × $400 + 100 × $350 = $75,000	$65,000
c. Maximum Income:	200 × $700 = $140,000	100 × $300 + 100 × $350 = $65,000	$75,000

8.21 (Harris Company; computations involving different cost flow assumptions.)

	Pounds	a. FIFO	b. Weighted Average	c. LIFO
Goods Available for Sale.........	13,500	$65,925	$65,925	$ 65,925
Less Ending Inventory...........	(2,500)	(13,075)[a]	(12,708)[c]	(11,350)[e]
Goods Sold...........................	11,000	$52,850[b]	$53,717[d]	$ 54,575[f]

[a](2,000 × $5.25) + (500 × $5.15) = $13,075.
[b](1,500 × $4.50) + (4,000 × $4.60) + (2,500 × $4.90) + (3,000 × $5.15) = $52,850.
[c]($65,925/13,500) × 2,500 = $12,208.
[d]($65,925/13,500) × 11,000 = $53,717.
[e](1,500 × $4.50) + (1,000 × $4.60) = $11,350.
[f](2,000 × $5.25) + (3,500 × $5.15) + (2,500 × $4.90) + (3,000 × $4.60) = $54,575.

8.22 (Moon Company; computations involving different cost flow assumptions.)

	Pounds	a. FIFO	b. Weighted Average	c. LIFO
Goods Available for Sale.........	41,000	$128,700	$128,700	$128,700
Less Ending Inventory...........	(12,500)	(37,830)[a]	(39,238)[c]	(40,430)[e]
Goods Sold...........................	28,500	$ 90,870[b]	$ 89,462[d]	$ 88,270[f]

[a](9,200 × $3.00) + (3,300 × $3.10) = $37,830.
[b](8,600 × $3.25) + (12,300 × $3.20) + (7,600 × $3.10) = $90,870.
[c]$128,700/41,000 = $3.139; 12,500 × $3.139 = $39,238.
[d]28,500 × $3.139 = $89,462.
[e](8,600 × $3.25) + (3,900 × $3.20) = $40,430.
[f](9,200 × $3.00) + (10,900 × $3.10) + (8,400 × $3.20) = $88,270.

Solutions

8.23 (Benton Company; over sufficiently long time spans, income equals cash inflows minus cash outflows; cost flow assumptions.)

a. FIFO

Year	Revenue			–	Cost of Goods Sold		=	Income
1	7,000 × $25 =	$	175,000		7,000 × $20 =	$ 140,000		$ 35,000
2	10,000 × $28 =		280,000		8,000 × $20 =	$ 160,000		
					2,000 × $22 =	44,000		
						$ 204,000		76,000
3	12,000 × $30 =		360,000		10,000 × $22 =	$ 220,000		
					2,000 × $24 =	48,000		
						$ 268,000		92,000
4	15,000 × $32 =		480,000		8,000 × $24 =	$ 192,000		
					7,000 × $26 =	182,000		
						$ 374,000		106,000
Totals...............			$1,295,000			$ 986,000		$ 309,000

b. LIFO

Year	Revenue			–	Cost of Goods Sold		=	Income
1	7,000 × $25 =	$	175,000		7,000 × $20 =	$ 140,000		$ 35,000
2	10,000 × $28 =		280,000		10,000 × $22 =	$ 220,000		60,000
3	12,000 × $30 =		360,000		10,000 × $24 =	$ 240,000		
					2,000 × $22 =	44,000		
						$ 284,000		76,000
4	15,000 × 32 =		480,000		7,000 × $26 =	$ 182,000		
					8,000 × $20 =	160,000		
						$ 342,000		138,000
Totals...............			$1,295,000			$ 986,000		$ 309,000

c. Over the four-year period, income is the same—cash inflows minus cash outflows—independent of the cost flow assumption. The cost flow assumption affects the timing of income recognition and this may well matter: it affects the timing of income tax payments, potential management bonuses, and potential violation of covenants in borrowing instruments and other contracts with outsiders, including labor contracts.

8.24 (Barnard Corporation; effect of LIFO on financial statements over several periods.)

a.

Year	Ending Inventory	
3	2,000 × $4,00	$ 8,000
4	(2,000 × $4.00) + (2,800 × $4.40)...............	$20,320
5	(2,000 × $4.00) + (2,800 × $4.40) + (1,200 × $4.75).................................	$26,020
6	(2,000 × $4.00) + (1,800 × $4.40)	$15,920
7	(2,000 × $4.00) + (1,800 × $4.40) + (1,700 × $5.85).................................	$25,865

b.

Year	Revenue		–	Cost of Goods Sold		=	Income
3	6,000 × $5.00 =	$ 30,000		6,000 × $4.00 =	$ 24,000		$ 6,000
4	8,200 × 5.50 =	45,100		8,200 × $4.40 =	$ 36,080		9,020
5	10,800 × 5.94 =	64,152		10,800 × $4.75 =	$ 51,300		12,852
6	17,200 × 6.65 =	114,380		15,000 × $5.32 =	$ 79,800		
				1,200 × $4.75 =	5,700		
				1,000 × $4.40 =	4,400		
					$ 89,900		24,480
	18,300 × $7.32 =	133,956		18,300 × $5.85 =	$107,055		26,901
Totals.................		$387,588			$308,335		$ 79,253

c.

Year	Income	Sales	Rate of income To Sales
3	$ 6,000	$ 30,000	20.0%
4	9,020	45,100	20.0%
5	12,852	64,152	20.0%
6	24,480	114,380	21.4%
7	26,901	133,956	20.0%

d. Barnard Corporation attempts to maintain a constant relation between replacement costs and selling prices. This relation held for each year. The income to sales percentage increased during Year 6, however, because the firm dipped into LIFO layers of earlier years. The firm matched selling prices during Year 6 with acquisition costs of Year 5 and Year 4, inflating the income to sales percentage.

8-11

8.25   (Chan Company; reconstructing financial statement data from information on effects of liquidations of LIFO layers.)

a. Cost of goods sold was $750,000 lower than it would have been had the firm maintained inventories at 200,000 units. The average cost of the 50,000 units removed from the beginning inventory was $15 (= $750,000/50,000 units) less than current cost: $26 − $15 = $11.

b. $11 × 50,000 units = $550,000 decline in inventory during the year. Beginning inventory must have been $550,000 + $600,000 (ending inventory) = $1,150,000.

8.26   (EKG Company; LIFO provides opportunity for income manipulation.)

a. Largest cost of goods sold results from producing 70,000 (or more) additional units at a cost of $20 each, giving cost of goods sold of $1,400,000.

b. Smallest cost of goods sold results from producing no additional units, giving cost of goods sold of $980,000 [= ($8 × 10,000) + ($15 × 60,000)].

c.

	Income Reported	
	Minimum	**Maximum**
Revenues ($30 × 70,000)	$2,100,000	$2,100,000
Less Cost of Goods Sold	(1,400,000)	(980,000)
Gross Margin	$ 700,000	$1,120,000

8.27   (Sears; analysis of annual report; usage of LIFO.)

a. Reported pretax income would have been higher by $230 million (= $670 million − $440 million).

b. After taxes, net income would increase $230 million × .66 = $151.8 million. $151.8/$606.0 = .25; so net income would be 25 percent larger than shown, or $757.8 million.

8.28   (Boise Cascade; identifying quantity and price changes.)

a. Inventory quantities increased during Year 10 because ending inventory for Year 10 exceeded ending inventory for Year 9. Thus, Boise Cascade added a new LIFO layer. Replacement cost decreased during Year 10 because the excess of current cost over LIFO cost decreased during the year, despite an increase in quantities.

b. Inventory quantities decreased during Year 11 because ending inventory for Year 11 is less than ending inventory for Year 10. Thus, Boise Cascade dipped into its Year 10 LIFO layer. Replacement cost increased during Year 11 because the excess of current cost over LIFO cost increased during the year, despite a decrease in quantities.

8.29 (Giles Computer Store; separating operating margin from holding gains.)

	FIFO	LIFO
a.		
Beginning Inventory (200 × $300)	$ 60,000	$ 60,000
Purchases (2,500 × $400)	1,000,000	1,000,000
Goods Available for Sale	$ 1,060,000	$ 1,060,000
Less Ending Inventory:		
(400 × $400)	(160,000)	
(200 × $300) + (200 × $400)		(140,000)
Cost of Goods Sold	$ 900,000	$ 920,000
b.		
Revenues (2,300 × $750)	$ 1,725,000	$ 1,725,000
Less Cost of Goods Sold	(900,000)	(920,000)
Gross Margin on Sales	$ 825,000	$ 805,000
c.		
Revenues	$ 1,725,000	$ 1,725,000
Less Replacement Cost of Goods Sold (2,300 × $400)	(920,000)	(920,000)
Operating Margin	$ 805,000	$ 805,000
Realized Holding Gains:		
Replacement Cost of Goods Sold	$ 920,000	$ 920,000
Less Historical Cost of Goods Sold	(900,000)	(920,000)
Realized Holding Gain	20,000	-0-
Gross Margin on Sales	$ 825,000	$ 805,000
d.		
Unrealized Holding Gains:		
Replacement Cost of Ending Inventory (400 × $500)	$ 200,000	$ 200,000
Less Historical Cost of Ending Inventory:		
(400 × $400)	(160,000)	
(200 × $300) + (200 × $400)		(140,000)
Unrealized Holding Gains	40,000	60,000
Total Realized Gross Margin and Unrealized Holding Gains	$ 865,000	$ 865,000

8.29 continued.

    e. The equality is not a coincidence. The choice of cost flow assumption does not affect the increase in wealth during a period. The choice affects only the amount of reported income. When unrealized gains are added to reported, realized gains, income is independent of the cost flow assumption for inventory.

8.30   (Warren Company; effect of inventory errors.)

a. None.	f. Understatement by $1,000.
b. None.	g. Understatement by $1,000.
c. Understatement by $1,000.	h. None.
d. Overstatement by $1,000.	i. None.
e. Overstatement by $1,000.	

8.31   (Hartison Corporation; detailed comparison of various choices for inventory accounting.)

	FIFO	LIFO	Weighted Average
Inventory, 1/1/Year 1	$ 0	$ 0	$ 0
Purchases for Year 1	25,600	25,600	25,600
Goods Available for Sale During Year 1	$ 25,600	$ 25,600	$ 25,600
Less Inventory, 12/31/Year 1	(6,400)[1]	(5,000)[2]	(5,565)[3]
Cost of Goods Sold for Year 1	$ 19,200	$ 20,600	$ 20,035
Inventory, 1/1/Year 2	$ 6,400 [1]	$ 5,000 [2]	$ 5,565 [3]
Purchases for Year 2	42,600	42,600	42,600
Goods Available for Sale During Year 2	$ 49,000	$ 47,600	$ 48,165
Less Inventory, 12/31/Year 2	(5,400)[4]	(3,000)[5]	(4,661)[6]
Cost of Goods Sold for Year 2	$ 43,600	$ 44,600	$ 43,504

[1] $(400 \times \$13) + (100 \times \$12) = \$6,400$.
[2] $500 \times \$10 = \$5,000$.
[3] $(\$25,600/2,300) \times 500 = \$5,565$.
[4] $300 \times \$18 = \$5,400$.
[5] $300 \times \$10 = \$3,000$.
[6] $(\$48,165/3,100) \times 300 = \$4,661$.

a.	$19,200.	d.	$43,600.
b.	$20,600.	e.	$44,600.
c.	$20,035.	f.	$43,504.

g.

	Cost of Goods Sold for Two Years
FIFO	$62,800
LIFO	65,200

8.31 g. continued.

The FIFO cost flow assumption results in reported pretax income which is higher by $2,400 (= $65,200 − $62,800) over the two-year period. After taxes, the difference is reduced to .60 × $2,400 = $1,440.

h. Management might prefer to report the higher net income from FIFO of $1,440. To do so, however, requires $960 (= .40 × $2,400) of extra income tax payments currently that could be postponed until Hartison Corporation dips further into its January Year 1 purchases. We think management should use LIFO for tax purposes and, because financial reports must conform to tax reporting, in this case the firm should use LIFO for financial reporting.

8.32   (Hartison Corporation; continuation of preceding problem introducing current cost concepts.)

a.

	FIFO	LIFO	Weighted Average
Sales (1,800 × $18)	$ 32,400	$ 32,400	$ 32,400
Less Cost of Goods Sold at Average Current Replacement Cost (1,800 × $12)	(21,600)	(21,600)	(21,600)
Operating Margin..............	$ 10,800	$ 10,800	$ 10,800
Realized Holding Gain:			
Cost of Goods Sold at Current Replacement Cost.	$ 21,600	$ 21,600	$ 21,600
Less Cost of Goods Sold at Acquisition Cost..........	(19,200)	(20,600)	(20,035)
Total Realized Holding Gain...............	$ 2,400	$ 1,000	$ 1,565
Conventional Gross Margin................................	$ 13,200	$ 11,800	$ 12,365
Unrealized Holding Gain:			
Ending Inventory at Current Replacement Cost (500 × $14)	$ 7,000	$ 7,000	$ 7,000
Less Ending Inventory at Acquisition Cost..........	(6,400)	(5,000)	(5,565)
Total Unrealized Holding Gain	$ 600	$ 2,000	$ 1,435
Less Unrealized Holding Gain at Beginning of Period.........................	--	--	--
Total Profit Including Holding Gain[a]	$ 13,800	$ 13,800	$ 13,800

[a]Total of operating margin, realized holding gain, and unrealized holding gain.

         Solutions

8.32 continued.

b.

	FIFO	LIFO	Weighted Average
Sales (2,800 × $24)	$ 67,200	$ 67,200	$ 67,200
Less Cost of Goods Sold at Average Current Replacement Cost (2,800 × $16)	(44,800)	(44,800)	(44,800)
Operating Margin..............	$ 22,400	$ 22,400	$ 22,400
Realized Holding Gain:			
Cost of Goods Sold at Current Replacement Cost.	$ 44,800	$ 44,800	$ 44,800
Less Cost of Goods Sold at Acquisition Cost..........	(43,600)	(44,600)	(43,504)
Total Realized Holding Gain	$ 1,200	$ 200	$ 1,296
Conventional Gross Margin	$ 23,600	$ 22,600	$ 23,696
Unrealized Holding Gain:			
Ending Inventory at Current Replacement Cost (300 × $18)	$ 5,400	$ 5,400	$ 5,400
Less Ending Inventory at Acquisition Cost..........	(5,400)	(3,000)	(4,661)
Total Unrealized Holding Gain	$ 0	$ 2,400	$ 739
Less Unrealized Holding Gain at Beginning of Period (see Part *a*.)..........	(600)	(2,000)	$ (1,435)
Increase (Decrease) in Unrealized Holding Gain during Year 2.................	$ (600)	$ 400	$ (696)
Total Profit Including Holding Gain........................	$ 23,000	$ 23,000	$ 23,000

c.		FIFO	LIFO	Weighted Average
	Operating Margin—Year 1..	$ 10,800	$ 10,800	$ 10,800
	—Year 2..	22,400	22,400	22,400
	Realized Holding Gain—			
	Year 1	2,400	1,000	1,565
	Year 2	1,200	200	1,296
	Unrealized Holding Gain at the End of Year 2	0	2,400	739
	Total Profit Including Holding Gain...........	$ 36,800	$ 36,800	$ 36,800

8.33 (Burton Corporation; detailed comparison of various choices for inventory accounting.)

	FIFO	LIFO	Weighted Average
Inventory, 1/1/Year 1.................	$ 0	$ 0	$ 0
Purchases for Year 1.................	14,400	14,400	14,400
Goods Available for Sale During Year 1..............................	$ 14,400	$ 14,400	$ 14,400
Less Inventory, 12/31/Year 1	(3,000)[1]	(2,000)[2]	(2,400)[3]
Cost of Goods Sold for Year 1.....	$ 11,400	$ 12,400	$ 12,000
Inventory, 1/1/Year 2.................	$ 3,000 [1]	$ 2,000 [2]	$ 2,400 [3]
Purchases for Year 2.................	21,000	21,000	21,000
Goods Available for Sale During Year 2..............................	$ 24,000	$ 23,000	$ 23,400
Less Inventory, 12/31/Year 2	(5,000)[4]	(6,200)[5]	(5,850)[6]
Cost of Goods Sold for Year 2.....	$ 19,000	$ 16,800	$ 17,550

[1] $200 \times \$15 = \$3,000$.
[2] $200 \times \$10 = \$2,000$.
[3] $(\$14,400/1,200) \times 200 = \$2,400$.
[4] $500 \times \$10 = \$5,000$.
[5] $(200 \times \$10) + (300 \times \$14) = \$6,200$.
[6] $(\$23,400/2,000) \times 500 = \$5,850$.

a. $11,400.
b. $12,400.
c. $12,000.

d. $19,000.
e. $16,800.
f. $17,550.

g. FIFO results in higher net income for Year 1. Purchase prices for inventory items increased during Year 1. FIFO uses older, lower purchase prices to measure cost of goods sold, whereas LIFO uses more recent, higher prices.

h. LIFO results in higher net income for Year 2. Purchase prices for inventory items decreased during Year 2. LIFO uses more recent, lower prices to measure cost of goods sold, whereas FIFO uses older, higher prices.

8.34 (Burton Corporation; continuation of preceding problem introducing current cost concepts.)

a.

	FIFO	LIFO	Weighted Average
Sales (1,000 × $25)	$ 25,000	$ 22,500	$ 25,000
Less Cost of Goods Sold at Average Current Replacement Cost (1,000 × $14)	(14,000)	(14,000)	(14,000)
Operating Margin..............	$ 9,000	$ 9,000	$ 9,000
Realized Holding Gain:			
Cost of Goods Sold at Current Replacement Cost.	$ 14,000	$ 14,000	$ 14,000
Less Cost of Goods Sold at Acquisition Cost..........	(11,400)	(12,400)	(12,000)
Total Realized Holding Gain..............	$ 2,600	$ 1,600	$ 2,000
Conventional Gross Margin................................	$ 11,600	$ 10,600	$ 11,000
Unrealized Holding Gain:			
Ending Inventory at Current Replacement Cost (200 × $16)	$ 3,200	$ 3,200	$ 3,200
Less Ending Inventory at Acquisition Cost..........	(3,000)	(2,000)	(2,400)
Total Unrealized Holding Gain	$ 200	$ 1,200	$ 800
Total Profit Including Holding Gain[a]	$ 11,800	$ 11,800	$ 11,800

[a]Total of operating margin, realized holding gain, and unrealized holding gain.

8.34 continued.

b.

	FIFO	LIFO	Weighted Average
Sales (1,500 × $22)	$ 33,000	$ 33,000	$ 33,000
Less Cost of Goods Sold at Average Current Replacement Cost (1,500 × $12)	(18,000)	(18,000)	(18,000)
Operating Margin..............	$ 15,000	$ 15,000	$ 15,000
Realized Holding Gain:			
Cost of Goods Sold at Current Replacement Cost.	$ 18,000	$ 18,000	$ 18,000
Less Cost of Goods Sold at Acquisition Cost..........	(19,000)	(16,800)	(17,550)
Total Realized Holding Gain (Loss).....	$ (1,000)	$ 1,200	$ 450
Conventional Gross Margin.................................	$ 14,000	$ 16,200	$ 15,450
Unrealized Holding Gain:			
Ending Inventory at Current Replacement Cost (500 × $10)	$ 5,000	$ 5,000	$ 5,000
Less Ending Inventory at Acquisition Cost..........	(5,000)	(6,200)	(5,850)
Total Unrealized Holding Gain (Loss)	$ 0	$ (1,200)	$ (850)
Less Unrealized Holding Gain at Beginning of Period (see Part a.)..........	(200)	(1,200)	(800)
Increase (Decrease) in Unrealized Holding Gain during Year 2.................	$ (200)	$ (2,400)	$ (1,650)
Total Profit Including Holding Gain.......................	$ 13,800	$ 13,800	$ 13,800

c.		FIFO	LIFO	Weighted Average
	Operating Margin—Year 1..	$ 9,000	$ 9,000	$ 9,000
	—Year 2..	15,000	15,000	15,000
	Realized Holding Gain (Loss)			
	Year 1	2,600	1,600	2,000
	Year 2	(1,000)	1,200	450
	Unrealized Holding Gain at the End of Year 2	0	(1,200)	(850)
	Total Profit Including Holding Gain (Loss) ..	$ 25,600	$ 25,600	$ 25,600

 Solutions

8.35 (Whitimore Corporation; effect of FIFO and LIFO on gross margin over several periods.)

a.

Year	Revenue	−	Cost of Goods Sold	=	Gross Margin
5	3,600 × $15.00 = $ 54,000		3,600 × $10 = $ 36,000		$ 18,000
6	8,000 × $18.00 = 144,000		(400 × $10) + (7,600 × $12) = 95,200		48,800
7	5,500 × $16.50 = 90,750		(1,400 × $12) + (4,100 × $11) = 61,900		28,850
8	10,000 × $15.00 = 150,000		(1,900 × $11) + (8,100 × $10) = 101,900		48,100

b.

Year	Revenue	−	Cost of Goods Sold	=	Gross Income
5	3,600 × $15.00 = $ 54,000		3,600 × $10 = $ 36,000		$ 18,000
6	8,000 × $18.00 = 144,000		8,000 × $12 = $ 96,000		48,000
7	5,500 × $16.50 = 90,750		5,500 × $11 = $ 60,500		30,250
8	10,000 × $15.00 = 150,000		(9,000 × $10) + (500 × $11) + (500 × $12) = $101,500		48,500

c.

		Change in Gross Margin FIFO	LIFO	Change in Sales
Year 6:	[($48,800/$18,000) − 1]	+171.1%		
	[($48,000/$18,000) − 1]		+166.7%	
	[($144,000/$54,000) − 1]			+171.7%
Year 7:	[($28,850/$48,800) − 1]	−40.9%		
	[($30,250/$48,000) − 1]		−37.0%	
	[($90,750/$144,000) − 1]			−37.0%
Year 8:	[($48,100/$28,850) − 1]	+66.7%		
	[($48,500/$30,250) − 1]		+60.3%	
	[($150,000/$90,750) − 1]			+65.3%

d. Whitimore Corporation consistently sets selling prices at 50 percent above replacement costs. Because LIFO uses more current acquisition costs to measure cost of goods sold than FIFO, LIFO's gross margin changes tend to track changes in sales. FIFO uses older acquisition costs to measure cost of goods sold. The gross margin under FIFO each period includes a larger realized holding gain or holding loss than LIFO, resulting in greater fluctuations in reported earnings. An exception to the generalization that LIFO tends to result in smother changes in gross margin each year than FIFO may occur when a LIFO firm dips into an old LIFO layer. Whitimore Corporation dipped into its LIFO layers during Year 8 but, in this case, its percentage change in the gross margin under LIFO is still less than under FIFO.

8.36   (Burch Corporation; reconstructing underlying events from ending inventory amounts [adapted from CPA examination].)

a.   Down. Notice that lower of cost or market is lower than acquisition cost (FIFO); current market price is less than cost.

b.   Up. FIFO means last-in, still-here. The last purchases (FIFO = LISH) cost $44,000 and the earlier purchases (LIFO = FISH) cost $41,800. Also, lower-of-cost-or-market basis shows acquisition costs which are greater than or equal to current cost.

c.   LIFO Cost. Other things being equal, the largest income results from the method that shows the largest *increase* in inventory during the year.

> Margin   = Revenues – Cost of Goods Sold
>   = Revenues – Beginning Inventory – Purchases + Ending Inventory
>   = Revenues – Purchases + Increase in Inventory.

Because the beginning inventory in Year 1 is zero, the method with the largest closing inventory amount implies the largest increase and hence the largest income.

d.   Lower of Cost or Market. The method with the "largest increase in inventory" during the year in this case is the method with the smallest decrease, because all methods show declines in inventory during Year 2. Lower of cost or market shows a decrease in inventory of only $3,000 during Year 2—the other methods show larger decreases ($3,800; $4,000).

e.   Lower of Cost or Market. The method with the largest increase in inventory: $10,000. LIFO shows a $5,400 increase while FIFO shows $8,000.

f.   LIFO Cost. The lower income for all three years results from the method that shows the smallest increase in inventory over the three years. Because all beginning inventories were zero under all methods, we need merely find the method with the smallest ending inventory at Year 3 year-end.

g.   FIFO lower by $2,000. Under FIFO, inventories increased $8,000 during Year 3. Under lower of cost or market, inventories increased $10,000 during Year 3. Lower of cost or market has a bigger increase—$2,000—and therefore lower of cost or market shows a $2,000 larger income than FIFO for Year 3.

8.37 (Wilson Company; LIFO layers influence purchasing behavior and provide opportunity for income manipulation.)

	Cost per Pound	Layer	Beginning Inventory Cost ($000)	+ Purchases Cost ($000)	– Ending Inventory Pounds	Cost ($000)	= Cost of Goods Sold ($000)
a.	(Controller)	Year 1	$ 60.0	---	2,000	$ 60.0	---
		Year 6	9.2	---	200	9.2	---
		Year 7	19.2	---	400	19.2	---
	7,000 @	Year 10	72.8	---	1,400	72.8	---
	$62/lb.	Year 11	---	$434.0	---	---	434.0
			$161.2	$434.0	4,000	$161.2	$434.0
b.	(Purchasing Agent)	Year 1	$ 60.0	---	600	$ 18.0	$ 42.0
		Year 6	9.2	---	---	---	9.2
		Year 7	19.2	---	---	---	19.2
	3,600 @	Year 10	72.8	---	---	---	72.8
	$62/lb.	Year 11	---	$223.2	---	---	223.2
			$161.2	$223.2	600	$ 18.0	$366.4

c.
Controller's Policy COGS $62/lb.	$ 434.00
Less Purchasing Agent's COGS	(366.40)
Controller's Extra Deductions	$ 67.60
Tax Rate: 40 Percent	x .40
Controller's Tax Savings	$ 27.04
Controller's Extra Cash Costs for Inventory: 3,400 @ $10/lb.	$ 34.00

d. The controller's policy does save taxes but not as much in taxes as the extra inventory costs. The purchasing agent's policy implies higher income from the date of this decision forward because the tax basis for cost of goods sold will be larger; see the older layers of cost retained under the controller's policy.

8.37 continued.

e. To maximize income for Year 11, liquidate all our LIFO inventory layers, 4,000 lbs. with total cost $161,200, and purchase only 3,000 lbs. at $62 each during Year 11. To minimize income, acquire 7,000 lbs. at $62 each.

Policy	Cost of Goods Sold for Year 11
Minimum Income:	
7,000 lbs. × $62	$ 434,000
Maximum Income:	
4,000 lbs. of Old Layer..	(161,200)
3,000 lbs. at $62..	(186,000)
Income Spread before Taxes	$ 86,800
Taxes at 40 Percent..	(34,720)
Income Spread after Taxes..	$ 52,080

By manipulating purchases of expensium, Wilson Company reports aftertax income anywhere in the range from $50,000 (by following the controller's policy) up to $102,080 (= $50,000 + $52,080) by acquiring only 3,000 lbs. and liquidating all LIFO layers.

8.38 (Deere & Company; interpreting disclosures relating to LIFO inventories.) (Amounts in Millions)

a. $20.8/(1 − .34) = $31.5 smaller. ✓

b. .34 × $31.5 = $10.7 million. ✓

c. .34[($1,885.0 − $760.9) − ($1,941.0 − $872.0)] = $18.7.

d. .34($1,885.0 − $760.9) = $382.2. Deere's actual tax savings is larger than $$382.2 because the income tax rate in earlier years exceeded 34 percent.

8.39 (Sankyo and Eli Lily; comparing gross margins using FIFO and LIFO cost flow assumptions.)

a. and b.

	Sankyo Average	Eli Lily LIFO	Eli Lily FIFO
Sales.................................	¥516,750	$ 6,452.4	$ 6,452.4
Cost of Goods Sold	(260,225)	(1,959.0)	(1,937.2)[a]
Gross Margin....................	¥256,525	$ 4,493.4	$ 4,515.2
Gross Margin Percentage ...	49.6%	69.6%	70.0%

[a]$1,959.0 + $86.9 − $108.7 = $1,937.2.

       Solutions

8.39 continued.

    c.   Eli Lily outperformed Sankyo during the current year in terms of profitability regardless of the cost flow assumption used. During periods of inflation and increasing inventory quantities, one would expect a lower gross margin percentage using LIFO than using FIFO. Thus, Lily's higher gross margin than Sankyo using LIFO understates its degree of superior profitability relative to the gross margins computed using FIFO. The gross margin percentage for Lily using a weighted average cost flow assumption would presumably be between the amounts computed under LIFO and FIFO, still superior to that for Sankyo.

d. and e.

	Sankyo Average	Eli Lily LIFO	Eli Lily FIFO
Cost of Goods Sold	¥ 260,225	$ 1,959.0	$ 1,937.0
Average Inventories:			
.5(¥79,186 + ¥86,347)	¥ 82,766.5		
.5($938.4 + $1,103.0)		$ 1,020.7	
.5($938.4 + $86.9 + $1,103.0 + $108.7)			$ 1,118.5
Inventory Turnover............	3.1	1.9	1.7

    f.   Sankyo turns its inventory over more quickly than Lily, regardless of the cost flow assumption used in the calculations. The inventory turnover of Lily based on the reported amounts (LIFO) overstates the likely physical turnover.

8.40   (E. I. duPont de Nemours & Company; analysis of disclosures from published financial reports on effects of changing from average cost to LIFO.)

    a. $378.2 [= 249.6/(1.00 − .34)] million. LIFO cost of goods sold was larger by $378.2 million, implying aftertax decrease in income of that amount multiplied by one minus the income tax rate.

    b.   The costs accumulated in earlier years enter cost of goods sold. In times of rising prices, such as those duPont faced, this means that the older costs are less than current costs, decreasing costs of goods sold and increasing income.

    c. $55.2 [= 36.4/(1.00 − .34)] million decrease in cost of goods sold.

    d.   The income tax rules impose a penalty for changing cost-flow assumptions for inventory and require LIFO conformity. duPont would have had to repay, perhaps in installments, all of its tax savings from the preceding year. Also, attesting auditors must approve changes in accounting policies, and it is hard to persuade them that switching back and forth between policies has any purpose other than income manipulation.

8.40 continued.

  e. $27.2 [= .34 × ($490 − $410)] million.

  f. Because of LIFO conformity rules and a company's preference for low tax payments, involving real cash flows, over the wish to report higher income in its financial statements. Also, the company may believe that LIFO reports better "matching" in years when no liquidations of LIFO layers occur.

8.41   (Bethlehem Steel; assessing the effect of LIFO versus FIFO on financial statements.) (Amounts in Millions)

  a.

	Year 9	Year 10	Year 11
Cost of Goods Sold: LIFO....	$4,399.1	$4,327.2	$4,059.7
Plus Excess of FIFO Cost over LIFO Values, Beginning of Year..................	530.1	562.5	499.1
Less Excess of FIFO Cost over LIFO Values, End of Year...........................	(562.5)	(499.1)	(504.9)
Cost of Goods Sold: FIFO....	$4,366.7	$4,390.6	$4,053.9

  b.

Cost of Goods Sold/Sales	Year 9	Year 10	Year 11
LIFO: $4,399.1/$5,250.9	83.8%		
$4,327.2/$4,899.2		88.3%	
$4,059.7/$4,317.9			94.0%
FIFO: $4,366.7/$5,250.9	83.2%		
$4,390.6/$4,899.2		89.6%	
$4,053.9/$4,317.9			93.9%

  c. Inventory quantities increased during Year 9 (LIFO ending inventory exceeds LIFO beginning inventory) but it is difficult to conclude for sure the direction of the change in manufacturing costs. It appears, however, that manufacturing costs increased during the year because cost of goods sold using LIFO exceeds cost of goods sold using FIFO. Inventory quantities increased again during Year 10 but it appears that manufacturing costs decreased, resulting in a higher cost of goods sold using FIFO than using LIFO. Clues that manufacturing costs decreased include (1) the excess of FIFO cost over LIFO values declined during Year 10, despite an increase in inventory quantities, and (2) ending inventory using FIFO is less that beginning inventory using FIFO, despite an increase in inventory quantities. Inventory quantities decreased during Year 11 but it appears that manufacturing costs increased. The principal clue for the latter conclusion is that the excess of FIFO

                        Solutions

8.41 c. continued.

cost over LIFO values increased during the year, despite a decrease in inventory quantities. The slightly higher cost of goods sold percentage using LIFO results from using higher manufacturing costs toward the end of Year 11 as well as dipping into the Year 10 LIFO layer priced at the higher manufacturing cost at the beginning of Year 10.

d.

Inventory Turnover Ratio	Year 9	Year 10	Year 11
LIFO: $4,399.1/.5($369.0 + $410.3)	11.3		
$4,327.2/.5($410.3 + $468.3)		9.9	
$4,059.7/.5($468.3 + $453.4)			8.8
FIFO: $4,366.7/.5($899.1 + $972.8)	4.7		
$4,390.6/.5($972.8 + $967.4)		4.5	
$4,053.9/.5($967.4 + $958.3)			4.2

e. The inventory turnover ratio for LIFO includes current cost data in the numerator and old cost data in the denominator, whereas this ratio under FIFO includes somewhat out-of-date cost data in the numerator and a mixture of out-of-date and current cost data in the denominator. The mismatching of cost data is less severe for FIFO than for LIFO because of the very old LIFO layers. Thus, the inventory turnover ratio using FIFO probably more accurately measures the actual rate of inventory turnover.

f.

Inventory Turnover Ratio	Year 8	Year 9	Year 10	Year 11
LIFO: $1,439.8/$870.1	1.65			
$1,435.2/$838.0		1.71		
$1,203.2/$831.4			1.45	
$957.8/$931.0				1.03
FIFO: $1,439.8 + (.66 ×				
$530.1)/$870.1	2.06			
$1,435.2 + (.66 ×				
$562.5)/$838.0		2.16		
$1,203.2 + (.66 ×				
$499.1/)/$831.4			1.84	
$957.8 + (.66 ×				
$504.9)/$931.0				1.39

8.41 continued.

g. The current ratio decreased between Year 9 and Year 11, suggesting increased short-term liquidity risk. The current ratio using a FIFO cost-flow assumption for inventories probably reflects better the potential of current assets to cover current liabilities because the FIFO inventory values use more recent cost data. The current ratio using FIFO inventory values still exceeds 1.0 at the end of Year 11, suggesting that short-term liquidity risk is not yet at a serious level. However, the sharp decrease during the three-year period coupled with a slower inventory turnover (see Part *d*. above) raise doubts about the future.

Note: The annual report indicates that the decreased current ratio occurs primarily because of reductions in cash that Bethlehem Steel Company needed to help finance its deteriorating operating position.

8.42 (General Motors Corporation; analysis of financial statement ratios affected by cost flow assumptions.)

a. Let w and x denote current liabilities at the ends of Year 2 and Year 1, respectively. Then,

$$w = \frac{\$14,043}{1.13} = \$12,427 \qquad\qquad x = \frac{\$13,714}{1.09} = \$12,582.$$

Let y and z denote the excess of FIFO over LIFO ending inventories for Year 2 and Year 1, respectively. If FIFO were used, then cash amounts required for income taxes would have been higher so that after tax (assuming a 34-percent rate), current assets would increase net by $(1.00 - .34)$ times the FIFO excess.

Year 2

$$\frac{\$14,043 + (1.00 - .34)y}{\$12,427} = 1.21$$

$.66y = (1.21 \times \$12,427) - \$14,043 = \$994$
$\quad y = \$994/.66 = \$1,506.$

Year 1

$$\frac{\$13,714 + (1.00 - .34)z}{\$12,582} = 1.18$$

$.66z = (1.18 \times \$12,582) - \$13,714 = \$1,133$
$\quad z = \$1,717.$

8.42 continued.

    b.   Cash flow was *reduced* by $72 million. The excess of FIFO over LIFO inventories *decreased* by $211 (= $1,717 − $1,506) million during Year 2. Therefore, FIFO pretax income is *less* than LIFO pretax income by $211 million. With income taxes computed at 34 percent, LIFO required extra income taxes (and, presumably, cash) of $72 (= .34 × $211) million.

    c.   Since GM adopted LIFO, LIFO pretax income has been less than FIFO pretax income by $1,717 million and, assuming an income tax rate of 34 percent, has saved cumulative income taxes of $584 (= .34 × $1,717) million.

8.43   (British Petroleum Company; calculating operating margins and realized holding gains.)

    a.   (Amounts in Millions of British Pounds)

	Year 8	Year 9	Year 10	Year 11
Sales	£ 25,922	£ 29,641	£ 33,039	£ 32,613
Replacement Cost of Goods Sold	(19,330)	(22,095)	(24,655)	(25,117)
Operating Margin	£ 6,592	£ 7,546	£ 8,384	£ 7,496
Realized Holding Gain:				
Replacement Cost of Goods Sold	£ 19,330	£ 22,095	£ 24,655	£ 25,117
Acquisition Cost of Goods Sold	(19,562)	(21,705)	(24,178)	(25,746)
Total	£ (232)	£ 390	£ 477	£ (629)
Gross Margin	£ 6,360	£ 7,936	£ 8,861	£ 6,867

    b.   **Operating Margin/Sales**

£6,592/£25,922	25.4%			
£7,546/£29,641		25.5%		
£8,384/£33,039			25.4%	
£7,496/£32,613				23.0%

Gross Margin/Sales

£6,360/£25,922	24.5%			
£7,936/£29,641		26.8%		
£8,861/£33,039			26.8%	
£6,867/£32,613				21.1%

8.43 continued.

   c. BP's operating margin to sales percentage fluctuates less than its gross margin to sales percentage. Perhaps BP provides the replacement cost of goods sold data to show the financial community that it prices its products at a relatively constant markup on replacement cost (except for Year 11). Variations in the gross margin percentage result from varying rates of change in oil prices over which BP has little, if any, control. The effects of these variations appear in realized holding gains and losses. Although BP's operating margin to sales percentage decreased in Year 11, the rate of decrease is not as large as the decrease in the gross margin to sales percentage. BP was able to almost maintain its historical operating margin percentage, despite decreases in petroleum costs.
   In years when significant increases in oil prices occur because of problems in the Middle East, these disclosures permit BP to show that most of the increase in its gross margin results from realized holding gains instead of increased operating margin. By including these disclosures each year, even when oil prices do not change much, BP educates the financial community regarding the effect of factors outside of its control on profitability.

8.44 (Olin Corporation; interpreting inventory disclosures.)

   a. $2,161 + (\$501 - \$320) - (\$474 - \$329) = \$2,197$.

   b. The quantities of inventory items increased since Olin Corporation added a new LIFO layer during the year (that is, the ending inventory under LIFO exceeds the beginning inventory under LIFO).

   c. The cost of inventory items decreased during the year. One clue is that the cost of goods sold under FIFO exceeds that under LIFO. A second clue is that the excess of FIFO over LIFO inventory at the end of the year is less than at the beginning of the year despite an increase in quantities.

   d. LIFO: $\$2,161/.5(\$320 + \$329) = 6.7$.
       FIFO: $\$2,197/.5(\$501 + \$474) = 4.5$.

   e. The difference in the rate of inventory turnover occurs because LIFO uses old costs in computing inventory amounts whereas FIFO uses more up-to-date costs. Both cost flow assumptions use relatively recent costs in the numerator of the ratio, although those for LIFO are more up-to-date.

                        Solutions

8.44 continued.

    f.   The amount for purchases in the numerator of the accounts payable turnover ratio should not differ between LIFO and FIFO, unless the firm accelerates purchases or production at the end of a year to avoid dipping into its LIFO layers. The average balance for accounts payable in the denominator of the ratio should not differ between LIFO and FIFO, unless the extra income taxes paid under FIFO (rising prices) or LIFO (falling prices) constrains a firm's ability to repay its suppliers.

CHAPTER 9

PLANT, EQUIPMENT, AND INTANGIBLE ASSETS: THE SOURCE OF OPERATING CAPACITY

Questions, Exercises, Problems, and Cases: Answers and Solutions

9.1   See the text or the glossary at the end of the book.

9.2   Maintenance services provided for selling and administrative activities appear as expenses of the current period. Maintenance services provided for manufacturing activities accumulate in Work-in-Process and Finished Goods Inventory accounts. These costs become expenses in the period of sale. Expenditures from any of these activities that increase the service life or service potential of assets beyond that originally expected increase the assets' depreciable base. Such expenditures become expenses as the firm recognizes depreciation during future years.

9.3   Generally accepted accounting principles use acquisition costs in the valuation of most assets. Accounting gives no recognition to the fact that some firms can acquire a particular asset for a lower price than other firms can acquire it. Part of the explanation relates to measuring the relevant cost savings. There is seldom a single, unique alternative price. Additionally, accounting views firms as generating income form using assets in operations, not from simply purchasing them.

The income effect of both recording procedures is a net expense of $250,000, the cash outflow to self-construct the warehouse. The generally accepted procedure recognizes $250,000 as depreciation expense over the life of the warehouse. The unacceptable procedure recognizes revenue of $50,000 upon completion of the warehouse and depreciation expense of $300,000 over the life of the warehouse.

9.4   a.   Over the life of the project, income is cash-in less cash-out. Capitalizing and then amortizing interest versus expensing it affects the timing but not the total amount of income. Capitalizing interest defers expense from the construction period to the periods of use, increasing income in the early years of construction and decreasing it in the periods of use, when depreciation charges are larger.

9.4 continued.

b. The "catch-up" described in the preceding part is indefinitely delayed. Reported income in each year increases by the policy of capitalizing interest. When the self-construction activity declines, then the reported income declines as a result of reduced capitalization of interest, but not before.

9.5 a. If the life of an asset is shorter than the accounting period (or that portion of the period remaining after the purchase of the asset), depreciation, as an accounting measurement problem, disappears. The difficulties increase as it becomes necessary to spread the cost of an asset over a number of periods of time. If the accounting period were ten years, fewer items would have to be spread, or "depreciated." If no asset lasted more than a year or two, accountants could make even annual depreciation calculations with considerable accuracy.

b. Depreciation accounting allocates the cost of long-lived assets to the periods of use in an orderly, reasonable manner. Charging depreciation does not "provide funds" for the firm. Selling the firm's products to customers provides funds.

9.6 a. Depreciation life is: $100,000/$10,000 per year = 10 years.

Age of the asset is: $60,000 accumulated depreciation charge divided by $10,000 depreciation per year = 6 years.

b. Age of the asset in years = accumulated depreciation at the end of a year divided by depreciation charge for the year.

9.7 Depreciation for years prior to the change in estimate is larger or smaller than it would have been if the firm had originally used the revised estimate. Depreciation for the current and future years is also smaller or larger than it would be if the firm corrected for the original misestimate retroactively. Thus, depreciation in no year of the assets' service life will show the appropriate depreciation for the actual depreciable life of assets.

9.8 The small amounts of certain expenditures often do not justify the record keeping cost of capitalization and amortization. Firms therefore expense all expenditures below a certain threshold amount.

9.9 The relevant question to apply generally accepted accounting principles is whether the expenditure maintained the originally expected useful life or extended that useful life. Firms should expense, as maintenance or repairs, expenditures that maintain the originally expected five-year life. In this case, the expenditure both maintains and extends the useful life. A portion of the expenditure should appear as an expense immediately (perhaps two-thirds) and a portion (perhaps one-third) should increase the depreciable base for the asset.

9.10   Accounting views sales of plant assets as peripheral to a firm's principal business activities. Revenues and expenses from a firm's principal business activities appear as sales revenue and cost of goods sold. Accounting nets the revenues and expenses from peripheral activities to show only the gain or loss.

9.11   Total expenses equal total cash expenditures. Full costing delays the recognition of expenses relative to successful efforts costing, but ultimately all expenditures to search for mineral resources become expenses.

9.12   Some critics of the required expensing of research and development (R & D) costs argue that there is little difference to justify the different accounting treatments. One possible explanation for the different treatment is the greater tangible nature of mineral resources relative to most R & D expenditures. Yet, some R & D expenditures result in tangible prototypes or products. Another possible explanation for the difference is the established market for most mineral resources versus the more unknown market potential for R & D expenditures.

9.13   Critics of the required expensing of research and development (R & D) costs argue that there is little rationale to justify the different accounting. One difference between the two cases is that firms make R & D expenditures for an uncertain future result (that is, the possibility of a patent), whereas less uncertainty exists for the purchase of a completed patent. A market transaction between an independent buyer and seller establish the existence and value of future benefits in the case of a purchased patent. Similar expenditures for R & D simply establish that a firm has made an expenditure.

9.14   (Classifying expenditure as asset or expense.)

   a.   Expense.

   b.   Expense.

   c.   Expense.

   d.   Asset (noncurrent).

   e.   Expense.

   f.   Expense or asset (noncurrent).

   g.   Product cost (current asset).

   h.   Equipment (noncurrent asset).

   i.   Expense.

9.14 continued.

j. Ore deposit (noncurrent asset).

k. Prepayment (current asset).

l. Marketable securities (current asset).

m. Product cost (current asset).

n. Asset (noncurrent).

o. Asset (noncurrent). Copyrights need not be expensed as developed.

9.15   (Bolton Company; cost of self-constructed assets.)

	Land	
	70,000	
(14)	2,000	
√	72,000	

	Office Building	
	20,000	
(4)	13,000	
√	33,000	

	Site Improvements	
(12)	5,000	
√	5,000	

	Factory Building		
(1)	200,000	7,000	(7)
(2)	12,000		
(3)	140,000		
(5)	6,000		
(8)	10,000		
(9)	8,000		
(10)	3,000[a]		
(11)	8,000[b]		
(13)	4,000		
(15)	1,000[a]		
√	385,000		

[a]The firm might expense these items. It depends on the rationality of the firm's "self-insurance" policy.

[b]The firm might prorate these items in part to the remodeling of the office building.

Item (6) is omitted because of *SFAS No. 34*.

Item (16) is omitted because no arm's length transaction occurred in which the firm earned a profit.

9.16   (New Hampshire Wood Stove Company; cost of self-developed product.)

The first four items qualify as research and development costs which the firm must expense in the year incurred. It might appear that the firm should capitalize the cost of the prototype because it acquires the prototype from an external contractor. However, completion of a prototype does not signify a viable product. Purchasing the prototype externally versus constructing it internally does not change the accounting.

   The firm should capitalize the legal fees to register and establish the patent as part of the cost of the patent. The firm might consider this cost as sufficiently immaterial to warrant treatment as an asset and expense it immediately.

   The firm should capitalize the cost of the castings and amortize them over the expected useful life of the wood stove product.

9.17   (Samson Chemical Company; amount of interest capitalized during construction.)

   a.   Average Construction = ($20,000,000 + $60,000,000)/2 = $40,000,000.

Relevant Loans	Interest Anticipated
$ 30,000,000 at .10	$3,000,000
10,000,000 at .08	800,000
$ 30,000,000	$3,800,000

   b.   Interest Expense... 7,000,000
             Interest Payable.......................................   7,000,000
        $30,000,000 × .10 + $50,000,000 × .08.

        Construction in Process................................. 3,800,000
             Interest Expense.......................................   3,800,000

9.18   (Nebok Company; capitalizing interest during construction.) (Amounts in Thousands)

   a.   Weighted average interest rate: $5,480/.5($51,500 + $49,700) = 10.83 percent.

        Weighted average balance in Construction in Process: .5($23,186 + $68,797) = $45,992.

        Interest Capitalized: .1083 × $45,992 = $4,981.

9.18 continued.

b. Interest Expense... 5,480
        Interest Payable.......................................   5,480

    Construction in Process................................ 4,981
        Interest Expense.......................................   4,981

c. Income before Interest Expense and Income
        Taxes.. $ 16,300
    Interest Expense ($5,480 – $4,981)........................... (499)
    Income before Income Taxes .... $ 15,801
    Income Tax Expense at 34 Percent.......................... (5,372)
    Net Income... $ 10,429

d. $16,300/$499 = 32.67 times.

e. $16,300/$5,480 = 2.97 times.

f. The interest coverage ratio in Part e. indicates the interest that the firm must pay and therefore provides a better measure for assessing risk.

9.19   (Galeway Motors; calculations for various depreciation methods.)

		Year 1	Year 2	Year 3
a.	Straight-Line Method .... ($29,600 – $2,600)/6 = $4,500.	$4,500	$4,500	$4,500
b.	Sum-of-the-Years'-Digits Method......................... (6 × 7)/2 = 21 sum-of-the-years'-digits.	$7,714	$6,429	$5,143
c.	Declining-Balance Method.. 33 percent rate.	$9,768	$6,545	$4,385
d.	Production Method............. $27,000/30,000 = $.90 per hour.	$4,050	$4,500	$4,950

(Luck Delivery Company; calculations for various depreciation methods.)

a. **Depreciation Charge (Straight-Line)**
Year 8	$ 6,000	(30,000/5)
Year 9	6,000	
Year 10	6,000	
Year 11	6,000	
Year 12	6,000	
	$30,000	

b. **Depreciation Charge (Double-Declining-Balance)**
Year 8	$12,000	($30,000 × .40)
Year 9	7,200	($18,000 × .40)
Year 10	4,320	($10,800 × .40)
Year 11	3,240	($6,480/2)
Year 12	3,240	(balance)
	$30,000	

c. **Depreciation Charge (Sum-of-the-Years'-Digits)**
Year 8	$10,000	($30,000 × 5/15)
Year 9	8,000	($30,000 × 4/15)
Year 10	6,000	($30,000 × 3/15)
Year 11	4,000	($30,000 × 2/15)
Year 12	2,000	($30,000 × 1/15)
	$30,000	

d. **ACRS (5-Year Class)**
Year 8	$ 6,000	(= $30,000 × .20)
Year 9	9,600	(= $30,000 × .32)
Year 10	5,760	(= $30,000 × .192)
Year 11	3,450	(= $30,000 × .115)
Year 12	3,450	(= $30,000 × .115)
Year 13	1,740	(= $30,000 × .058)
	$30,000	

e. **Depreciation Charge (Sum-of-the-Years'-Digits)**
Year 8	3/4 × $10,000			=	$ 7,500
Year 9	3/4 × $ 8,000	+	1/4 × $10,000 =		8,500
Year 10	3/4 × $ 6,000	+	1/4 × $ 8,000 =		6,500
Year 11	3/4 × $ 4,000	+	1/4 × $ 6,000 =		4,500
Year 12	3/4 × $ 2,000	+	1/4 × $ 4,000 =		2,500
Year 13			1/4 × $ 2,000 =		500
					$30,000

                                     Solutions

9.21 (Calculations for various depreciation methods.)

		Year 1	Year 2	
	a.	$10,000	$10,000	($450,000 − $50,000)/40 = $10,000.
	b.	$22,000	$19,800	($220,000 × 2/20) = $22,000; ($198,000 × 2/20) = $19,800.
	c.	$20,000	$16,000	($80,000 − $20,000) × 5/15 = $20,000; ($80,000 − $20,000) × 4/15 = $16,000.
	d.	$18,750	$15,937.50	$125,000 × 1.5/10 = $18,750; $106,250 × 1.5/10 = $15,937.50.
	e.	$ 3,333	$ 3,333	($24,000 − $4,000)/6 = $3,333.
	f.	$ 4,800	$ 7,680	$24,000 × .20 = $4,800; $24,000 × .32 = $7,680.

9.22 (United Express; production or use depreciation.)

a. ($22,600 − $2,600)/100,000 miles = $.20 per mile.

	Miles at $.20 Each	Depreciation Charge
Year 6.....................	14,000 Miles	$ 2,800
Year 7.....................	34,000 Miles	6,800
Year 8.....................	<u>32,000 Miles</u>	<u>6,400</u>
	80,000 Miles	$ 16,000

b. **June 16, Year 9**

Depreciation Expense.....................................	3,600	
Accumulated Depreciation		3,600

18,000 (= 98,000 − 80,000) miles at $.20 per mile = $3,600. Accumulated Depreciation is now $19,600 (= $.20 × 98,000 miles).

Cash..	2,600	
Accumulated Depreciation............................	19,600	
Loss on Sale of Truck....................................	400	
Truck..		22,600

9.23 (Fast Pace Shipping Company; revision of estimated service life changes depreciation schedule.)

Summary of the depreciation charges under the two methods:

	a. Straight-Line	b. Sum-of-the-Years'-Digits
Year 7	$ 3,600[a]	$ 6,545[c]
Year 8	3,600[a]	5,891[d]
Year 9	4,800[b]	6,733[e]
Year 10...........................	4,800[b]	5,610[f]
	$16,800	$24,779

[a]($40,000 – $4,000)/10 = $3,600.
[b]($40,000 – $3,600 – $3,600 – $4,000)/6 = $4,800.
[c][($40,000 – $4,000)/10/55] = $6,545.
[d][($40,000 – $4,000)/9/55] = $5,891.
[e]($40,000 – $6,545 – $5,891 – $4,000)/6/21 = $6,733.
[f]($40,000 – $6,545 – $5,891 – $4,000)/5/21 = $5,610.

9.24 (Fort Manufacturing Corporation; journal entries for revising estimate of life.)

a. Work-in-Process Inventory............................ 600
    Accumulated Depreciation 600
    ($45,000 – $1,800)/144 = $300 per month.

b. Work-in-Process Inventory............................ 3,600
    Accumulated Depreciation 3,600
    12 × $300 = $3,600.

c. Depreciation to 1/1/Year 15 = 62 × $300 = $18,600.
    Remaining depreciation = $45,000 – $18,600 – $960 = $25,440.
    Remaining life = 168 months – 62 months = 106 months as of 1/1/Year 15.
    Depreciation charge per month = $25,440/106 = $240.

    Work-in-Process Inventory............................ 2,880
    Accumulated Depreciation 2,880

d. By March 31, Year 20, the machine has been on the new depreciation schedule for Year 15 through Year 19 plus 3 months or 63 months altogether. Accumulated depreciation is $18,600 + (63 × $240) = $15,190; $18,600 + $15,120 = $33,720.

Book value is $45,000 – $33,720 = $11,280; loss is $1,280.

Journal entries are:

 Solutions

9.24 d. continued.

Work-in-Process Inventory............................ 720
    Accumulated Depreciation 720
3 × $240 = $720; to bring depreciation up to date
as of 3/31/Year 20.

Cash.. 10,000
Accumulated Depreciation............................ 33,720
Loss on Disposal of Machinery....................... 1,280
    Machinery... 45,000

9.25   (Neptune Equipment Corporation; retirement of plant assets.)

a.

	Depreciation Charge for the Year	Accumulated Depreciation at July 1
Year 4—Year 5	$2,000	$ 2,000
Year 5—Year 6	2,000	4,000
Year 6—Year 7	2,000	6,000
	$6,000	

b. **9/30/Year 7**
Work-in-Process Inventory............................ 500
    Accumulated Depreciation 500
3 months' depreciation since 6/30/Year 7:
$2,000/4 = $500.

9/30/Year 7
Cash on Hand... 2,700
Accumulated Depreciation............................ 6,500
Loss on Sale of Machinery............................. 400
    Machinery... 9,600
$6,000 + $500 = $6,500.

c. **12/31/Year 7**
Work-in-Process Inventory............................ 1,000
    Accumulated Depreciation 1,000
6 months' depreciation since 6/30/Year 7:
$2,000/2 = $1,000.

12/31/Year 7
Cash on Hand... 2,700
Accumulated Depreciation............................ 7,000
    Machinery... 9,600
    Gain on Sale of Machinery........................ 100
$6,000 + $1,000 = $7,000.

9.26   (Wilcox Corporation; working backwards to derive proceeds from disposition of plant assets.)

Cost of Equipment Sold: $400,000 + $230,000 − $550,000 = $80,000.
Accumulated Depreciation
  on Equipment Sold: $180,000 + $50,000 − $160,000 = $70,000.
Book Value of Equipment
  Sold: $80,000 − $70,000 = $10,000.
Proceeds of Sale: $10,000 + $4,000 = $14,000.

9.27   (Checker's Pizza Company; use of a single asset account or separate asset accounts affects classification of expenditures as repairs or improvements.)

a.

		Expenses		
Single Asset	Depreciation			
Account	Truck	Engine	Repairs	Total
Year 1	$ 4,500	---	---	$ 4,500
Year 2	4,500	---	$ 5,000	9,500
Year 3	4,500	---	---	4,500
Year 4	4,500	---	---	4,500
Totals......	$ 18,000		$ 5,000	$ 23,000

b. **Separate Asset Accounts**

	Truck	Engine		Total
Year 1	$ 3,250[a]	$ 2,500[b]	---	$ 5,750
Year 2	3,250	2,500	---	5,750
Year 3	3,250	2,500	---	5,750
Year 4	3,250	2,500	---	5,750
Totals.......	$ 13,000	$ 10,000		$ 23,000

[a]($18,000 − $5,000)/4.   [b]$5,000/2.

9.28   (Journal entries to correct accounting errors.)

a. Depreciation Expense................................... 375
        Accumulated Depreciation 375
    $3,000 × .25 × 6/12 = $375.

    Accumulated Depreciation............................. 1,875
    Loss on Disposal of Equipment....................... 325
        Store Equipment....................................... 2,200
    $3,000 × .25 × 2.5 = $1,875. $3,200 + $3000 − $4,000
    = $2,200.

b. Accumulated Depreciation............................ 5,000
        Truck... 5,000

                               Solutions

9.28 continued.

   c. Depreciation Expense... 60
        Accumulated Depreciation   60
        $1,200 × .10 × 6/12 = $60.

        Accumulated Depreciation............................ 270
            Theft Loss   270
        $1,200 × .10 × 27/12 = $270.

9.29   (Boston Can Corporation; journal entries for depreciable asset transactions.)

3/31/Year 6
Depreciation Expense.................................... 350
    Accumulated Depreciation.............................   350
($12,000 – $800)/8 = $1,400 per year; 3/12 × $1,400 = $350.

3/31/Year 6
Cash 4,000
Accumulated Depreciation 7,350
Loss on Sale 650
    Machinery (Old)......................................   12,000
($1,400 × 5) + $350 = $7,350.

Machinery (New)... 16,000
    Notes Payable..   6,000
    Cash...   10,000

12/31/Year 6
Interest Expense.. 450
    Interest Payable.....................................   450
$6,000 × .10 × 9/12 = $450.

Depreciation Expense...................................... 1,125
    Accumulated Depreciation.............................   1,125
($16,000 – $1,000)/10 = $1,500 per year; 9/12 × $1,500 = $1,125.

9.30   (Effects of transactions on statement of cash flows.)

a. The journal entry to record this transaction is as follows:

Cash..	3,000	
Accumulated Depreciation............................	6,000	
Loss on Sale of Machine................................	1,000	
Machine...		10,000

The debit to the Cash account means that Line (9) increases by $3,000. Sales of plant assets are investing transactions, so Line (4) increases by $3,000. The loss on the sale reduces net income, so Line (1) decreases by $1,000. Because we show the full cash proceeds of $3,000 on Line (4), we must offset the effect of the $1,000 reduction on Line (1). Thus, Line (2) increases by $1,000. The net effect of the entries on Lines (1) and (2) is zero.

b. The journal entry to record this transaction is as follows:

Cash..	5,000	
Accumulated Depreciation............................	6,000	
Machine...		10,000
Gain on Sale of Machine.............................		1,000

The debit to the Cash account means that Line (9) increases by $5,000. Sales of plant assets are investing transactions, so Line (4) increases by $5,000. The gain on the sale increases net income, so Line (1) increases by $1,000. Because we show the full cash proceeds of $5,000 on Line (4), we must offset the effect of the $1,000 increase on Line (1). Thus, Line (3) increases by $1,000. The net effect of the entries on Lines (1) and (3) is zero.

c. The journal entry to record this transaction is as follows:

Machine (New)...	8,000	
Accumulated Depreciation (Old)......................	6,000	
Machine (Old)		10,000
Cash		4,000

The credit to the Cash account reduces Line (9) by $4,000. Acquisitions of plant assets are investing transactions, so Line (5) increases by $4,000. Because this entry does not involve an income statement account, there is no effect on the Operating section of the statement of cash flows.

d. The journal entry to record this transaction is as follows:

Loss from Fire..	50,000	
Accumulated Depreciation............................	40,000	
Warehouse...		90,000

9.30 d. continued.

Because this entry does not involve an entry to the Cash account there is no effect on Line (9). The loss from the fire reduces net income, so Line (1) decreases by $50,000. We must offset this loss if the net effect on Line (9) is to be zero. Thus, Line (2) increases by $50,000 for the loss that does not use cash.

e. The journal entry to record this transaction is as follows:

Loss from Fire	60,000	
Inventory		60,000

This entry does not involve a debit or credit to the Cash account so Line (9) is not affected. The loss from the fire reduces net income, so Line (1) decreases by $60,000. We must offset this loss if the net effect on Line (9) is to be zero. Thus, Line (2) increases by $60,000 for the decrease in inventories.

9.31 (Allocation of cost in "basket" purchases.)

a.
Land—East Tract	16,200	
Land—West Tract	10,800	
Cash		27,000

To record purchase and legal fees.

If both offers were *bona fide*, then the land appears to be worth $30,000 in separate five-acre plots; 18/30 of the cost of the land is allocated to the east half and 12/30 to the west half.

Cash	18,000	
Land—East Tract		16,200
Gain on Sale of Land		1,800

b.
Land—East Tract	10,800	
Land—West Tract	16,200	
Cash		27,000

Cash	15,000	
Loss on Sale of Land	1,200	
Land—West Tract		16,200

The value of the land as two plots ($25,000) appears to be less than its value as one plot ($27,000). The firm recognizes a loss of $1,200 on the sale of the West Tract. Conservatism suggests the recognition of another $800 loss on the East Tract.

9.32   (Stith Equipment Company; accounting for plant asset transactions.)

a. **January 2, Year 1**

Land	20,000	
Building	60,000	
Equipment	40,000	
Cash		120,000

b. **December 31, Year 1**

Depreciation Expense	6,300	
Accumulated Depreciation		6,300

($60,000 – $6,000)/20 = $2,700; ($40,000 – $4,000)/10 = $3,600.

c. **June 30, Year 6**

Depreciation Expense	450	
Accumulated Depreciation		450

($10,000 – $1,000)/10 = $900 per year.

June 30, Year 6

Cash	6,000	
Accumulated Depreciation	4,950	
Equipment		10,000
Gain on Sale of Equipment		950

$900 × 5.5 years = $4,950.

d. **December 31, Year 6**

Depreciation Expense	4,725	
Accumulated Depreciation		4,725

Book Value of Building on January 1, Year 6:
  $60,000 – ($2,700 × 5) = $46,500.
Depreciation on Building for Year 6:
  ($46,500 – $6,000)/20 = $2,025.
Depreciation on Equipment for Year 6:
  ($30,000 – $3,000)/10 = $2,700.

e. **June 30, Year 8**

Depreciation Expense	900	
Accumulated Depreciation		900

($20,000 – $2,000)/10 = $1,800 per year.

June 30, Year 8

Cash	5,000	
Accumulated Depreciation	13,500	
Loss on Sale of Equipment	1,500	
Equipment		20,000

$1,800 × 7.5 years = $13,500.

9.32 continued.

    f.   **December 31, Year 10**

Depreciation Expense	2,925	
Accumulated Depreciation		2,925

Depreciation on building, $2,025 (see Part *d*.).
Depreciation on equipment, ($10,000 − $1,000)/10
= $900.

Accumulated Depreciation	9,000	
Loss on Retirement of Equipment....................	1,000	
Equipment		10,000

9.33   (Deutsch Lufthansa AG; depreciation calculations affect net income; working backwards to derive depreciable assets' costs.)

The improvements in pretax income is DM 280 million marks:

First Six Months Pretax Loss....................	DM 542 million marks
First Nine months Pretax Loss.................	262
Loss Reduction in Third Quarter	DM 280 million marks

Let C = Cost of aircraft.
Then $[.75(C - .05C)/10)] - [.75(C - .15C/12] = 280$ million marks
C = 15,450 million marks.

Proof

		Amounts in Millions of Deutsch Marks	
		Old Calculations	New Calculations
(1)	Depreciation Lives in Years	10	12
(2)	Salvage Value Percentage of Cost	.05	.15
(3)	Depreciation Cost	15,450.0	15,450.0
(4)	Salvage Value = [2] × [3]	772.5	2,317.5
(5)	Cost Less Salvage	14,677.5	13,132.5
(6)	Depreciation for Year = [5] ÷ [1]	1,467.8	1,094.4
(7)	Depreciation for Nine Months = [6] × .75	1,100.8	820.8
(8)	Depreciation Savings for Nine Months = [7] Old − [7] New	280.0	

9.34 (American Airlines; effect on net income of changes in estimates for depreciable assets.)

Income has been about $180 million (= .06 × $3 billion) per year.

Reconciliation of Plant Data:

Airplanes Cost...	$ 2,500,000,000
Less Salvage Value (10%).......................................	250,000,000
Depreciable Basis...	$ 2,250,000,000
Divided by 10-Year Life Equals Yearly Depreciation Charges..	$ 225,000,000
Times 4 Years Equals Accumulated Depreciation..........	$ 900,000,000
Plus Net Book Value	1,600,000,000
Airplanes Cost..	$ 2,500,000,000

New Depreciation Charge:

Net Book Value...	$ 1,600,000,000
Less Salvage Value (12% of Cost)	300,000,000
Depreciation Basis..	$ 1,300,000,000
Divided by 10 (= 14 − 4) Years Equals Revised Yearly Depreciation Charge	$ 130,000,000

Increase in Pretax Income:

Old Depreciation Charges...	$ 225,000,000
New Depreciation Charges	130,000,000
	$ 95,000,000
Multiplied by (1 − tax rate) = 1 − .34 = .66.......................	X .66
Increase in Aftertax Income..	$ 62,700,000

Income will rise by about 35 percent (= $62.7/$180.0).

9.35 (Cord Manufacturing Company; composite depreciation versus individual-item depreciation.)

a.

Machine Tool (1)	Percentage of Joint Cost (2)	Cost Allocated to Total (2) × $72,000 (3)	Cost to Renovate and Install	Total Cost to Be Capitalized
A	33.3%	$ 24,000	$1,500	$ 25,500
B	44.4%	32,000	2,400	34,400
C	22.2%	16,000	2,000	18,000
	100.0%[a]	$ 72,000	$5,900	$ 77,900

[a]Amounts above do not sum to 100% due to rounding.

9.35 continued.

b. **Year 1**

Work-in-Process Inventory............................	13,050	
Accumulated Depreciation—Tool A.............		4,250
Accumulated Depreciation—Tool B		4,300
Accumulated Depreciation—Tool C		4,500

$25,500/6 = $4,250; $34,400/8 = $4,300; $18,000/4 = $4,500.

Year 5

Work-in-Process Inventory............................	8,550	
Accumulated Depreciation—Tool A.............		4,250
Accumulated Depreciation—Tool B		4,300

Year 8

Work-in-Process Inventory............................	4,300	
Accumulated Depreciation—Tool B		4,300

c. $77,900/8 = $9,737.50 per year.

d. Assumption of *a*.. The cumulative depreciation charges are always larger. Thus, the cumulative taxable income and tax payments would be smaller until the tenth year. The present value of the tax payments would be less for any positive interest rate.

9.36 (The Mead Corporation; interpreting disclosures regarding plant assets.)

a.

Property, Plant and Equipment........................	315.6	
Cash		315.6
Depreciation Expense.....................................	188.1	
Accumulated Depreciation		188.1
Cash (Given)	38.7	
Loss on Sale of Property, Plant and Equipment (Plug)..	19.9	
Accumulated Depreciation ($1,803.7 + $188.1 − x = $1,849.3; x = $142.5)..................................	142.5	
Property, Plant and Equipment ($3,824.0 + $315.6 − x = $3,938.5; x = $201.1).............		201.1

b. .5($3,824.0 + $3,938.5)/$188.1 = 20.6 years.

c. .5($1,803.7 + $1,849.3)/$188.1 = 9.7 years.

d. $4,557.5/.5($2,020.3 + $2,089.5) = 2.2.

9.36 continued.

    e. $\$4,557.5/.5(\$1,013.8^a + \$1,108.0^b) = 4.3.$

          [a]$\$3,824.0 - \$2,810.2 = \$1,013.8.$
          [b]$\$3,938.5 - \$2,830.5 = \$1,108.0.$

9.37   (PepsiCo; interpreting disclosures regarding income taxes.)

    a.

Property, Plant and Equipment	2,253.2	
Cash		2,253.2
Depreciation Expense	1,200.0	
Accumulated Depreciation		1,200.0
Cash	55.3	
Accumulated Depreciation ($\$5,394.4 + \$1,200.0 - x = \$6,247.3$; $x = \$347.1$)	347.1	
Property, Plant and Equipment ($\$14,250.0 + \$2,253.2 - y = \$16,130.1$; $y = \$373.1$)		373.1
Gain on Sale of Property, Plant and Equipment (Plug)		29.3

    b. $.5(\$14,250.0 + \$16,130.1)/\$1,200.0 = 12.7$ years.

    c. $.5(\$5,394.4 + \$6,247.3)/\$1,200.0 = 4.9$ years.

    d. $\$28,472.4/.5(\$8,855.6 + \$9,882.8) = 3.0.$

    e. $\$28,472.4/.5(\$7,231.2^a + \$8,393.9^b) = 3.6.$

          [a]$\$14,250.0 - \$7,018.8 = \$7,231.2.$
          [b]$\$16,130.1 - \$7,736.7 = \$8,393.4.$

           Solutions

9.38   (Grand Met; accounting for plant asset revaluations.)

a. **December 31, Year 3 to Year 5**
    Depreciation Expense 10,000
        Accumulated Depreciation 10,000
    £10,000 = £50,000/5.

b. **January 1, Year 6**
    Equipment 5,000
        Revaluation Allowance............................... 5,000

    Current Market Value.. £ 25,000
    Book Value: £50,000 – (£10,000 × 3)............................... (20,000)
                                                                      £   5,000

c. **December 31, Year 6 and Year 7**
    Depreciation Expense 10,000
    Revaluation Allowance.................................... 2,500
        Accumulated Depreciation 12,500
    £2,500 = £5,000/2.

d. The revaluation and subsequent depreciation of the revaluation had
    no effect on net income. At the end of Year 7 just prior to removing
    the equipment form the books, the accounts appear as follows:

    Equipment (£50,000 + £5,000)... £ 55,000
    Accumulated Depreciation (£10,000 × 5) + (£2,500 × 2)......   55,000
    Revaluation Allowance [£5,000 – (£2,500 × 2)].................   -0-

9.39 (Consumer Products Company; capitalizing versus expensing advertising costs: effects on financial statements and rate of return.)

a. Rate of Return on Assets Assuming Advertising Costs Are Expensed in the Year Incurred:

Year	Other Income	Revenue from Advertising Campaign	Expenses for Advertising Campaign	Net Income	Payments to Owner	Addition to (Subtraction from) Total Assets	Total Assets End of Year	Rate of Return
1	$ 45,000	---	$(24,000)	$ 21,000	$ 45,000	$(24,000)	$276,000	7.61%
2	45,000	$ 10,000	---	55,000	47,000	8,000	284,000	19.37%
3	45,000	10,000	---	55,000	47,000	8,000	292,000	18.84%
4	45,000	10,000	---	55,000	47,000	8,000	300,000	18.33%
	$180,000	$ 30,000	$(24,000)	$186,000	$186,000	$ -0-		

b. Rate of Return on Assets Assuming Advertising Costs Are Capitalized:

Year	Other Income	Revenue from Advertising Campaign	Expenses for Advertising Campaign	Net Income	Payments to Owners	Addition to (Subtraction from) Total Assets	Total Assets End of Year	Rate of Return
1	$ 45,000	---	$ (8,000)	$ 45,000	$ 45,000	$ -0-	$300,000	15.00%
2	45,000	$ 10,000	(8,000)	47,000	47,000	-0-	300,000	15.67%
3	45,000	10,000	(8,000)	47,000	47,000	-0-	300,000	15.67%
4	45,000	10,000	(8,000)	47,000	47,000	-0-	300,000	15.67%
	$180,000	$ 30,000	$(24,000)	$186,000	$186,000	$ -0-		

c. Management has made the right decision to pursue the campaign. We know that the advertising campaign was profitable from our answer to Part b. above. We think the accounting in Part b. is better than in Part a., but not all accountants would agree. Most, in fact, would require expensing as in Part a. above.

 Solutions

9.40   (General Mills; expensing versus capitalizing advertising costs for firm advertising every year.)

	Year 1	Year 2	Year 3	Year 4
a. Expense Costs as Incurred				
Other Income.................	$ 30,000	$30,000	$30,000	$ 30,000
Additional Income from Advertising:				
First Year's Ads......	36,000	36,000	36,000	
Second Year's Ads...		36,000	36,000	36,000
Third Year's Ads.....			36,000	36,000
Fourth Year's Ads...				36,000
Advertising Expense.......	(90,000)	(90,000)	(90,000)	(90,000)
Net Income (Loss)..........	$(24,000)	$12,000	$48,000	$ 48,000

	Year 1	Year 2	Year 3	Year 4
b. Capitalize and Amortize Over 3 Years (Including Year of Occurrence)				
Other Income.................	$ 30,000	$ 30,000	$ 30,000	$ 30,000
Additional Income from Advertising:				
First Year's Ads......	36,000	36,000	36,000	
Second Year's Ads...		36,000	36,000	36,000
Third Year's Ads.....			36,000	36,000
Fourth Year's Ads...				36,000
Advertising Amortization Expense:				
First Year's Ads......	(30,000)	(30,000)	(30,000)	
Second Year's Ads...		(30,000)	(30,000)	(30,000)
Third Year's Ads.....			(30,000)	(30,000)
Fourth Year's Ads...				(30,000)
Net Income....................	$ 36,000	$ 42,000	$ 48,000	$ 48,000
Advertising Asset on Balance Sheet:				
First Year's Ads......	$ 60,000	$ 30,000		
Second Year's Ads...		60,000	$ 30,000	
Third Year's Ads.....			60,000	$ 30,000
Fourth Year's Ads...				60,000
Total...........................	$ 60,000	$ 90,000	$ 90,000	$ 90,000

9.40 continued.

    c. The expensing policy leads to higher expenses, lower income, and lower asset totals in the first two years. After that, the two policies are the same. When the firm ceases to advertise, the policy of expensing will show higher income in the two years when the benefits of prior advertising continue, but there are no matching expenses. There are no expenses under Policy (1), but Policy (2) continues to show amortization expense.

    d. The income under the two policies will continue to be the same if there is no growth or change in policy. Policy (2) will show a lower rate of return on total assets and a lower rate of return on stockholders' equity than will Policy (1) because the asset and equity totals are larger under Policy (2) than under Policy (1). When there is growth in advertising amounts over time and corresponding growth in income, Policy (2) will always appear worse than will Policy (1).

9.41   (Ross Laboratories; valuation of brand name.) (Dollar amounts in millions.)

			Part a.	Part b.
(1)	Operating Margin		$ 600.0	$ 600.0
	Employed Physical Capital $500.0			
	Subtract Pretax Profit on Physical Capital Required at 10 (Part *a.*) or 20 (Part *b.*)		(50.0)	(100.0)
(2)	Profit Generated by Brand		$ 550.0	$ 500.0
	Subtract Income Taxes at 40 Percent		(220.0)	(200.0)
(3)	Net Brand Profits		$ 330.0	$ 300.0
	Multiply by Aftertax Capitalization Factor		12.0	8.0
(4)	Estimate of Brand Value		$3,960.0	$2,400.0

9.42 (May Department Stores; improvements versus repairs or maintenance.)

a. **January 2**

Building (or Displays).....................................	28,000	
Cash		28,000

To record cost of new displays.

December 31

Depreciation Expense.....................................	24,000	
Accumulated Depreciation on Building.........		24,000

$24,000 = 1/7 \times [(\$800,000 - \$660,000 + \$28,000)] = 1/40 \times \$800,000 + 1/7 \times \$28,000$.

b. **January 2**

Loss..	28,000	
Building (or Accumulated Depreciation on Building)...		28,000

Recognize loss from destruction.

Building (or Accumulated Depreciation on Building)	28,000	
Cash..		28,000

To recognize cost of new windows.

These two entries are equivalent to, and could be replaced by:

Loss..	28,000	
Cash		28,000

December 31

Depreciation Expense.....................................	20,000	
Accumulated Depreciation		20,000

Depreciation for year on remaining $140,000 over 7 years = $800,000/40 years.

c. Same as *b.* above.

d. The authors split on this one. Some favor the treatment in Part *a.*, while others favor the treatment in Part *b.* or Part *c.*. Those favoring Part *a.* point to the voluntary nature of the decision to replace the windows rather than to close down. Presumably society as a whole benefits from use of shatter-proof windows or else regulations would not require them. If future benefits to society as a whole result and the firm decides to make the expenditure, an asset results which the firm will depreciate over its estimated service life. It would be improper, some say, to charge the entire cost of making future operations possible to this year. They cite the enormous expenditures for antipollution equipment as being similar.

9.42 d. continued.

Those favoring the treatment in Part *b.* argue that regulators require this expenditure to maintain the service potential of the building assets at the same level as before passage of the law. They see no essential difference between the economic effects of destruction by natural disaster (Part *b.*), man-made disaster (Part *c.*), and another form of man-made "disaster" (Part *d.*). It may seem antisocial to say that the passage of a law results in damage no different from vandalism, but the economic consequences to the owner of the business are the same in Parts *c.* and *d.*, and so they urge immediate expensing. They agree that the enormous expenditures for antipollution equipment are also a loss (at least to the degree that costs exceed firm-specific benefits) even though most firms do not expense such items.

The holders of the opposing (capitalize) view see a significant difference between natural (or man-made) disasters and democratic social decision, which they view as not being "man-made disasters."

e. If you believe that Part *d.* is like Part *a.*, then so is Part *e.* like Part *a.*. If you believe that Part *d.* is like Parts *b.* and *c.*, then the loss here should be only $21,000 (= $28,000 − $7,000). Depreciation expense for each of the last seven years is $21,000 [= ($140,000 + $7,000)/7 years].

9.43   (Epstein Company; accounting for intangibles.)

a. The issue here is the length of the amortization period. In spite of the fact that the company plans to make and sell indefinitely, the fair market value of $100,000 attached to the property right is allocable only to the next three years of use. After that, anyone can use the patent. Thus, we would amortize this patent over three years.

b. The same problem and reasoning above leads us to use a five-year life.

c. The amortization period here is theoretically indefinite, but APB *Opinion No. 17* does not permit a period longer than forty years.

d. In Year 2, we should debit expense and credit asset for the diminution in the value of the trade secret. This amount will be hard to estimate. The auditor may argue that the secret has lost all of its value and will require the write off of the remaining book value.

       Solutions

9.43 continued.

e. The firm should capitalize the film as an asset and write it off over its economic life. This is an easy statement to make, but the estimate of life might be as short as three years or as long as the firm sells thyristors, which appears to be the indefinite future. The firm will pick a number and be prepared to give in to the auditor who asks for a shorter life. Management will lack any sound arguments as to what the life should be. We would argue only with the immediate expensing of the film's cost.

Sheldon L. Epstein, former patent counsel of Brunswick Corporation, suggested this question to us. His reaction to the above answers is as follows:

a. The trademark registration is simple proof of ownership in the United States which the company could renew again and again for twenty-year periods. Because trademark rights will continue to exist as long as the company properly uses the mark, the amortization period is theoretically infinite. However, APB *Opinion No. 17* requires that the amortization period be no longer than 40 years. In the event that the company discontinues the use of the mark or loses the exclusive right to use the mark, the firm should write off the unamortized amount in the year in which the event occurs. Where the company owns a foreign trademark, the right to exclusive use may be dependent on a valid registration, and loss or expiration of the registration could require complete amortization in the year when such an event occurs. Note that trademarks receive a different accounting treatment from that given patents because trademarks can have an infinite life while patents expire on a known date.

b. The design patent grants the company the right to exclude others from manufacturing, using or selling the same or similar containers for 5 years. After that, anyone is free to copy the design. Therefore, the privilege of exclusivity diminishes with time and the value should be amortized over the remaining life of the patent.

c. I agree with your answer.

d. I agree with your answer but with the caveat that its value depends on what the competitor does with its knowledge of the trade secret. If it does nothing, then there is little or no loss of value. If it uses it for the purpose of competition, then its value diminishes by the present value of anticipated lost profits and the accountant should recognize the value lost in the year the event occurs. If a competitor publishes the trade secret, then all of its value is lost.

9.43 continued.

    e.   The answer is generally correct; however, note that the accounting treatment for copyrights lies somewhere between that used for patents and that used for trademarks. Under the copyright law, it is possible for the copyright to extend for periods well beyond 40 years or for a substantially shorter period (as would be the case for an old work). The important point is to ask what the remaining life of the exclusive privilege is and, in the case of a work licensed by the company from an individual, when the right reverts to the author (35 years). For example, copyrights in new works last for the life of the author plus 50 years except for anonymous or pseudonymous works for which the period is the first of 75 years from publication or 100 years from creation. For older works, many will expire on December 31, 2002; however, there are a number of exceptions.

9.44   (Capitalizing versus expensing; if capitalized, what amortization period?)

    a.   If the firm makes this expenditure to secure future benefits, then there is an argument for capitalizing it. The entries would be:

Building (or Fire Escapes)..............................	28,000	
Cash		28,000

To capitalize improvements.

Depreciation Expense....................................	4,000	
Accumulated Depreciation		4,000

One year's amortization of improvements based on a seven-year life.

A somewhat more logical view is that the firm made the expenditure to maintain the service potential that it had planned previously. It obtains no additional benefits beyond those planned. See the discussion in Problem 9.42 above. The expenditure is a result of new legislation, so this view results in the following entry at the time the law is passed:

Loss from New Legislation............................	28,000	
Building (or Accumulated Depreciation).......		28,000

To recognize loss.

When the expenditure is made, the entry is:

Building (or Fire Escapes)............................	28,000	
Cash		28,000

To capitalize expenditure for fire escapes.

         Solutions

9.44 a. continued.

This second treatment results in immediate recognition of the loss, and subsequent depreciation of the building improvements and fire escapes is the same as before the law was passed.

b. Building.. 1,050,000
    Investment in General Electric Stock............   100,000
    Gain on Disposal of Investment....................   950,000

In the case of widely traded stock, the stock market valuation is probably a better guide than is the appraisal value of a single building.

c. Building.. 1,000,000
    Investment in Small Timers Stock................   100,000
    Gain on Disposal of Investment....................   900,000

For thinly traded issues, the appraisal value of the building may be a more reliable guide. Many people think that investors cannot sell large blocks of such stock at once, except at a discount from the quoted price per share. We would not argue with the same answer as Part *b.* above.

d. Garages..   18,000
    Cash   18,000
To capitalize improvements to garages.

Depreciation Expense.....................................   900
    Accumulated Depreciation..........................   900
$18,000/20 years = $900 per year.

The useful life of the improvements in this case is likely to be as long as the useful lives of the garages. A case can be made, however, for amortization over five or ten years.

e. See the glossary at *reserve-recognition accounting*.

Successful-Efforts Accounting Would Be:

Drilling Expense...   9,000,000
Oil Well   1,000,000
    Cash..   10,000,000

Full-Cost Accounting Would Be:

Oil Well   10,000,000
    Cash..   10,000,000

9.44 e. continued.

Reserve-Recognition Accounting Would Be:

Oil Well	40,000,000	
Cash..		10,000,000
Revenue from Successful Exploration		
Efforts...		30,000,000

Reserve-recognition accounting provides the most up-to-date or current valuation for the oil well. However, because accountants generally base asset valuations on acquisition cost, the choice is between successful-efforts and full costing. The principal argument for full costing is that firms must incur the costs of many dry holes in order to find a few productive holes. The cost of the dry holes is, therefore, a cost of finding productive ones and capitalization is appropriate. The principal argument for successful-efforts costing is that firms capitalize expenditures leading to future benefits (productive hole) but expense expenditures not creating future benefits (dry holes), consistent with the usual accounting for assets and expenses.

f.	Advertising Expense	400,000	
	Cash		400,000

Firms generally immediately expense expenditures on advertising. Theoretically, the firm should capitalize some portion of the expenditures as an asset because the company probably would not spend on advertising unless it expected future benefits. However, firms seldom follow the more theoretically sound procedure in practice due to the difficulty of identifying and measuring the future benefits.

g.	Research Expense..	1,500,000	
	Cash		1,500,000

This is the treatment required by FASB *Statement No. 2*, although we criticize it. The company has a proven record of success with its research and it would not continue the research expenditures unless it expected future benefits. Capitalization of these benefits on the balance sheet and subsequent amortization is at least a theoretically superior treatment.

9.44 continued.

h. Charitable Contribution (Expense)................... 250,000
    Cash 250,000

Although some indirect future benefit may come to the company, it is too indefinite to justify recognition. We wonder, though, if companies give away money without some expectation of future benefit.

i. Machine Tools... 6,000,000
    Cash 6,000,000
To set up asset account.

Depreciation of Machine Tools (a production
    cost) 2,000,000
      Machine Tools... 2,000,000
Amortize over 3 years, the life of the automobile model. An alternative entry debits the Inventory account.

The tools will be obsolete in three years; their physical life of six years is irrelevant. For some reason, automobile manufacturers do not show accumulated depreciation on special tools in published statements; credits appear to go directly to the asset account.

j. (Dollar Amounts in Millions)

Start of Year
Plant Assets (Airbuses) 100
    Cash 100
To record purchase of airplanes.

Plant Assets (Spare Parts)............................ 20
    Cash 20
To record spare parts as plant assets, not as inventory. This is the point of the question. Because the spare parts are giving up their future benefits as the firm uses the airplanes, we treat their cost as plant assets. At the end of the useful life of the airplanes, the spare parts will be worthless. We think they should be depreciated over the life of the airplanes, not accounted for like an inventory of parts which the firm can use in various alternative ways. Nothing in the chapter alerts the student to this treatment and many, if not most, will set up the asset as inventory.

9.44 j. continued.

(Dollar Amounts in Millions)

End of Year

Depreciation Expense..	12	
Accumulated Depreciation		12

Depreciation on plant assets for 1/10 of useful life costing $120 (= $100 + $20) in total. This treatment is consistent with that described in the preceding entry.

Whether or not the instructor or students agree with us, the point is worth discussing. Is the cost of spare parts acquired solely for use with a plant asset and therefore treated like plant assets or like inventory?

k. (Dollar Amounts in Millions)

End of Year

Depreciation Expense..	12	
Accumulated Depreciation		12

The entry made for the same reason as in the preceding question. We think the following entries, which result from treating the spare parts as inventory, are wrong:

Depreciation Expense..	10	
Accumulated Depreciation		10
Repair Expense...	1	
Spare Parts Inventory		1

9.45 (Recognizing and measuring impairment losses.)

a. The loss occurs because of an adverse action by a governmental entity. The undiscounted cash flows of $50 million are less than the book value of the building of $60 million. An impairment loss has therefore occurred. The market value of the building of $32 million is less than the book value of $60 million. Thus, the amount of the impairment loss is 28 million (= $60 million − $32 million). The journal entry to record the impairment loss is (in millions):

Loss from Impairment....................................	28	
Accumulated Depreciation..........................	20	
Building		48

9.45 a. continued.

This entry records the impairment loss, eliminates the accumulated depreciation, and writes down the building to its market value of $32 million (= $80 − $48).

b. The undiscounted cash flows of $70 exceed the book value of the building of $60 million. Thus, no impairment loss occurs according to the definition in FASB *Statement No. 121*. An **economic** loss occurred but GAAP does not permit it to be recognized.

c. The loss arises because the accumulated costs significantly exceed the amount originally anticipated. The undiscounted future cash flows of $22 million exceed the book value of the building of $25 million. Thus, an impairment loss has occurred. The impairment loss recognized equals $9 million (= $25 million − $16 million). The journal entry is (in millions):

Loss from Impairment	9	
Construction in Process		9

d. The loss occurs because of a significant decline in the market value of the patent. FASB *Statement No. 121* requires the accountant to combine the patent and goodwill in measuring the loss. The undiscounted future cash flows of $18 million are less than the book value of the patent and goodwill of $34 million (= $20 + $14). Thus, an impairment loss occurred. The amount of the loss is $22 million (= $34 million − $52 million). The journal entry to record the loss is:

Loss from Impairment	22	
Goodwill		14
Patent		8

Statement No. 121 requires the reduction of goodwill to zero before a firm writes down the identifiable intangible asset (patent) in the amount of the impairment loss.

e. The loss occurs because of a significant change in the business climate for Chicken Franchisees. One might question whether this loss is temporary or permanent. Evidence from previous similar events (for example, Tylenol) suggests that consumers soon forget or at least forgive the offending company. The FASB reporting standard discusses but rejects the use of a permanency criterion in identifying impairment losses. Thus, an impairment loss occurs in this case because the future undiscounted cash flows of $6 million from the franchise rights exceed the book value of the franchise rights of $10 million. Note that Chicken Franchisees must separate the cash flows associated with the preparing and selling of chicken in its physical facilities from the cash flows associated with the

9.45 e. continued.

Chicken Delight franchise name. The amount of the impairment loss is $7 million (= $10 million – $3 million). The journal entry is (in millions):

Impairment Loss...	7	
Franchise Rights.......................................		7

This entry assumes that Chicken Franchisees does not use an Accumulated Amortization account.

9.46 (Ormes Company; preparing statement of cash flows.) A T-account worksheet for Ormes Company for Year 2 appears after the statement of cash flows.

ORMES COMPANY
Statement of Cash Flows
For Year 2

Operations:		
Net Income..	$ 60,000	
Addbacks and Additions:		
Bad Debt Expense....................................	20,000	
Depreciation Expense	39,000	
Loss on Sale of Equipment.....................	8,000	
Amortization Expense.............................	15,000	
Increase in Accounts Payable................	27,000	
Subtractions:		
Gain on Sale of Patent	(125,000)	
Increase in Accounts Receivable	(29,200)	
Increase in Inventories	(25,000)	
Cash Flow from Operations...........................		$ (10,200)
Investing:		
Sale of Patents...	$ 125,000	
Sale of Property, Plant and Equipment......	10,000	
Acquisition of Patent.................................	(75,000)	
Acquisition of Property, Plant and Equipment..	(62,900)	
Cash Flow from Investing..............................		(2,900)
Financing:		
Common Stock Issued	$ 43,900	
Dividends...	(25,000)	
Cash Flow from Financing		18,900
Change in Cash..		$ 5,800
Cash, Beginning of Year 2		25,700
Cash, End of Year 2.......................................		$ 31,500

Supplementary Information

Ormes Company issued $30,000 of its common stock in the acquisition of property, plant and equipment during Year 2.

9.46 continued.

Cash

√	25,700		

Operations

(1)	60,000	125,000	(5)
(7)	20,000	29,200	(9)
(11)	39,000	25,000	(10)
(12)	8,000		
(13)	15,000		
(14)	27,000		

Investing

(5)	125,000	62,900	(3)
(12)	10,000	75,000	(6)

Financing

(15)	43,900	25,000	(2)

√	31,500	

Accounts Receivable

√	120,000		
(9)	29,200	19,200	(8)
√	130,000		

Allowance for Uncollectable Accounts

		2,400	√
(8)	19,200	20,000	(7)
		3,200	√

Inventory

√	175,000	
(10)	25,000	
√	200,000	

Property, Plant and Equipment

√	247,300		
(3)	62,900	40,000	(12)
(4)	30,000		
√	300,200		

Accumulated Depreciation

		78,000	√
(12)	22,000	39,000	(11)
		95,000	√

Patents

(6)	75,000	
√	75,000	

9.46 continued.

Accumulated Amortization		
--		
	15,000	(13)
	15,000	√

Accounts Payable		
	155,000	√
	27,000	(14)
	182,000	√

Common Stock		
	100,000	√
	30,000	(4)
	43,900	(15)
	173,900	√

Retained Earnings				
			232,600	√
(2)	25,000		60,000	(1)
			267,600	√

 Solutions

CHAPTER 10

LIABILITIES: INTRODUCTION

Questions, Exercises, Problems, and Cases: Answers and Solutions

10.1   See the text or the glossary at the end of the book.

10.2   a.   Yes; amount of accrued interest payable.

        b.   Yes. In spite of the indefiniteness of the time of delivery of the goods or services and the amount, the balance sheet reports a liability in the amount of the cash received.

        c.   No; accounting does not record executory promises.

        d.   Yes; at the present value, calculated using the yield rate at the time of issue, of the remaining coupon and principal payments.

        e.   Yes; at the expected, undiscounted value of future service costs arising from all sales made prior to the balance sheet date. The income statement includes warranty expense because of a desire to match all expenses of a sale with the sale; presumably one reason the firm sold the product was the promise of free repairs. When recognizing the expense, the accountant credits a liability account to recognize the need for the future expenditures.

        f.   No. If the firm expected to lose a reasonably estimable amount in the suit, then it would show an estimated liability.

        g.   Yes, assuming statutes or contracts require the restoration. The present value of an estimate of the costs is the theoretically correct answer, but many accountants would use the full amount undiscounted.

        h.   No; viewed as executory.

        i.   Airlines should recognize an expense and a liability for the estimated costs of providing the free flight during the periods when customers use flight services at regular fares. The airlines argue that they incur virtually no incremental cost for the free flight because the customer uses otherwise unused capacity. Thus, the airlines do not recognize an obligation for their frequent flyer programs.

       Solutions

10.3   The store should recognize the loss as soon as it is probable that it has incurred a liability and it can reasonably estimate the amount of the loss. Whether the store recognizes a loss at the time of the injury on July 5, Year 6, depends on the strength of the case the store feels it has against the customer's claims. If the floor was wet because a broken bottle had remained on the floor for several hours and was not cleaned up, then the store may feel it is probable that it has incurred a liability. If, on the other hand, the customer fell while running down a dry, uncluttered aisle while trying to shop quickly, then the store may feel that it is probable that it has not incurred a liability. Attorneys, not accountants, must make these probability assessments.

     If the store does not recognize a loss at the time of the injury, the next most likely time is June 15, Year 7, when the jury renders its verdict. Unless attorneys for the store feel that it is highly probable that the court will reverse the verdict on appeal, the store should recognize the loss at this time.

     If attorneys feel that the grounds for appeal are strong, then the next most likely time is on April 20, Year 8, when the jury in the lower court reaches the same verdict as previously. This is the latest time in this case at which the store should recognize the loss. If the store had recognized a loss on June 15, Year 7, it would recognize only the extra damage award in Year 8.

10.4   The expected value of the liability is $90,000 in both cases ($.90 \times \$100,000 = \$90,000$; $.09 \times \$1 \times 1,000,000 = \$90,000$). Accounting would probably report the liability from the lawsuit as $100,000 and the liability for the coupons as $90,000. This inconsistency seems curious since the two situations differ only with respect to the number of possible outcomes (that is, all or nothing with respect to the lawsuit, whereas the coupon redemption rate conceivably ranges from one to one million).

10.5   Suppliers often grant a discount if customers pay within a certain number of days after the invoice date, in which case this source of funds has an explicit interest cost. Suppliers who do not offer discounts for prompt payment often include an implicit interest change in the selling price of the product. Customers in this second category should delay payment as long as possible because they are paying for the use of the funds. Firms should not delay payment to such an extent that it hurts their credit rating and raises their cost of financing.

10.6   The school should accrue the salary in ten monthly installments of $36,000 each at the end of each month, September through June. It will have paid $30,000 at the end of each of these months, so that by the end of the reporting year, it reports a current liability of $60,000 [$= \$360,000 - (10 \times \$30,000)$].

10.7 There are two principal explanations. First, the obligation to customers in the event the firm does not publish the magazines is $45,000. Second, recognition of a liability of $32,000 requires a remaining credit of $13,000 to some other account. Recognizing the $13,000 as income is inappropriate because the publisher has not yet rendered the required services. Including the $13,000 is some type of Deferred Income account (a liability) has the same effect on total liabilities as reporting the Advance from Customers at $45,000.

10.8 It is cheaper (and, therefore, more profitable) to repair a few sets than to have such stringent quality control that the manufacturing process produces zero defectives. An allowance is justified when firms expect to have warranty costs. Manufacturers of TV sets for space travel or heart pacemakers should strive for zero defects.

10.9 **Similarities:** The accountant makes estimates of future events in both cases. The accountant charges the cost of estimated uncollectibles or warranties to income in the period of sale, not in the later period when specific items become uncollectible or break down. The income statement reports the charge against income as an expense in both cases, although some accountants report the charge for estimated uncollectibles as a revenue contra (and we prefer it that way).

Differences: The balance sheet account showing the expected costs of future uncollectibles reduces an asset account, while that for estimated warranties appears as a liability.

10.10 The coupon rate and par value of the bonds, the market rate of interest, and the market's opinion of the firm as a borrower. If the coupon rate is 8 percent, the market rate is 12 percent and the market views the firm as a relatively poor credit risk, the bonds will sell at a price to yield say, 15 percent. This means that the firm will receive less than the par value of the bonds it issues. We are told that when bonds are brought to the market, the investment banker attempts to set the coupon rate so the bonds will sell close to par.

10.11 a. Par value and face value are always synonymous.

b. Par value appears on the bond certificate and serves as the base for computing the periodic coupon interest payment. The book value is the same as the par value whenever the market-required interest rate on the date of issue equals the coupon interest rate. The book value will exceed the par value when the coupon rate exceeds the market rate at the time of issue. The par value will exceed the book value when the market rate exceeds the coupon rate at the time of issue.

10.11 continued.

    c.   Book value equals the present value of future cash flows on a bond discounted at the market-required interest rate at the time of issue. Current market value equals the present value of future cash flows on a bond discounted at the interest rate the market currently requires to induce purchase of the bond. The book value exceeds the current market value when the market interest rate at the time of issue was lower than the current market interest rate. The current market value will exceed the book value when the current market interest rate is lower than the market interest rate at the time of issue.

10.12   Accountants initially record assets at acquisition cost and then allocate this amount to future periods as an expense. Changes in the market value of most assets (except for use of the lower-of-cost-or-market method for inventories and the market value method for marketable securities and investments in securities) do not appear in the accounting records. Similarly, using the market interest rate at the time of issue to account for bonds results in an initial liability equal to the amount of cash received and a subsequent liability that reflects amortization of this initial amount. Changes in the market value of bonds do not appear in the accounting records.

10.13   Interest expense as a percentage of the book value of a liability at the beginning of a period equals the market interest rate at the time debt was issued. Accountants use this interest rate throughout the life of the debt under the effective interest method. The amount of interest expense will change if the book value changes each period. The latter occurs if the firm issues debt at an amount exceeding or less than par or if each periodic payment includes a repayment of a portion of the principal.

10.14   With bond financing, the firm borrows the entire principal, $1 million, for the entire term of the loan. With lease or mortgage financing, the firm repays part of the principal with each payment. Thus, the effective amount borrowed decreases over time and interest expenses should also decrease, even though the borrowings use the same rate.

10.15   Zero coupon bonds offer no cash payments to the investor until maturity. The issuer benefits by delaying cash payments. The issuer also gets a tax deduction for interest expense (that is, amortization of bond discount) during the period the bonds are outstanding even though it has no immediate cash outflow for interest. The investor locks in a yield at the time of purchase. The investor need not worry about having to invest periodic coupon payments during the life of the bonds. Thus, the investor avoids the risk of interest rate changes. The disadvantage to the investor is that the amortization of bond discount during the life of the bonds is taxable income even though the investor receives no cash. Most investors in zero coupon bonds do not pay taxes (for example, pension funds).

10.16 The call premium, which typically declines as bonds approach maturity, compensates bondholders for the loss of interest payments when a firm calls, or buys back, some of its outstanding bonds before the maturity date. The call premium protects the bondholder from redemption by the issuer if interest rates in the market decline by reasonably small amounts.

10.17 When market interest rates change, so do market values of bonds. When interest rates rise, bond prices decline, but book values of bonds remain unchanged. Firms can issue new bonds at current market rates and use the proceeds to retire outstanding bonds previously issued when rates were lower, and accountants record this transaction as a gain. The gain actually occurred as market rates rose and the burden of the debt fell. This is an unrealized holding gain in historical cost accounting. Because management can time bond retirements, management can time income recognition. This possibility explains in part the requirement that firms report gains and losses on bond retirements as extraordinary items in the income statement.

10.18 (McGee Associates; journal entries for payroll.)

a.
Wage and Salary Expense	700,000	
U.S. Withholding Taxes Payable		126,000
State Withholding Taxes Payable		35,000
FICA Taxes Payable		42,000
Wages and Salaries Payable		497,000

Amounts payable to and for employees.

Wage and Salary Expense	107,800	
FICA Taxes Payable		42,000
FUTA Taxes Payable to U.S. Government		14,000
FUTA Taxes Payable to State Government		7,000
Payable to Profit Sharing Fund		28,000
Vacation Liability		16,800

Employer's additional wage expense; estimated vacation liability is $16,800 (= 1.20 × $14,000).

b. $807,800 = $700,000 + $107,800.

10.19 (PepsiCo; computations and journal entries for income taxes payable.)

Income Taxes at .35 × $1,900 million = $665.0 million.
Income Taxes at .35 × $2,010 million = $703.5 million.
Income Taxes at .35 × $1,940 million = $679.0 million.
Income Taxes at .35 × $1,950 million = $682.5 million.
Income Taxes at .35 × $2,000 million = $700.0 million.

 Solutions

10.19 continued.

a. (Amounts in Millions)

(1)   **Tax Returns**

Date	Estimated Taxes for Year	Cumulative Payments Due	Payment
4/15/Y1	$ 665.00	$ 166.25[a]	$ 166.25
6/15/Y1	703.50	351.75[b]	188.50
9/15/Y1	679.00	509.25[c]	154.50
12/15/Y1	682.50	682.50	173.25
12/31/Y1	700.00	--	--
3/15/Y2	700.00	700.00	17.50
			$ 700.00

[a]$1/4 \times \$665.0$ million. [b]$1/2 \times \$703.5$ million. [c]$3/4 \times \$679.0$ million.

(2)   **Financial Statements**

Date	Tax Expense for Quarter	Cumulative Tax Expense
3/31/Y1	$ 166.25	$ 166.25
6/30/Y1	188.50	351.75
9/30/Y1	154.50	509.25
12/31/Y1	190.75	700.00
For Year................	$ 700.00	

b. (Amounts in Millions)

Year 1

March 31

Tax Expense...	166.25	
Taxes Payable..		166.25

April 15

Taxes Payable..	166.25	
Cash		166.25

June 15

Prepaid Taxes...	188.50	
Cash		188.50

June 30

Tax Expense...	188.50	
Prepaid Taxes		188.50

10.19 b. continued.

Sept. 15
Prepaid Taxes... 154.50
    Cash 154.50

Sept. 30
Tax Expense.. 154.50
    Prepaid Taxes 154.50

Dec. 15
Prepaid Taxes... 173.25
    Cash 173.25

Dec. 31
Tax Expense.. 190.75
    Prepaid Taxes 173.25
    Taxes Payable... 17.50

Year 2

March 15
Taxes Payable.. 17.50
    Cash 17.50

c. (Amounts in Millions)

Date	Cash	Prepaid Income Taxes	Income Taxes Payable		Tax Expense
Year 1					
March 31				166.25	166.25
April 15	166.25		166.25		
June 15	188.50	188.50			
June 30			188.50		188.50
Sept. 15	154.50	154.50			
Sept. 30			154.50		154.50
Dec. 15	173.25	173.25			
Dec. 31			173.25	17.50	190.75
		√ 0		17.50√	√ 700.00
Year 2					
March 15	17.50		17.50		

10.20   (Delicious Cafeteria; journal entries for coupons.)

a. **January**

Cash	50,100	
Sales Revenue		48,000
Coupon Liability		2,100

| Coupon Liability.. | 1,600 | |
| Sales Revenue .... | | 1,600 |

February

Cash..	50,700	
Sales Revenue		48,500
Coupon Liability		2,200

| Coupon Liability.. | 2,300 | |
| Sales Revenue .... | | 2,300 |

March

Cash..	52,400	
Sales Revenue		50,000
Coupon Liability		2,400

| Coupon Liability.. | 2,100 | |
| Sales Revenue .... | | 2,100 |

b. The Coupon Liability account has a balance of $4,700 (= $4,000 + $2,100 − $1,600 + $2,200 − $2,300 + $2,400 − $2,100) on March 31.

10.21   (Abson Corporation; journal entries for service contracts.)

a. **1/31–3/31**

| Cash.. | 180,000 | |
| Service Contract Fees Received in Advance.... | | 180,000 |

To record sale of 300 annual contracts.

3/31

| Service Contract Fees Received in Advance....... | 22,500 | |
| Contract Revenues.................................... | | 22,500 |

To recognize revenue on 300 contracts sold during the first quarter; 1.5/12 × $180,000.

1/01–3/31

| Service Expenses.. | 32,000 | |
| Cash (and Other Assets and Liabilities)......... | | 32,000 |

10.21 a. continued.

4/01–6/30

Cash..	300,000	
Service Contract Fees Received in Advance....		300,000
To record sale of 500 annual contracts.		

6/30

Service Contract Fees Received in Advance.......	82,500	
Contract Revenues......................................		82,500

To recognize revenue on 500 contracts sold and
300 contracts outstanding:

   First Quarter:

      3/12   X $ 180,000 = $45,000

   Second Quarter:

      1.5/12 X $ 300,000 = <u>37,500</u>

                                       <u>$82,500</u>

4/01–6/30

Service Expenses...	71,000	
Cash (and Other Assets and Liabilities)........		71,000

7/01–9/30

Cash..	240,000	
Service Contract Fees Received in Advance....		240,000
To record sale of 400 annual contracts.		

9/30

Service Contract Fees Received in Advance.......	150,000	
Contract Revenues......................................		150,000

To recognize revenue on 400 contracts sold and
800 contracts outstanding from prior sales.

   First Quarter Sales:

      3/12   X $180,000 = $ 45,000

   Second Quarter Sales:

      3/12   X $300,000 =   75,000

   Third Quarter Sales:

      1.5/12 X $240,000 =   <u>30,000</u>

                                = <u>$ 150,000</u>

7/01–9/30

Service Expenses...	105,000	
Cash (and Other Assets and Liabilities)........		105,000

   10-9   **Solutions**

10.21 continued.

b. Balances in Service Contract Fees Received in Advance Account:

January 1	--
Less First Quarter Expirations	$ (22,500)
Plus First Quarter Sales	180,000
March 31	$ 157,500
Less Second Quarter Expirations	(82,500)
Plus Second Quarter Sales	300,000
June 30	$ 375,000
Less Third Quarter Expirations	(150,000)
Plus Third Quarter Sales	240,000
September 30	$ 465,000
Less Fourth Quarter Expirations	(195,000)
Plus Fourth Quarter Sales	120,000
December 31	$ 390,000

OR

Contracts	X	Balance Remaining	X	$ 600	=	Amount
300	X	1.5/12	X	$ 600	=	$ 22,500
500	X	4.5/12	X	$ 600	=	112,500
400	X	7.5/12	X	$ 600	=	150,000
200	X	10.5/12	X	$ 600	=	105,000
						$ 390,000

10.22 (Maypool Corporation; journal entries for estimated warranty liabilities and subsequent expenditures.)

a. **Year 1**

Accounts Receivable	1,200,000	
Sales		1,200,000
Estimated Warranty Liability	12,000	
Cash		12,000
Expenditures actually made.		
Warranty Expense	48,000	
Estimated Warranty Liability		48,000
(.01 + .03) × $1,200,000.		

10.22 a. continued.

Year 2

Accounts Receivable	1,500,000	
Sales Revenue		1,500,000

Estimated Warranty Liability	50,000	
Cash		50,000

Expenditures actually made.

Warranty Expense	60,000	
Estimated Warranty Liability		60,000

$(.01 + .03) \times \$1,500,000$.

b. $\$46,000 = \$48,000 - \$12,000 + \$60,000 - \$50,000$.

10.23 (Global Motors Corporation; journal entries for estimated warranty liabilities and subsequent expenditures.)

a. **Year 1**

Cash	800,000	
Sales Revenue		800,000

Estimated Warranty Liability	22,000	
Cash		13,200
Parts Inventory		8,800

Warranty Expense	48,000	
Estimated Warranty Liability		48,000

$.06 \times \$800,000 = \$48,000$.

Year 2

Cash	1,200,000	
Sales Revenue		1,200,000

Estimated Warranty Liability	55,000	
Cash		33,000
Parts Inventory		22,000

Warranty Expense	72,000	
Estimated Warranty Liability		72,000

$.06 \times \$1,200,000 = \$72,000$.

10.23 a. continued.

Year 3

Cash	900,000	
Sales Revenue		900,000
Estimated Warranty Liability	52,000	
Cash		31,200
Parts Inventory		20,800
Warranty Expense	54,000	
Estimated Warranty Liability		54,000

.06 × $900,000 = $54,000.

b. $48,000 − $22,000 + $72,000 − $55,000 + $54,000 − $52,000 = $45,000.

10.24 (Sung Company; journal entry for short-term note payable.)

a. **12/01**

Cash	50,000	
Notes Payable		50,000

12/31

Interest Expense	250	
Interest Payable		250

$50,000 × .06 × 30/360 = $250.

1/30

Interest Expense	250	
Interest Payable		250

1/30

Notes Payable (Original Note)	50,000	
Interest Payable	500	
Notes Payable (New Note)		50,000
Cash		500

    Note: Omitting the entries to the Notes Payable account above is also acceptable.

3/2

Notes Payable	50,000	
Interest Expense	250	
Cash		50,250

10.24 continued.

b. The entry to complete the accrual of interest (30 days) is the first entry under both alternatives. It is:

Interest Expense	250	
Interest Payable		250

(1) **1/30**

Notes Payable (Original Note)	50,000	
Interest Payable	500	
Cash		50,500

(2) **1/30**

Notes Payable (Original Note)	30,000	
Interest Payable	500	
Notes Payable (New Note)		30,500

10.25 (Blaydon Company; amortization schedule for note where explicit interest differs from market rate of interest.)

a. **Amortization Schedule for a Three-Year Note with a Maturity Value of $40,000, Calling for 8-Percent Annual Interest Payments, Yield of 12 Percent per Year**

Year (1)	Book Value Start of Year (2)	Interest Expense for Period (3)a	Payment (4)	Interest Added to (Subtracted from) Book Value (5)	Book Value End of Year (6)
0					$ 36,157
1	$ 36,157	$ 4,339	$ 3,200	$ 1,139	37,296
2	37,296	4,476	3,200	1,276	38,572
3	38,572	4,628	43,200	(38,572)	-0-

a(3) = (2) X .12, except in Year 3 where it is a plug.

b.

Computer	36,157	
Note Payable		36,157

To record purchase.

Annual Journal Entry for Interest and Principal

Dr. Interest Expense.. Amount in Col. (3)		
Cr. Cash		Amount in Col. (4)
Cr. Note Payable		Amount in Col. (5)*

*In third year, the firm debits Note Payable for $38,572.

10.26   (Skinner Corporation; computing the issue price of bonds.)

a.

Required Cash Flows	Present Value Factor for 6 Percent Discount Rate Compounded Semi-annually for 10 Years	Present Value of Required Cash Flows
$ 10,000,000 at End of 10 Years	.55368[a]	$ 5,536,800
$400,000 Every Six Months for 10 Years	14.87747[b]	5,950,988
Issue Price		$11,487,788

[a]Table 2, 3-percent column and 20-period row.
[b]Table 4, 3-percent column and 20-period row.

b.

Required Cash Flows	Present Value Factor for 8 Percent Discount Rate Compounded Semi-annually for 10 Years	Present Value of Required Cash Flows
$ 10,000,000 at End of 10 Years	.45639[a]	$ 4,563,900
$400,000 Every Six Months for 10 Years	13.59033[b]	5,436,132
Issue Price		$10,000,032[c]

[a]Table 2, 4-percent column and 20-period row.
[b]Table 4, 4-percent column and 20-period row.
[c]Difference from $10,000,000 due to rounding.

c.

Required Cash Flows	Present Value Factor for 10 Percent Discount Rate Compounded Semi-annually for 10 Years	Present Value of Required Cash Flows
$ 10,000,000 at End of 10 Years	.37689[a]	$ 3,768,900
$400,000 Every Six Months for 10 Years	12.46221[b]	4,984,884
Issue Price		$ 8,753,784

[a]Table 2, 5-percent column and 20-period row.
[b]Table 4, 5-percent column and 20-period row.

10.27 (Computing the issue price of bonds.)

a. $1,000,000 × .23138[a] .... $ 231,380
$60,000 × 15.37245[b] 922,347
    Issue Price $1,153,727

[a]Table 2, 5-percent column and 30-period row.
[b]Table 4, 5-percent column and 30-period row.

b. $75,000 × 17.29203[a] $1,296,902

[a]Table 4, 4-percent column and 30-period row.

c. $1,000,000 × .17411[a] .... $ 174,110

[a]Table 2, 6-percent column and 30-period row.

10.28 (O'Brien Corporation; computing the issue price of bonds and interest expense.)

a. $8,000,000 × .30656[a] $2,452,480
$320,000 × 23.11477[b] 7,396,726
    Issue Price $9,849,206

[a]Table 2, 3-percent column and 40-period row.
[b]Table 4, 3-percent column and 40-period row.

b. .03 × $9,849,206 = $295,476.

c. .03($9,849,206 + $295,476 − $320,000) = $294,740.

d. Book Value: ($9,849,206 + $295,476 − $320,000 +
    $294,740 − $320,000) $9,799,422

e. $8,000,000 × .32523[a] $2,601,840
$320,000 × 22.49246[b] 7,197,587
    Present Value $9,799,427

[a]Table 2, 3-percent column and 38-period row.
[b]Table 4 3-percent column and 38-period row.

The difference between the book value in Part *d.* and the present value in Part *e.* results from rounding present value factors.

                      Solutions

10.29 (Robinson Company; computing the issue price of bonds and interest expense.)

a.

$5,000,000 × .37689[a]	....	$1,884,450
$200,000 × 12.46221[b]	....	2,492,442
Issue Price	....	$4,376,892

[a]Table 2, 5-percent column and 20-period row.
[b]Table 4, 5-percent column and 20-period row.

b. .05 × $4,376,892 = $218,845.

c. .05($4,376,892 + $218,845 − $200,000) = $219,787.

d. $4,376,892 + $218,845 − $200,000 + $219,787 − $200,000 = $4,415,524.

e.

$5,000,000 × .41552[a]	....	$2,077,600
$200,000 × 11.68959[b]	....	2,337,918
Present Value	....	$4,415,518

[a]Table 2, 5-percent column and 18-period row.
[b]Table 4, 5-percent column and 18-period row.

The difference between the book value in Part *d.* and the present value in Part *e.* results from rounding present value factors.

10.30 (Florida Edison Company; using bond tables; computing interest expense.)

a. $885,301; see Table 5, 10-year row, 12-percent column.

b. $53,118 = .06 × $885,301.

c. $53,305 = .06 × $888,419; see Table 5, 9.5-year row, 12-percent column.

d. $926,399; see Table 5, 5-year row, 12-percent column.

e. $55,584 = .06 × $926,399.

10.31 (Centrex Company; using bond tables.)

Refer to Table 6.

a. $1,084,658; 25-year row; 11-percent column.

b. $1,080,231; 20-year row; 11-percent column.

c. $1,072,669; 15-year row; 11-percent column.

10.31 continued.

d. $1,072,669; same answer is *not* coincidental.

e. ($1,000,000 × .06) − ($1,004,739 − $1,000,000) = $60,000 − $4,739 = $55,261; 0.5-year row; 11-percent column.

f. $934,707; 15-year row; 13-percent column.

g. 10 percent compounded semiannually; scan 10-year row to find 112.46.

10.32 (Margie Rogers; partial amortization schedule for mortgage.)

Date	Total Paid	Interest	Principal	Balance
Month 0				$ 112,000.00
1	$ 802.40	$ 560.00[a]	$ 242.40	111,757.60
2	802.40	558.79	243.61	111,513.99
3	802.40	557.57	244.83	111,269.16
4	802.40	556.35	246.05	111,023.11

[a].005 × balance at beginning of the month.

10.33 (Womack Company; amortization schedule for bonds.)

a.
$100,000 × .67556[a]	$ 67,556
$5,000 × 8.11090[b]	40,555
Issue Price...	$ 108,111[c]

[a]Table 2, 4-percent column and 10-period row.
[b]Table 4, 4-percent column and 10-period row.
[c]Also see Table 5.

b.

Six-Month Period	Liability at Start of Period	Interest at 4 Percent for Period	Coupon at 5% of Par	Increase in Book Value of Liability	Liability at End of Period
0					$ 108,111
1	$ 108,111	$ 4,324	$ 5,000	$ 676	107,435
2	107,435	4,297	5,000	703	106,732
3	106,732	4,269	5,000	731	106,001
4	106,001	4,240	5,000	760	105,241
5	105,241	4,210	5,000	790	104,451
6	104,451	4,178	5,000	822	103,629
7	103,629	4,145	5,000	855	102,774
8	102,774	4,111	5,000	889	101,885
9	101,885	4,075	5,000	925	100,960
10	100,960	4,040[a]	5,000	960	100,000
Total.................		$41,889	$50,000	$8,111	

[a]Does not equal .04 × $100,960 due to rounding.

 Solutions

10.33 continued.

    c.   Book Value of Bonds: $10,363.

Bonds Payable...	10,363	
Extraordinary Loss on Bond Retirement.......		63
Cash..		10,300

10.34   (Seward Corporation; amortization schedule for bonds.)

    a. $100,000 × .74622[a]... $ 74,622

        $4,000 × 5.07569[b]... 20,303

        Issue Price.. $ 94,925

[a]Table 2, 5-percent column and 6-period row.
[b]Table 4, 5-percent column and 6-period row.

b.

Six-Month Period	Liability at Start of Period	Interest at 5 Percent for Period	Coupon at 4% of Par	Increase in Book Value of Liability	Liability at End of Period
0					$ 94,925
1	$ 94,925	$ 4,746	$ 4,000	$ 746	95,671
2	95,671	4,784	4,000	784	96,455
3	96,455	4,823	4,000	823	97,278
4	97,278	4,864	4,000	864	98,142
5	98,142	4,907	4,000	907	99,049
6	99,049	4,951	4,000	951	100,000
Total.................		$29,075	$24,000	$5,075	

    c. **January 2, Year 1**

Cash	94,925	
Bonds Payable		94,925

        June 30, Year 1

Interest Expense.......................................	4,746	
Interest Payable		4,000
Bonds Payable		746

        July 1, Year 1

Interest Payable..	4,000	
Cash		4,000

        December 31, Year 1

Interest Expense.......................................	4,784	
Interest Payable		4,000
Bonds Payable		784

    d.

Bonds Payable (.20 × $98,142)...........................	19,628	
Loss on Retirement of Bonds...........................	772	
Cash		20,400

10.35   (Brooks Corporation; journal entries to account for bonds.)

a. $100,000 × .55368[a].. $ 55,368
    $4,000 × 14.87747[b]...   59,510
        Issue Price... $114,878

[a]Table 2, 3-percent column and 20-period row.
[b]Table 4, 3-percent column and 20-period row.

b. **January 2, Year 2**
    Cash 114,878
        Bonds Payable   114,878

    June 30, Year 2
    Interest Expense (.03 × $114,878) 3,446
    Bonds Payable..   554
        Cash   4,000

    December 31, Year 2
    Interest Expense [.03 × ($114,878 – $554)]........... 3,430
    Bonds Payable..   570
        Cash   4,000

c. Book Value: $114,878 – $554 – $570 = $113,754.
    Market Value:
        $100,000 × .41552[a] .... $ 41,552
        $4,000 × 11.68959[b]...   46,758
            Total Market Value... $ 88,310

[a]Table 2, 5-percent column and 18-period row.
[b]Table 4, 5-percent column and 18-period row.

    Bonds Payable.. 113,754
        Cash   88,310
        Gain on Bond Retirement   25,444

10.36   (Central Appliance; allowance method for warranties; reconstructing transactions.)

a. $720,000 = $820,000 (Goods Available for Sale) – $100,000 (Beginning Inventory).

b. $700,000 = $820,000 (Goods Available for Sale) – $120,000 (Ending Inventory).

c. $21,000 = $6,000 (Cr. Balance) + $15,000 (Dr. Balance).

                       Solutions

10.36 continued.

d. $20,000 = $5,000 (Required Cr. Balance) + $15,000 (Existing Dr. Balance).

e.
Dr. Estimated Liability for Warranty Repairs .. 21,000
  Cr. Various Assets Used for Repairs...........   21,000
Repairs made during Year 2.

Dr. Warranty Expense 20,000
  Cr. Estimated Liability for Warranty Re-
    pairs   20,000
Expense recognition for Year 2.

Dr. Cost of Goods Sold 700,000
  Cr. Merchandise Inventory........................   700,000
Cost of goods sold is goods available for sale less ending inventory.

10.37 (Time Warner Inc.; accounting for zero-coupon debt; see *The Wall Street Journal* for December 8, 1992.)

a. $483 million = $1,550 million/3.20714; see table 1, 6-percent column, 20-period row.

b. 5.8 percent = ($1,550/$500)$^{1/20}$ − 1 = 3.10$^{1/20}$ − 1. That is, for each dollar of the initial issue proceeds (of the $500 million), Time Warner must pay $3.10 (= $1,550/$500) at maturity of the notes. You can find the periodic interest rate to make $1.00 grow to $3.10 in 20 periods by trial and error or by using the exponential function on your computer or calculator. Note that you can state an equation to solve, as follows:

$$(1 + r)^{20} = 3.10; \text{ solve for } r.$$

You can see from Table 1 that 5.8 percent is approximately correct.

c. $28 million = .07 × $400 million.

d. $101.4 million. Ask, first, what must the book value of the notes be at the end of Year 19. Then, compute interest for the year on that amount. The book value of the loan at the end of Year 19 must be $1,448.6 (= $1,550/1.07) million. Interest for one year at 7 percent on $1,448.6 million is $101.4 (= .07 × $1,448.6 = $1,550.0 − $1,448.6) million. You can check this approach to finding the answer by noting that:

$$\$1,448.6 \times 1.07 = \$1,550.0.$$

10.38   (Aggarwal Corporation; accounting for long-term bonds.)

a.   **Interest Expense**
First Six Months: .05 × $301,512 = $15,076.
Second Six Months: .05($301,512 + $15,076) = $15,829.
Book value of bonds on December 31, Year 4: $301,512 + $15,076 + $15,829 = $332,417.

b.   **Book Value of Bonds on December 31, Year 3**
Interest:
   $ 35,000 × 8.11090 = $ 283,882   (Table 4, 10 periods and 4%)
Principal:
   $1,000,000 × .67556 =   675,560   (Table 2, 10 periods and 4%)
      Total........................ $ 959,442

Book Value of Bonds, December 31, Year 3.................... $ 959,442
Add Interest Expense for Year 4................................. X
Subtract Coupon Payments during Year 4..................... (70,000)
Book Value of Bonds, December 31, Year 4................... $ 966,336

Interest expense for Year 4 is $76,894.

c.   **Book Value of Bonds on July 1, Year 4**
Book Value of Bonds, December 31, Year 3.................... $1,305,832
Plus Interest Expense for First Six Months of Year 4: .03
   × $1,305,832.. 39,175
Subtract Coupon Payment during First Six Months of
   Year 4... (45,000)
Book Value of Bonds, July 1, Year 4 .... $1,300,007
Book Value of One-Half of Bonds................................. $ 650,004

   Bonds Payable.. 650,004
      Cash   526,720
      Gain on Bonds Retirement   123,284

d.   **Interest Expense for Second Six Months**
.03 × $650,004 = $19,500.

10.39   (Wal-Mart Stores; accounting for long-term bonds.)

a.   .06 × $83,758,595... $ 5,025,516
      .06($83,758,595 + $5,025,516 − $4,500,000)...................... 5,057,047
                                                                              $10,082,563

b.   Interest Expense... $10,082,563
      Interest Payable... 9,000,000
      Increase in Bonds Payable....................................... $ 1,082,563
      Book Value, January 31, Year 11............................... 83,758,595
      Book Value, January 31, Year 12............................... $84,841,158

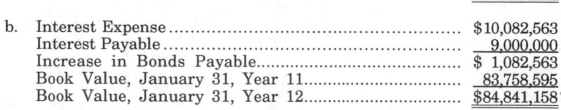

10.39 continued.

    c.   Present Value = Maturity Value × Present Value Factors.
          $162,395,233 = Maturity Value × (4 percent, 11 periods).
          $175,646,684 = Maturity Value × (4 percent, 9 periods).
          Maturity Value = $250,000,000.

    d.   The book value equals the par value, so the initial market yield is the stated interest yield of 9.25 percent compounded semiannually.

10.40   (Maloney Corporation; accounting for long-term bonds.)

    a. $10,000,000 × .20829[a] $2,082,900
         $300,000 × 19.79277[b] 5,937,831
          Issue Price... $8,020,731

        [a]Table 2, 4-percent column and 40-period row.
        [b]Table 4, 4-percent column and 40-period row.

    b.   .04 × $8,020,731.. $ 320,829
         .04($8,020,731 + $320,829 − $300,000) 321,662
          Interest Expense.. $ 642,491

    c.   **January 2, Year 8**

Cash	8,020,731	
Bonds Payable		8,020,731

        June 30, Year 8

Interest Expense	320,829	
Cash		300,000
Bonds Payable		20,829

        December 31, Year 8

Interest Expense	321,662	
Cash		300,000
Bonds Payable		21,662

10.40 continued.

    d. **Market Value**

$4,000,000 × .23138[a]	$ 925,520
$120,000 × 15.37245[b]	1,844,694
Total Market Value	$2,770,214

[a]Table 2, 5-percent column and 30-period row.
[b]Table 4, 5-percent column and 30-period row.

Book Value

$4,000,000 × .30832[a]	$1,233,280
$120,000 × 17.29203[b]	2,075,044
Total Book Value	$3,308,324

[a]Table 2, 4-percent column and 30-period row.
[b]Table 4, 4-percent column and 30-period row.

Bonds Payable	3,308,324	
Cash		2,770,214
Gain on Bond Retirement		538,110

    e. Book Value on January 2, Year 13 after Retirement in Part *d.*:

$6,000,000 × .30832	$1,849,920
$180,000 × 17.29203	3,112,565
Total Book Value	$4,962,485

Interest Expense for Year 13:

.04 × $4,962,485	$ 198,499
.04($4,962,485 + $198,499 − $180,000)	199,239
Total Interest Expense	$ 397,738

10.41   (Quaker Oats Company; managing income and the debt-equity ratio through bond retirement.)

    a. $25,200,000 = .63 × $40,000,000 of cash must be raised to retire old issue.

                                                              Dollars in Thousands

Cash	25,200	
Bonds Payable—9 Percent		25,200
Issue of new bonds.		
Bonds Payable—5 Percent	40,000	
Cash		25,200
Gain on Bond Retirement (Extraordinary		
Item)		14,800
Income Tax Expense	5,920	
Cash		5,920
.40 × $14,800.		

                                                Solutions

10.41 continued.

b. Income increases by $8,880,000 [= (1 – .40) × $14,800,000], or by about 110 percent (= $8,880/$8,000) to about $15 million. Retained Earnings increases by $8,880,000.

c. Debt-equity ratio ($ in 000):

$$\frac{\$5,000 + \$25,200}{\$5,000 + \$25,200 + \$35,000 + \$8,880} = \frac{\$30,200}{\$74,080} = 40.8\%.$$

10.42 (FNB/OOPS; accounting for bonds in a troubled-debt restructuring.)

a. Present value of newly-promised cash flows at 20 percent, compounded semiannually = $2,563,903.

Present value of 50 semiannual payments of $1 discounted at 10 percent per period = 9.91481; see Table 4, 50-period row, 10-percent column.
9.91481 × $250,000 .... $2,478,703

Present value of $1 paid 50 periods hence, discounted at 10 percent per period = .00852; see Table 2, 50-period row, 10-percent column.
.00852 × $10,000,000 85,200
$2,563,903

b. Present value of newly-promised cash flows at 12 percent, compounded semiannually = $4,483,365.

Present value of 50 semiannual payments of $1 discounted at 6 percent per period = 15.76186; see Table 4, 50-period row, 6-percent column.
15.76186 × $250,000 .... $3,940,465

Present value of $1 paid 50 periods hence, discounted at 6 percent per period = .05429; see Table 2, 50-period row, 10-percent column.
.05429 × $10,000,000 542,900
$4,483,365

c. FNB would recognize a loss of $7,436,097 (= $10,000,000 – $2,563,903) under the first method. This would be followed by interest revenue of $12,500,000 (= 50 × $250,000) from cash receipts plus interest revenue from amortization of discount of $7,436,097. Total income under the first method would be $–7,436,097 for write down in 1990 plus $12,500,000 for cash receipts plus $7,436,097 for interest revenue from amortization; total income equal to $12,500,000.

Solutions 10-24

10.42 c. continued.

Under the second method, FNB would recognize a loss of $5,516,635 (= $10,000,000 − $4,483,365). This would be followed by interest revenue of $12,500,000 (= 50 × $250,000) from cash receipts plus interest revenue from amortization of discount of $5,516,635. Total income under the second method would be $12,500,000 (= $−5,516,635 + $12,500,000 + $5,516,635).

Under the third method, income over the next twenty years would be $12,500,000 (= 50 × $250,000) for cash receipts.

Over long enough time spans, accounting income is equal to cash receipts. But note that the timing of income recognition varies drastically as a function of the treatment chosen.

d. We prefer the first method, because we think the troubled-debt restructuring results from an arm's length transaction. FASB *Statement No. 114*, however, requires the use of the second method.

10.43 (Discounting warranty obligations.)

a. **Year 1**

Warranty Expense	2,000,000	
Estimated Warranty Liability		2,000,000

Year 2

Estimated Warranty Liability	500,000	
Cash and Other Accounts		500,000

Year 3

Estimated Warranty Liability	600,000	
Cash and Other Accounts		600,000

Year 4

Estimated Warranty Liability	900,000	
Cash and Other Accounts		900,000

b. The present value of the future cost amounts on December 31, Year 1, discounted as 10 percent, is $1,626,594, computed as follows:

Year 2:	$500,000 × .90909	$	454,545
Year 3:	$600,000 × .82645		495,870
Year 4:	$900,000 × .75131		676,179
	Total		$1,626,594

10.43 b. continued.

Year 1
Warranty Expense 1,626,594
    Estimated Warranty Liability 1,626,594

Year 2
Interest Expense 162,659
    Estimated Warranty Liability 162,659
.10 × $1,626,594 = $162,659.

Year 2
Estimated Warranty Liability 500,000
    Cash and Other Accounts 500,000

Year 3
Interest Expense 128,925
    Estimated Warranty Liability 128,925
.10($1,626,594 + $162,659 − $500,000) = $128,925.

Year 3
Estimated Warranty Liability 600,000
    Cash and Other Accounts 600,000

Year 4
Interest Expense 81,818
    Estimated Warranty Liability 81,818
.10($1,626,594 + $162,659 − $500,000 + $128,925 −
$600,000) = .10 × $818,178 = $81,818.

Year 4
Estimated Warranty Liability 899,996
Interest Expense   4
    Cash and Other Accounts 900,000

There is a rounding error of $4 in the Estimated Warranty Liability account at the end of Year 4. Interest expense for Year 4, therefore, increases by $4.

c. The firm must first acquire for cash the goods and services provided under the warranty plan. Thus, even though customers will receive goods and services, the firm must expend cash at some point. To be consistent with monetary liabilities, accounting would discount these amounts to their present value.

10.44   (Effects on statement of cash flows.)

a. The journal entry to record this transaction is:

Cash 100,000
    Bonds Payable   100,000

The debit to the Cash account results in an increase of $100,000 in Line (9). Issuing debit is a financing activity, so Line (6) increases by $100,000.

b. The journal entry for this transaction is:

Building 100,000
    Bonds Payable   100,000

The transaction does not affect the Cash account, so Line (9) does not change. This transaction does not affect net income, so Line (1) does not change. This transaction does not appear in the statement of cash flows but in a note to the financial statements.

c. The journal entry to record this transaction is:

Bonds Payable.. 100,000
    Cash   90,000
    Extraordinary Gain on Bond Retirement   10,000

The Cash account decreases, so Line (9) decreases by $90,000. Retiring bonds is a financing activity, so Line (7) increases by $90,000. The extraordinary gain increases net income, so Line (1) increases by $10,000. Because this gain does not provide an operating source of cash, Line (3) increases by $10,000 to offset the gain and result in a zero net effect on cash flow from operations.

d. The journal entry for this transaction is:

Bonds Payable 100,000
Extraordinary Loss on Bond Retirement...........   5,000
    Cash   105,000

The Cash account decreases, so Line (9) decreases by $105,000. Calling bonds is a financing activity, so Line (7) increases by $105,000. The extraordinary loss reduces net income, so Line (1) decreases by $5,000. Because this loss does not use an operating cash flow, Line (2) increases by $5,000 to offset the loss and result in a zero net effect on cash flow from operations.

       Solutions

10.44 continued.

e. The journal entry to record this transaction is:

Interest Expense (= .06 X $90,000)	5,400	
Cash (= .05 X $100,000)		5,000
Bonds Payable		400

The Cash account decreases by $5,000, so Line (9) decreases by $5,000. Net income decreases by $5,400 for interest expense, so Line (1) decreases by $5,400. Because the firm uses only $5,000 cash for this expense, Line (2) increases by $400 for the portion of the expense that does not use cash.

f. The journal entry to record this transaction is:

Interest Expense (= .06 X $90,000)	5,250	
Bonds Payable..	750	
Cash (= .06 X $100,000)		6,000

The Cash account decreases by $6,000, so Line (9) decreases by $6,000. Net income decreases by $5,250, so Line (1) decreases by $5,250. Because the firm uses more cash than the amount of interest expense, Line (3) increases by $750. The total effect on cash flow from operations is $6,000 (= $5,250 + $750).

10.45　(Branaire Company; preparing statement of cash flows.) A T-account work sheet for Branaire Company appears after the statement of cash flows.

BRANAIRE COMPANY
Statement of Cash Flows
Year 2

Operations:

Net Income	$ 53,000	
Addbacks and Additions:		
Depreciation Expense	48,000	
Loss on Bond Retirement	3,000	
Bad Debt Expense	9,000	
Increase in Accounts Payable	11,000	
Subtractions:		
Gain on Sale of Equipment	(4,900)	
Amortization of Bond Premium	(5,000)	
Increase in Accounts Receivable	(15,900)	
Increase in Inventories	(12,000)	
Cash Flow from Operations		$ 86,200
Investing:		
Sale of Property, Plant and Equipment	$ 19,900	
Acquisition of Property, Plant and Equipment	(57,300)	
Cash Flow from Investing		(37,400)
Financing:		
Issue of Bonds	$ 50,000	
Retirement of Bonds	(73,000)	
Dividends	(30,000)	
Cash Flow from Financing		(53,000)
Change in Cash		$ (4,200)
Cash, January 1, Year 2		47,000
Cash, December 31, Year 2		$ 42,800

Supplementary Information

Branaire Company issued $11,000 of common stock during Year 2 to acquire property, plant and equipment.

　10-29

10.45 continued.

Cash

√ 47,000

Operations

(1)	53,000	4,900	(5)
(4)	48,000	5,000	(9)
(7)	3,000	15,900	(12)
(10)	9,000	12,000	(13)
(14)	11,000		

Investing

(5)	19,900	57,300	(6)

Financing

(8)	50,000	30,000	(2)
		73,000	(7)

√ 42,800

Accounts Receivable				Allowance for Un-collectible Accounts				Inventory		
√	80,000					1,200	√	√	110,000	
(12)	15,900	8,900	(11)	(11) 8,900		9,000	(10)	(13)	12,000	
√	87,000					1,300	√	√	122,000	

Property, Plant and Equipment				Accumulated Depreciation				Accounts Payable		
√	474,000					189,800	√		70,000	√
(3)	11,000	60,100	(5)	(5) 45,100		48,000	(4)		11,000	(3)
(6)	57,300									
√	482,200					192,700	√		81,000	√

Bonds Payable			Common Stock			Retained Earnings		
	195,000	√		100,000	√		155,000	√
(7) 70,000	50,000	(8)		11,000	(3)	(2) 30,000	53,000	(1)
(9) 5,000								
	170,000	√		111,000	√		178,000	√

CHAPTER 11

LIABILITIES: OFF-BALANCE-SHEET FINANCING, LEASES, DEFERRED INCOME TAXES AND RETIREMENT BENEFITS

Questions, Exercises, Problems, and Cases: Answers and Solutions

11.1   See the text or the glossary at the end of the book.

11.2   One premise underlying this statement is that the notes provide sufficient information to permit the analyst to make an informed judgment about the nature of the obligation or commitment and its associated risks. Current disclosures of off-balance-sheet commitments aggregate similar transactions, making an informed judgment about individual items difficult. Even if the disclosure permitted an informed judgment, the question arises as to whether information processing costs for analysts would decrease if firms actually recognized these items as liabilities. The counter argument to recognition of off-balance-sheet liabilities is that they differ in their risk characteristics relative to liabilities appearing on the books; thus disclosure in the notes is more appropriate than recognition in the balance sheet.

11.3   Using an executory contract to achieve off-balance-sheet financing results in the recognition of neither an asset (for example, leased assets) nor a liability (for example, lease liability) on the balance sheet. Using an asset sale with recourse results in a decrease in an asset (for example, accounts receivable) and an increase in cash. In both cases, no liability appears on the balance sheet.

11.4   The party with the risks and rewards of ownership effectively owns the asset, whatever the legal niceties. The asset should appear on the balance sheet of the owner. The capital lease criteria attempt to state unambiguously who has economic ownership.

11.5   The distinction depends upon which criteria of the lease made it a capital lease. The major difference is that at the end of a lease term the asset reverts to the lessor in a capital lease, whereas at the end of the installment payments, the asset belongs to the purchaser. The criteria for capitalizing a lease are such that the expected value of the asset when it reverts to the lessor is small, but misestimates can occur. In most other respects, capital leases and installment purchases are similar in economic substance.

11-1

11.6 The differences are minor. The lessee's asset is Leasehold on the one hand and Actual Asset (Plant) on the other. The liability will have different titles. The effect on income is the same for both transactions.

11.7 Expenses are gone assets. The measure of expense over the life of a lease is the total outflow of cash to discharge the obligation. The accounting for leases, either operating or capital, does not change the total cash outflow, only the timing of the recognition of asset expirations.

11.8 Rent revenue for the lessor will equal rent expense for the lessee on an operating lease. Likewise, interest revenue for the lessor should equal interest expense for the lessee on a capital lease. The principal difference between the lessor and lessee is that the lessor recognizes its cost to acquire or manufacture the leased asset as depreciation expense under an operating lease or as cost of goods sold under a capital lease. The lessor also recognizes revenue under a capital lease equal to the "selling price" of the lease asset on the date of signing the lease.

11.9 Deferred tax accounting matches against pre-tax book income each period the income taxes a firm has to pay currently plus (minus) the income taxes the firm expects to pay (save) in the future when revenues and expenses that appear in book income now appear in tax returns later.

11.10 This statement is incorrect. In order for deferred taxes to be a loan, there must be a cash receipt at the inception of the loan and a cash disbursement at the maturity date. The entries for deferred taxes are as follows:

When Timing Differences Originate:

Income Tax Expense...	X	
Deferred Tax Liability......................................		X

When Timing Differences Reverse:

Deferred Tax Liability..	X	
Income Tax Expense		X

There are no cash flows involved and, therefore, no loan.

Another approach is to raise the question: How would cash flows have differed if a firm used the same methods of accounting for book as it used for tax? The response is that cash flows would have been the same even though deferred income taxes would have been eliminated. Thus, recognizing or not recognizing deferred taxes has no incremental effect on cash flows and, therefore, cannot represent a loan situation.

11.11   The Congress defines the manner in which firms calculate taxable income and income taxes payable. Corporations pay the income taxes each year that the income tax law legally requires them to pay. The amount shown for Deferred Tax Liability is not a liability. It represents the cumulative tax savings from using different methods of accounting for financial reporting and income tax purposes. The Congress and the FASB permit such differences in accounting methods because the objectives of income taxation and financial reporting differ. The income taxation system attempts to raise revenues in an equitable manner. Generally accepted accounting principles attempt to measure operating performance and financial position. If the Congress feels that it should not permit such differences, it should legislate either (1) that firms prepare their financial statements in conformance with the accounting methods used for tax purposes, or (2) that they compute taxable income in accordance with the accounting methods used for financial reporting purposes. Both approaches result in eliminating the Deferred Tax Liability account. Given the differences in objectives of the two reporting systems, it seems undesirable for Congress to take either of the actions indicated above. Congress should merely recognize that Deferred Tax Liability is not a liability but the result of accountants' attempts to obtain meaningful measures of operating performance over time.

11.12   Unlike Accounts Payable or Bonds, which "roll over" and new obligations replace them, the deferred tax liability does not arise from specific transactions. A firm computes taxes on operations as a whole, not on specific transactions. The analyst should attempt to ascertain when the firm is likely to pay the deferred taxes. Then the analyst should use the present value of those payments as the amount of the debt. If, as is likely, a stable or growing firm is never likely to pay the deferred taxes (for example, as with depreciation charges), then the present value of the payments is zero, and the analyst should exclude the "liability" from the amount of debt. (This results in larger shareholders' equity.)

11.13   Deferred tax assets arise when a firm recognizes revenue earlier for tax purposes than book purposes or expenses later for tax purposes than for book purposes. Deferred tax assets provide for lower taxable income in the future relative to book income and, therefore, future tax savings.

11.14   The valuation allowance reduces deferred tax assets to the amount a firm expects to realize in tax savings in the future. The use of a valuation allowance provides a more conservative measure of assets at each balance sheet date than if no valuation allowance were used. The most conservative measure of deferred tax liabilities occurs without a valuation allowance (that is, larger liabilities and larger income tax expense).

       Solutions

11.15   The difference arises for two principal reasons: tax rate differences and permanent differences. The income tax rate on state, municipal and foreign income likely differs from the statutory U.S. tax rate. Also, firms recognize various revenues and expenses for book purposes that never appear (for example, interest on state and municipal bonds) or appear in smaller amounts (for example, dividends received from domestic subsidiaries) in taxable income.

11.16   The matching convention suggests that firms recognize as expenses each period all costs actually incurred currently or expected to be incurred in the future to generate the current period's revenues. Employees provide labor services each period in return for both current compensation (salary, health care benefits) and compensation deferred until retirement (pensions, health care benefits). The absence of deferred compensation arrangements would presumably lead employees to demand higher current compensation to permit them to fund their own retirement plans. Thus, firms must match current compensation and the present value of deferred compensation against the current period's revenues.

11.17   Laws require firms to contribute funds to an independent trustee to manage on behalf of employees. The employer cannot use these funds for its general corporate purposes. Firms must, however, report an underfunded accumulated benefit obligation on the balance sheet as a liability.

11.18   One defines outputs (defined benefit) whereas the other defines inputs (defined contribution). Actuaries can design both to have the same expected costs with the same payment patterns by the company.

Immediate funding for defined-contribution plans transfers all accounting problems subsequent to funding to the plan trustee. The defined-benefit plan could similarly transfer obligations to the pension fund by immediate cash payments, but the company would ultimately be responsible for making up any shortages caused by deviations of earnings or mortality from expectations. But the firm could insure against those deviations. The essential difference then appears to be the prior service obligation problem—the adoption and sweetenings that cause obligations to arise instantaneously, even though not immediately for accounting purposes.

11.19   Pension fund assets appear when a firm funds its pension plan faster than it expenses it. Pension fund liabilities appear either (a) when a firm expenses its pension plan faster than it funds it, or (b) has an underfunded accumulated benefit obligation.

11.20   Both the accumulated and projected benefit obligations equal the present value of amounts firms expect to pay to retired employees, taking into consideration employee turnover, mortality, and interest, rates. Both obligations base the benefit calculation on employees accumulated service as of the valuation date. The accumulated benefit obligation computes the benefit based on current salaries whereas the projected benefit obligation uses the salary levels expected to affect the final calculation of the annual pension to retired employees.

11.21   Some accountants argue that the projected benefit obligation provides a more accurate measure of the amount a firm ultimately expects to pay to retired employees than the accumulated benefit obligation. The requirements of FASB *Statement No. 87* for measuring pension expense implicitly support this conclusion. The offsetting debit for the pension liability might be an intangible asset, an expense account, or retained earnings. The argument for debiting an intangible asset relates to having a happier work force that will likely be more productive in the future (underfunded projected benefit obligations often arise because firms increase, or sweeten, pension benefits). The argument for debiting an expense is that all costs must appear in the income statement of some period before transferring to retained earnings. The argument for debiting retained earnings is that pension expenses of previous years were understated.

11.22   The result occurs when all other components of pension expense net to zero. The interest cost will offset the expected return on assets when pension assets equal the projected benefit obligation and the expected return on pension assets equals the discount rate used to compute the projected benefit obligation. The amortization component will be zero if all past performance of the pension plan exactly coincided with expectations (for example, asset returns, employee turnover and mortality assumptions).

11.23   (Cypres Appliance Store; using accounts receivable to achieve off-balance sheet financing.)

a. (1) **January 2, Year 2**
         Cash 89,286
            Bank Loan Payable   89,286
         To record bank loan.

         December 31, Year 2
         Cash 100,000
            Accounts Receivable   100,000
         To record collections from customers.

         Interest Expense (= .12 × $89,286) 10,714
         Bank Loan Payable 89,286
            Cash   100,000
         To record interest expense on loan for
         Year 2 and repayment of the loan.

    (2) Cash 89,286
         Loss from Sale of Accounts Receivable 10,714
            Accounts Receivable   100,000
         To record sale of accounts receivable; alternative title for the loss account is interest expense.

b. Both transactions result in an expense of $10,714 for Year 2 for this financing. Both transactions result in an immediate increase in cash. Liabilities increase for the collateralized loan, whereas an asset decreases for the sale.

c. Cypres Appliance Store must attempt to shift credit and interest rate risk to the bank. The bank should have no rights to demand additional receivables if interest rates increase or uncollectible accounts appear. Likewise, Cypres Appliance Store should have no rights to buy back the accounts receivable if interest rates decline. The bank of course will not both lend on the receivables and purchase the receivables at the same price because it incurs different amounts of risk in each case.

11.24   (P. J. Lorimar Company; using inventory to achieve off-balance sheet financing.)

a.   (i)   **January 2, Year 5**

Cash..	300,000	
Bank Loan Payable		300,000
To record bank loan.		

December 31, Year 5

Interest Expense (= .10 × $300,000).............	30,000	
Bank Loan Payable		30,000
To record interest expense for Year 5.		

December 31, Year 6

Cash..	363,000	
Sales Revenue		363,000
To record sale of tobacco inventory.		

Cost of Goods Sold.....................................	200,000	
Inventory		200,000
To record cost of tobacco inventory sold.		

Interest Expense (= .10 × $330,000).............	33,000	
Bank Loan Payable	330,000	
Cash...		363,000
To record interest expense for Year 6 and repayment of loan.		

(ii)   **January 2, Year 5**

Cash..	300,000	
Sales Revenue		300,000
To record "sale" of tobacco to bank.		

Cost of Goods Sold.....................................	200,000	
Inventory		200,000
To record cost of tobacco "sold".		

b.   Both transactions result in a total of $100,000 income for the two years combined. The collateralized loan shows $163,000 gross profit from the sale in Year 6 and interest expense of $30,000 in Year 5 and $33,000 in Year 6. The "sale" results in $100,000 gross profit in Year 5. Cash increases by $300,000 in both transactions. Liabilities increase for the collateralized loan, whereas an asset decreases for the sale.

       Solutions

11.24 continued.

    c. P. J. Lorimar Company must shift the risk of changes in storage costs for Year 5 and Year 6 and the selling price for the tobacco at the end of Year 6 to the bank. The firm should not guarantee a price or agree to cover insurance and other storage costs. Of course, the bank will not both lend on the inventory and "purchase" the inventory for $300,000 because it incurs different amounts of risk in each case.

11.25   (Boeing and American; applying the capital lease criteria.)

    a. This lease is a capital lease because the lease period of 20 years exceeds 75 percent of the expected life of the aircraft. The lease does not meet any other capital lease criteria. The aircraft reverts to Boeing at the end of 20 years. The present value of the lease payments when discounted at 10 percent is $51.1 million ($6 million X 8.51356), which is less than 90 percent of the fair market value of $60 million.

    b. This lease is not a capital lease because the present value of the lease payments of $54.8 million (= $7.2 million X 7.60608) exceeds 90 percent of the $60 million fair market value of the aircraft.

    c. The lease is not a capital lease. The present value of the required lease payments of $36.9 million (= $5.5 million X 6.71008) is less than 90 percent of the market value of the aircraft. The life of the lease is less than 75 percent of the expected useful life of the aircraft. The purchase option price coupled with the rental payments provides Boeing with a present value of all cash flows of $62.4 million [= ($5.5 million X 6.71008) + ($55 million X .46319)], so there does not appear to be a bargain purchase option.

    d. This lease is not a capital lease. The present value of the minimum required lease payments is $50.9 million (= $6.2 million X 8.20141). The fee contingent on usage could be zero, so the calculations exclude it. The life of the lease is less than 75 percent of the useful life of the aircraft. The aircraft reverts to Boeing at the end of the lease period.

11.26   (Fedup Delivery Services; preparing lessee's journal entries for an operating and a capital lease.)

    a. This lease is a capital lease because the present value of the lease payments of $24,688 (= $820 X 30.10751) exceeds 90 percent of the market value of the leased asset ($24,000). The life of the lease is less than 75 percent of the life of the leased property and the property reverts to Chrysler at the end of the lease period, so the lease fails these criteria for a capital lease.

11.26 continued.

b.   **Time of Signing Lease**
     No Entry.

     End of Each Month   ✓
     Rent Expense...   820
        Cash...   820
     To record monthly rental expense and pay-
     ment.

c.   **Time of Signing Lease**
     Asset—Leasehold......................................   24,688
        Liability—Present Value of Lease Obligation.   24,688
     To record capital lease.

     End of First Month
     Interest Expense (= .01 × $24,688)....................   246.88
     Liability—Present Value of Lease Obligation....   573.12
        Cash...   820.00
     To record interest expense and cash payment
     for first month; the book value of the lease lia-
     bility is now $24,114.88 (= $24,688.00 – $573.12).

     Depreciation Expense 685.78
        Accumulated Depreciation.......................   685.78
     To record depreciation expense for the first
     month of $685.78 (= $24,688/36).

     End of Second Month
     Interest Expense (= .01 × $24,114.88)................   241.15
     Liability—Present Value of Lease Obligation....   578.85
        Cash...   820.00
     To record interest expense and cash payment
     for the second month.

     Depreciation Expense 685.78
        Accumulated Depreciation.......................   685.78
     To record depreciation expense for the second
     month.

11.27 (Baldwin Products; preparing lessee's journal entries for an operating lease and a capital lease.)

a. This lease does not satisfy any of the criteria for a capital lease, so it is an operating lease. The leased asset reverts to the lessor at the end of the lease period. The life of the lease (3 years) is less than 75 percent of the expected useful life of the leased asset (5 years). The present value of the lease payments of $24,018 (= $10,000 × 2.40183) is less than 90 percent of the market value of the leased asset of $30,000.

b. **December 31, of Each Year**

Rent Expense	10,000	
Cash		10,000

To record annual rent expense and cash payment.

c. **January 2, Year 6**

Asset—Leasehold	24,018	
Liability—Present Value of Lease Obligation.		24,018

To record capital lease.

December 31, Year 6

Interest Expense (= .12 × $24,018)	2,882	
Liability—Present Value of Lease Obligation....	7,118	
Cash		10,000

To record interest expense and cash payment for Year 6. The book value of the lease liability is now $16,900 (= $24,018 − $7,118).

Depreciation Expense or Work-in-Process Inventory ($24,018/3)	8,006	
Accumulated Depreciation		8,006

To record depreciation expense for Year 6.

December 31, Year 7

Interest Expense (= .12 × $16,900)	2.028	
Liability—Present Value of Lease Obligation....	7,972	
Cash		10,000

To record interest expense and cash payment for Year 7. The book value of the lease liability is now $8,928 (= $16,900 − $7,972).

Depreciation Expense or Work-in-Process Inventory	8,006	
Accumulated Depreciation		8,006

To record depreciation expense for Year 7.

11.27 c. continued.

December 31, Year 8

Interest Expense (= .12 × $8,928)......................	1.072	
Liability—Present Value of Lease Obligation....	8,928	
Cash...		10,000

To record interest expense and cash payment
for Year 8. Interest expense does not precisely
equal .12 × $8,928 due to rounding.

Depreciation Expense on Work-in-Process Inventory...	8,006	
Accumulated Depreciation......................		8,006

To record depreciation expense for Year 8.

d. Operating Lease Method: Rent Expense (= $10,000 × 3)....   <u>$ 30,000</u>

Capital Lease Method: Interest Expense (= $2,882 +	
$2,028 + $1,072)	$ 5,982
Depreciation (= $8,006 × 3)...	<u>24,018</u>
Total Expenses	<u>$ 30,000</u>

11.28 (Sun Microsystems; preparing lessor's journal entries for an operating lease and a capital lease.)

a. This lease is a capital lease. The life of the lease equals the expected useful life of the property. The present value of the lease payments of $12,000 [= $4,386.70 + ($4,386.70 × 1.73554)] equals the market value of the leased asset.

b. **Beginning of Each Year**

Cash..	4,386.70	
Rental Fees Received in Advance................		4,386.70

To record cash received in advance from lessee.

End of Each Year

Rental Fees Received in Advance	4,386.70	
Rent Revenue		4,386.70

To record rent revenue for each year.

Depreciation Expense	2,400.00	
Accumulated Depreciation.........................		2,400.00

To record annual depreciation (= $7,200/3).

       Solutions

11.28 continued.

c. **January 2, Year 2**

Cash..	4,386.70	
Lease Receivable (= $4,386.70 × 1.73554).............	7,613.30	
Sales Revenue..		12,000.00

To record "sale" of work station..

Cost of Goods Sold..	7,200.00	
Inventory..		7,200.00

To record cost of work station "sold".

December 31, Year 2

Lease Receivable (= .10 × $7,613.30)...................	761.33	
Interest Revenue..		761.33

To record interest revenue for Year 2.

January 2, Year 3

Cash..	4,386.70	
Lease Receivable.......................................		4,386.70

To record cash received at the beginning of
Year 3. The book value of the receivable is now
$3,987.93 (= $7,613.30 + $761.33 – $4,386.70).

December 31, Year 3

Lease Receivable (= .10 × $3,987.93)...................	398.77	
Interest Revenue..		398.77

To record interest revenue for Year 3. Interest
revenue is slightly less than .10 × $3,987.93 due
to rounding of present value factors. The book
value of the receivable is now $4,386.70 (=
$3,987.93 + $398.77).

January 2, Year 4

Cash..	4,386.70	
Lease Receivable.......................................		4,386.70

To record cash received for Year 4.

11.29   (Ingersoll-Rand; preparing journal entries for income tax expense.)

a. **Year 9**

Income Tax Expense....................................	67,400	
Deferred Tax Liability...................................	43,575	
Cash or Income Tax Payable.......................		110,975

Year 10

Income Tax Expense....................................	90,000	
Deferred Tax Liability...................................	15,537	
Cash or Income Tax Payable.......................		105,537

Year 11

Income Tax Expense....................................	118,800	
Deferred Tax Liability.................................		14,185
Cash or Income Tax Payable.......................		104,615

b. Taxable income exceeds book income for Year 9 and Year 10 but taxable income was less than book income for Year 11. Ingersoll-Rand probably reduced its expenditures on new depreciable assets during Year 9 and Year 10 so that depreciation expense for financial reporting exceeded depreciation deducted in computing taxable income. Ingersoll-Rand increased its capital expenditures during Year 11 so that depreciation deducted in computing taxable income exceeded depreciation expense recognized for financial reporting.

11.30   (L.A. Gear; preparing journal entries for income tax expense.)

a. **Year 4**

Income Tax Expense....................................	34,364	
Deferred Tax Asset ($17,621 – $12,763)	4,858	
Deferred Tax Liability ($6,270 – $4,967)		1,303
Cash or Income Tax Payable.......................		37,919

Year 5

Income Tax Expense....................................	16,376	
Deferred Tax Asset ($17,329 – $17,621)..........		292
Deferred Tax Liability ($9,470 – $6,270)		3,200
Cash or Income Tax Payable.......................		12,884

Year 6

Cash or Income Tax Receivable.......................	17,184	
Deferred Tax Liability ($3,785 – $9,470)..............	5,685	
Deferred Tax Asset ($17,187 – $17,329)..........		142
Income Tax Expense (Credit).......................		22,727

11.30 continued.

b. Book income and taxable income were both positive for Year 4. Taxable income exceeded book income. The deferred tax asset related to uncollectible accounts increased, suggesting an increased sales level for the year. The deferred tax liability for depreciation increased, suggesting that L.A. Gear increased its level of capital expenditures. The net effect of these two temporary differences is more expenses for book purposes than for tax purposes.

Book income and taxable income were both positive in Year 5. In this year book income exceeded taxable income. The decline in total income tax expense coupled with a small decrease in the deferred tax asset relating to uncollectible accounts suggests a decline in sales for the year. L.A. Gear continues to acquire depreciable assets, causing its deferred tax liability to increase. The net effect of these two temporary differences is more expenses for tax purposes than for book purposes.

Book income and taxable income were both negative in Year 6. The loss for book purposes exceeded the loss for tax purposes. The small decline in the deferred tax asset related to uncollectible accounts suggests flat or declining sales. The decline in the deferred tax liability suggests a cutback in capital expenditures. Straight-line depreciation for book purposes exceeded accelerated depreciation for financial reporting. The net effect of the two temporary differences is more expenses for book purposes than for tax purposes.

11.31   (Kleen Cleaners; measuring income tax expense.)

Year 7

Income Tax Expense (Plug)	236	
Deferred Tax Asset [= .40($260 – $200)]....................	24	
Deferred Tax Liability [= .40($550 – $500)]		20
Cash or Income Tax Payable (= .40 × $600)		240

To record income tax expense for Year 7.

Year 8

Income Tax Expense (Plug)	264	
Deferred Tax Liability [= .40($400 – $550)]................	60	
Deferred Tax Asset [= .40($200 – $260)]		24
Cash or Income Tax Payable (= .40 × $750)		300

To record income tax expense for Year 8.

11.32   (Computer Electronics Corporation; measuring income tax expense.)

Year 4

Income Tax Expense (Plug)	850	
Deferred Tax Asset[a]	70	
Deferred Tax Liability [= .40($1,200 − $900)]		120
Cash or Income Tax Payable (= .40 × $2,000)		800

[a]Deferred Tax Asset:

January 1, Year 4: [= (.4 × $600) − $50]	$ 190
December 31, Year 4: [= (.4 × $800) − $60]	260
Increase for Year 4	$ 70

Year 5

Income Tax Expense (Plug)	955	
Deferred Tax Asset[a]	25	
Deferred Tax Liability [= .40($1,250 − $1,200)]		20
Cash or Income Tax Payable (= .40 × $2,400)		960

[a]Deferred Tax Asset:

December 31, Year 4: [= (.4 × $800) − $60]	$ 260
December 31, Year 5: [= (.4 × $900) − $75]	285
Increase for Year 5	$ 25

11.33   (Sung Company; computations and journal entries for income taxes with both temporary and permanent differences.)

a.   **Year 1**

Income Tax Expense (.40 × $560,000)	224,000	
Deferred Tax Liability (.40 × $40,000)	16,000	
Income Tax Payable—Current (.40 ×		
$600,000)		240,000

Year 2

Income Tax Expense (.40 × $500,000)	200,000	
Deferred Tax Liability (.40 × $50,000)		20,000
Income Tax Payable—Current (.40 ×		
$450,000)		180,000

Year 3

Income Tax Expense (.40 × $620,000)	248,000	
Deferred Tax Liability (.40 × $6,000)		24,000
Income Tax Payable—Current (.40 ×		
$560,000)		224,000

11-15

11.33 continued.

b. **Year 1**
Income Tax Expense (.40 × $550,000).................. 220,000
    Deferred Tax Liability (.40 × $50,000).............. 20,000
    Income Tax Payable—Current (.40 ×
        $600,000).. 240,000

Year 2
Income Tax Expense (.40 × $490,000).................. 196,000
    Deferred Tax Liability (.40 × $40,000).............. 16,000
    Income Tax Payable—Current (.40 ×
        $450,000).. 180,000

Year 3
Income Tax Expense (.40 × $610,000).................. 244,000
    Deferred Tax Liability (.40 × $50,000).............. 20,000
    Income Tax Payable—Current (.40 ×
        $560,000).. 224,000

11.34   (Beneish Company; deriving permanent and temporary differences from financial statement disclosures.)

a.	Income Tax Expense	=	Income Taxes Currently Payable	+	Change in Deferred Tax Liability
	$78,000	=	$24,000	+	X
	X	=	$54,000		

Temporary Differences   = Changes in Deferred Tax Liability/.40

= $54,000/.40

= $135,000

Because income tax expense exceeds income taxes payable, book income exceeded taxable income.

b. Taxable Income: $24,000/.40...................................... $ 60,000
Temporary Differences 135,000
Book Income before Taxes Excluding Permanent Differences.. $ 195,000
Permanent Differences (Plug)..................................... 36,000
Book Income before Taxes (Given)............................. $ 159,000

The amortization of goodwill of $36,000 for book purposes and zero for tax purposes causes taxable income to exceed book income.

11.35   (Woodward Corporation; effect of temporary differences on income taxes.)

a.

	Year 1	Year 2	Year 3	Year 4
Other Pre-Tax Income.........	$ 35,000	$ 35,000	$35,000	$35,000
Income before Depreciation from Machine....................	25,000	25,000	25,000	25,000
Depreciation Deduction:				
.33 × $50,000......................	(16,500)			
.44 × $50,000......................		(22,000)		
.15 × $50,000......................			(7,500)	
.08 × $50,000......................				(4,000)
Taxable Income	$ 43,500	$ 38,000	$52,500	$56,000
Tax Rate............................	.40	.40	.40	.40
Income Taxes Payable	$ 17,400	$ 15,200	$21,000	$22,400

b.

Financial Reporting	Year 1	Year 2	Year 3	Year 4
Book Value, January 1.........	$ 50,000	$ 37,500	$25,000	$12,500
Depreciation Expense	(12,500)	(12,500)	(12,500)	(12,500)
Book Value, December 31	$ 37,500	$ 25,000	$12,500	$ --
Tax Reporting				
Tax Basis, January 1...........	$ 50,000	$ 33,500	$11,500	$ 4,000
Depreciation Deduction........	(16,500)	(22,000)	(7,500)	(4,000)
Tax Basis, December 31........	$ 33,500	$ 11,500	$ 4,000	$ --

c.

	Year 1	Year 2	Year 3	Year 4
Book Value of Machine	$ 37,500	$ 25,000	$12,500	$ --
Tax Basis of Machine...........	(33,500)	(11,500)	(4,000)	--
Difference...........................	$ 4,000	$ 13,500	$ 8,500	$ --
Tax Rate.............................	.40	.40	.40	--
Deferred Tax Liability..........	$ 1,600	$ 5,400	$ 3,400	$ --

d.

	Year 1	Year 2	Year 3	Year 4
Income Tax Payable (from Part a.)	$ 17,400	$ 15,200	$21,000	$22,400
Change in Deferred Tax Liability:				
$1,600 – $0	1,600			
$5,400 – $1,600....................		3,800		
$3,400 – $5,400....................			(2,000)	
$0 – $3,400				(3,400)
Income Tax Expense	$19,000	$19,000	$19,000	$19,000

                                      Solutions

11.35 continued.

e. **Year 1**

Income Tax Expense	19,000	
Cash or Income Tax Payable		17,400
Deferred Tax Liability		1,600

Year 2

Income Tax Expense	19,000	
Cash or Income Tax Payable		15,200
Deferred Tax Liability		3,800

Year 3

Income Tax Expense	19,000	
Deferred Tax Liability	2,000	
Cash or Income Tax Payable		21,000

Year 4

Income Tax Expense	19,000	
Deferred Tax Liability	3,400	
Cash or Income Tax Payable		22,400

11.36 (Dominiak Company; reconstructing information about income taxes.)

DOMINIAK COMPANY
Illustrations of Timing Differences and Permanent Differences

	Financial Statements	Type of Difference	Income Tax Return
Operating Income Except Depreciation	$ 360,000 (6)	--	$ 360,000 (4)
Depreciation	(270,000) (g)	Timing	(300,000) (3)
Municipal Bond Interest	70,000 (5)	Permanent	--
Taxable Income	--		$ 60,000 (2)
Pretax Income	$ 160,000 (g)		
Income Taxes Payable at 40 Percent			$ 24,000
Income Tax Expense at 40 Percent of $90,000 = $160,000 – $70,000, Which Is Book Income Excluding Permanent Differences	(36,000) (g)		
Net Income	$ 124,000 (1)		

11.36 continued.

Order and derivation of computations:
(g) Given.
(1) $124,000 = $160,000 – $36,000.
(2) $60,000 = $24,000/.40.
(3) Timing difference for depreciation is ($36,000 – $24,000)/.40 = $30,000. Because income taxes payable are less than income tax expense, we know that depreciation deducted on tax return exceeds depreciation expense on financial statements. Thus, the depreciation deduction on the tax return is $300,000 = $270,000 + $30,000.
(4) $360,000 = $300,000 + $60,000.
(5) Taxable income on financial statements is $90,000 = $36,000/.40. Total financial statement income before taxes, including permanent differences, is $160,000. Hence, permanent differences are $160,000 – $90,000 = $70,000.
(6) $160,000 + $270,000 – $70,000 = $360,000. See also (4), for check.

11.37   (Merck; interpreting pension disclosures.)

(Amounts in Millions)
a. Pension Expense.. 73.7
        Pension Liability....................................... 73.7

    Pension Liability ($35.1 + $73.7 – $42.0).......... 66.8
        Cash.. 66.8

b. Pension Expense.. 64.3
        Pension Liability....................................... 64.3

    Pension Liability ($42.0 + $64.3 – $18.8).......... 87.5
        Cash.. 87.5

c. Annual returns were a negative $52 million in Year 8, significantly less than expected returns of $112 million (+ $164.0 – $52.0). Actual returns of $231.8 million in Year 9 significantly exceeded expected returns of $102.3 million (= $231.8 – $129.5).

d. Merck experienced an actuarial gain during Year 8 which it must amortize over future years. The gain in Year 8 did not occur because actual returns on pension assets during Year 8 were less than expected. Amortization of this difference increases, not reduces, future pension expense. Thus, Merck's projected benefit obligation must have decreased during Year 8 because of (1) an increase in the discount rate, (2) a decrease in the assumed rate of compensation cost increases, (3) faster employee turnover, or (4) shorter life expectancies. Amortization of the actuarial gain from Year 8 reduces pension expense in Year 9 and later years.

                                       Solutions

11.38   (May Department Stores; interpreting pension disclosures.)

   a. Pension Expense..   19
       Prepaid Pension Asset ($25 – $21)   4
           Cash   23

   b. May Department Stores has funded its pension plan faster than it
       has recognized pension expense. Despite this faster funding, the
       firm still has an underfunded projected benefit obligation.

11.39   (International Paper Company; interpreting pension disclosures.)
        (Amounts in Millions)

   a. Pension Expense..   77
       Prepaid Pension Asset ($586 – $507)   79
           Cash   156

   b. Possible reasons for the increased overfunded projected benefit
       obligation include:

       (1) A decrease in the assumed rate of compensation increases
            during Year 5, which caused the projected benefit obligation to
            increase less rapidly than otherwise.

       (2) An increase in the discount rate that caused the projected
            benefits obligation to decrease.

       (3) Accelerated funding of the projected benefit obligation ($156)
            relative to pension expense ($77), which puts more assets in the
            pension fund.

11.40   (Effects of leases on statement of cash flows.)

   a. The journal entry to record this transaction is:

       Depreciation Expense.....................................   10,000
           Accumulated Depreciation   10,000

       Because this entry does not involve a debit or credit to the Cash
       account, Line (9) does not change. Depreciation expense reduces net
       income, so Line (1) decreases by $10,000. The recognition of
       depreciation expense does not affect cash, so Line (2) increases by
       $10,000.

   b. The journal entry for this transaction is:

       Cash...   19,925
           Rent Revenue   19,925

       The debit to Cash results in an increase of $19,925 in Line (9). The
       credit to Rent Revenue increases Line (1), net income, by $19,925.

11.40 continued.

    c.   The journal entry to record this transaction is:

| Rent Revenue | 19,925 | |
| Cash | | 19,925 |

The credit to Cash results in an decrease of $19,925 in Line (9). The debit to Rent Expense reduces Line (1), net income, by $19,925.

    d.   The journal entry for this transaction is:

| Leasehold Asset | 100,000 | |
| Lease Liability | | 100,000 |

This transaction does not involve a change in cash, so Line (9) does not change. The entry does not affect net income, so Line (1) does not change. This transaction is an investing and financing activity that would appear in the statement of cash flows but in a supplementary schedule or note to the financial statements.

    e.   The journal entry to record this transaction is:

Interest Expense	15,000	
Lease Liability	4,925	
Cash		19,925

This entry results in a reduction in Cash, so Line (9) decreases by $19,925. Line (1) decreases by $15,000 for interest expense and Line (7) increases by $4,925 for the reduction in the lease liability. Thus, $15,000 of the reduction in cash appears in the operating section and $4,925 appears in the financing section of the statement of cash flows.

11.41   (Effects of income taxes on statement of cash flows.)

    a.   The entry to record this event is:

Income Tax Expense (.4 X $200,000)	80,000	
Income Tax Payable (.4 X $150,000)		60,000
Deferred Tax Liability (.4 X $50,000)		20,000

This entry does not involve a change in Cash, so Line (9) does not change. The debit to income tax expense reduces Line (1), net income, by $80,000. Line (2) increases by $60,000 for the increases in a current operating liability. Line (2) also increases by $20,000 for the addback of an expense that does not use cash. Thus, the effect on cash flow from operations is zero.

        Solutions

11.41 continued.

   b. The journal entry for this event is:

   Income Tax Expense (.4 × $300,000)................. 120,000
   Deferred Tax Asset (.4 × $40,000)..................... 16,000
      Cash (.4 × $340,000) 136,000

   This entry reduces Cash, so Line (9) decreases by $136,000. The
   recognition of income tax expense reduces Line (1), net income, by
   $120,000. Line (3) increases by $16,000 for an expense that used more
   cash than the amount of the expense.

   c. The journal entry and explanation for this part are the same as in
       Part *b.* above. Line (1) decreases by $120,000, Line (3) increases by
       $16,000, and Line (9) decreases by $136,000.

   d. The journal entry is:.

   Cash.. 10,000
      Interest Revenue 10,000

   Interest on municipal bonds is nontaxable, so recognition of income
   taxes on the interest revenue is inappropriate (a permanent
   difference). The Cash account increases, so Line (9) increases by
   $10,000. The recognition of interest revenue increases Line (1), net
   income, by $10,000.

11.42 (Wal-Mart Stores; financial statement effects of operating and capital
       leases.)

   a. Interest Expense (= .11 × $1,694.2).................   186.4
       Liability—Present Value of Lease Obligation
          (Plug)..   18.3
             Cash (Given) 204.7

   b. Rent Expense 249.3
          Cash...   249.3

11.42 continued.

    c. **January 31, Year 9**

Asset—Leasehold.....................................	1,586.5	
Liability—Present Value of Lease Obligation...		1,586.5
To capitalize operating leases.		

       January 31, Year 10

Interest Expense (= .12 × $1,586.5).................	190.4	
Liability—Present Value of Lease Obligation..	58.9	
Cash...		249.3
To record interest expense and cash payment on capitalized operating leases.		
Depreciation Expense.................................	105.8	
Accumulated Depreciation.......................		105.8
To record depreciation expense on capitalized operating leases; $105.8 = $1,586.5/15.		

11.43   (American Airlines; financial statement effect of operating and capital leases.)

(Amounts in Millions)

    a.

Capital Lease Liability, January 31, Year 10......................	$2,233
Interest Expense for Year 11 (= .08 × $2,233).......................	179
Cash Payment for Year 11..	(268)
New Leases Signed during Year 11 (Plug).........................	259
Capital Lease Liability, January 31, Year 11.....................	$2,403

    b.

Leasehold Asset, January 31, Year 10.............................	$1,716
New Leases Capitalized during Year 11 (from Part c.)........	259
Depreciation Expense for Year 11 (Plug).........................	(97)
Leasehold Asset, January 31, Year 11.............................	$1,878

    c. **December 31, Year 11**

Interest Expense	179	
Liability—Present Value of Lease Obligation.......	89	
Cash..		268
Depreciation Expense or Work-in-Process Inventory..	97	
Accumulated Depreciation.........................		97
Asset—Leasehold...	259	
Liability—Present Value of Lease Obligation....		259

            Solutions

11.43 continued.

  d. **December 31, Year 11**
      Rent Expense 946
        Cash.. 946

  e. **December 31, Year 10**
      Asset—Leasehold.. 7,793
        Liability—Present Value of Lease Obligation.... 7,793
      To capitalize operating leases as if they were
      capital leases.

      December 31, Year 11
      Interest Expense (= .10 × $7,793)........................ 779
      Liability—Present Value of Lease Obligation....... 167
        Cash.. 946
      To record interest expense and cash payment
      for capitalized operating leases.

      Depreciation Expense or Work-in-Process In-
        ventory.. 354
          Accumulated Depreciation......................... 354
      To record depreciation for Year 11; ($354 =
      $7,793/22).

      Asset—Leasehold.. 538
        Liability—Present Value of Lease Obligation.... 538
      To record present value of new leases; $7,793 + X
      − $167 = $8,164; X = $538.

11.44   (Carom Grocery Store; comparison of borrow/buy with operating and capital leases.)

  a. $100,000/3.79079 = $26,379.725 = $26,380.

Carom Grocery Store Amortization Schedule

Year	Start of Year Balance	Interest (10%)	Payment	Reduction	End of Year Balance
1	$100,000	$ 10,000	$ 26,380	$ 16,380	$ 83,620
2	83,620	8,362	26,380	18,018	65,602
3	65,602	6,560	26,380	19,820	45,782
4	45,782	4,578	26,380	21,802	23,980
5	23,980	2,398	26,380	23,982	(2)

11.44 continued.

    b. (1) Asset—Computer System.
             Asset Contra—Accumulated Depreciation on Computer System.
             Liability—Bonds Payable and Interest Payable.

       (2) None.

       (3) Asset—Leasehold for Computer System.
             Asset Contra—Accumulated Amortization of Leasehold (not required.)
             Liability—Present Value of Lease Obligations.
             Liability Contra—Discount on Lease Obligations (required only if previous account shows gross rentals.

    c. $150,000 = $100,000 + (.10 \times $100,000 \times 5).

    d. (1) Operating: $131,900 = $26,380 \times 5.
       (2) Capital: $131,900.

    e. The method of accounting for a lease affects only the timing of expenses, not their total. Expenses under Plan (1) are larger because the firm borrows $100,000 for the entire 5 years, whereas under Plan (2) it pays the loan with part of each lease payment; with smaller average borrowing, interest expense is smaller.

    f. (1) $30,000 = $20,000 depreciation plus $10,000 bond interest.
       (2) Operating-lease Method: $26,380.
             Capital-lease Method: $30,000 = $20,000 amortization + $10,000 lease interest.

    g. (1) $30,000.
       (2) Operating: $26,380.
             Capital: $22,400 (or $22,398) = $20,000 + $2,400.

                    Solutions

11.44 g. continued.

CAROM GROCERY STORE SUMMARY (Not Required)

	Year 1	Year 2	Year 3	Year 4	Year 5	Total
Plan 1						
Depreciation Expense.........	$20,000	$20,000	$20,000	$20,000	$20,000	$ 100,000
Interest Expense.........	10,000	10,000	10,000	10,000	10,000	50,000
Total...........	$30,000	$30,000	$30,000	$30,000	$30,000	$ 150,000
Plan 2 (Operating)						
Lease Expense...	$26,380	$26,380	$26,380	$26,380	$26,380	$ 131,900
Plan 2 (Financing)						
Amortization Expense.........	$20,000	$20,000	$20,000	$20,000	$20,000	$ 100,000
Interest Expense.........	10,000	8,362	6,560	4,578	2,400*	31,900
Total...........	$30,000	$28,362	$26,560	$24,578	$22,400	$ 131,900

*Plug to correct for rounding errors. By computations, this number is
$2,398 = $26,380/1.10.

11.45 (U.S. Airlines; financial statement effects of capitalizing operating leases.)

	American	Delta	United
a. $7,878/($7,878 + $3,380)	70.0%		
$3,121/($3,121 + $1,827)		63.1%	
$3,617/($3,617 − $267)....................			108.0%
b. ($7,878 + $8,164)/($7,878 + $8,164 + $3,380)	82.6%		
($3,121 + $7,307)/($3,121 + $7,307 + $1,827)		85.1%	
($3,617 + $10,645)/($3,617 + $10,645 − $267).................................			101.9%

c. The airlines have high debt ratios without including operating leases. Inclusion of the operating leases in liabilities probably violates debt covenants of these airlines.

d. The lease period probably runs for less than 75 percent of the useful life of their equipment or the lessor incurs the salvage value risk.

11.45 continued.

    e.   The airlines often operate at a loss and are unable to take advantage of depreciation deductions. The airlines hope to obtain lower lease payments by allowing the lessor to claim the depreciation deductions for tax purposes.

11.46   (Deere & Company; interpreting income tax disclosures.) (Amounts in Millions)

    a.

Income Tax Expense......................................	182	
Deferred Tax Asset (= $82 – $77)......................	5	
Deferred Tax Liability (= $375 – $312).............		63
Income Tax Payable or Cash........................		124

    b.   Book income before income taxes exceeded taxable income because income tax expense exceeds income taxes currently payable. Also, the deferred tax accounts on the balance sheet experienced a net credit change of $58 million (= $63 – $5) during Year 10, suggesting larger book income than taxable income.

    c.

Deferred Tax Asset (= $149 – $82)	67	
Deferred Tax Asset (= $342 – $375)....................	33	
Income Tax Payable....................................		95
Income Tax Expense (Credit).......................		5

    d.   Book loss before income taxes was smaller than taxable income. Also, the deferred tax accounts on the balance sheet experienced a net debit change of $100 million (= $67 + $33) during Year 11, suggesting smaller book income (loss) than taxable income.

    e.   The decline in book income before income taxes between Year 10 and Year 11 suggests the possibility of a slowdown in sales growth. Revenue recognized for tax purposes using the installment method exceeds revenue recognized at the time of sale for book purposes, resulting in a decrease in the deferred tax liability relating to installment sales. The increase in the deferred tax assets relating to uncollectible accounts and sales rebates and allowances suggest weak economic conditions, causing Deere to increase its provisions for these items for book purposes.

    f.   Deere shows a deferred tax asset relating to pension, suggesting that Deere's pension expenses have exceeded pension contributions.

    g.   The deferred tax asset related to pension decreased during Year 10, suggesting that Deere's pension contribution exceeded pension expense.

        Solutions

11.46 continued.

    h.   Change in Deferred Tax Liability Relating to Depreciable
           Assets (= \$215 – \$208)..   \$ 7
        Income Tax Rate...   ÷ .35
        Temporary Difference for Year 11...............................   \$ 20
        Book Depreciation..   209
        Tax Depreciation..   \$ 229

    i.   Deere must amortize goodwill for book purposes but cannot amortize goodwill for tax purposes (that is, goodwill is a permanent difference). The computation of income taxes on pretax book income at the statutory tax rates assumes that Deere receives a tax saving from recognizing goodwill. The addition for goodwill eliminates the tax saving included in the statutory tax rate computation on the first line of the tax reconciliation.

11.47   (Sun Microsystems; interpreting income tax disclosures.) (Amounts in Millions)

    a.   Income Tax Expense...............................   67
        Deferred Tax Asset (= \$150 – \$142).........................   8
        Deferred Tax Liability (= \$7 – \$14)   7
            Income Tax Payable or Cash (= \$38 + \$38 + \$6)   82

    b.   Book income before income taxes was less than taxable income because there is a net debit change (= \$8 + \$7) in the deferred tax accounts on the balance sheet.

    c.   Income Tax Expense...............................   88
        Deferred Tax Asset (= \$174 – \$150).........................   24
            Deferred Tax Liability (= \$27 – \$7).......................   20
            Income Tax Payable or Cash (= \$28 + \$60 + \$4)   92

    d.   Book income before income taxes was less than taxable income because there is a net debit change (= \$24 – \$20) in the deferred tax accounts on the balance sheet.

    e.   Income Tax Expense...............................   167
        Deferred Tax Asset (= \$195 – \$174).........................   21
        Deferred Tax Liability (= \$25 – \$27).........................   2
            Income Tax Payable or Cash (= \$123 + \$57 + \$10) ...   190

    f.   Taxable income exceeds book income (loss) before income taxes. The deferred tax accounts on the balance sheet experienced a net debit change (= \$21 + \$2) during Year 7.

11.47 continued.

    g. Sun's pension contribution was less than its pension expense for Year 7 because its deferred tax asset for pensions increased during the year.

    h. Sun probably decreased its capital expenditures during Year 7 because depreciation for book purposes exceeded depreciation for tax purposes (that is, the deferred tax liability relating to depreciation temporary differences decreased during Year 7).

11.48   (General Products Company; interpreting income tax disclosures.)

    a. Book income was likely less than taxable income because the deferred tax accounts on the balance sheet experienced a net debit change during Year 3.

    b. Book income was likely larger than taxable income because the deferred tax accounts on the balance sheet experienced a net credit change during Year 4.

    c. The sales of products on account and under warranty plans increased continually during the three-year period. Estimated bad debt expense on each year's sales exceeded actual write-off of uncollectible accounts arising from the current and previous years' sales. Estimated warranty expense on products sold each year exceeded actual expenditures for warranties and products sold during the current and previous years.

    d.

Change in Deferred Tax Liability Relating to Temporary Depreciable Assets (= $213 − $155)	$ 58
Income Tax Rate	÷ .35
Excess of Tax Depreciation Over Book Depreciation	$165.7

11.49 (Equilibrium Company; behavior of deferred income tax account when a firm acquires new assets every year.)

TAX DEPRECIATION (ACRS)

Year	Units Acquired	1	2	3	4	5	6	7
1	1	$2,400	$3,840	$2,280	$1,440	$1,320	$720	$0
2	1		2,400	3,840	2,280	1,440	1,320	720
3	1			2,400	3,840	2,280	1,440	1,320
4	1				2,400	3,840	2,280	1,440
5	1					2,400	3,840	2,280
6	1						2,400	3,840
7	1							2,400

	1	2	3	4	5	6	7
a. Annual Depreciation	$2,400	$6,240	$8,520	$9,960	$11,280	$12,000	$12,000
b. Straight Line Depreciation = $2,000 per Machine per Year	2,000	4,000	6,000	8,000	10,000	12,000	12,000
c. Difference	$400	$2,240	$2,520	$1,960	$1,280	$0	$0
d. Increase in Deferred Tax (40%)	$160	$896	$1,008	$784	$512	$0	$0
e. Balance of Deferred Income Taxes	$160	$1,056	$2,064	$2,848	$3,360	$3,360	$3,360

f. The Deferred Income Taxes account balance will remain constant at $3,360 so long as the firm continues this replacement policy.

11.50　(American Home Products; interpreting pension disclosures.)

(Amounts in Millions)

a.

Pension Fund Assets, December 31, Year 5	$ 668.0
Actual Return on Pension Investments (Given)	113.4
Employer Contribution [= $35.3 − ($37.8 − $19.5)]............	17.0
Payments to Retirees (Plug)...	(55.1)
Pension Fund Assets, December 31, Year 6	$ 743.3

b.

Pension Benefit Obligation, December 31, Year 5............	$ 700.9
Interest Cost (Given)...	59.5
Service Cost (Given)...	31.5
Payments to Retirees (from Part *a*.)	(55.1)
Actuarial Gain (Plug)..	89.9
Projected Benefit Obligation, December 31, Year 6	$ 826.7

c. The decreased compensation inflation assumption decreased the projected benefit obligation (resulting in an actuarial gain) more than the decreased discount rate increased the projected benefit obligation.

d. Actual return of $113.4 million exceeds the expected return by $56.6 million, so pension fund performance exceeded expectations.

11.51　(Bristol-Myers Squibb; interpreting pension disclosures.)

(Amounts in Millions)

a.

	Year 8	Year 9
Pension Assets, Beginning of Year	$ 1,511	$ 1,381
Plus Actual Return on Pension Assets..........	(52)	335
Plus Contributions Received.......................	21[a]	89[b]
Less Payments to Retired Employees (Plug) ...	(99)	(111)
Pension Assets, End of Year	$ 1,381	$ 1,674

[a]$14 + ($35 − $28) = $21.
[b]$56 + ($68 − $35) = $89.

b.

	Year 8	Year 9
Projected Benefit Obligation, Beginning of Year	$ 1,407	$ 1,453
Plus Interest Cost	120	133
Plus Service Cost	73	82
Less Payments to Retired Employees (from Part *a*.)...	(99)	(111)
Plus (Minus) Actuarial Losses (Gains) (Plug)..	(48)	173
Projected Benefit Obligation, End of Year.......	$ 1,453	$ 1,730

Solutions

11.51 continued.

c. Pension assets generated a net loss of $52 million during Year 8, significantly less than the expected return of $181 million (= $233 – $52). Pension assets generated a higher return during Year 8 ($335 million) than the expected return of $166 million (= $335 – $169).

d. Pension fund performance fell significantly short of expectations during Year 8. Firms do not recognize such poor performance immediately in measuring pension expense but amortize it over future years. Note that the increase in discount rate from 8.8 percent to 9.1 percent causes the projected benefit obligation to decline and provides for an unamortized actuarial gain. The change in the unamortized experience and actuarial gain (loss) during Year 8 appears below:

Unamortized Experience and Actuarial Gain at Beginning of Year 8	$ 76
Plus Actuarial Gain from Change in Discount Rate (Plug)...	48
Less Experience Loss from Investment Performance Less than Expectations	(233)
Plus Amortization for Year	2
Unamortized Experience and Actuarial Loss at End of Year 8..	$(107)

e. The change in the unamortized experience and actuarial gain (loss) during Year 9 appears below:

Unamortized Experience and Actuarial Loss at Beginning of Year 8	$(107)
Less Actuarial Loss During Year 9 (Plug)......................	(173)
Plus Experience Gain from Investment Performance Exceeding Expectations...	169
Plus Amortization for Year	7
Unamortized Experience and Actuarial Loss at End of Year 9..	$(104)

The decrease in the discount rate caused the projected benefit obligation to increase, resulting in an actuarial loss. Bristol-Myers Squibb may have also changed other actuarial assumptions to help explain the large actuarial loss for Year 9.

f. The pension asset on the balance sheet indicates that Bristol-Myers Squibb has funded its pension plan faster than it has expensed pension costs. There is no necessary relation between the employers expensing versus funding policies and the overall funded status of the pension plan.

Solutions   11-32

11.52   (Brion Company; attempts to achieve off-balance-sheet financing.)

[The chapter does not give sufficient information for the student to know the GAAP answers. The six items are designed to generate a lively discussion.]

Transfer of Receivables with Recourse *SFAS No. 77* (1983) sets out the following criteria to treat a transfer of receivables with recourse as a sale: (1) the seller (Brion) surrenders control of the future economic benefits and risks of the receivables, and (2) the purchaser of the receivables (Credit Company) cannot require the seller to repurchase the receivables except as set out in the original provision, and (3) the seller can estimate its obligation under the recourse provision.

Brion Company retains control of the future economic benefits. If interest rates decrease, Brion can borrow funds at the lower interest rate and repurchase the receivables. Because the receivables carry a fixed interest return, Brion enjoys the benefit of the difference between the fixed interest return on the receivables and the lower borrowing cost. If interest rates increase, Brion will not repurchase the receivables. Credit Company bears the risk of interest rate increases because of the fixed interest return on the receivables. The control of who benefits from interest rate changes and who bears the risk resides with Brion Company. Brion Company also bears credit risk in excess of the allowance. Thus, this transaction does not meet the first two criteria as a sale. Brion Company should report the transaction as a collateralized loan.

Product Financing Arrangement *SFAS No. 49* (1981) provides that firms recognize product financing arrangements as liabilities if (1) the arrangement requires the sponsoring firm (Brion) to purchase the inventory at specified prices and (2) the payments made to the other entity (Credit Company) cover all acquisition, holding, and financing costs.

Brion Company agrees to repurchase the inventory at a fixed price, thereby incurring the risk of changing prices. The purchase price formula includes a fixed interest rate, so Brion enjoys the benefits or incurs the risk of interest rate changes. Brion also controls the benefits and risk of changes in storage costs. Thus, Brion treats this product financing arrangement as a collateralized loan.

11-33

11.52 continued.

Throughput Contract *SFAS Statement No. 49* (1981) treats throughput contracts as executory contracts and does not require their recognition as a liability. Note, however, the similarity between a product financing arrangement (involving inventory) and a throughput contract (involving a service). Brion Company must pay specified amounts each period regardless of whether it uses the shipping services. The wording of the problem makes it unclear as to whether the initial contract specifies a selling price (railroad bears risk of operating cost increases) or whether the selling price is the railroad's current charges for shipping services each period (Brion bears risk of operating cost increases). It seems unlikely that the railroad would accept a fixed price for all ten years. Thus, it appears that Brion incurs a commitment to make highly probable future cash payments in amounts that cover the railroad's operating and financing costs. This transaction has the economic characteristics of a collateralized loan, even though GAAP permits treatment as an executory contract.

Construction Joint Venture The construction loan appears as a liability of the books of Chemical, the joint entity. Because Brion and Mission each own 50 percent of Chemical, neither company consolidates Chemical's financial statements with their own. (Chapter 13 discusses consolidated financial statements.) Thus, the loan will not appear on either Brion's or Mission's balance sheet by way of their accounting for their investment in Chemical.

GAAP treats the commitment to pay one-half of the operating and debt service costs as an executory contract, similar to the throughput contract. Even though the probability of making future cash payments is high, GAAP concludes that a liability does not arise until the firm receives future benefits from Chemical.

The only way that Brion will recognize a liability is if the debt guarantee gives rise to a loss contingency. If Mission defaults on its share of operating and debt service costs, the probability of Brion having to repay the loan increases sufficiently to warrant recognition of a liability. It is difficult to see the logic of GAAP in recognizing the full liability in this case while not recognizing one-half of the liability in situations described in the preceding paragraphs. In both cases, the probability of future cash outflows is high.

Research and Development Partnership *SFAS No. 68* (1982) requires firms to recognize financings related to research and development (R & D) as liabilities if (1) the sponsoring firm (Brion) must repay the financing regardless of the outcome of the R & D work, or (2) the sponsoring firm, even in the a absence of a loan guarantee, bears the risk of failure of the R & D effort.

11.52 continued.

   Brion guarantees the bank loan in this case regardless of the outcome of the R &D effort and therefore must recognize a liability (satisfies first criterion above). It does not matter whether Brion has an option or an obligation to purchase the results of the R & D effort.

   If Brion did not guarantee the bank loan, then the second criterion above determines whether Brion recognizes a liability. If Brion has the option to purchase the results of the R & D work, it does not bear the risk of failure and need not recognize a liability. If Brion has the obligation to purchase the results, it recognizes a liability for the probable amount payable. The problem does not make it clear whether the amount payable includes the unpaid balance of the loan or merely the value of the R & D work (which could be zero). It seems unlikely that the bank would lend funds for the R & D work without some commitment or obligation by Brion to repay the loan.

Hotel Financing Brion Company will recognize a liability for the hotel financing only if its debt guarantee satisfies the criteria for a loss contingency. It appears in this case that the probability of Brion having to make payments under the loan guarantee is low. The hotel is profitable and probably generating cash flows. In addition, the bank can sell the hotel in the event of loan default to satisfy the unpaid balance of the loan. Thus, Brion's loan guarantee is a third level of defense against loan default. If default does occur and the first two lines of defense prove inadequate to repay the loan in full, then Brion would recognize a liability for the unpaid portion.

CHAPTER 12

SHAREHOLDERS' EQUITY

Questions, Exercises, Problems, and Cases: Answers and Solutions

12.1   See the text or the glossary at the end of the book.

12.2   The common shareholder would not likely receive an amount equal to the amounts in the common shareholders' equity accounts. The amounts in these accounts reflect acquisition cost valuations for assets. The firm might sell assets for more or less than their book values, with the common shareholders thereby receiving more or less than the amount in the common shareholders' equity accounts. Furthermore, the bankruptcy and liquidation process requires legal and other costs not now reflected on the balance sheet. The asset sales must generate sufficient cash to pay these costs before the common shareholders receive any residual cash.

12.3   Ordinarily, the shareholders of a corporation have no personal responsibility for the debts of the corporation. By endorsing the note, the president of the corporation becomes personally liable in case the corporation defaults. If the firm was a partnership, the president as a general partner would be personally liable for this debt in any case, as well as other liabilities of the partnership. The personal endorsement may, however, provide a higher priority claim against personal assets.

12.4   Firms have issued securities in recent years (for example, convertible bonds and redeemable preferred stock) that have both debt and equity characteristics. A clear distinction between liabilities and shareholders' equity no longer exists. Firms might list various claims against a firm's assets in decreasing order of priority in the case of bankruptcy with no distinction between liabilities and shareholders' equity. Alternatively, firms might create a third category that includes securities with both debt and equity characteristics and include it between liabilities and shareholders' equity on the balance sheet.

12.5   There is no reason to expect a newly organized firm to issue common shares at a price more than par value except to take advantage of some state laws which permit the distribution of Additional Paid-in Capital. The firm may issue additional shares of an old issue at more than par value in order to effect adjustments between old and new shareholders. If the company has been successful, new shareholders may have to contribute more than the amount contributed (par) by the original shareholders who invested when the business had not yet established its profitability.

12.6   The par value of preferred, rather than the amount contributed, serves as a basis for measuring the dividend rate and the amount of preference as to assets in event of liquidation. The par value of common stock may have legal significance in certain states, but it has no economic significance. Firms declare dividends based on the number of common shares outstanding, not on the par value of the common stock.

12.7   The three provisions provide different benefits and risks to the issuing firm and the investor and should sell at different prices. Callable preferred stock should sell for less than convertible preferred stock. The issuing firm gains benefits with an option to call, or repurchase, the preferred stock and must thereby accept a lower issue price. The investor gains benefits with an option to convert into capital stock and must pay a higher price. The mandatory redemption requirement makes the preferred stock more like debt than shareholders' equity. Its market price depends on market interest rates for similar maturity debt (versus the 4 percent yield on the preferred stock) and the rank-ordering priority of the preferred stock in bankruptcy.

12.8   The question addresses the tradeoff between relevance and reliability frequently encountered in accounting. Financial statement users desire information that helps them assess the economic value of firms. Information about the value of options is relevant information for this purpose. The measurement of the value of options is subject to varying degrees of subjectivity. Reliability decreases as subjectivity increases. Likewise, the usefulness of relevant information decreases as reliability decreases.

12.9   All three items permit their holder to acquire shares of common stock at a set price. Their values depend on the difference between the market price and the exercise price on the exercise date and the length of the exercise period. Firms grant stock options to employees, grant stock rights to current shareholders and either sell stock warrants on the open market or attach them to a debt or preferred stock issue. The issuance of stock options and stock rights does not result in an immediate cash inflow, whereas the issuance of a stock warrant usually does. Accountants credit a Stock Warrant account if the value of the stock warrant is objectively measurable. At the time of exercise of all these items, the accountant records the cash proceeds as a capital contribution.

12.10   The managers of a firm have knowledge of the plans and risks of the firm that external investors may not possess. Although laws prevent firms from taking advantage of this "inside information," inclusion of gains from treasury stock transactions in net income might motivate firms to buy and sell treasury stock to improve reported earnings. Excluding these gains from net income removes this incentive. Also, the accounting for the acquisition of treasury stock (that is, a reduction from total shareholders' equity) has the same effect on shareholders' equity as a retirement of the capital stock. The reissue of the treasury stock for more than its acquisition cost does not result in a gain any more than the issue of common stock for more than par value represents a gain.

12.11   Most firms acquire treasury stock with the intention of reissuing the stock upon the exercise of stock options or warrants or the conversion of debt or preferred stock into common stock. Thus, treasury stock typically does not remain as treasury stock for an extended period. The fallacy in this explanation is that firms destroy the stock certificates underlying shares purchased as treasury stock, the same as for retired stock, and issue new stock certificates to purchasers of the treasury stock, the same as for newly issued stock.

12.12   The president is right, but the shareholders may prefer that the firm pay a cash dividend rather than force the shareholders to sell off some shares to raise funds. The president's point is that they do not lose out in any fundamental sense by not receiving dividends, since their equity in the firm increases (absolutely, not proportionately) as a result and, presumably, the market price of the shares increases. Furthermore, shareholders save a set of personal income taxes. The statement is somewhat self-serving, but this process does simplify raising additional capital.

12.13   Yes. Earnings do not necessarily indicate the availability of idle cash funds for distribution. The corporation may have insufficient cash to meet maturing obligations, additional working capital requirements in connection with increasing accounts receivable and inventory replacement, replacements of equipment, or other such expenditures.

12.14   As the Retained Earnings account has grown, so has the firm's net assets. The firm has likely invested these assets in plant, not in cash and temporary marketable securities. The firm is unlikely to have cash in the amount of the increase in retained earnings available for paying dividends. If the firm had regularly declared stock dividends (to capitalize into the contributed capital accounts amounts permanently invested in plant assets), then the balance in the Retained Earnings account might better indicate the ability to pay cash dividends. But then, of course, the Retained Earnings account would have a smaller balance.

         Solutions

12.15 In the case of a cash dividend, the shareholder now holds the investment in two parts—cash and stock certificates. The sum of the cash and the book value of the stock after the dividend declaration equals the book value of the stock before the firm declared the dividend. It is common to speak of a cash dividend as income, but it is merely the conversion of a portion of the shareholder's investment into a different form. In a sense, the shareholder earns income on the investment when the corporation earns its income. Because of the realization test for income recognition in accounting, however, the shareholders do not recognize income (except under the equity method discussed in Chapter 13) until the firm distributes cash. A stock dividend does not even improve the marketability of the investment, although when a firm issues preferred shares to common shareholders or vice versa, shareholders may view the situation as similar to a cash dividend. The stock dividend capitalizes a portion of retained earnings.

12.16 An error in previously-issued financial statements results from oversights or errors which the firm should not have made given reasonable diligence in accessing available information at the time. Accountants restate the previously-issued financial statements to correct the error. A change in an accounting estimate results from *new* information that suggests that the original estimate was inaccurate as judged *ex post*. Accountants adjust for changes in estimates during the current and future periods instead of restating previously-issued financial statements.

12.17 Prior-period adjustments are direct debits or credits to Retained Earnings for information resolving uncertainty from earlier accounting periods. Some accountants suspect that if management were allowed to use prior-period adjustments for the resolution of past uncertainty, all "bad" news would find its way into the financial statements via prior-period adjustments, never having appeared in the income statement originally issued for any period. For example, firms might take an optimistic view with respect to the depreciable life of assets, showing low periodic depreciation charges in each year's income statement. When the firm discovers that the assets will last a shorter time than projected, there is a direct debit to Retained Earnings and a credit to Accumulated Depreciation for the catch-up. These accountants think that all losses (gains are seldom a problem; why?) should appear in income as discipline for managements that might wish to report favorably on their own performances.

12.18 (Journal entries to record the issuance of capital stock.)

a. Cash... 625,000
    Common Stock (= 25,000 × $10)..................... 250,000
    Additional Paid-in Capital (= 25,000 × $15)...... 375,000

b. Cash... 1,000,000
    Preferred Stock.. 1,000,000

12.18 continued.

c. Land... 180,000
     Common Stock (= 12,000 × $1).....................   12,000
     Additional Paid-in Capital (= 12,000 × $14)......   168,000

The market value of the stock seems a better indicator of the value of the land than either the assessed value or the asking price.

d. No entry.

e. Cash.. 180,000
     Common Stock (= 3,000 × $10).....................   30,000
     Additional Paid-in Capital (= 3,000 × $50)........   150,000

f. Bonds Payable.. 300,000
     Common Stock (= 10,000 × $10)   100,000
     Additional Paid-in Capital..........................   200,000

g. Bonds Payable.. 300,000
   Loss on Conversion of Bonds...........................   50,000
     Common Stock (= 10,000 × $10)   100,000
     Additional Paid-in Capital (= 10,000 × $25)......   250,000

12.19 (Journal entries for the issuance of common stock.)

a. Inventory 250,000
   Land 160,000
   Building... 1,200,000
   Equipment... 390,000
     Common Stock (= 40,000 × $15).....................   600,000
     Additional Paid-in Capital 1,400,000

b. Cash.. 500,000
     Redeemable Preferred Stock   500,000

c. Cash (= 20,000 × $18)................................... 360,000
   Common Stock Warrants (= 20,000 × $2).............   40,000
     Common Stock (= 20,000 × $1).....................   20,000
     Additional Paid-in Capital   380,000

d. Preferred Stock (= 20,000 × $100)...................... 2,000,000
     Common Stock (= 50,000 × $10).....................   500,000
     Additional Paid-in Capital 1,500,000

       Solutions

12.20 (Vertovec Corporation; journal entries for employee stock option.)

a. **December 31, Year 3**
No entry.

October 15, Year 5

Cash..	375,000	
Common Stock (= 15,000 × $10)		150,000
Additional Paid-in Capital (= 15,000 × $15)......		225,000

November 30, Year 6

Cash..	125,000	
Common Stock (= 5,000 × $10)		50,000
Additional Paid-in Capital (= 5,000 × $15)........		75,000

b. **December 31, Year 3**

Compensation Expense...................................	100,000	
Common Stock Options (= 20,000 × $5)...........		100,000

October 15, Year 5

Cash..	375,000	
Common Stock Options (= 15,000 × $5)	75,000	
Common Stock (= 15,000 × $10)		150,000
Additional Paid-in Capital...........................		300,000

November 30, Year 6

Cash..	125,000	
Common Stock Options (= 5,000 × $5).................	25,000	
Common Stock (= 5,000 × $10)		50,000
Additional Paid-in Capital...........................		100,000

12.21 (Haskins Corporation; journal entries for stock warrants.)

February 26, Year 6

Cash	120,000	
Common Stock Warrants (= 40,000 × $3).............		120,000

June 6, Year 7

Cash (= 30,000 × $40)	1,200,000	
Common Stock Warrants (= 30,000 × $3)..................	90,000	
Common Stock (= 30,000 × $5)		150,000
Additional Paid-in Capital...............................		1,140,000

February 26, Year 8

Common Stock Warrants (= 10,000 × $3)..................	30,000	
Additional Paid-in Capital...............................		30,000

12.22 (Higgins Corporation; journal entries for convertible bonds.)

a. **1/02/Year 1**

Cash..	1,000,000	
Convertible Bonds Payable		1,000,000
To record the issue of convertible bonds.		

1/02/Year 5

Convertible Bonds Payable..............................	1,000,000	
Common Stock—$1 Par		40,000
Additional Paid-in Capital..........................		960,000
To record conversion using book value of bonds.		

b. **1/02/Year 1**

Cash	1,000,000	
Convertible Bonds Payable........................		685,139.78
Additional Paid-in Capital........................		314,860.22

Issue of 10-percent semiannual coupon convertible bonds at a time when the firm could issue ordinary 10-percent bonds for $685,139.78 when the market interest rate is 15 percent compounded semiannually.

Supporting Computations

$50,000 × 12.59441..	$629,720.43
$1,000,000 × .05542..	<u>55,419.35</u>
Issue Price..	<u>$685,139.78</u>

Also see Table 6 at the back of the book.

12.23 (Huerta Corporation; journal entries for treasury stock transactions.)

a.
Treasury Stock...	240,000	
Cash (= 8,000 × $30).....................................		240,000

b.
Cash (= 3,000 × $32)...	96,000	
Treasury Stock (= 3,000 × $30)......................		90,000
Additional Paid-in Capital		6,000

c.
Treasury Stock...	190,000	
Cash (= 5,000 × $38).....................................		190,000

d.
Land..	200,000	
Treasury Stock [= (5,000 × $30) + (1,000 × $38)]...		188,000
Additional Paid-in Capital		12,000

e.
Cash (= 4,000 × $36)...	144,000	
Additional Paid-in Capital	8,000	
Treasury Stock (= 4,000 × $38)......................		152,000

12.24   (Melissa Corporation; journal entries for treasury stock transactions.)

a. Treasury Stock.. 120,000
        Cash (= 10,000 × $12)   120,000

b. Bonds Payable... 72,000
        Treasury Stock (= 6,000 × $12)   72,000

c. Treasury Stock... 300,000
        Cash (= 20,000 × $15)   300,000

d. Land.. 540,000
        Treasury Stock [= (4,000 × $12) + (20,000 ×
            $15)]...   348,000
        Common Stock (= 6,000 × $5)   30,000
        Additional Paid-in Capital............................   162,000

12.25   (Uncertainty Corporation; journal entries to correct errors and adjust for changes in estimates.)

a. Retained Earnings... 12,000
        Patent (or Accumulated Amortization).........   12,000
    To correct error from neglecting to amortize
    patent during previous year.

b. Accumulated Depreciation............................ 7,000
        Retained Earnings.....................................   7,000
    To eliminate the balance in accumulated depre-
    ciation relating to the machine sold and convert
    a $4,000 loss on the sale to a $3,000 gain.

c. Depreciation Expense..................................... 50,000
        Accumulated Depreciation   50,000
    Book value on January 1, Year 13 is $1,600,000
    [= $2,400,000 − ($80,000 × 10)]. The revised
    annual depreciation is $50,000 (= $1,600,000/32).

d. Bad Debt Expense... 10,000
        Allowance for Uncollectible Accounts   10,000
    To adjust the balance in the allowance account
    to the amount needed to cover estimated un-
    collectibles.

12.26   (Journal entries for cash dividends.)

a. Retained Earnings... 4,600
        Dividends Payable—Preferred Stock..............   4,600
    2,300 shares at $2.

12.26 continued.

b. Retained Earnings 30,000
      Dividends Payable—Common Stock 30,000
    10,000 shares at $3.

c. Dividends Payable—Preferred Stock 4,600
      Cash 4,600

d. Dividends Payable—Common Stock 30,000
      Cash 30,000

12.27   (Journal entries for dividends.)

a. Retained Earnings 16,000
      Dividends Payable—Preferred Stock............. 16,000
    Dividend of $2.50 per share on 6,400 shares.

b. Dividends Payable—Preferred Stock 16,000
      Cash 16,000

c. Retained Earnings 250,000
      Common Stock 250,000

d. No entry.

12.28   (Watt Corporation; journal entries for dividends.)

a. **March 31, Year 6**
    Retained Earnings 10,000
      Dividends Payable 10,000
    $10,000 = 20,000 × $.50.

b. **April 15, Year 6**
    Dividends Payable 10,000
      Cash 10,000

c. **June 30, Year 6**
    Retained Earnings (= 2,000 × $20) 40,000
      Common Stock (= 2,000 × $15) 30,000
      Additional Paid-in Capital 10,000

d. **September 30, Year 6**
    Retained Earnings 11,000
      Dividends Payable 11,000
    $11,000 = 22,000 × $.50.

e. **October 15, Year 6**
    Dividends Payable 11,000
      Cash 11,000

12.28 continued.

    f.   **December 31, Year 6**

Additional Paid-in Capital	165,000	
Common Stock (= 11,000 × $15)		165,000

12.29   (Effects on statement of cash flows.)

    a.   The journal entry to record this transaction is:

Cash..	200,000	
Common Stock		200,000

The Cash account increases, so Line (9) increases by $200,000. Issuing common stock is a financing activity, so Line (6) increases by $200,000.

    b.   The journal entry to record this transaction is:

Common Stock..	50,000	
Additional Paid-in Capital	25,000	
Cash		75,000

The Cash account decreases, so Line (9) decreases by $75,000. Repurchasing common stock is a financing activity, so Line (7) increases by $75,000.

    c.   The journal entry to record this transaction using the book value method is:

Convertible Bonds Payable..............................	100,000	
Common Stock		10,000
Additional Paid-in Capital...........................		90,000

The journal entry to record this transaction under the market value method is:

Convertible Bonds Payable..............................	100,000	
Loss on Conversion of Bonds...........................	140,000	
Common Stock		10,000
Additional Paid-in Capital...........................		230,000

The Cash account does not change under either method of recording the transaction. The transaction does not appear on the statement of cash flows when the firm uses the book value method. When the firm uses the market value method, net income on Line (1) decreases for the loss. Line (2) increases to add back the loss to net income since it does not affect cash. The firm reports this financing transaction in a supplementary schedule or note.

12.29 continued.

d. The journal entry to record this transaction is:

Cash.. 15,000
Additional Paid-in Capital 5,000
   Treasury Stock 20,000

The Cash account increases, so Line (9) increases by $15,000. Issuing treasury stock is a financing transaction, so Line (6) increases by $15,000.

e. The journal entry to record this transaction is:

Retained Earnings.. 300,000
   Common Stock 1,000
   Additional Paid-in Capital.......................... 299,000

Because this transaction does not affect the Cash account, it does not appear in the statement of cash flows.

f. The journal entry to record this transaction is:

Retained Earnings.. 70,000
   Dividends Payable..................................... 70,000

Because this transaction does not affect the Cash account, it does not appear in the statement of cash flows.

g. The journal entry to record this transaction is:

Dividends Payable.. 70,000
   Cash 70,000

The Cash account decreases, so Line (9) decreases by $70,000. Paying dividends is a financing activity, so Line (8) increases by $70,000.

h. The journal entry to record this transaction is:

Cash.. 20,000
   Common Stock 1,000
   Additional Paid-in Capital.......................... 19,000

The Cash account increases, so Line (9) increases by $20,000. Issuing common stock under a stock rights plan is a financing activity, so Line (6) increases by $20,000.

 Solutions

12.30 (Wilson Supply Company; transactions to incorporate and run a business.)

a. **1/02**
   Cash.. 9,000
      Common Stock—$30 Stated Value................   9,000
   300 shares × $30 = $9,000.

b. **1/06**
   Cash.. 60,000
      Common Stock—$30 Stated Value................   60,000
   2,000 shares × $30 = $60,000.

c. **1/08**
   Cash.. 400,000
      Preferred Stock—Par   400,000
   4,000 shares × $100 = $400,000.

d. **1/09**
   No entry.

e. **1/12**
   Inventories... 50,000
   Land.. 80,000
   Building.. 210,000
   Equipment 120,000
      Preferred Stock—Par   100,000
      Common Stock—Stated Value.....................   360,000

f. **7/03**
   Retained Earnings...................................... 20,000
      Dividends Payable on Preferred Stock............   20,000
   $100 × (.08/2) × (4,000 + 1,000) shares = $20,000.

g. **7/05**
   Cash.. 825,000
      Common Stock—$30 Stated Value................   750,000
      Additional Paid-in Capital........................   75,000
   25,000 shares × $33 = $825,000.

h. **7/25**
   Dividends Payable on Preferred Stock............... 20,000
      Cash   20,000

i. **10/02**
   Retained Earnings...................................... 39,300
      Dividends Payable on Common Stock   39,300
   $1 × (300 + 2,000 + 12,000 + 25,000) shares =
   $39,300.

12.30 continued.

  j. **10/25**
    Dividends Payable on Common Stock................ 39,300
     Cash   39,300

12.31 (Hutchins Company; transactions to incorporate and run a business.)

  a. No formal entry is required.

  b. **July 8, Year 1**
    Cash... 240,000
     Common Stock   240,000
    6,000 shares issued at $40 per share.

  c. **July 9, Year 1**
    Accounts Receivable.................................... 20,000
    Inventories.. 30,000
    Land... 40,000
    Buildings.. 50,000
    Equipment 20,000
     Common Stock   160,000
    4,000 shares issued at $40 per share.

  d. **July 13, Year 1**
    Cash... 80,000
     Preferred Stock—Par   80,000

  e. **Dec. 31, Year 1**
    Income Summary.. 75,000
     Retained Earnings...................................   75,000

  f. **Jan. 4, Year 2**
    Retained Earnings...................................... 31,600
     Dividends Payable on Preferred Stock...........   1,600
     Dividends Payable on Common Stock   30,000
    $800 \times \$2 = \$1,600; 10,000 \times \$3 = \$30,000$.

  g. **Feb. 1, Year 2**
    Dividends Payable on Preferred Stock............... 1,600
    Dividends Payable on Common Stock................ 30,000
     Cash   31,600

  h. **July 2, Year 2**
    Retained Earnings...................................... 1,600
     Dividends Payable on Preferred Stock...........   1,600

  i. **Aug. 1, Year 2**
    Dividends Payable on Preferred Stock............... 1,600
     Cash   1,600

  12-13   **Solutions**

12.32   (Conrad Company; reconstructing transactions involving shareholders' equity.)

a. $30,000 par value/$10 per share = 3,000 shares.

b. $3,600/180 = $20 per share.

c. 300 − 180 = 120 shares.

d. If the Additional Paid-in Capital is $15,720, then $15,000 [= 3,000 × ($15 − $10)] represents contributions in excess of par value on original issue of 3,000 shares. Then, $720 (= $15,720 − $15,000) represents the credit to Additional Paid-in Capital when it reissued the treasury shares.

The $720 represents 120 shares reissued times the excess of reissue price over acquisition price:

$$120(\$X - \$20) = \$720, \text{ or } X = \$26.$$

The shares were reissued for $26 each.

e. (1) Cash (3,000 × $15) 45,000

Capital Stock ($10 Par Value)................		30,000
Additional Paid-in Capital		15,000

(2) Treasury Shares 6,000

Cash (300 × $20)....................................		6,000

(3) Cash (120 × $26)..................................... 3,120

Treasury Shares (120 × $20)		2,400
Additional Paid-in Capital		720

12.33   (Gorman Company; reconstructing transactions involving shareholders' equity.)

a. $100,000 par value/$5 per share = 20,000 shares.

b. $33,600/1,200 = $28 per share.

c. 2,000 − 1,200 = 800 shares.

12.33 continued.

    d. If the Additional Paid-in Capital is $509,600, then $500,000 [= 20,000 × ($30 − $5)] represents contributions in excess of par value on original issue of 20,000 shares. Then, $9,600 (= $509,600 − $500,000) represents the credit to Additional Paid-in Capital when it reissued the treasury shares.

        The $9,600 represents 800 shares reissued times the excess of reissue price over acquisition price:

$$800(\$X - \$28) = \$9,600, \text{ or } X = \$40.$$

The shares were reissued for $40 each.

    e. (1)

Cash..	600,000	
Capital Stock ($5 Par Value).................		100,000
Additional Paid-in Capital		500,000

        (2)

Treasury Shares	56,000	
Cash..		56,000

        (3)

Cash..	32,000	
Treasury Shares................................		22,400
Additional Paid-in Capital		9,600
800 × $40 = $32,000.		

12.34   (General Electric Company; dilutive effects of stock options.)

    a. 2.7 million shares × $77 = $207.9 million.

    b. 2.7 million shares × $54 = $145.8 million.

    c. Shareholders are $62.1 million better off with a public issue than with a private issue. $207.9 million − $145.8 million = 2.7 million shares × ($77 − $54) = $62.1 million.

    d. The unwary reader might mistakenly infer from GE's explanation that exercised options do not dilute the equity of other shareholders. Holders will not exercise options unless the market price at time of exercise exceeds the exercise price. At the time of exercise, the firm issues shares at a price less than it would realize if it issued the shares to the general public. The $62.1 million dilution in shareholders' equity is the realized amount of compensation expense that GE incurred when it granted the options. If GAAP permitted the firm to recognize compensation expense when it granted the options, the amount of expense would be the present value of the estimate of the eventual dilution or perhaps a measure of the services rendered by the employees. GE's shareholders are better off if the employees who were granted the options worked harder than they otherwise would have and produced more than $62.1 million of aftertax income since the time of the grant. Otherwise, shareholders were hurt.

            Solutions

12.35 (Alcher Company; accounting for detachable warrants.)

a. The warrants reduced the amount borrowed, but not the interest rate. In reality, see Part *b.* below, the Company borrowed $855,812 at an interest rate of 12 percent per year and issued detachable warrants for $144,188. One cannot ascertain whether or not this was a fair price for the option under the circumstances from the available data.

b.
Present Value of $80,000 in arrears for 5 years discounted at 12% is 3.60478 × $80,000	$ 288,382
Present Value of $1,000,000 paid in 5 years discounted at 12% is .56743 × $1,000,000	567,430
Present Value of loan repayments is...........................	$ 855,812

The remaining $144,188 must be for the option. Thus, the entry to reflect the economics of the situation is:

Cash..	1,000,000	
Note Payable...		855,812
Additional Paid-in Capital............................		144,188

At each interest payment date, the entry is:

Interest Expense...	80,000 + X	
Cash		80,000
Note Payable...		X

Where X is the increase in interest expense to recognize increase in book value of the note.

End of Year	X = Increase in Note Payable[a]	Remaining Loan
0	--	$ 855,812
1	$22,697	878,509
2	25,421	903,930
3	28,472	932,402
4	31,888	964,290
5	35,710	1,000,000

[a]= (.12 × Amount in Last Column for Preceding Year) – $80,000, except in Year 5 where it is the amount required to give $1,000,000 in last column.

c.
Cash..	400,000	
Common Stock—$5 Par		100,000
Additional Paid-in Capital...........................		300,000

20,000 × $5 = $100,000. 20,000 × ($20 – $5) = $300,000.

12.35 continued.

    d.   Yes. The firm could issue the same shares to other investors for $45 per share. This does not mean that shareholders were hurt by the entire transaction. They gambled with the lending-investor and "lost." If the option was fairly priced at $144,188, then all sides were treated fairly.

    e.   During the life of the loan, disclosure of the amount of the options outstanding and their exercise price would enable the reader of financial statements to see the potential dilution of earnings overhanging the company.

12.36   (Chris Corporation; comprehensive review of accounting for shareholders' equity.)

a. and b.

    See following page.

    c.   (1) The acquisition of treasury shares, the declaration of dividends, and the incurrence of a net loss reduce total book value.

          (2) The issue of common shares for a price less than current book value per share (for example, under stock option plans), the acquisition of treasury shares for a price greater than current book value per share, and the sale or reissue of treasury shares at a price less than their acquisition cost (at a "loss") reduce book value per share.

 Solutions

JOURNAL ENTRY

a.

b.

(1)	Retained Earnings	150,000	
	Common Stock (5,000 × $10)		50,000
	Additional Paid-in Capital (5,000 × $20)		100,000
(2)	Common Stock ($10 Par Value)	500,000	
	Common Stock ($5 per Share)		500,000
(3)	Treasury Stock	125,000	
	Cash (5,000 × $25)		125,000
(4)	Treasury Stock	75,000	
	Cash (5,000 × $15)		75,000
(5)	Cash (5,000 × $35)	175,000	
	Treasury Stock (5,000 × $25)		125,000
	Additional Paid-in Capital		50,000
(6)	Cash (5,000 × $20)	100,000	
	Additional Paid-in Capital	25,000	
	Treasury Stock (5,000 × $25)		125,000
(7)	Cash (5,000 × $15)	75,000	
	Additional Paid-in Capital	50,000	
	Treasury Stock (5,000 × $25)		125,000
(8)	Cash (5,000 × $15)	75,000	
	Common Stock (5,000 × $10)		50,000
	Additional Paid-in Capital		25,000
(9)	Cash (5,000 × $50)	250,000	
	Common Stock (5,000 × $10)		50,000
	Additional Paid-in Capital		200,000
(10)	Bonds Payable	150,000	
	Common Stock (10,000 × $10)		100,000
	Additional Paid-in Capital		50,000
(11)	Bonds Payable	150,000	
	Loss on Conversion of Bonds	20,000	
	Common Stock		100,000
	Additional Paid-in Capital		70,000

BOOK VALUE PER SHARE
(Numerator is Total Book Value)

$\dfrac{\$2,250,000}{50,000} = \$45.00$ per share.

(1) $\dfrac{\$2,250,000}{55,000} = \$40.91$ per share.

(2) $\dfrac{\$2,250,000}{100,000} = \$22.50$ per share.

(3) $\dfrac{\$2,125,000}{45,000} = \$47.22$ per share.

(4) $\dfrac{\$2,175,000}{45,000} = \$48.33$ per share.

(5) $\dfrac{\$2,300,000}{50,000} = \$46.00$ per share.

(6) $\dfrac{\$2,225,000}{50,000} = \$44.50$ per share.

(7) $\dfrac{\$2,200,000}{50,000} = \$44.00$ per share.

(8) $\dfrac{\$2,325,000}{55,000} = \$42.27$ per share.

(9) $\dfrac{\$2,500,000}{55,000} = \$45.45$ per share.

(10) $\dfrac{\$2,400,000}{60,000} = \$40.00$ per share.

(11) $\dfrac{\$2,400,000}{60,000} = \$40.00$ per share.

12.37   (Neslin Company; reconstructing events affecting shareholders' equity.)

a.   (1) Issue of 20,000 shares of common stock at $52 per share for cash or other assets.

(2) Acquisition of 4,000 shares of treasury stock for $55 per share.

(3) Reissue of 3,000 shares of treasury stock for $48 per share.

(4) Reissue of 1,000 shares of treasury stock for $60 per share.

(5) Net income of $2,400,000 closed to Retained Earnings.

(6) Dividends declared of $10 per share.

b.   (1) Cash.. 1,040,000
            Common Stock.............................   200,000
            Additional Paid-in Capital.............   840,000

(2) Treasury Stock............................... 220,000
            Cash..   220,000

(3) Cash.. 144,000
       Additional Paid-in Capital................ 21,000
            Treasury Stock............................   165,000

(4) Cash.. 60,000
            Treasury Stock............................   55,000
            Additional Paid-in Capital............   5,000

(5) Income Summary........................... 2,400,000
            Retained Earnings   2,400,000

(6) Retained Earnings.......................... 1,200,000
            Cash or Dividends Payable   1,200,000

12.38   (Wal-Mart Stores; journal entries for changes in shareholders' equity.)

(1) Income Summary.................................... 1,291,024
        Retained Earnings   1,291,024

(2) Retained Earnings.................................... 158,889
        Dividends Payable or Cash...........................   158,889

(3) Cash.. 3,820
        Common Stock   66
        Additional Paid-in Capital...........................   3,754

(4) Additional Paid-in Capital............................ 56,680
        Common Stock   56,680

(5) Investment in Securities............................... 274,696
        Common Stock   1,037
        Additional Paid-in Capital...........................   273,659

(6) Treasury Stock..................................... 25,826
        Cash   25,826

12.39   (Wellington Company; journal entries for changes in shareholders' equity.)

(1) Income Summary....................................... 210,500
        Retained Earnings   210,500

(2) Retained Earnings..................................... 120,000
        Cash or Dividends Payable   120,000

(3) Bonds Payable.................................... 70,000
        Common Stock   6,270
        Additional Paid-in Capital...........................   63,730

(4) Cash.. 950
        Common Stock   73
        Additional Paid-in Capital...........................   877

(5) Retained Earnings..................................... 62,810
        Common Stock   5,604
        Additional Paid-in Capital...........................   57,206

(6) Treasury Stock..................................... 48,600
        Cash   48,600

(7) Cash.. 40,530
        Additional Paid-in Capital 2,170
        Treasury Stock   42,700

12.40 (Baiman Corporation; preparing a statement of cash flows.)

a.

		Cash		
√	45,000			

Operations

(1)	48,000	15,000	(9)	
(4)	28,000	20,000	(10)	
(5)	4,000			
(6)	3,000			
(12)	1,000			
(14)	7,000			

Investing

(5)	8,000	45,000	(11)	

Financing

(8)	12,000	39,000	(2)	
(13)	4,000	25,000	(16)	
(15)	38,000			
√	54,000			

Accounts Receivable—Net			Inventory	
√	160,000	√	115,000	
(9)	15,000	(10)	20,000	
√	175,000	√	135,000	

Property, Plant and Equipment			Accumulated Depreciation	
√	265,000		120,000	√
(3)	20,000	30,000 (5)	(5) 18,000	28,000 (4)
(11)	45,000			
√	300,000		130,000	√

Accounts Payable			Dividends Payable	
	105,000	√	10,000	√
	1,000	(12)	4,000	(13)
	106,000	√	14,000	√

 Solutions

12.40 a. continued.

Bonds Payable				Convertible Bonds Payable			
	90,000	√				50,000	√
	3,000	(6)	(7)	50,000			
	93,000	√				--	√

Deferred Income Taxes				Preferred Stock			
	20,000	√				60,000	√
	7,000	(12)					
	27,000	√				60,000	√

Common Stock (Par)				Additional Paid-in Capital			
	25,000	√				65,000	√
	4,000	(3)				16,000	(3)
	10,000	(7)				40,000	(7)
	8,000	(15)				2,000	(8)
						30,000	(15)
	47,000	√				153,000	√

Retained Earnings				Treasury Stock			
		55,000	√	√	15,000		
(2)	39,000	48,000	(1)	(16)	25,000	10,000	(8)
		64,000	√	√	30,000		

12.40 continued.

b.

BAIMAN CORPORATION
Statement of Cash Flows
For Year 2

Operations:		
Net Income	$ 48,000	
Addbacks and Additions:		
Depreciation Expense......................	28,000	
Loss on Sale of Equipment................	4,000	
Amortization of Bond Discount..........	3,000	
Increase in Accounts Payable...........	1,000	
Increase in Deferred Income Tax		
Liability......................................	7,000	
Subtractions:		
Increase in Accounts Receivable.......	(15,000)	
Increase in Inventories....................	(20,000)	
Cash Flow from Operations.....................		$ 56,000
Investing:		
Sale of Investment in Roy Company	$ 8,000	
Acquisition of Property, Plant and		
Equipment......................................	(45,000)	
Cash Flow from Investing......................		(37,000)
Financing:		
Issue of Common Stock........................	$ 38,000	
Reissue of Treasury Stock	12,000	
Reacquisition of Common Stock............	(25,000)	
Dividends Paid ($39,000 – $4,000)...........	(35,000)	
Cash Flow from Financing.....................		(10,000)
Net Change in Cash		$ 9,000
Cash, January 1, Year 2		45,000
Cash, December 31, Year 2.....................		$ 54,000

Supplementary Information

1. Holders of convertible bonds with a book value of $50,000 exercised their option to convert their bonds into shares of common stock.

2. The firm issued common shares with a market value of $20,000 in the acquisition of a machine.

12.41   (Case for discussion: value of stock options.)

The correct answer is *b.* $10 – $100. An option to buy a share for price $X cannot ever be worth more than $X per share, so options to purchase 10,000 for $.01 each cannot ever be worth more than $.01 × 10,000 = $100. We use this question in Silicone Valley to introduce the topic (it hardly needs introduction there) to executives skeptical of measuring option values. They invariably overestimate the cost to the company of granting options and this overestimate makes them not like counting the cost of their issue as compensation expense.

CHAPTER 13

LONG-TERM INVESTMENTS IN CORPORATE SECURITIES

Questions, Exercises, Problems, and Cases: Answers and Solutions

13.1   See the text or the glossary at the end of the book.

13.2   Firms acquire marketable equity securities classified as *Investments* for their long-term return. Although unrealized capital gains and losses are an element of this return, the firm will not recognize them for perhaps many years in the future. Unrealized losses (gains) in the short run may end up as realized gains (losses) in the long run.

We find fault with this reasoning. In an efficient capital market, current market prices reflect the present value of expected future cash flows from owning the security *given currently available information*. A decrease in market price below acquisition cost suggests that the market expects the cash flows to be either smaller or more spread out in the future or else the market requires a higher rate of return. Until the information available to the market changes, economists view this decrease in value as permanent (that is, the market price is an equilibrium price). Thus, the notion that market price may increase in the long run is irrelevant. It may just as well decrease when new information becomes available.

13.3   a.   These accounts are both shareholders' equity accounts and reflect the change in the market value of securities since acquisition.

b.   Dividend Revenue is an income statement account. It reflects the revenue recognized when a firm uses the market-value method. Equity in Earnings of Unconsolidated Affiliates is also an income statement account. It reflects the revenue recognized when a firm uses the equity method.

c.   Equity in Earnings of Unconsolidated Affiliate is an income statement account. It reflects the revenue earned by a minority, active investor in an investee accounted for using the equity method. Minority Interest in Earnings of Consolidated Subsidiary is an account appearing on the consolidated income statement of a parent and its majority-owned, active investee. It represents the external, minority interest in the earnings of the investee.

13-1

13.3 continued.

    d. Minority Interest in Earnings of Consolidated Subsidiary is an income statement account. It reflects the external, minority interest in the earnings of a majority-owned consolidated subsidiary. Minority Interest in Net Assets of Consolidated Subsidiary is a balance sheet account. It reflects the external, minority interest in the net assets of a consolidated subsidiary.

13.4 Dividends represent revenues under the market-value method and a return of capital under the equity method.

13.5 Under the equity method, the change each period in the net assets, or shareholders' equity, of the subsidiary appears on the one line, Investment in Subsidiary, on the balance sheet. When the parent consolidates the subsidiary, changes in the individual assets and liabilities that comprise the net asset change appear in the individual consolidated assets and liabilities. Likewise, under the equity method, the investor's interest in the investee's earnings appears in one line on the income statement, Equity in Earnings of Unconsolidated Subsidiary. When the parent consolidates the subsidiary, the individual revenues and expenses of the subsidiary appear in consolidated revenues and expenses.

13.6 If Company A owns less than, or equal to, 50 percent of Company B's voting stock, it is a minority investor in Company B. If Company A owns more than 50 percent of Company C, it is a majority investor in Company C. The entities holding the remainder of the voting stock of Company C are minority investors. Their minority interest appears on the consolidated balance sheet of Company A and Company C.

13.7 When the investor uses the equity method, total assets include the Investment in Subsidiary account. The investment account reflects the parent's interest in the *net* assets (assets minus liabilities) of the subsidiary. When the investor consolidates the subsidiary, total consolidated assets include all of the subsidiary's assets. Consolidated liabilities include the liabilities of the subsidiary. Thus, total assets on a consolidated basis exceed total assets when the investor uses the equity method.

13.8 (Apollo Corporation; amount of income recognized under various methods of accounting for investments.)

a. and b.
    $3.0 million = .15($20 million).

    c. $24 million = .30($80 million).

    d. $22 million = .30($80 million) − ($80 million/40).*

    *The equity method recognizes amortization of goodwill.

13.9   (Trusco; balance sheet and income effects of alternative methods of accounting for investments.)

Part	Investment	Net Income
a.	$40 million	$2 million
b.	$39 million	$2 million
c.	$45 million	$2 million
d.	$129 million[a]	$15 million[b]
e.	$168 million[c]	$14 million[d]

[a]$120 million + .30($50 million – $20 million) = $129 million.

[b].30 × $50 million = $15 million.

[c]$160 million + .30($50 million – $20 million) – ($40 million/40) = $168 million.

[d](.30 × $50 million) – ($40 million/40) = $14 million.

13.10   (Randle Corporation; journal entries to apply the market value method for long-term investments in securities.)

April 10, Year 1

Investment in Securities (M)	37,000	
Cash...		37,000

July 11, Year 1

Investment in Securities (N)	31,000	
Cash...		31,000

September 29, Year 1

Investment in Securities (O)	94,000	
Cash...		94,000

December 31, Year 1

Cash	7,900	
Dividend Revenue...		7,900

December 31, Year 1

Unrealized Holding Loss on Investments in Securities (SE)...	9,000	
Investment in Securities (M).........................		2,000
Investment in Securities (O).........................		7,000

December 31, Year 1

Investment in Securities (N)	7,000	
Unrealized Holding Gain on Investment in Securities (SE)...		7,000

                                  Solutions

13.10 continued.

October 15, Year 2

Cash	43,000	
Investment in Securities (M)		37,000
Realized Gain on Sale of Investment in Securities (IncSt)		6,000

October 31, Year 2 or December 31, Year 2

Investment in Securities (M)	2,000	
Unrealized Holding Loss on Investment in Securities (SE)		2,000

December 31, Year 2

Cash	5,600	
Dividend Revenue		5,600

December 31, Year 2

Investment in Securities (N)	7,000	
Unrealized Holding Gain on Investment in Securities (SE)		7,000

December 31, Year 2

Investment in Securities (O)	2,000	
Unrealized Holding Loss on Investment in Securities (SE)		2,000

13.11 (Blake Company; journal entries to apply the market value method to long-term investments in securities.)

July 2, Year 4

Investment in Securities (G)	42,800	
Cash		42,800

October 19, Year 4

Investment in Securities (H)	29,600	
Cash		29,600

October 29, Year 4

Cash	89,700	
Realized Loss on Sale of Investments in Securities (IncSt)	4,000	
Investment in Securities (F)		93,700

October 29, Year 4 or December 31, Year 4

Investment in Securities (F)	2,500	
Unrealized Holding Loss on Investment in Securities (SE)		2,500

13-4

13.11 continued.

December 31, Year 4

Unrealized Holding Loss on Investment in Securities (SE)......	4,500	
Investment in Securities (G)		4,500

December 31, Year 4

Investment in Securities (H)	2,000	
Unrealized Holding Gain on Investment in Securities (SE)		2,000

February 9, Year 5

Investment in Securities (I)	18,100	
Cash......		18,100

September 17, Year 5

Cash	32,300	
Investment in Securities (H)		29,600
Realized Gain on Sale of Investment in Securities (IncSt)		2,700

September 17, Year 5 or December 31, Year 5

Unrealized Holding Gain on Investment in Securities (SE)......	2,000	
Investment in Securities (H)		2,000

December 31, Year 5

Unrealized Holding Loss on Investment in Securities (SE)......	1,400	
Investment in Securities (G)		1,400

December 31, Year 5

Investment in Securities (I)	2,600	
Unrealized Holding Gain on Investment in Securities (SE)		2,600

13.12   (Wood Corporation; journal entries to apply the equity method of accounting for investments in securities.)

January 2

Investment in Securities (Knox)	350,000	
Investment in Securities (Vachi)	196,000	
Investment in Securities (Snow)	100,000	
Cash......		646,000

13.12 continued.

December 31

Investment in Securities (Knox)	35,000	
Investment in Securities (Vachi)	12,000	
Investment in Securities (Snow)		4,800
Equity in Earnings of Affiliates		42,200

$(.50 \times \$70,000) + (.30 \times \$40,000) - (.20 \times \$24,000) = \$42,200$.

December 31

Cash	19,800	
Investment in Securities (Knox)		15,000
Investment in Securities (Vachi)		4,800

$(.50 \times \$30,000) + (.30 \times \$16,000) = \$19,800$.

December 31

Amortization Expense	3,000	
Investment in Securities (Vachi)		2,000
Investment in Securities (Snow)		1,000

$\$196,000 - (.30 \times \$520,000) = \$40,000$; $\$40,000/20 = \$2,000$. $\$100,000 - (.20 \times \$400,000) = \$20,000$; $\$20,000/20 = \$1,000$.

13.13 (Stebbins Corporation; journal entries to apply the equity method of accounting for investments in securities.)

a. **January 1, Year 1**

Investment in Securities (R)	250,000	
Investment in Securities (S)	325,000	
Investment in Securities (T)	475,000	
Cash		1,050,000

December 31, Year 1

Investment in Securities (R)	50,000	
Investment in Securities (S)	48,000	
Investment in Securities (T)		75,000
Equity in Earnings of Affiliates		23,000

$(.25 \times \$200,000) + (.40 \times \$120,000) - (.50 \times \$150,000) = \$23,000$.

December 31, Year 1

Cash	63,250	
Investment in Securities (R)		31,250
Investment in Securities (S)		32,000

$(.25 \times \$125,000) + (.40 \times \$80,000) = \$63,250$.

13.13 a. continued.

December 31, Year 1

Amortization Expense	3,750	
Investment in Securities (R)		2,500
Investment in Securities (S)		1,250

$250,000 − (.25 × $800,000) = $50,000; $50,000/20 = $2,500. $325,000 − (.40 × $750,000) = $25,000; $25,000/20 = $1,250. $475,000 − (.50 × $950,000) = 0.

December 31, Year 2

Investment in Securities (R)	56,250	
Investment in Securities (S)	30,000	
Investment in Securities (T)	25,000	
Equity in Earnings of Affiliates		111,250

(.25 × $225,000) + (.40 × $75,000) − (.50 × $50,000) = $111,250.

December 31, Year 2

Cash	64,500	
Investment in Securities (R)		32,500
Investment in Securities (S)		32,000

(.25 × $130,000) + (.40 × $80,000).

December 31, Year 2

Amortization Expense	3,750	
Investment in Securities (R)		2,500
Investment in Securities (S)		1,250

b.

Cash	330,000	
Loss on Sale of Investments	6,500	
Investment in Securities (S)		336,500

$325,000 + $48,000 − $32,000 − $1,250 + $30,000 − $32,000 − $1,250 = $336,500.

 13.14 (Mulherin Corporation; journal entries under various methods of accounting for investments.)

a. **January 2**

Investment in Hanson	320,000	
Investment in Maloney	680,000	
Investment in Quinn	2,800,000	
Cash		3,800,000

To record acquisition of investments.

a. continued.

December 31

Cash..	6,000	
Dividend Revenue.................................		6,000

To record dividend from Hanson: .15 × $40,000 = $6,000.

December 31

Unrealized Holding Loss on Investment in Securities (SE)	15,000	
Investment in Hanson.........................		15,000

To apply the market value method to the investment in Hanson.

December 31

Investment in Maloney...........................	150,000	
Equity in Earnings of Maloney		150,000

To recognize share of Maloney's earnings; .30 × $500,000 = $150,000.

December 31

Cash..	54,000	
Investment in Maloney........................		54,000

To recognize share of Maloney's dividends; .30 × $180,000 = $54,000.

December 31

Amortization Expense............................	2,000	
Investment in Maloney........................		2,000

To amortize excess acquisition cost for Maloney; $680,000 − (.30 × $2,000,000) = $80,000; $80,000/40 = $2,000.

December 31

Investment in Quinn..............................	600,000	
Equity in Earnings of Quinn..................		600,000

To recognize share of Quinn's earnings.

December 31

Cash..	310,000	
Investment in Quinn..........................		310,000

To recognize share of Quinn's dividends.

December 31

Amortization Expense............................	20,000	
Investment in Quinn..........................		20,000

$2,800,000 − $2,000,000 = $800,000; $800,000/40 = $20,000.

b.
Common Stock (Quinn).............................	200,000	
Additional Paid-in Capital (Quinn)	800,000	
Retained Earnings (Quinn)...........................	690,000	
Equity in Earnings of Quinn (Mulherin)...........	600,000	
Goodwill	780,000	
Investment in Quinn (Mulherin).................		3,070,000

$2,800,000 + $600,000 − $310,000 − $20,000 =
$3,070,000.

13.15   (Packard Corporation; consolidation policy and principal consolidation concepts.)

a.   Packard Corporation should consolidate French Software Systems and Credit Corporation or, under exceptional circumstances, use the market value method.

b.
Canadian Electronics ....(.75 × $120,000) =	$ 90,000	
French Software Systems........................(.80 × 60,000) =	48,000	
Credit Corporation ....(.90 × 144,000) =	129,600	
Total Income from Subsidiaries................................	$ 267,600	

c.   Minority Interest shown under accounting assumed in problem:

Canadian Electronics..............................(.25 × $120,000) =	$ 30,000	
French Software Systems....................................(None) =	--	
Credit Corporation...(None) =	--	
	$ 30,000	

Packard Corporation subtracts the minority interest in computing net income.

d.   Canadian Electronics, no increase because already consolidated.

French Software Systems increase by 80 percent of net income less dividends:
.80 × ($96,000 − $60,000) = $28,800.

Credit Corporation, no increase because equity method results in the same income statement effects as do consolidated statements. Net income of Packard Corporation would be:

$1,228,800 = $1,200,000 (as reported) + $28,800 (increase).

         Solutions

13.15 continued.

    e. Minority Interest shown if Packard Corporation consolidated all companies:

Canadian Electronics............................(.25 × $120,000) =	$ 30,000
French Software Systems ....(.20 × 96,000) =	19,200
Credit Corporation ....(.10 × 144,000) =	14,400
	$ 63,600

13.16 (Clinton Corporation; equity method and consolidation elimination entries.) (Amounts in Millions.)

    a. Investment in Stock of Dole Computer.............. 500

        Cash 500

To record acquisition of shares of common stock.

Investment in Stock of Dole Computer.............. 100

    Equity in Earnings of Dole Computer 100

To accrue Dole Computer's earnings for the year.

Cash or Dividends Receivable......................... 30

    Investment in Stock of Dole Computer........... 30

To recognize dividends received or receivable.

Amortization Expense.................................... 2

    Investment in Stock of Dole Computer........... 2

To amortize goodwill; $2 = ($500 − $420)/40.

    b. Common Stock.. 300

Retained Earnings ($120 − $30) 90

Equity in Earnings of Dole Computer................ 100

Goodwill 78

    Investment in Stock of Dole Computer........... 568

To eliminate investment account.

Accounts Payable.. 3

    Accounts Receivable.................................... 3

To eliminate intercompany receivable and liability.

13.17   (Low Company; equity method and consolidation elimination entries.)

a. Investment in Stock of Denver Company........... 550,000
        Cash   550,000
    To record acquisition of common stock.

    Investment in Stock of Denver Company........... 120,000
        Equity in Earnings of Denver Company.........   120,000
    To accrue 100 percent share of Denver Company's earnings.

    Cash or Dividends Receivable........................ 40,000
        Investment in Stock of Denver Company   40,000
    To accrue dividends received or receivable.

b. Common Stock... 200,000
    Retained Earnings ($350 – $40) 310,000
    Equity in Earnings of Denver Company 120,000
        Investment in Stock of Denver Company   630,000
    To eliminate investment account; $630,000 =
    $550,000 + $120,000 – $40,000.

13.18   (Joyce Company and Vogel Company; equity method and consolidation work sheet entries.)

a. **Joyce Company's Books**

    (1) Investment in Stock of Vogel Company...... 420,000
             Cash..   420,000
         To record acquisition of common stock.

    (2) Accounts Receivable.............................. 29,000
             Sales Revenue.....................................   29,000
         To record intercompany sales on account.

    (2) Cost of Goods Sold................................. 29,000
             Inventories...   29,000
         To record cost of intercompany sales.

    (3) Advance to Vogel Company...................... 6,000
             Cash..   6,000
         To record advance to Vogel Company.

    (4) Cash... 16,000
             Accounts Receivable............................   16,000
         To record collections on account from
         Vogel Company.

         Solutions

13.18 a. continued.

(5)	Cash...	4,000	
	Advance to Vogel Company..................		4,000
	To record collection of advance from Vogel Company.		

(6)	Cash...	20,000	
	Investment in Stock of Vogel Company...		20,000
	To record dividend from Vogel Company.		

(7)	Investment in Stock of Vogel Company......	30,000	
	Equity in Earnings of Vogel Company....		30,000
	To accrue 100 percent share of Vogel Company's net income.		

(8)	Amortization Expense	1,000	
	Investment in Stock of Vogel Company...		1,000
	To record amortization of goodwill; $1,000 = ($420,000 − $380,000)/40.		

Vogel Company's Books

(1)   No entry.

(2)	Inventories...	29,000	
	Accounts Payable...............................		29,000
	To record intercompany purchase of materials on account.		

(3)	Cash...	6,000	
	Advance from Joyce Company..............		6,000
	To record advance from Joyce Company.		

(4)	Accounts Payable..................................	16,000	
	Cash...		16,000
	To record payment for purchases on account.		

(5)	Advance from Joyce Company..................	4,000	
	Cash...		4,000
	To record repayment of advance.		

(6)	Retained Earnings	20,000	
	Cash...		20,000
	To record declaration and payment of dividend.		

(7)   No entry.

13.18 continued.

    b.

Common Stock..	300,000	
Retained Earnings ($80,000 – $20,000)...............	60,000	
Equity in Earnings of Vogel Company	30,000	
Goodwill	39,000	
Investment in Stock of Little Company		429,000

To eliminate investment account; $429,000 = $420,000 + $30,000 – $20,000 – $1,000.

Accounts Payable..	13,000	
Accounts Receivable..................................		13,000

To eliminate intercompany receivable and payable.

Advance from Joyce Company.........................	2,000	
Advance to Little Company		2,000

To eliminate intercompany advance.

13.19   (Working backwards to consolidation relations.)

    a. $80,000 = ($156,000 – $100,000)/.70.

    b.   73 percent = ($156,000 – $100,000)/$77,000.

    c. $56,000 = ($156,000 – $100,000).

13.20   (Dealco Corporation; working backwards from consolidated income statements.) (Amounts in Millions.)

    a. $56/$140 = 40 percent.

    b.   [.40 × (1 – .20) × $140] = $44.80.

    c.   [1 – ($42/$280)] = 1 – .15 = 85 percent.

        Solutions

13.21 (Water Company and Soluble Company; financial statement effects of purchase and pooling-of-interests methods.)

a. (Amounts in Millions)

	(1) Purchase Method	(2) Pooling-of-Interests Method
Assets:		
Current Assets	$ 350	$ 350
Property, Plant and Equipment (Net).	650	600
Goodwill	100	--
Total Assets	$1,100	$ 950
Equities:		
Liabilities	$ 570	$ 570
Common Stock	380[a]	150[b]
Retained Earnings	150	230[c]
Total Equities	$1,100	$ 950

[a]$100 + $280 = $380.
[b]$100 + $50 = $150.
[c]$150 + $80 = $230.

b. (Amounts in Millions)

	(1) Purchase Method	(2) Pooling-of-Interests Method
Precombination Net Income	$80	$80
Additional Depreciation Expense:		
$50/5	(10)	--
Goodwill Amortization:		
$100/25	(4)	--
Revised Projected Net Income	$66	$80

13.22 (Bristol-Myers and Squibb; financial statement effects of purchase and pooling-of-interests method.)

a. (Amounts in Millions)

	(1) Purchase Method	(2) Pooling-of-Interests Method
Assets, Except Goodwill	$ 8,273	$8,273
Goodwill	11,469[a]	--
Total Assets	$19,742	$8,273
Liabilities	$ 3,325	$3,325
Shareholders' Equity	16,417[b]	4,948[c]
Total Equities	$19,742	$8,273

[a]$12,870 – $1,401 = $11,469.
[b]$3,547 + $12,870 = $16,417.
[c]$3,547 + $1,401 = $4,948.

13.22 continued.

b. (Amounts in Millions)

	(1) Purchase Method	(2) Pooling-of-Interests Method
Precombination Projected Consolidated Net Income	$1,748	$1,748
Goodwill Amortization:		
$11,469/40	(287)	--
Revised Projected Net Income	$1,461	$1,748

c. These firms will prefer the pooling-of-interests method because it results in higher future earnings and rates of return on assets and on shareholders' equity.

 (Effect of transactions on the statement of cash flows.)

a. The journal entry to record this transaction is:

Cash.. 7,000
   Dividend Revenue.. 7,000

The Cash account increases, so Line (9) increases by $7,000. Net income increases, so Line (1) increases by $7,000.

b. The journal entry to record this event is:

Unrealized Holding Loss on Investment in
   Securities (SE)... 2,000
     Investments in Securities......................... 2,000

The Cash account does not change so there is no effect on Line (9). Net income does not change so there is no effect on Line (1). The firm would disclose this event in a supplementary schedule or note if the amount was material.

c. The journal entry to record this transaction is:

Cash (.40 X $10,000)...................................... 4,000
Investment in Affiliate [.40($25,000 − $10,000)]... 6,000
   Equity in Earnings of Affiliate (.40 X $25,000).. 10,000

The Cash account increases in the amount of the dividend, so Line (9) increases $4,000. Net income on Line (1) increases by $10,000 for the equity in earnings. Because the firm recognizes more revenue ($10,000) than the cash received ($4,000), it must increase Line (3) by $6,000 to convert net income to cash flow from operations.

   13-15

continued.

d. The journal entry to record this event is:

Equity in Loss of Affiliate (.40 X $12,500)   5,000
    Investment in Affiliate   5,000

There is no effect on the Cash account so Line (9) does not change. Net income decreases for the share of the loss so Line (1) decreases by $5,000. Because the loss does not use cash, Line (2) increases by $5,000 when converting net income to cash flow from operations.

e. The journal entry to record this event is:

Amortization Expense   2,000
    Investment in Affiliate   2,000

There is no effect on the Cash account so Line (9) does not change. Net income on Line (1) decreases for amortization expense. Because the amortization expense does not reduce cash, Line (2) increases by $2,000 when converting net income to cash flow from operations.

 13.24   (Effect of errors on financial statements.)

	Assets	Liabilities	Shareholders' Equity	Net Income
a.	U/S	No	U/S	U/S
b.	O/S	No	O/S	No
c.	O/S	No	O/S	O/S
d.	O/S	No	O/S	O/S
e.	No	No	No	No
f.	O/S	O/S	No	No
g.	No	No	O/S	O/S ?

 13.25   (Rockwell Corporation; journal entries and consolidation work sheet entries for various methods of accounting for intercorporate investments.)

a. Investment in Stock of Company R   648,000
    Cash   648,000
To record acquisitions of shares of Company R.

Cash and Dividends Receivable   48,000
    Dividend Revenue   48,000
To record dividends received or receivable.

13.25 a. continued.

Unrealized Holding Loss on Investment in Securities (SE)	24,000	
Investment in Stock of Company R		24,000

To write down investment in stock of Company R account to market value; $24,000 = $648,000 − $624,000.

b.
Investment in Stock of Company S	2,040,000	
Cash		2,040,000

To record acquisitions of shares of Company S.

Investment in Stock of Company S	360,000	
Equity in Earnings of Company S..................		360,000

To accrue share of Company S's earnings; $360,000 = .30 × $1,200,000.

Cash and Dividends Receivable........................	144,000	
Investment in Stock of Company S		144,000

To record dividends received or receivable.

Amortization Expense.....................................	24,000	
Investment in Stock of Company S		24,000

To record amortization of goodwill implicit in purchase price; $24,000 = ($2,040,000 − $1,800,000)/10.

c.
Investment in Stock of Company T...................	6,000,000	
Cash		6,000,000

To record acquisitions of shares of Company T.

Investment in Stock of Company T...................	1,200,000	
Equity in Earnings of Company T		1,200,000

To accrue earnings of Company T; $1,200,000 = 100% × $1,200,000.

Cash and Dividends Receivable........................	480,000	
Investment in Stock of Company T		480,000

To record dividends received or receivable.

d.
Common Stock..	2,400,000	
Retained Earnings ($3,600,000 − $480,000)	3,120,000	
Equity in Earnings of Company T.....................	1,200,000	
Investment in Stock of Company T................		6,720,000

To eliminate investment account on consolidation work sheet.

13.25 continued.

   e. Common Stock... 2,400,000
       Retained Earnings 4,320,000
          Investment in Stock of Company T................   6,720,000
       To eliminate investment account on consolida-
       tion work sheet.

   f. Investment in Stock of Company T................... 6,600,000
          Cash   6,600,000
       To record acquisitions of shares of Company T.

       Investment in Stock of Company T................... 1,200,000
          Equity in Earnings of Company T   1,200,000
       To accrue earnings of Company T.

       Cash and Dividends Receivable........................   480,000
          Investment in Stock of Company T   480,000
       To record dividends received or receivable.

       Amortization Expense.....................................   60,000
          Investment in Stock of Company T   60,000
       To record amortization of goodwill implicit in
       purchase price; $60,000 = (\$6,600,000 −
       \$6,000,000)/10.

   g. Common Stock... 2,400,000
       Retained Earnings ($3,600,000 − $480,000) 3,120,000
       Equity in Earnings of Company T..................... 1,200,000
       Goodwill   540,000
          Investment in Stock of Company T................   7,260,000
       To eliminate investment account on consolida-
       tion work sheet; $7,260,000 = $6,600,000 +
       $1,200,000 − $480,000 − $60,000.

13.26   (Peak Company and Valley Company; preparing a consolidation work sheet.)

   a. See next page.

   b. Common Stock (Valley)...................................   5
       Retained Earnings (Valley).............................   41
       Equity in Earnings of Valley Company (Peak)....   10
       Goodwill   18
          Investment in Stock of Valley Company
             (Peak)   74

13.26 continued.

a.

PEAK COMPANY AND VALLEY COMPANY
Consolidation Work Sheet
(Amounts in Thousands)

	Peak Company Debit	Peak Company Credit	Valley Company Debit	Valley Company Credit	Adjustments and Eliminations Debit	Adjustments and Eliminations Credit	Consolidated Debit	Consolidated Credit
Cash	$ 13		$ 6				$ 19	
Accounts Receivable	42		20			$10 (2)	52	
Investment in Stock of Valley Company	56		--			56 (1)	--	
Other Assets	143		85				228	
Cost of Goods Sold	320		90				410	
Selling and Administrative Expenses	44		20				64	
Income Tax Expense	12		5				17	
Accounts Payable		$ 80		$ 25	(2) $10			$ 95
Bonds Payable		50		30				80
Common Stock		10		5	(1) 5			10
Retained Earnings		80		41	(1) 41			80
Sales Revenue		400		125				525
Equity in Earnings		10		--	(1) 10			--
Totals	$ 630	$ 630	$ 226	$ 226	$66	$66	$ 790	$ 790

(1) To eliminate the investment account.
(2) To eliminate intercompany receivables and payables.

13-19

13-27 (Company P and Company S; preparing a consolidation work sheet.)

a.

COMPANY P AND COMPANY S
Consolidation Work Sheet
(Amounts in Thousands)

	Company A Debit	Company A Credit	Company B Debit	Company B Credit	Adjustments and Eliminations Debit	Adjustments and Eliminations Credit	Consolidated Debit	Consolidated Credit
Receivables...............	$ 60		$ 40			$ 12 (3)	$ 88	
Investment in Stock of Company S..................	272		--			272 (1)	--	
Other Assets...............	496		352				848	
Cost of Goods Sold........	1,160		496			40 (2)	1,616	
Other Expenses...........	280		112				392	
Accounts Payable.........		$ 72		$ 48	(3) $ 12			$ 108
Other Liabilities..........		88		72				160
Common Stock............		160		80	(1) 80			160
Retained Earnings........		316		160	(1) 160			316
Sales Revenue............		1,600		640	(2) 40			2,200
Equity in Earnings of Company S................		32			(1) 32			--
Totals..................	$2,268	$2,268	$1,000	$1,000	$ 324	$ 324	$2,944	$2,944

(1) Eliminate investment account.
(2) Eliminate intercompany sales.
(3) Eliminate intercompany receivables and payables.

13.27 continued.

b.

COMPANY P AND COMPANY S
Consolidated Statement of Income
and Retained Earnings
For Year 2

Sales Revenue	$2,200,000
Expenses:	
Cost of Goods Sold	$1,616,000
Other Expenses	392,000
Total	$2,008,000
Net Income	$ 192,000
Less Dividends Declared	(40,000)
Increase in Retained Earnings for Year 2	$ 152,000
Retained Earnings, December 31, Year 1	356,000[a]
Retained Earnings, December 31, Year 2	$ 508,000

[a]$316,000 retained earnings on December 31, Year 2 + $40,000 dividend declared during year 2.

COMPANY P AND COMPANY S
Consolidated Balance Sheet
December 31, Year 2

Assets

Receivables	$ 88,000
Other Assets	848,000
Total	$ 936,000

Equities

Accounts Payable	$ 108,000
Other Liabilities	160,000
Common Stock	160,000
Retained Earnings	508,000
Total	$ 936,000

 Solutions

13.28   (Sly Company and Sims Company; preparing a consolidation work sheet.)

SLY COMPANY AND SIMS COMPANY
Consolidation Work Sheet
(Amounts in Thousands)

	Sly Company Debit	Sly Company Credit	Sims Company Debit	Sims Company Credit	Adjustments and Eliminations Debit	Adjustments and Eliminations Credit	Consolidated Debit	Consolidated Credit
Cash.............................	$ 12,000		$ 5,000				$ 17,000	
Accounts Receivable.......	25,000		15,000			$ 7,500 (2)	32,500	
Investment in Sims Company Stock................	78,000		--			78,000 (1)	--	
Other Assets..................	85,000		80,000				165,000	
Goodwill.......................	--		--		(1) $18,000		18,000	
Current Liabilities..........		$ 45,000		$ 40,000	(2) 7,500			$ 77,500
Common Stock................		50,000		10,000	(1) 10,000			50,000
Retained Earnings...........		105,000		50,000	(1) 50,000			105,000
Totals....................	$ 200,000	$ 200,000	$ 100,000	$ 100,000	$85,500	$85,500	$ 232,500	$ 232,500

(1) Eliminate investment account.
(2) Eliminate intercompany obligations.

13.29 (Company S and Company J; preparing a consolidation work sheet subsequent to year of acquisition.)

COMPANY S AND COMPANY J
Consolidation Work Sheet
December 31, Year 2
(Amounts in Thousands)

	Company S Debit	Company S Credit	Company J Debit	Company J Credit	Adjustments and Eliminations Debit	Adjustments and Eliminations Credit	Consolidated Debit	Consolidated Credit
Cash..............................	$ 36.00		$ 26.00				$ 62.00	
Accounts and Notes Receivable	180.00		50.00			$ 16.40 (2)	213.60	
Inventories	440.00		250.00				690.00	
Investment in Stock of Company J	726.00		--			726.00 (1)	--	
Plant Assets....................	600.00		424.00				1,024.00	
Accounts and Notes Payable..........................		$ 110.00		$ 59.00	(2) $ 16.40			$ 152.60
Other Liabilities		286.00		22.00				308.00
Common Stock.................		1,200.00		500.00	(1) 500.00			1,200.00
Capital Contributed in Excess of Stated Value		--		100.00	(1) 100.00			--
Retained Earnings............		386.00		69.00	(1) 69.00			386.00
Goodwill.........................					(1) 57.00		57.00	
Totals...................	$1,982.00	$1,982.00	$ 750.00	$ 750.00	$ 724.40	$ 724.40	$2,046.60	$2,046.60

(1) Eliminate investment account.
(2) Eliminate intercompany obligations.

13-23 Solutions

13.30 (Hatfield Corporation and McCoy Corporation; effect of purchase and pooling-of-interests methods on financial statements.)

a. HATFIELD CORPORATION AND McCOY CORPORATION
Consolidated Balance Sheet
January 1, Year 8

	(1) Purchase Method	(2) Pooling-of-Interests Method
Assets at Historical Cost	$ 3,500	$3,500
Asset Revaluation	400	--
Goodwill	200	--
Total Assets	$ 4,100	$3,500
Liabilities	$ 1,500	$1,500
Common Stock ($1 Par)	150[a]	150[a]
Additional Paid-in Capital	1,750[b]	750[c]
Retained Earnings	700	1,100[d]
Total Equities	$ 4,100	$3,500

[a]$100,000 + (50,000 × $1) = $150,000.
[b]$400,000 + (50,000 × $27) = $1,750,000.
[c]$400,000 + ($100,000 + $300,000 − $50,000) = $750,000.
[d]$700,000 + $400,000 = $1,100,000.

b. HATFIELD CORPORATION AND McCOY CORPORATION
Consolidated Income Statement
First Year After Merger

	(1) Purchase Method	(2) Pooling-of-Interests Method
Sales	$14,000	$14,000
Other Revenues	125	125
Total Revenues	$14,125	$14,125
Expenses Except Income Taxes	(11,125)	(11,125)
Taxable Income	$ 3,000	$ 3,000
Tax Expense at 40%	(1,200)	(1,200)
Amortization of Increased Asset Costs	(80)[a]	--
Amortization of Goodwill	(10)[b]	--
Net Income	$ 1,710	$ 1,800
Earnings per Share	$11.40[c]	$12.00[c]

[a]$400,000/5 = $80,000.
[b]$200,000/20 = $10,000.
[c]Based on 150,000 shares.

13.31-33 (General Electric Company; effects of consolidating companies with different asset and equity structures.)

a. [Dollars in Millions]

	Parent's Books	Subsidiary's Books	Adjustments and Eliminations		Consolidated
			Debit	Credit	
Year 1 (31)					
Assets Except Investments................	$6,008.5	$2,157.0			$8,165.5
Investment in G.E.C.S.	190.0	—		$190.0 (1)	—
Total................	$6,198.5	$2,157.0			$8,165.5
Liabilities...............	$3,644.9	$1,967.0			$5,611.9
Shareholders' Equity	2,553.6	190.0	(1) $190.0		2,553.6
Total................	$6,198.5	$2,157.0			$8,165.5
Year 2 (32)					
Assets Except Investments................	$6,655.9	$2,358.7			$9,014.6
Investment in G.E.C.S................	231.9	—		$231.9 (1)	—
Total...............	$6,887.8	$2,358.7			$9,014.6
Liabilities...............	$4,086.0	$2,126.8			$6,212.8
Shareholders' Equity	2,801.8	231.9	(1) $231.9		2,801.8
Total...............	$6,887.8	$2,358.7			$9,014.6
Year 3 (33)					
Assets Except Investments................	$7,141.8	$2,789.5			$9,931.3
Investment in G.E.C.S................	260.0	—		$260.0 (1)	—
Total...............	$7,401.8	$2,789.5			$9,931.3
Liabilities...............	$4,317.2	$2,529.5			$6,846.7
Shareholders' Equity	3,084.6	260.0	(1) $260.0		3,084.6
Total...............	$7,401.8	$2,789.5			$9,931.3

(1) To eliminate investment account.

13.31-33 continued.

b. and c.

Single-Company Books
(Dollar Amounts in Millions)

	Part b. Equity Method			**Part c. Consolidated Statements**		
	Year 1 (31)	Year 2 (32)	Year 3 (33)	Year 1 (31)	Year 2 (32)	Year 3 (33)
(1) Rate of Return on Total Assets:						
Numerator (Net Income)	$ 328.5	$ 471.8	$ 530.0	$ 328.5	$ 471.8	$ 530.0
Denominator (12/31 Assets)	$6,198.5	$6,887.8	$7,401.8	$8,165.5	$9,014.6	$9,931.3
Rate of Return	5.30%	6.85%	7.16%	4.02%	5.23%	5.34%
(2) Debt Equity Ratio:						
Numerator (Liabilities)	$3,644.9	$4,086.0	$4,317.2	$5,611.9	$6,212.8	$6,846.7
Denominator (12/31 Assets)	$6,198.5	$6,887.8	$7,401.8	$8,165.5	$9,014.6	$9,931.3
Ratio	58.8%	59.3%	58.3%	68.7%	68.9%	68.9%

13.31-33 continued.

    d. Notice that the rate of return on assets is smaller after consolidating the subsidiary. The total income from the equity method is the same as consolidated net income. (The equity method is often called a one-line consolidation for this reason.) Total assets are larger under consolidation. Hence, the rate of return on assets is smaller. This result holds in general for credit subsidiaries.

        The debt-equity ratios are higher for the consolidated statements than from using the equity method for G.E. This result holds in general.

        In general, when one compares financial ratios for companies with different kinds of structures, one must analyze carefully the separate component companies before drawing valid comparisons and inferences from them.

13.34   (Coke and Pepsi; effect of intercorporate investment policies on financial statements.)

    a. Coke as Reported: $[\$1,364 + (1 - .34)(\$231)]/\$9,280 = 16.3\%$.
       Coke's Bottlers: $[\$290 + (1 - .34)(\$452)]/\$11,110 = 5.3\%$.
       Coke and Bottlers
       Consolidated: $[\$1,364 + (1 - .34)(\$231 + \$452) + .51(\$290)]/\$18,675 = 10.5\%$.

    Pepsi as Reported: $[\$1,091 + (1 - .34)(\$689)/\$15,637 = 9.9\%$.

    b. Coke as Reported: $(\$4,296 + \$1,133)/\$9,280 = 58.5\%$.
       Coke's Bottlers: $(\$2,752 + \$4,858)/\$11,110 = 68.5\%$.
       Coke and Bottlers
       Consolidated: $(\$7,048 + \$5,991)/\$18,675 = 69.8\%$.

    Pepsi as Reported: $(\$3,264 + \$7,469)/\$15,637 = 68.6\%$.

    c. The rate of return on assets using reported amounts suggests that Coke is considerably more profitable than Pepsi. This measure of the rate of return on assets includes Coke's 49 percent interest in the earnings of its bottlers but does not include Coke's 49 percent interest in the assets of these bottlers. Coke's rate of return on assets with its bottlers consolidated includes 100 percent of the net income and assets of these bottlers. Thus, Coke appears only slightly more profitable than Pepsi during Year 8.

        Coke's liabilities to assets ratio is less than the corresponding ratio for its bottlers. On a comparable measurement basis with Pepsi, Coke has slightly more debt in its capital structure instead of approximately 14.7 percent less debt as indicated by the reported amounts $[14.7\% = (68.6\% - 58.5\%)/68.6\%]$.

13.34 continued.

    d. Coke's intercorporate investment policy permits it to report higher profitability and lower debt ratios than if it held a sufficient ownership percentage to consolidate its bottlers. Coke's 49 percent ownership probably permits it to exert control over its bottlers because (1) the remaining 51 percent is widely-held by many individuals and institutions, and (2) Coke maintains exclusive contracts with its bottlers that tie their success to Coke's success. Thus, one might argue that consolidation reflects the economic reality of the relationship better than use of the equity method.

13.35   (Cherry Corporation; preparing a statement of cash flows.)

a.

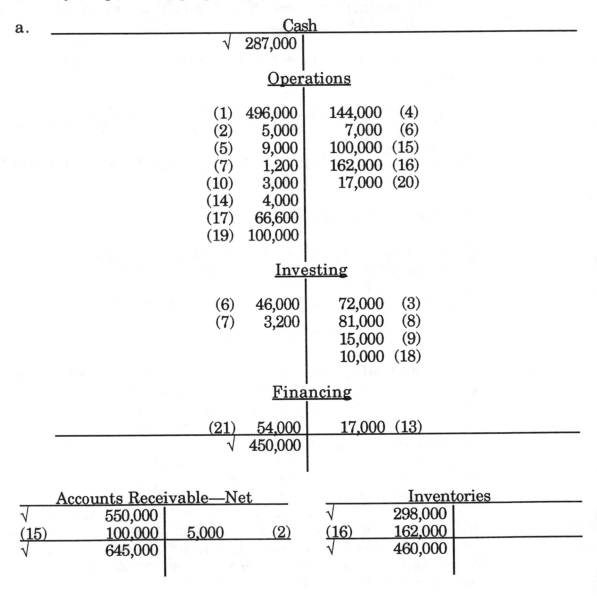

13.35 a. continued.

Investments—Roy Co.			
√	39,000		
		39,000	(6)
√	0		

Investments—Zuber Co.			
√	0		
(3)	111,300		
(4)	144,000	9,000	(5)
√	246,300		

Plant Assets			
√	381,000		
(8)	81,000	22,000	(7)
(9)	15,000		
√	455,000		

Accumulated Depreciation			
		144,000	√
(7)	17,600	66,600	(17)
		193,000	√

Patents (Net)			
√	19,000		
(18)	10,000	3,000	(10)
√	26,000		

Dividends Payable			
		0	√
		181,000	(12)
		181,000	√

Accounts Payable			
		70,000	√
		100,000	(19)
		170,000	√

Accrued Liabilities			
		41,800	√
(20)	17,000		
		24,800	√

Long-Term Bonds Payable			
		133,000	√
(13)	17,000	4,000	(14)
		54,000	(21)
		174,000	√

Common Stock			
		700,000	√
		24,000	(3)
		28,000	(11)
		752,000	√

Additional Paid-in Capital—Common			
		9,600	√
		4,800	(3)
		5,600	(11)
		20,000	√

Preferred Stock			
		53,000	√
		7,000	(3)
		60,000	√

Additional Paid-in Capital—Preferred			
		2,500	√
		3,500	(3)
		6,000	√

Retained Earnings			
		420,100	√
(11)	33,600	496,000	(1)
(12)	181,000		
		701,500	√

13.35 a. continued.

Explanation of entries in work sheet (not required):

(1) Net income of $496,000.
(2) Bad debt expense of $5,000.
(3) Issue of preferred shares totaling $10,500 (= 3,500 × $3), issue of common shares totaling $28,800 (= 2,400 × $12), and expenditure of $72,000 cash in the acquisition of 45 percent of Zuber, $111,300 = $10,500 + $28,800 + $72,000.
(4) Share of earnings of Zuber; $144,000 (= .45 × $320,000).
(5) Reduce investment for dividends declared by Zuber; $9,000 (= .45 × $20,000).
(6) Gain on sale of Roy; $7,000 (= $46,000 – $39,000).
(7) Loss on sale of plant; $1,200 (= $22,000 – $17,600 – $3,200).
(8) Acquire new plant for $81,000.
(9) Acquire new plant (major improvements) for $15,000; plug in Plant Assets account.
(10) Amortization of patents; $3,000.
(11) Stock dividend; .04 × 70,000 × $12 = $33,600.
(12) Dividends declared; $181,000 (= $145,000 + $36,000).
(13) Retire bonds at book value.
(14) Amortization of bond discount of $4,000 does not use cash.
(15) Plug for net increase in receivables.
(16) Plug for net increase in inventories.
(17) Plug for net increase in accumulated depreciation; an addback for expense not using cash.
(18) Acquire new patents (net) for $10,000; plug in Patents (Net) account.
(19) Plug for net increase in accounts payable.
(20) Plug for net decrease in accrued liabilities.
(21) Plug for issue of new bonds.

13.35 continued.

b.

CHERRY CORPORATION
Statement of Cash Flows
For Year 6

Operations:		
Net Income	$ 496,000	
Additions:		
Bad Debt Expense	5,000	
Loss on Sale of Plant Asset................	1,200	
Amortization of Patent......................	3,000	
Amortization of Discount..................	4,000	
Depreciation Expense.......................	66,600	
Increase in Accounts Payable	100,000	
Subtractions:		
Equity in Undistributed Earnings......	(135,000)	
Gain on Sale of Investment...............	(7,000)	
Increase in Accounts Receivable	(100,000)	
Increase in Inventories....................	(162,000)	
Decrease in Accrued Liabilities.........	(17,000)	
Cash Flow from Operations.....................		$ 254,800
Investing:		
Sale of Investment in Roy Company	$ 46,000	
Sale of Plant Asset.............................	3,200	
Acquisition of Investment in Zuber		
Company...	(72,000)	
Acquisition of Plant Assets...................	(81,000)	
Major Repairs to Plant Assets	(15,000)	
Acquisition of Patent	(10,000)	
Cash Flow from Investing......................		(128,800)
Financing:		
Issue of Bonds	$ 54,000	
Redemption of Bonds...........................	(17,000)	
Cash Flow from Financing.....................		37,000
Net Change in Cash		$ 163,000
Cash, January 1, Year 6		287,000
Cash, December 31, Year 6....................		$ 450,000

Supplementary Information

During Year 6 Cheery Corporation acquired 45 percent of the common stock of Zuber Company for $111,300, comprising $72,000 cash, $10,500 of preferred stock, and $28,800 of common stock.

CHAPTER 14

STATEMENT OF CASH FLOWS: ANOTHER LOOK

Problems and Cases: Answers and Solutions

14.1   (Effects of transactions on statement of cash flows.)

a.   The journal entry to record this transaction is:

Retained Earnings	15,000	
Dividends Payable		3,000
Cash		12,000

The credit to the Cash account reduces Line (9) by $12,000. Paying dividends is a financing activity so Line (8) increases by $12,000.

b.   The journal entry to record this transaction is:

Cash	75,000	
Bank Loan Payable		75,000

The debit to the Cash account increases Line (9) by $75,000. Borrowing is a financing activity so Line (6) increases by $75,000.

c.   The journal entry to record this transaction is:

Cash	20,000	
Accumulated Depreciation	35,000	
Machinery		40,000
Gain on Sale of Machinery		15,000

The debit to the Cash account results in an increase in Line (9) of $20,000. Selling machinery is an investing activity so Line (4) increases by $20,000. The gain on the sale increases net income on Line (1) by $15,000. Because the full cash proceeds is an investing activity, Line (3) increases by $15,000 to subtract from net income a revenue that did not provide an operating source of cash.

14.1 continued.

d. The journal entry for this transaction is:

Rent Expense...	28,000	
Cash..		28,000

The credit to the Cash account reduces Line (9) by $28,000. The recognition of rent expense reduces net income on Line (1) by $28,000. Paying rent is an operating transaction so the accountant makes no adjustment to net income when computing cash flow from operations.

e. The journal entry to record this transaction is:

Marketable Securities.....................................	39,000	
Cash..		39,000

The credit to the Cash account reduces Line (9) by $39,000. Purchasing marketable securities is an investing transaction so Line (5) increases by $39,000.

f. The journal entry to record this transaction is:

Accumulated Depreciation.............................	14,000	
Truck..		14,000

Because this transaction does not affect either the Cash account on Line (9) or net income on Line (1), it does not appear on the statement of cash flows.

g. The journal entry to record this event is:

Unrealized Holding Loss of Marketable Securities (SE)..	8,000	
Marketable Securities.............................		8,000

Because this entry does not affect either the Cash account on Line (9) or net income on Line (1), it does not appear on the statement of cash flows. The firm discloses in a supplementary schedule or note the write down of marketable equity securities totaling $8,000.

14.1 continued.

h. The journal entry to record this transaction is:

Interest Expense..	15,000	
Bonds Payable..		500
Cash...		14,500

The credit to the Cash account results in a decrease in Line (9) of $14,500. The recognition of interest expense reduces net income on Line (1) by $15,000. Because the firm used only $14,500 of cash for this expense, Line (2) increases by $500 for the portion of the expense that did not use cash.

i. The journal entry for this event is:

Amortization Expense.................................	22,000	
Goodwill..		22,000

This entry does not involve the Cash account so Line (9) does not change. The recognition of amortization expense reduces net income on Line (1) by $22,000. Because this expense requires no cash outflow, Line (2) increases by $22,000 to convert net income to cash flow from operations.

j. The journal entry to record this transaction is:

Building..	400,000	
Note Payable..		360,000
Cash...		40,000

The credit to the Cash account reduces Line (9) by $40,000. Acquiring a building is an investing transaction so Line (5) increases by $40,000. The firm discloses in a supplementary schedule or note the acquisition of a building by assuming a mortgage for $360,000.

k. The journal entry for this event is:

Bad Debt Expense.......................................	32,000	
Allowance for Uncollectible Accounts.........		32,000

This entry does not involve the Cash account so Line (9) does not change. The recognition of bad debt expense reduces net income on Line (1) by $32,000. Because this expense does not use cash, Line (2) increases by $32,000 to convert net income to cash flow from operations.

14-3

14.1 continued.

l. The journal entry for this event is:

Allowance for Uncollectible Accounts.............. 28,000
    Accounts Receivable 28,000

This event does not affect the Cash account so Line (9) does not change. The event also does not affect net income so Line (1) does not change. Thus, the event would not normally appear in the statement of cash flows. An alternative acceptable answer is Line (2) increases by $28,000 and Line (3) increases by $28,000.

m. The journal entry to record this transaction is:

Cash... 15,000
    Equity in Earnings of Affiliate.................... 12,000
    Investment in Securities 3,000

The debit to the Cash account results in an increase in Line (9) of $15,000. The recognition of equity in earnings increases net income on Line (1) by $12,000. Because the firm received $3,000 more cash than its equity in earnings, Line (2) increases by $3,000 when converting net income to cash flow from operations. An alternative acceptable answer for the increase in Line (2) of $3,000 is that Line (2) increases by $15,000 for the dividend received and Line (3) increases by $15,000 to subtract the equity in earnings.

n. The journal entries to record this transaction are:

Cash.. 22,000
Realized Loss on Sale of Marketable Secur-
    ities (IncSt).. 3,000
        Marketable Securities............................. 25,000

Marketable Securities.................................... 2,000
    Unrealized Holding Loss on Marketable
        Securities (SE)....................................... 2,000

The debit to the Cash account results in an increase in Line (9) of $22,000. Selling marketable securities is an investing transaction so Line (4) increases by $22,000. The recognition of a realized loss on the sale reduces net income on Line (1) by $3,000. Because the loss does not use cash, the accountant increases Line (2) by $3,000 to add back the loss to net income when converting net income to cash flow from operations.

14.1 continued.

o. The journal entry to record this transaction is:

Preferred Stock	10,000	
Common Stock		2,000
Additional Paid-in Capital		8,000

This transaction affects neither the Cash account [Line (9)] nor net income [Line (1)]. Thus, it would not appear on the statement of cash flows. The firm discloses in a supplementary schedule or note the conversion of preferred stock into common stock totaling $10,000.

p. The journal entry to record this transaction is:

Legal Expense	5,000	
Land		5,000

The transaction does not affect the Cash account so Line (9) does not change. The recognition of legal expense reduces net income on Line (1) by $5,000. Because this expense does not use cash, Line (2) increases by $5,000 to convert net income to cash flow from operations.

q. The journal entry for this transaction is:

Rental Fees Received in Advance	8,000	
Rent Revenue		8,000

This entry does not affect the Cash account so Line (9) does not change. The recognition of rent revenue increases net income on Line (1) by $8,000. Because this revenue does not increase cash during the current period, Line (3) increases by $8,000 to convert net income to cash flow from operations.

r. The journal entry to record this event is:

Long-Term Debt	30,000	
Current Portion of Long-Term Debt		30,000

This entry affects neither the Cash account [Line (9)] nor net income [Line (1)] and would therefore not appear on the statement of cash flows.

14.1 continued.

s.   The journal entry to record this event is:

Contracts in Process.................................... 15,000
   Contract Revenue   15,000

This entry does not affect the Cash account so Line (9) does not change. The recognition of contract revenue increases net income on Line (1) by $15,000. Because this revenue does not result in a change in cash, Line (3) increases by $15,000 to convert net income to cash flow from operations.

t.   The journal entry to record this transaction is:

Land... 50,000
   Donated Capital (SE)   50,000

This transaction affects neither the Cash account [Line (9)] nor net income [Line (1)] and therefore does not appear on the statement of cash flows. The firm discloses in a supplementary schedule or note the donation of land by a governmental agency totaling $50,000.

u.   The journal entry to record this event is:

Unrealized Holding Loss on Investments in
   Securities (SE)....................................... 8,000
      Investments in Securities.......................   8,000

This transaction affects neither the Cash account [Line (9)] nor net income [Line (1)] so would not appear on the statement of cash flows. The firm discloses in a supplementary schedule or note the write down of marketable equity investments totaling $8,000.

v.   The journal entry to record the recognition of depreciation is:

Inventories 60,000
   Accumulated Depreciation........................   60,000

The journal entry to record the sale of the inventory items is:

Cost of Goods Sold 60,000
   Inventories   60,000

These entries do not affect the Cash account so Line (9) does not change. The recognition of cost of goods sold containing depreciation reduces net income on Line (1) by $60,000. Because this expense does not use cash, Line (2) increases by $60,000 to convert net income to cash flow from operations.

14.1 continued.

w. The journal entry to record this transaction is:

Warranty Expense	35,000	
Estimated Warranty Liability.....................		35,000

This entry does not affect the Cash account so Line (9) does not change. The recognition of warranty expense reduces net income on Line (1) by $35,000. Because this expense does not use cash, Line (2) increases by $35,000 to convert net income to cash flow from operations.

x. The journal entry to record this transaction is:

Estimated Warranty Liability	28,000	
Cash..		28,000

The credit to the Cash account reduces Line (9) by $28,000. Using cash to service a warranty is an operating transaction. This entry does not affect net income on Line (1) this period. Thus, Line (3) increases by $28,000 to convert net income to cash flow from operations.

y. The journal entry to record this event is:

Income Tax Expense....................................	80,000	
Deferred Tax Liability..................................	20,000	
Cash..		100,000

The credit to the Cash account results in a reduction in Line (9) of $100,000. The recognition of income tax expense reduces net income on Line (1) by $80,000. Because the firm used more cash this period than the amount of income tax expense, Line (3) increases by $20,000 when converting net income to cash flow from operations.

z. The journal entry to record this event is:

Loss from Writedown of Inventories................	18,000	
Inventories		18,000

This entry does not affect the Cash account so Line (9) does not change. The recognition of the writedown reduces net income on Line (1) by $18,000. Because the writedown did not use cash, Line (2) increases by $18,000 to convert net income to cash flow from operations.

14.2   (Alcoa; working backwards from statement of cash flows.)

(2) Cash (Operations—Depreciation Expense Add-
     back).. 664.0
        Accumulated Depreciation..........................   664.0

(3) Cash (Operations—Deferred Tax Addback)...... 82.0
        Deferred Income Tax Liability.....................   82.0

(4) Investment in Affiliates............................... 47.1
        Cash (Operations—Equity in Undistributed
        Earnings Subtraction) 47.1

(5) Cash (Investing—Sale of Marketable Secur-
&   ities).. 49.8
(11)   Cash (Operations—Gain on Sale of Mar-
           ketable Securities Subtraction)..............   20.8
           Marketable Securities 29.0

(6) Cash (Operations—Decrease in Accounts Re-
     ceivable).. 74.6
        Accounts Receivable 74.6

(7) Inventories... 198.9
        Cash (Operations—Increase in Inventories).   198.9

(8) Prepayments 40.3
        Cash (Operations—Increase in Prepay-
        ments)...   40.3

(9) Cash (Operations—Decrease in Accounts Pay-
     able) 33.9
        Accounts Payable 33.9

(10) Other Current Liabilities.............................. 110.8
        Cash (Operations—Decrease in Other Cur-
        rent Liabilities).......................................   110.8

(12) Marketable Securities.................................... 73.2
        Cash (Investing—Acquisition of Marketable
        Securities) 73.2

(13) Property, Plant and Equipment....................... 875.7
        Cash (Investing—Acquisition of Property,
        Plant and Equipment)..............................   875.7

(14) Investments in Securities............................. 44.5
        Cash (Investing—Acquisition of Subsid-
        iaries) 44.5

14.2 continued.

   (15) Cash (Financing—Common Stock Issued to Employees).. 34.4

         Common Stock.. 34.4

   (16) Treasury Stock 100.9

         Cash (Financing—Repurchase of Common Stock) 100.9

   (17) Retained Earnings 242.9

         Cash (Financing—Dividends Paid to Shareholders).. 242.9

   (18) Cash (Financing—Additions to Short-Term Borrowing).. 127.6

         Notes Payable.. 127.6

   (19) Cash (Financing—Additions to Long-Term Borrowing).. 121.6

         Bonds Payable.. 121.6

   (20) Bonds Payable.. 476.4

         Cash (Financing—Payments to Long-Term Borrowing) 476.4

   (21) Property, Plant and Equipment...................... 76.9

         Mortgage Payable.................................... 76.9

   (22) Property, Plant and Equipment...................... 98.2

         Capitalized Lease Obligation 98.2

   (23) Convertible Bonds Payable............................ 47.8

         Common Stock.. 47.8

14.3   (Ingersoll-Rand; working backwards from statement of cash flows.)

   (2) Cash (Operations—Depreciation Expense Add-back)... 179.4

         Accumulated Depreciation...................... 179.4

   (3) Cash (Investing—Sale of Property, Plant, and
&   Equipment 26.5
(12)   Property, Plant and Equipment (Net) 22.9

         Cash (Operations—Gain on Sale Subtraction)....................................... 3.6

   (4) Investment in Securities.............................. 41.5

         Cash (Operations—Equity in Earnings Subtraction) 41.5

         Solutions

14.3 continued.

(5)	Cash (Operations—Deferred Taxes Addback)...	15.1	
	Deferred Income Taxes................................		15.1
(6)	Cash (Operations—Decrease in Accounts Receivable)...	50.9	
	Accounts Receivable		50.9
(7)	Inventories..	15.2	
	Cash (Operations—Increase in Inventories).		15.2
(8)	Other Current Assets	33.1	
	Cash (Operations—Increase in Other Current Assets)		33.1
(9)	Accounts Payable......................................	37.9	
	Cash (Operations—Decrease in Accounts Payable)...		37.9
(10)	Cash (Operations—Increase in Other Current Liabilities)...	19.2	
	Other Current Liabilities........................		19.2
(11)	Property, Plant and Equipment......................	211.7	
	Cash (Investing—Acquisition of Property, Plant and Equipment)...........................		211.7
(13)	Marketable Securities.................................	4.6	
	Cash (Investing—Acquisition of Marketable Securities)		4.6
(14)	Cash (Investing—Advances from Equity Companies)..	18.4	
	Advances from Equity Companies		18.4
(15)	Short-Term Debt......................................	81.5	
	Cash (Financing—Repayment of Short-Term Debt)..		81.5
(16)	Cash (Financing—Issue of Long-Term Debt)....	147.6	
	Long-Term Debt Payable...........................		147.6
(17)	Long-Term Debt Payable	129.7	
	Cash (Financing—Repayment of Long-Term Debt)		129.7

14.3 continued.

(18) Cash (Financing—Issue of Common Stock
  under Option Plan)..................................... 47.9
   Common Stock, Additional Paid-in
    Capital..   47.9

(19) Cash (Financing—Sale of Treasury Stock)....... 59.3
   Treasury Stock, Additional Paid-in
    Capital..   59.3

(20) Retained Earnings 78.5
   Cash (Financing—Dividends Paid).............   78.5

(21) Leasehold Asset... 147.9
   Capitalized Lease Obligation 147.9

(22) Preferred Stock 62.0
   Common Stock, Additional Paid-in Capital...   62.0

(23) Investments in Securities............................. 94.3
   Common Stock, Additional Paid-in Capital...   94.3

14.4 See solution to Problem 7.49.

14.5 See solution to Problem 9.46.

14.6 See solution to Problem 12.40.

14.7 See solution to Problem 13.35.

     Solutions

14.8 (Warren Corporation; preparing a statement of cash flows.)

a.

		Cash			
	√	223,200			

Operations

Net Income	(5)	234,000	
Loss on Sale of Machinery	(1b)	15,600	
Amortize Patent	(2b)	5,040	
Decrease in Accounts Receivable	(7)	18,000	
Bad Debt Expense	(8)	2,400	
Decrease in Inventories	(9)	66,000	
Depreciation Expense	(11)	106,800	
Amortize Leasehold Improvements	(12)	10,800	
Increase in Accounts Payable	(13)	153,360	

Investing

Sale of Machinery	(1b)	57,600	463,200	(1a)	Acquisition of Machinery
			2,400	(2a)	Payment for Patent Defense
			180,000	(10)	Acquisition of Securities

Financing

		13,200	(3)	Retirement of Preferred Stock
		60,000	(15)	Provision for Current Portion of Serial Bonds

	√	174,000	

14.8 a. continued.

Accounts Receivable			Allowance for Un-collectible Accounts				Inventory		
√ 327,600				20,400 √		√ 645,600			
	3,600 (6)	(6) 3,600	2,400 (8)				66,000 (9)
	18,000 (7)						
√ 306,000			19,200 √		√ 579,600		

Securities Held for Plant Expansion			Machinery and Equipment (Cost)			Accumulated Depreciation		
√ -0-		√ 776,400				446,400 √	
(10) 180,000		(1a) 463,200	127,200 (1b)	(1b) 54,000	106,800 (11)	
√ 180,000		√ 1,112,400			499,200 √	

Leasehold Improvements			Allowance for Amortization			Patents		
√ 104,400				58,800 √	√ 36,000		
			10,800 (12)	(2a) 2,400	5,040 (2b)	
√ 104,400			69,600 √	√ 33,360		

Accounts Payable			Dividends Payable			Bonds Payable (Current)		
	126,000 √			-- √			60,000 √	
	153,360 (13)			48,000 (4)	(15) 60,000	60,000 (14)	
	279,360 √			48,000 √			60,000 √	

6-Percent Serial Bonds Payable			Preferred Stock			Common Stock		
	360,000 √			120,000 √			600,000 √	
(14) 60,000		(3) 12,000					
	300,000 √			108,000 √			600,000 √	

Retained Earnings		
	321,600 √	
(4) 48,000	234,000 (5)	
(3) 1,200		
	506,400 √	

14-13

14.8 continued.

b.

WARREN CORPORATION
Statement of Cash Flows
For the Year Ending December 31, Year 5

Operations:

Net Income...	$ 234,000	
Loss on Sale of Machinery	15,600	
Depreciation	106,800	
Amortization of Leasehold Improvements..	10,800	
Amortization of Patents............................	5,040	
Bad Debt Expense	2,400	
Decrease in Accounts Receivable...............	18,000	
Decrease in Inventories............................	66,000	
Increase in Accounts Payable....................	153,360	
Cash Flow from Operations		$ 612,000
Investing:		
Sale of Machinery....................................	$ 57,600	
Payment of Legal Fee for Patent Defense	(2,400)	
Acquisition of Securities for Plant Expansion...	(180,000)	
Acquisition of Machinery	(463,200)	
Cash Flow from Investing		(588,000)
Financing:		
Retirement of Serial Bonds	$ (60,000)	
Retirement of Preferred Stock	(13,200)	
Cash Flow from Financing		(73,200)
Net Change in Cash....................................		$ (49,200)
Cash, January 1, Year 5.............................		223,200
Cash, December 31, Year 5		$ 174,000

14.9 (Roth Company; preparing a statement of cash flows.)

a.

Cash

√ 37,950

Operations

Net Income	(1)	95,847	3,600	(2)	Gain on Sale of Marketable Securities
Bond Discount Amortization	(6)	225			
Amortize Goodwill	(8)	180	16,050	(4)	Gain on Condemnation of Land
Depreciation	(11)	1,875	37,500	(9)	Increase in Accounts Receivable
Increase in Income Taxes Payable	(15)	51,924			
Deferred Taxes	(16)	504	26,250	(10)	Increase in Inventories
			8,820	(12)	Equity in Earnings
			5,835	(13)	Decrease in Accounts Payable

Investing

Sale of Marketable Securities	(2)	17,400	122,250	(5)	Acquisition of Equipment
Proceeds from Condemnation of Land	(4)	48,000			

Financing

Issuance of Bonds	(7)	97,500
	√	131,100

Marketable Securities	
√ 24,000	
	13,800 (2)
√ 10,200	

Accounts Receivable	
√ 36,480	
(9) 37,500	
√ 73,980	

Inventory	
√ 46,635	
(10) 26,250	
√ 72,885	

Land	
√ 60,000	
	31,950 (4)
√ 28,050	

Building	
√ 375,000	
√ 375,000	

Equipment	
√ -0-	
(5) 122,250	
√ 122,250	

14.9 a. continued.

Accumulated Depreciation			Investment in 30-Percent Owned Co.			Other Assets	
	22,500 √		√ 91,830			√ 22,650	
	1,875 (11)		(12) 8,820	180 (8)			
	24,375 √		√ 100,470			√ 22,650	

Accounts Payable			Dividends Payable			Income Taxes Payable	
	31,830 √			-0- √			-0- √
(13) 5,835				12,000 (14)			51,924 (15)
	25,995 √			12,000 √			51,924 √

Other Liabilities			Bonds Payable			Deferred Income Taxes	
	279,000 √			71,550 √			765 √
				225 (6)			504 (16)
				97,500 (7)			
	279,000 √			169,275 √			1,269 √

Preferred Stock			Common Stock			Dividends Declared	
	45,000 √			120,000 √		√ -0-	
(3) 45,000				45,000 (3)		(14) 12,000	
	-0- √			165,000 √		√ 12,000	

Unrealized Holding Loss on Marketable Securities			Retained Earnings	
√ 750				124,650 √
				95,847 (1)
√ 750				220,497 √

14.9 continued.

b.   ROTH COMPANY
                      Statement of Cash Flows
               For the Three Months Ended March 31, Year 7

Operations:
   Net Income.. $ 95,847
   Bond Discount Amortization..................... 225
   Goodwill Amortization............................ 180
   Depreciation 1,875
   Deferred Income Taxes........................... 504
   Increase in Income Taxes Payable 51,924
   Gain on Sale of Marketable Securities .... (3,600)
   Gain on Condemnation of Land .... (16,050)
   Equity in Earnings................................. (8,820)
   Increase in Accounts Receivable............... (37,500)
   Increase in Inventories........................... (26,250)
   Decrease in Accounts Payable................... (5,835)
Cash Flow from Operations .... $ 52,500
Investing:
   Proceeds from Sale of Marketable Securi-
     ties .... $ 17,400
   Proceeds from Condemnation of Land........ 48,000
   Acquisition of Equipment .... (122,250)
Cash Flow from Investing .... (56,850)
Financing:
   Issue of Bonds...................................... $ 97,500
Cash Flow from Financing 97,500
Net Change in Cash.................................. $ 93,150
Cash, January 1 Year 7.............................. 37,950
Cash, March 31, Year 7.............................. $ 131,100

Supplementary Information
Holders of the firm's preferred stock converted shares with a book value of $45,000 into shares of common stock.

   14-17   **Solutions**

14.10 (Biddle Corporation; preparing a statement of cash flows.)

a.

Cash					
√	45,000				

Operations

Income from Continuing Operations	(14)	54,500	35,000	(7)	Increase in Accounts Receivable
Loss on Sale of Equipment	(4)	2,000	20,000	(8)	Increase in Inventories
Depreciation	(9)	10,000	5,000	(12)	Decrease in Accrued Liabilities
Amortization	(10)	1,500			
Increase in Accounts Payable	(11)	30,000			
Deferred Income Taxes	(13)	20,000			

Extraordinary Gain or Loss

Income from Extraordinary Items	(14)	6,000	6,000	(3)	Gain on Retirement of Bonds Net of Income Taxes

Investing

Sale of Equipment	(4)	9,500	42,500	(6)	Acquisition of Land

Financing

			19,000	(3)	Retirement of Bonds, Including Income Taxes
			1,000	(5)	Dividends

√	50,000			

Accounts Receivable—Net			
√	70,000		
(7)	35,000		
√	105,000		

Inventories			
√	110,000		
(8)	20,000		
√	130,000		

Land			
√	100,000		
(2)	20,000		
(6)	42,500		
√	162,500		

14.10 a. continued.

Plant and Equipment		Accumulated Depreciation		Patents	
√ 316,500			50,000 √	√ 16,500	
	26,500 (4)	(4) 15,000	10,000 (9)		1,500 (10)
√ 290,000			45,000 √	√ 15,000	

Accounts Payable		Accrued Liabilities		Deferred Income Taxes	
	100,000 √		105,000 √		50,000 √
	30,000 (11)	(12) 5,000			20,000 (13)
	130,000 √		100,000 √		70,000 √

Long-term Bonds		Common Stock		Additional Paid-in Capital	
	90,000 √		105,000 √		85,000 √
(3) 25,000			10,500 (1)		21,000 (1)
			9,500 (2)		10,500 (2)
	65,000 √		125,000 √		116,500 √

Retained Earnings	
	73,000 √
(1) 31,500	60,500 (14)
(5) 1,000	
	101,000 √

 Solutions

14.10 continued.

b.

BIDDLE CORPORATION
Statement of Cash Flows
For the Year Ended December, Year 2

Operations:

Income from Continuing Operations.........	$ 54,500	
Loss on Sale of Equipment	2,000	
Depreciation	10,000	
Amortization	1,500	
Deferred Income Taxes...........................	20,000	
Increase in Accounts Payable..................	30,000	
Increase in Accounts Receivable..............	(35,000)	
Increase in Inventories..........................	(20,000)	
Decrease in Accrued Liabilities................	(5,000)	
Cash Flow from Operations		$ 58,000
Investing:		
Sale of Equipment....................................	$ 9,500	
Acquisition of Land.................................	(42,500)	
Cash Flow from Investing		(33,000)
Financing:		
Retirement of Bonds..............................	$ (19,000)	
Dividends	(1,000)	
Cash Flow from Financing........................		(20,000)
Net Change in Cash..................................		$ 5,000
Cash, January 1, Year 2.............................		45,000
Cash, December 31, Year 2		$ 50,000

Supplementary Information
During Year 2, Biddle Corporation issued common stock with a market value of $20,000 in the acquisition of land.

14.11 (Plainview Corporation; preparing a statement of cash flows.)

a.

Cash					
√	165,300				

Operations

Income from Continuing Operations	(1)	239,580	17,000	(5)	Gain on Sale of Marketable Securities
Loss from Fire	(6)	35,000	131,100	(12)	Increase in Inventories
Equity in Loss	(9)	17,920	1,400	(13)	Increase in Prepayments
Decrease in Accounts Receivable—Net	(11)	59,000	1,500	(18)	Decrease in Accrued Payables
Depreciation	(15)	79,900	500	(20)	Deferred Taxes
Increase in Accounts Payable	(16)	24,800			
Increase in Income Taxes Payable	(19)	66,500			

From Extraordinary Items

Loss on Retirement of Bonds	(21)	3,000	3,000	(1)	Extraordinary Loss

Investing

Sale of Marketable Securities	(5)	127,000	28,000	(8)	Acquisition of Machinery
Building Sold	(7)	4,000	103,400	(10)	Acquisition of Marketable Securities
Bond Sinking Funds Utilized	(14)	63,000			

Financing

Sale of Treasury Stock	(3)	6,000	130,000	(2)	Dividends
Issuance of Debentures	(22)	125,000	145,000	(17)	Payment of Note Payable—Current
			313,000	(21)	Retirement of Bonds

√	142,100				

14.11 a. continued.

Marketable Securities
√ 129,200	
(10) 103,400	110,000 (5)
√ 122,600	

Accounts Receivable—Net
√ 371,200	
	59,000 (11)
√ 312,200	

Inventories
√ 124,100	
(12) 131,100	
√ 255,200	

Prepayments
√ 22,000	
(13) 1,400	
√ 23,400	

Bond Sinking Fund
√ 63,000	
	63,000 (14)
√ -0-	

Investment in Subsidiary
√ 152,000	
	17,920 (9)
√ 134,080	

Plant and Equipment—Net
√ 1,534,600	
(6) 65,000	100,000 (6)
(8) 28,000	4,000 (7)
	79,900 (15)
√ 1,443,700	

Accounts Payable
	213,300 √
	24,800 (16)
	238,100 √

Notes Payable—Current
	145,000 √
(17) 145,000	
	-0- √

Accrued Payables
	18,000 √
(18) 1,500	
	16,500 √

Income Taxes Payable
	31,000 √
	66,500 (19)
	97,500 √

Deferred Income Taxes
	128,400 √
(20) 500	
	127,900 √

6-Percent Mortgage Bonds
	310,000 √
(21) 310,000	
	-0- √

8-Percent Debentures
	-0- √
	125,000 (22)
	125,000 √

Common Stock
	950,000 √
	83,500 (4)
	1,033,500 √

Additional Paid-in Capital
	51,000 √
	16,700 (4)
	67,700 √

Unrealized Holding Gain on Marketable Securities
	2,500 √
	2,500 √

Retained Earnings
	755,700 √
(2) 130,000	236,580 (1)
(3) 3,000	
(4) 100,200	
	759,080 √

Treasury Stock
√ 43,500	
	9,000 (3)
√ 34,500	

14.11 continued.

b.

PLAINVIEW CORPORATION
Statement of Cash Flows
For the Year Ended December, Year 5

Operations:

Income from Continuing Operations.........	$ 239,580	
Loss from Fire.........	35,000	
Equity in Loss of Subsidiary	17,920	
Depreciation	79,900	
Gain on Sale of Marketable Securities.........	(17,000)	
Deferred Income Taxes.........	(500)	
Decrease in Accounts Receivable—Net.......	59,000	
Increase in Accounts Payable.........	24,800	
Increase in Income Taxes Payable	66,500	
Increase in Inventories.........	(131,100)	
Increase in Prepayments	(1,400)	
Decrease in Accounts Payable.........	(1,500)	
Cash Flow from Operations		$ 371,200

Investing:

Marketable Securities Sold.........	$ 127,000	
Building Sold	4,000	
Bond Sinking Funds Utilized	63,000	
Acquisition of Marketable Securities.........	(103,400)	
Acquisition of Machinery	(28,000)	
Cash Flow from Investing.........		62,600

Financing:

Sale of Treasury Stock	$ 6,000	
Issue of Debentures	125,000	
Dividends	(130,000)	
Retirement of Bonds.........	(313,000)	
Payment of Short-Term Note.........	(145,000)	
Cash Flow from Financing.........		(457,000)
Net Change in Cash.........		$ (23,200)
Cash, January 1, Year 5.........		165,300
Cash, December 31, Year 5		$ 142,000

 Solutions

14.12 (UAL Corporation; preparing and interpreting the statement of cash flows.)

a. T-account work sheet for Year 9.

	Cash		
√	1,087		

	Operations		
(1)	324	106	(4)
(3)	517	147	(7)
(11)	56	39	(8)
(15)	42	67	(9)
(17)	12	49	(16)

	Investing		
(4)	1,199	1,568	(2)
(10)	40	957	(6)

	Financing		
(12)	325	110	(13)
(18)	4	98	(19)
√	465		

	Marketable Securities			Accounts Receivable			Inventories	
√	--		√	741		√	210	
(5)	85		(7)	147		(8)	39	
(6)	957							
√	1,042		√	888		√	249	

	Prepayments			Property, Plant and Equipment			Accumulated Depreciation	
√	112		√	7,710			3,769	√
(9)	67		(2)	1,568	1,574 (4)	(4) 481	517	(3)
√	179		√	7,704			3,805	√

	Other Assets			Accounts Payable			Short-Term Borrowing	
√	610				540 √		121	√
		40 (10)			56 (11)		325	(12)
√	570				596 √		446	√

14.12 a. continued.

Current Portion Long-Term Debt			Advances from Customers			Other Current Liabilities		
	110	√		619	√		1,485	√
(13) 110	84	(14)		42	(15)	(16) 49		
	84	√		661	√		1,436	√

Long-Term Debt			Deferred Tax Liability			Other Noncurrent Liabilities		
	1,418	√		352	√		715	√
(14) 84				12	(17)		4	(18)
	1,334	√		364	√		719	√

Common Stock			Unrealized Holding Gain on Marketable Securities			Retained Earnings		
	119	√		--	√		1,188	√
				85	(5)		324	(1)
	119	√		85	√		1,512	√

Treasury Stock		
√	14	
(19)	98	
√	112	

14.12 continued.

a. T-account work sheet for Year 10.

		Cash		
√	465			

		Operations		
(1)	101	286	(4)
(3)	560	25	(7)
(15)	182	74	(8)
(16)	390	30	(9)
(18)	4	44	(11)

		Investing		
(4)	1,697	2,821	(2)
		17	(6)
		35	(10)

		Financing		
(12)	1	84	(13)
(17)	230		
(19)	2		
(20)	5		
√	221		

Marketable Securities				Accounts Receivable				Inventories		
√	1,042			√	888			√	249	
(5)	7			(7)	25			(8)	74	
(6)	17									
√	1,066			√	913			√	323	

Prepayments				Property, Plant and Equipment				Accumulated Depreciation		
√	179			√	7,704					3,805	√
(9)	30			(2)	2,821	1,938	(4)	(4)	527	560	(3)
√	209			√	8,587					3,838	√

14.12 a. continued.

Other Assets		
√	570	
(10)	35	
√	605	

Accounts Payable		
	596	√
(11)	44	
	552	√

Short-Term Borrowing

	446	√
	1	(12)
	447	√

Current Portion Long-Term Debt

	84	√
(13)	84	89 (14)
	89	√

Advances from Customers

	661	√
	182	(15)
	843	√

Other Current Liabilities

	1,436	√
	390	(16)
	1,826	√

Long-Term Debt		
	1,334	√
(14)	89	230 (17)
	1,475	√

Deferred Tax Liability

	364	√
	4	(18)
	368	√

Other Noncurrent Liabilities

	719	√
	2	(19)
	721	√

Common Stock		
	119	√
	1	(20)
	120	√

Additional Paid-in Capital

	48	√
	4	(20)
	52	√

Unrealized Holding Gain on Marketable Securities

	85	√
	7	(5)
	92	√

Retained Earnings		
	1,512	√
	101	(1)
	1,613	√

Treasury Stock		
√	112	
√	112	

14.12 continued.

b.　　Comparative Statement of Cash Flows for UAL Corporation
(Amounts in Millions)

	Year 9	Year 10
Operations:		
Net Income...	$ 324	$ 101
Depreciation Expense............................	517	560
Deferred Income Taxes..........................	12	4
Gain on Sale of Property, Plant and Equipment..	(106)	(286)
(Increase) Decrease in Accounts Receivable..	(147)	(25)
(Increase) Decrease in Inventories............	(39)	(74)
(Increase) Decrease in Prepayments..........	(67)	(30)
Increase (Decrease) in Accounts Payable ...	56	(44)
Increase (Decrease) in Advances from Customers..	42	182
Increase (Decrease) in Other Current Liabilities..	(49)	390
Cash Flow from Operations	$ 543	$ 778
Investing:		
Sale of Property, Plant and Equipment	$ 1,199	$ 1,697
Acquisition of Property, Plant and Equipment..	(1,568)	(2,821)
Acquisition of Marketable Securities..........	(957)	(17)
(Increase) Decrease in Other Noncurrent Assets..	40	(35)
Cash Flow from Investing	$(1,286)	$ 1,176)
Financing:		
Increase in Short-Term Borrowing............	$ 325	$ 1
Increase in Long-Term Borrowing............	--	230
Increase in Common Stock.......................	--	5
Decrease in Long-Term Borrowing............	(110)	(84)
Acquisition of Treasury Stock....................	(98)	--
Increase in Other Noncurrent Liabilities ...	4	2
Cash Flow from Financing.........................	$ 121	$ 154
Net Change in Cash....................................	$ (622)	$ (244)
Cash, January 1...	1,087	465
Cash, December 31....................................	$ 465	$ 221

14.12 continued.

c. During Year 9, cash flow from operations exceeded net income primarily because of the noncash expense for depreciation. Cash flows from operations and from the sale of property, plant and equipment were sufficient to finance capital expenditures. UAL Corporation used the excess cash flow as well as cash from additional short-term borrowing to repay long-term debt and reacquire treasury stock. It invested the remaining excess cash flow in short-term marketable securities. Although the balance in the cash account declined during Year 9, the combined balance in cash and marketable securities actually increased.

Net income declined in Year 10 relative to Year 9 but cash flow from operations increased. The increase occurred because UAL Corporation received increased cash advances from customers and stretched its other current liabilities. Cash flow from operations and from the sale of property, plant and equipment were insufficient to finance capital expenditures. UAL Corporation increased long-term borrowing and decreased the balance in its cash account to finance these capital expenditures.

One additional item to note for UAL Corporation is the significant turnover of aircraft each year. The airline sold older aircraft at a gain and replaced them with newer aircraft.

14.13 (Scott Paper Company; preparing and interpreting the statement of cash flows.)

a. T-account work sheet for Year 9.

Cash

√	374		

Operations

(1)	376	221	(7)
(6)	306	31	(8)
(9)	2	112	(10)
(12)	54	59	(11)
(14)	72	5	(17)
(18)	87		

Investing

(7)	5	92	(3)
(13)	8	775	(4)

Financing

(5)	449	59	(2)
		129	(16)
		201	(19)

√	49		

Accounts Receivable			Inventories			Prepayments	
√	611		√	522		√	108
(10)	112		(11)	59			54 (12)
√	723		√	581		√	54

Investments in Affiliates			Property, Plant and Equipment			Accumulated Depreciation	
√	254		√	5,272		2,160	√
(3)	92	2 (9)	(4) 775	78 (7)	(7) 74	306	(6)
(8)	31						
√	375		√	5,969		2,392	√

Other Assets			Accounts Payable		Current Portion Long-Term Debt	
√	175			920 √		129 √
(7)	220	8 (13)		72 (14)	(16) 129	221 (15)
√	387			992 √		221 √

14.13 a. continued.

Other Current Liabilities			Long-Term Debt			Deferred Income Taxes		
	98 √			1,450 √			607 √	
(17) 5			(15) 221	449 (5)			87 (18)	
	93 √			1,678 √			694 √	

Common Stock			Retained Earnings			Treasury Stock		
	629 √			1,331 √	√	15		
(19) 201			(2) 59	376 (1)			15	
	428 √			1,648 √	√	15		

a. T-account work sheet for Year 10.

Cash

√	49			

Operations

(1)	169	19	(8)
(7)	346	38	(9)
(10)	5	106	(11)
(14)	186	154	(12)
		10	(17)
		26	(18)

Investing

(3)	86	931	(4)
(8)	21	78	(13)

Financing

(5)	890	59	(2)
(19)	4	221	(16)
√	114		

Accounts Receivable			Inventories			Prepayments		
√	723		√	581		√	54	
(11)	106		(12)	154				
√	829		√	735		√	54	

14.13 a. continued.

Investments in Affiliates		
√	375	
(9)	38	86 (3)
		5 (10)
√	322	

Property, Plant and Equipment		
√	5,969	
(4)	931	42 (8)
(6)	221	
√	7,079	

Accumulated Depreciation		
		2,392 √
(8)	40	346 (7)
		2,698 √

Other Assets		
√	387	
(13)	78	
√	465	

Accounts Payable		
		992 √
		186 (14)
		1,178 √

Current Portion Long-Term Debt		
		221 √
(16)	221	334 (15)
		334 √

Other Current Liabilities		
		93 √
(17)	10	
		83 √

Long-Term Debt		
		1,678 √
(15)	334	890 (5)
		221 (6)
		2,455 √

Deferred Income Taxes		
		694 √
(18)	26	
		668 √

Common Stock		
		428 √
		4 (19)
		432 √

Retained Earnings		
		1,648 √
(2)	59	169 (1)
		1,758 √

Treasury Stock		
√	15	
√	15	

14.13 continued.

a. T-account work sheet for Year 11.

Cash

√	114		

Operations

(6)	353	142	(1)
(7)	34	30	(8)
(9)	32	2	(12)
(10)	159	45	(17)
(11)	164	7	(18)
(14)	136		

Investing

(7)	114	13	(3)
		315	(4)
		19	(13)

Financing

(5)	36	59	(2)
(19)	8	334	(16)
√	184		

Accounts Receivable				Inventories				Prepayments		
√	829			√	735			√	54	
		159	(10)			164	(11)	(12)	2	
√	670			√	571			√	56	

Investments in Affiliates				Property, Plant and Equipment				Accumulated Depreciation		
√	322			√	7,079				2,698	√
(3)	13	32	(9)	(4)	315	222	(7)	(7)	74	353 (6)
(8)	30									
√	333			√	7,172				2,977	√

Other Assets			Accounts Payable			Current Portion Long-Term Debt		
√	465			1,178	√		334	√
(13)	19			136	(14)	(16) 334	158	(15)
√	484			1,314	√		158	√

14.13 a. continued.

Other Current Liabilities			Long-Term Debt			Deferred Income Taxes		
	83 √			2,455 √			668 √	
(17) 45			(15) 158	36 (5)	(18) 7			
	38 √			2,333 √			661 √	

Common Stock		Retained Earnings			Treasury Stock	
	432 √		1,758 √ √		15	
	7 (19)	(1) 142				1 (19)
		(2) 59				
	439 √		1,557 √ √		14	

b.

SCOTT PAPER COMPANY
Statement of Cash Flows
(Amounts in Millions)

	Year 9	Year 10	Year 11
Operations:			
Net Income (Loss)	$ 376	$ 169	$ (142)
Depreciation Expense	306	346	353
Loss (Gain) on Sale of Property, Plant and Equipment	(221)	(19)	34
Equity in Undistributed Earnings of Affiliates	(29)	(33)	2
Increase (Decrease) in Deferred Income Taxes	87	(26)	(7)
(Increase) Decrease in Accounts Receivable	(112)	(106)	159
(Increase) Decrease in Inventories....	(59)	(154)	164
(Increase) Decrease in Prepayments	54	--	(2)
Increase (Decrease) in Accounts Payable	72	186	136
Increase (Decrease) in Other Current Liabilities	(5)	(10)	(45)
Cash Flow from Operations	$ 469	$ 353	$ 652
Investing:			
Sale of Property, Plant and Equipment	$ 5	$ 21	$ 114
Acquisition of Property, Plant and Equipment	(775)	(931)	(315)
(Increase) Decrease in Investments in Affiliates	(92)	86	(13)
(Increase) Decrease in Other Assets..	8	(78)	(19)
Cash Flow from Investing	$ (854)	$ (902)	$ (233)

14.13 b. continued.

Financing:

Issue of Long-Term Debt..................	$ 449	$ 890	$ 36
Sale of Common Stork or Treasury Stock..	--	4	8
Redemption of Long-Term Debt.........	(129)	(221)	(334)
Redemption of Common Stock Warrants...	(201)	--	--
Dividends.......................................	(59)	(59)	(59)
Cash Flow from Financing.................	$ 60	$ 614	$ (349)
Net Change in Cash	$ (325)	$ 65	$ 70
Cash, January 1...............................	374	49	114
Cash, December 31...........................	$ 49	$ 114	$ 184

Supplementary Information
During Year 10, Scott Paper Company assumed a mortgage payable of $221 million in the acquisition of property, plant and equipment.

c. The pattern of cash flows for Year 9 is typical of a growing, capital-intensive firm. Cash flow from operations exceeds net income because of the addback of depreciation expense. Book income before taxes exceeds taxable income, resulting in a deferral of taxes payable. Accounts receivable and inventories increased to support the growth, while accounts payable increased to finance the increased inventories. Scott made significant capital expenditures during the year for which it had to rely in part on external debt financing.

The pattern of cash flows for Year 10 is similar to that for Year 9, again typical of a growing firm. In this case, however, cash flow from operations declines relative to Year 9 because of reduced net income. The reduced net income occurs in part because of a smaller gain on sale of property, plant and equipment and in part because of larger depreciation and administrative expenses. Scott financed its increased capital expenditures with additional long-term borrowing.

The pattern of cash flows for Year 11 is typical of a firm that stopped growing. Sales and net income declined, the result of under-utilizing manufacturing capacity. Cash flow from operations increased, however, because Scott collected receivables and decreased its investment in inventories. It also stretched its accounts payable. Cash flow from operations was more than sufficient to finance a reduced level of capital expenditures and repay long-term dept.

 Solutions

14.14 (L.A. Gear; interpreting the statement of cash flows.)

a. The rate of increase in net income suggests that L.A. Gear grew rapidly during the three-year period. Increased investments in accounts receivable and inventories used operating cash flow. Increases in supplier credit did not fully finance the increased working capital investments, resulting in negative cash flow from operations.

b. During Year 7, L.A. Gear sold marketable securities and borrowed short term to finance the negative cash flow from operations. Accounts receivable and inventories convert into cash within one year, so short-term financing is appropriate. Selling marketable securities to help finance these working capital investments suggests that the revenue from these securities was less than the cost of additional short-term borrowing.

   During Year 8, L.A. Gear relied on short-term borrowing to finance its working capital needs, matching the term structure of its financing with the term structure of its assets.

   During Year 9, L.A. Gear issued additional common stock to finance its working capital needs. Several explanations for this switch in financing are possible. First, the proportion of debt in the capital structure may have reached a point after the borrowing in Year 8 that lenders considered the firm unduly risky, thereby raising the cost of additional borrowing. Second, L.A. Gear may have expected continuing rapid growth and wished to infuse a more permanent form of capital than short-term debt into the capital structure. Third, short-term borrowing rates might have increased significantly relative to long-term rates and L.A. Gear chose to access longer term sources of capital.

c. L.A. Gear is growing rapidly, so that new capacity additions exceed depreciation recognized on existing capacity.

d. L.A. Gear is not very capital intensive. The firm uses independent manufacturers in East Asia and markets its products through independent retailers. Thus, its property, plant and equipment serves primarily its administrative needs.

e. L.A. Gear has few fixed assets that might serve as collateral for such borrowing. The principal collateral is short-term, so lenders likely prefer to extend short-term financing.

14.15   (Campbell Soup Company; interpreting the statement of cash flows.)

a. Campbell uses suppliers and other creditors to finance its working capital needs. Consumer foods is a mature industry in the United States, so Campbell's modest growth rate does not require large incremental investments in accounts receivable and inventories.

b. (1) Capital expenditures have declined slightly each year, suggesting little need to add productive capacity.

(2) Depreciation expense is a growing percentage of acquisitions of property, plant and equipment, suggesting slower growth in manufacturing capacity.

(3) Substantial trading in marketable securities each year. Mature, profitable firms tend to accumulate cash beyond their operating needs and invest in marketable securities until they need cash.

(4) Acquisition of another business in Year 8. Firms in mature industries grow by acquiring other firms. Campbell financed this acquisition in part by selling marketable securities.

c. (1) Increases in long-term debt approximately equal repayments of long-term debt, particularly for Year 7 and Year 8. Mature firms tend to roll over debt as long as they remain in the no-growth phase.

(2) Campbell repurchased a portion of its common stock with excess cash.

(3) Dividends have grown in line with increases in net income and represent approximately a 37 percent payout rate relative to net income.

     Solutions

CHAPTER 15

SIGNIFICANCE AND IMPLICATIONS OF ALTERNATIVE ACCOUNTING PRINCIPLES

Questions, Exercises, Problems, and Cases: Answers and Solutions

15.1   See the text or the glossary at the end of the book.

15.2   This question emphasizes the dual dimensions of the standard-setting process that standard-setting bodies must reconcile. Such bodies need a conceptual foundation to guide their selection of accounting principles if the resulting financial statements are to have internal consistency and external usefulness over time. Such bodies cannot simply respond to various preparers and users on each issue addressed and hope to achieve the consistency and usefulness objectives stated above. Standard-setting bodies must recognize, however, the political nature of the standard-setting process and communicate on an on-going basis with its various constituencies. Such bodies may need to convince one or more constituencies of the desirability of a particular standard.

15.3   This question gets to the issue of uniformity versus flexibility in generally accepted accounting principles. One might argue that when the economic effects of a transaction on two firms are the same, the firms should use the same accounting method for the transaction. The firms should not have latitude to choose from among several alternative methods. On the other hand, when the economic effects of a transaction on two firms are different, the firms should have latitude to use different accounting methods. GAAP should not compel the firms to use the same method and inaccurately report the economic effects. In both cases, the economic effects should drive the *degree* of uniformity versus flexibility.

15.4   Because most firms select accounting methods for tax purposes that minimize the present value of income tax payments, this proposal would likely result in greater uniformity in financial statements. However, one might question the usefulness and meaningfulness of the resulting financial statements. The Congress sets income tax laws to accomplish certain governmental policies and not necessarily to measure accurately the economic effects of various transactions.

15-1

15.5   This question relates to the use of the cash basis versus the accrual basis of accounting. Chapter 3 discussed the deficiencies of the cash basis of accounting as a periodic measure of operating performance and the benefits of the accrual basis (more timely recognition of revenue, better matching of expenses with associated revenues). One of the "costs" of the accrual basis, however, is that it requires the allocation of revenues and expenses to periods of time. These allocations are the subject content of generally accepted accounting principles.

15.6   This statement is correct with respect to the *amount* of net income. Conservatism and profit maximizations relate to the *timing* of its recognition. Analysts use net income as a measure of the operating performance of a firm over time. The timing of income recognition affects the trend in earnings and thus the strategy a firm follows in selecting its accounting methods.

15.7   Net income over long time periods equals cash inflows minus cash outflows from operating and investing activities. Alternative accounting principles affect merely the timing of revenue and expense recognition. One accounting principle may report high revenues and expenses in early years and another accounting principle may report high revenues and expenses in later years. The first accounting principle produces higher (or lower) earnings in each of the early years as well as cumulatively during each year. At some point, the second accounting principle produces higher (or lower) earnings in each year but the first method continues to report higher (or lower) cumulative earnings until earnings under the second accounting principle catch up.

15.8   Alternative accounting methods differentially affect the statement of cash flows. Cash flow differences generally occur when two firms use different methods of accounting on their tax returns. If the methods used by two firms on their tax returns are the same but on their financial statements are different, then their balance sheets and income statements will differ. Their statements of cash flows will differ under the indirect method only with respect to the adjustments made to convert net income to cash flow from operations. They will report identical amounts of cash flow from operations, however.

15.9   There are two responses to this question:

1.   If the market reacts quickly and unbiasedly, then *someone* does the analysis. Sophisticated security analysts who trade continually in the markets likely perform the financial statement analysis.

2.   There are settings outside of the organized securities markets where financial statement analysis is beneficial. These include banks lending to business customers, governments contemplating antitrust actions, labor unions considering negotiating strategy, and so on.

15.10   (Identifying generally accepted accounting principles.)

a. FIFO cost flow assumption.

b. Allowance method.

c. Equity method.

d. Capital lease method.

e. Weighted-average cost flow assumption.

f. Effective interest method.

g. Lower-of-cost-or-market valuation basis.

h. Direct write-off method.

i. Double-declining-balance method.

j. Market value method.

k. Percentage-of-completion method.

l. Allowance method.

m. LIFO cost flow assumption.

n. Operating lease method.

o. FIFO cost flow assumption.

p. Market value method.

q. Straight line method.

r. FIFO cost flow assumption.

s. Operating lease method.

t. LIFO cost flow assumption.

u. Capital lease method.

v. LIFO cost flow assumption.

15.11   (Identifying generally accepted accounting principles.)

    a. Direct write-off method of accounting for uncollectible accounts.

    b. Market value method of accounting for either marketable securities or long-term investments in securities.

    c. Market value method for marketable securities.

    d. Equity method of accounting for long-term investments.

    e. Allowance method of accounting for uncollectible accounts.

    f. Operating method of accounting for leases by lessee.

    g. Equity method of accounting for long-term investments.

    h. Allowance method of accounting for uncollectible accounts.

    i. Lower-of-cost-or-market valuation basis for inventories. In most cases, the debit entry is made to cost of goods sold.

    j. Capital lease method of accounting for long-term leases by lessee.

15.12   (Identifying generally accepted accounting principles.)

    a. Lower-of-cost-or-market method.

    b. LIFO.

    c. FIFO.

    d. Market value method.

    e. Equity method.

    f. Sum-of-the-years' digits.

    g. Sum-of-the-years' digits. Conservatism is defined in terms of *cumulative* reported earnings rather than earnings for a single year.

    h. Capital lease method.

    i. Operating lease method.

15.13   (West Company and East Company; impact of capitalizing and amortizing versus expensing when incurred.)

a. and b. see following two pages.

c.   When R & D costs are constant each year, the largest difference in R & D expense occurs in the first year. For Year 5 and thereafter, R & D expense is the same whether the firm expenses the costs when incurred or capitalizes and then amortizes them over five years. The amount shown on the balance sheet as Deferred R &D Costs increases each year for four years when the firm uses the deferral method but stabilizes beginning in Year 5. The cumulative earnings are $200 million greater under the deferral than the immediate expense procedure as long as R & D costs remain at $100 million per year.

   When R & D costs increase each year, the effects are different. R & D expense under the immediate expensing procedure continues to be larger than under the deferral method. Likewise, the amount shown on the balance sheet each year as Deferred R & D Costs continues to increase each year. The larger is the increase in R & D costs each year, the larger will be the difference in R & D expense and deferred R & D costs between the immediate expensing and deferral methods.

15-5

15.13 continued.

(Amounts in Millions)

a.

	Year 1	2	3	4	5	6
R & D Expense						
West Company	$100	$100	$100	$100	$100	$100
East Company:						
Year 1 Costs	$ 20	$ 20	$ 20	$ 20	$ 20	$ 20
Year 2 Costs		20	20	20	20	20
Year 3 Costs			20	20	20	20
Year 4 Costs				20	20	20
Year 5 Costs					20	20
Year 6 Costs						20
Total Expense	$ 20	$ 140	$ 60	$ 80	$ 100	$ 100
Deferred R & D Costs						
West Company	$ 0	$ 0	$ 0	$ 0	$ 0	$ 0
East Company:						
Year 1 Costs	$ 80	$ 60	$ 40	$ 20	$ 20	$ 20
Year 2 Costs		80	60	40	40	40
Year 3 Costs			80	60	60	60
Year 4 Costs				80	80	80
Year 5 Costs						
Year 6 Costs						
Total Deferred Costs	$ 80	$ 140	$ 180	$ 200	$ 200	$ 200

15-6

b.

R & D Expense

			Year			
	1	2	3	4	5	6
West Company	$100	$120	$140	$160	$180	$200
East Company:						
Year 1 Costs	$ 20	$ 20	$ 20	$ 20	$ 20	
Year 2 Costs		24	24	24	24	$ 24
Year 3 Costs			28	28	28	28
Year 4 Costs				32	32	32
Year 5 Costs					36	36
Year 6 Costs						40
Total Expense.........	$ 20	$ 44	$ 72	$ 104	$ 140	$ 160

Deferred R & D Costs

			Year			
	1	2	3	4	5	6
West Company	$ 0	$ 0	$ 0	$ 0	$ 0	$ 0
East Company:						
Year 1 Costs	$ 80	$ 60	$ 40	$ 20		
Year 2 Costs		96	72	48	$ 24	
Year 3 Costs			112	84	56	$ 28
Year 4 Costs				128	96	64
Year 5 Costs					144	108
Year 6 Costs						160
Total Deferred Costs......	$ 80	$ 156	$ 224	$ 280	$ 320	$ 360

15.14 (Humble Company and Huff Company; impact of alternative accounting principles on two firms.)

a.

Comparative Income Statements
For the Year Ending December 31, Year 1

	Humble Company		Huff Company	
	Financial Statement	Tax Return	Financial Statement	Tax Return
Sales Revenue	$2,700,000	$2,700,000	$2,700,000	$2,700,000
Expenses:				
Cost of Goods Sold	$1,239,000a	$1,239,000a	$1,221,000b	$1,221,000b
Depreciation on Equipment	500,000c	293,700	275,000	293,700
Sales Promotion	375,000	375,000	93,750	375,000
Selling, General and Administrative	150,000	150,000	150,000	150,000
Expenses before Income Taxes	$2,264,000	$2,057,700	$1,739,750	$2,039,700
Net Income before Income Taxes	$ 436,000	$ 642,300	$ 960,250	$ 660,300
Income Tax Expense	130,800d		288,075d	
Net Income	$ 305,200		$ 672,175	

a[$1,641,000 – (30,000 × $8.00) + (20,000 × $8.10)] = $1,239,000.
b$1,641,000 – (50,000 × $8.40) = $1,221,000.
c10/55 × $2,750,000 = $500,000.

dComputation of Income Tax Expense

Income Taxes Payable—Current:
  Humble Company: .30 × $642,300................ $ 192,690
  Huff Company: .30 × $660,300................ $ 198,090
Credits (Debits) to Deferred Income Taxes:
  Humble Company: Dr. .30($293,700 – $500,000)................ (61,890)
  Huff Company: Cr. .30($293,700 – $275,000) + ($375,000 – $93,750)................ 89,985
Total Income Tax Expense................ $ 130,800 / $ 288,075

15.14 continued.

b.

Comparative Balance Sheet
December 31, Year 1

	Humble Company	Huff Company
Assets		
Cash	$ 639,848	$ 635,528
Accounts Receivable	1,300,000	1,300,000
Merchandise Inventory	402,000	420,000
Equipment (at Acquisition Cost)	2,750,000	2,750,000
Less Accumulated Depreciation	(500,000)	(275,000)
Deferred Sales Promotion Costs	--	281,250
Deferred Tax Asset	61,890	--
Total Assets	$4,653,738	$5,111,778
Equities		
Accounts Payable	$ 310,000	$ 310,000
Income Taxes Payable	38,538	39,618
Deferred Tax Liability	--	89,985
Common Shares	500,000	500,000
Additional Paid-in Capital	3,500,000	3,500,000
Retained Earnings	305,200	672,175
Total Equity	$4,653,738	$5,111,778

 Solutions

15.14 continued.

c.

Comparative Statement of Cash Flows
For the Year Ended December 31, Year 1

	Humble Company	Huff Company
Operations:		
Net Income	$ 305,200	$ 672,175
Depreciation Expense	500,000	275,000
Portion of Income Tax Expense Not		
Currently Payable	--	89,985
Increase in Accounts Payable	310,000	310,000
Increase in Income Tax Payable	38,538	39,618
Excess of Cash Used for Sales Promotion		
over Amount Recognized as Expense ..	--	(281,250)
Excess of Income Tax Paid over Income		
Tax Expense	(61,890)	--
Increase in Accounts Receivable	(1,300,000)	(1,300,000)
Increase in Merchandise Inventories	(402,000)	(420,000)
Cash Flow from Operations	$ (610,152)	$ (614,472)
Investing:		
Acquisition of Equipment	(2,750,000)	(2,750,000)
Financing:		
Issue of Common Stock	4,000,000	4,000,000
Net Change in Cash	$ 639,848	$ 635,528
Cash, January 1	0	0
Cash, December 31	$ 639,848	$ 635,528

d. Cash on December 31, Year 1: Humble Company .... $ 639,848
Additional Income Taxes Currently Payable by Huff
Company: $198,090 − $192,690 .... (5,400)
Portion of Additional Income Taxes Not Yet Paid:
$39,618 − $38,538 1,080
Cash on December 31, Year 1: Huff Company .... $ 635,528

15.15 - (Brown Corporation; impact of two sets of alternative accounting principles on net income and cash flows.)

a.

BROWN CORPORATION
Income Statements Under Alternative Principles
For the Year Ending December 31, Year 1

	Set A Financial Statement	Set A Tax Return	Set B Financial Statement	Set B Tax Return
Sales Revenue	$ 504,000	$ 504,000	$ 504,000	$ 504,000
Expenses:				
Cost of Goods Sold	$ 335,250 [1]	$ 335,250 [1]	$ 315,750 [2]	$ 315,750 [2]
Depreciation on Equipment	22,500 [3]	16,073	11,250 [4]	16,073
Training	37,500	37,500	7,500	37,500
Selling, General and Administrative	60,000	60,000	60,000	60,000
Goodwill	3,750	--	1,250	--
Expenses before Income Taxes	$ 459,000	$ 448,823	$ 395,750	$ 429,323
Net Income before Income Taxes	$ 45,000	$ 55,177	$ 108,250	$ 74,677
Income Tax Expense—Current	16,553 [5]		22,403 [7]	
Income Tax Expense—Deferred	(1,928) [6]		10,447 [8]	
Net Income	$ 30,375		$ 75,400	

[1] (37,500 × $2.40) + (15,000 × $2.20) + (22,500 × $2.10) + (82,500 × $2.00) = $335,250.

[2] (150,000 × $2.00) + (7,500 × $2.10) = $315,750.

[3] .20 × $112,500 = $22,500.

[4] $112,500/10 = $11,250.

[5] .30 × $55,177 = $16,553.

[6] .30 × ($16,073 − $22,500) = −$1,928.

[7] .30 × $74,677 = $22,403.

[8] .30($16,073 − $11,250) + .30($37,500 − $7,500) = $1,447 + $9,000 = $10,447.

Solutions

15.15 continued.

b.
BROWN CORPORATION
Cash Flow from Operations
For Year 1

	Set A	Set B
Net Income..	$ 30,375	$ 75,400
Additions:		
Depreciation Expense	22,500	11,250
Goodwill Amortization	3,750	1,250
Excess of Income Tax Expense over		
Amount Currently Payable..............	--	10,447
Increase in Accounts Payable...............	30,200	30,200
Increase in Income Taxes Payable........	4,138	5,601
Subtractions:		
Excess of Cash Used for Training over		
Amount Reported as an Expense.......	--	(30,000)
Excess of Income Taxes Currently Pay-		
able over Income Tax Expense	(1,928)	--
Increase in Accounts Receivable...........	(120,000)	(120,000)
Increase in Merchandise Inventories....	(135,000)	(154,500)
Cash Used for Operations........................	$ (165,965)	$ (170,352)

c. Cash Flow from Operations, Set A.................................... $(165,965)

Additional Income Taxes Currently Payable Under Set
  B: $22,403 – $16,553 .... (5,850)

Portion of Additional Income Taxes Not Yet Paid:
  $5,601 – $4,138.. 1,463

Cash Flow from Operations, Set B .... $(170,352)

15.16 (Chicago Corporation; comprehensive review problem.)

a. Balance, January 1, Year 2.. $100,000

Provision for Year 2 120,000

Less Balance, December 31, Year 2............................ (160,000)

Write-offs during Year 2.. $ 60,000

b.

	LIFO	FIFO
Beginning Inventory	$ 1,500,000	$ 1,800,000
Purchases...	5,300,000	5,300,000
Available for Sale	$ 6,800,000	$ 7,100,000
Less Ending Inventory..........................	(1,800,000)	(1,700,000)
Cost of Goods Sold	$ 5,000,000	$ 5,400,000
Net Sales...	$13,920,000	$13,920,000
Less Cost of Goods Sold	(5,000,000)	(5,400,000)
Gross Profit...	$ 8,920,000	$ 8,520,000

15.16 continued.

c. The quantity of inventory increased because the LIFO ending inventory is larger than the LIFO beginning inventory. The prices of the inventory items decreased because the FIFO ending inventory is less than the FIFO beginning inventory despite an increase in quantity during the year.

d. None of the companies declared dividends during Year 2 because the changes (increases) in the investment accounts equal the amounts recognized as Chicago Corporation's equity in the earnings of these companies.

e.
Investment in Chicago Finance Corporation....	1,800,000	
Investment in Rosenwald Company................	125,000	
Investment in Hutchinson Company..............	75,000	
Equity in Earnings of Chicago Finance Corporation		1,800,000
Equity in Earnings of Rosenwald Company		125,000
Equity in Earnings of Hutchinson Company		75,000

f. Year 1: $4,000,000 \times 2/40 = \$200,000$.
Year 2: $(\$4,000,000 - \$200,000) \times 2/40 = \$190,000$.

g.
Cash...	400,000	
Accumulated Depreciation...........................	800,000	
Machinery and Equipment.......................		1,000,000
Gain on Sale of Machinery and Equipment..		200,000

h.
Interest Expense..	288,000	
Bonds Payable (= $3,648,000 – $3,600,000)		48,000
Cash (= .06 × $4,000,000)		240,000

i. Effective interest rate × $3,600,000 = $288,000. The effective interest rate = 8 percent. Chicago Corporation issued these bonds for less than their face value because the coupon rate of 6 percent is less than the market interest rate at the time of issue of 8 percent.

j. Difference between book and taxable depreciation = $150,000/.30 = $500,000.

Because the Deferred Tax Liability account increased, tax depreciation must be $500,000 larger than depreciation for financial reporting.

15.16 continued.

k. Cash... 1,000,000
    Treasury Shares...   400,000
    Additional Paid-in Capital.........................   600,000

l. Acquisition Cost.. $1,250,000
  Less Book Value..   (750,000)
  Accumulated Amortization.. $ 500,000

Because the patent is being amortized at the rate of $125,000 per year, the patent was acquired four years before the balance sheet date (= $500,000/$125,000).

m. If Chicago Corporation owns less than 20 percent of the common stock of Hutchinson Company, it must use the market-value method. Chicago Corporation would show the Investment in Hutchinson account at its market value of $200,000 (= $175,000 + $25,000) and show a $25,000 amount in the Unrealized Holding Gain on Investment in Securities account in the shareholders' equity section of the balance sheet. Hutchinson Company did not declare dividends during the year. Thus, net income of Chicago Corporation would decrease by the $75,000 equity in Hutchinson Company's earnings during Year 2 recognized under the equity method. Consolidated retained earnings would, therefore, be $75,000 less than as now stated. In the statement of cash flows, there would be $75,000 smaller net income and no subtraction of $75,000 for the equity in earnings of Hutchinson Company.

n. Capitalized Lease Obligation 80,000
  Interest Expense.. 90,000
    Cash...   170,000

Amortization of Leased Property Rights........... 150,000
    Accumulated Amortization.......................   150,000
Total expense would be $240,000 (= $90,000 + $150,000).

o. The income statement would show a $200,000 loss from the price decline, and retained earnings would be $200,000 less than as shown. The Inventories account would be shown at $1,600,000 instead of $1,800,000. There would be an addback for the loss on the statement of cash flows because the loss did not use cash.

15.16 continued.

p. Basic earnings per share $= \dfrac{\$4,400,000 - \$120,000}{1,600,000} = \$2.675$.

Fully diluted earnings per share $= \dfrac{\$4,400,000}{1,600,000 + ?} = \$2.20$.

The number of common shares that would be issued is 400,000.

q.

	Cash		
√	200,000		

	Operations		
(1)	4,000,000	100,000	(3)
(11)	1,000,000	300,000	(4)
(12)	125,000	1,800,000	(5)
(13)	75,000	125,000	(6)
(14)	150,000	75,000	(7)
(16)	60,000	200,000	(9)
(17)	130,000	20,000	(15)
(18)	50,000		
(19)	260,000		
(20)	48,000		
(23)	170,000		

	Investing		
(9)	400,000	100,000	(8)
		1,700,000	(10)

	Financing		
(24)	1,000,000	2,200,000	(2)
		968,000	(21)
		80,000	(22)
√	400,000		

	Accounts Receivable	
√	500,000	
(3)	100,000	
√	600,000	

	Merchandise Inventory	
√	1,500,000	
(4)	300,000	
√	1,800,000	

15-15

15.16 q. continued.

Prepayments

√	200,000	
√	200,000	

Investment in Chicago Finance Corp.

√	2,200,000	
(5)	1,800,000	
√	4,000,000	

Investment in Rosenwald Corp.

√	900,000	
(6)	125,000	
√	1,025,000	

Investment in Hutchinson Corp.

√	100,000	
(2)	75,000	
√	175,000	

Land

√	400,000	
(8)	100,000	
√	500,000	

Building

√	4,000,000	
√	4,000,000	

Machinery and Equipment

√	7,300,000		
(10)	1,700,000	1,000,000	(9)
√	8,000,000		

Property Rights Under Lease

√	1,500,000	
√	1,500,000	

Accumulated Depreciation

		3,800,000	√
(9)	800,000	1,000,000	(11)
		4,000,000	√

Patent

√	875,000		
(2)		125,000	(12)
√	750,000		

Goodwill

√	1,125,000		
		75,000	(13)
√	1,050,000		

Accounts Payable

		400,000	√
		150,000	(14)
		550,000	√

Accrued Liabilities

		660,000	√
(15)	20,000		
		640,000	√

Salaries Payable

		240,000	√
		60,000	(16)
		300,000	√

15.16 q. continued.

Income Taxes Payable		
	300,000	√
	130,000	(17)
	430,000	√

Rent Received in Advance		
	0	√
	50,000	(18)
	50,000	√

Other Current Liabilities		
	200,000	√
	260,000	(19)
	460,000	√

Bonds Payable		
	3,600,000	√
	48,000	(20))
	3,648,000	√

Equipment Mortgage Payable

		1,300,000	√
(21)	968,000		
		332,000	√

Capitalized Lease Obligation

		1,100,000	√
(22)	80,000		
		1,020,000	√

Deferred Tax Liability		
	1,400,000	√
	170,000	(23)
	1,570,000	√

Convertible Preferred Stock		
	2,000,000	√
	2,000,000	√

Common Stock		
	2,000,000	√
	2,000,000	√

Additional Paid-in Capital		
	2,400,000	√
	600,000	(24)
	3,000,000	√

Retained Earnings

		2,800,000	√
(2)	2,200,000	4,400,000	(1)
		5,000,000	√

Treasury Stock

√	1,400,000		
		400,000	(24)
√	1,000,000		

r. The total shareholders' equity of Chicago Corporation is not an accurate measure of the value or worth of the firm for the following reasons.

(1) The balance sheet does not include such resources of the firm as superior managerial expertise, a well-trained labor force, or goodwill.

15.16 r. continued.

(2) The balance sheet shows assets at acquisition cost (net of accumulated depreciation or amortization in some instances). These amounts will likely differ from the current replacement costs or net realizable value of these assets.

(3) The total liabilities of Chicago Corporation do not include uncapitalized long-term operating leases. The liabilities do include Deferred Tax Liability. However, if the firm continues to grow, it is questionable whether Chicago Corporation will have to pay these taxes.

(4) Chicago Corporation reports the long-term debt at the present value of the future cash flows discounted at the market rate on the date of issue. The current market values of these obligations may differ significantly from their book values.

s.(1) *For Narrowing:*

(1) Lead to better interfirm and interperiod comparisons of financial statement data.

(2) Make financial statements easier to understand, because the reader will not need to be familiar with as many accounting methods.

(3) Reduces opportunities for management to manipulate earnings by selecting or changing accounting principles.

s.(2) *For Continuing Present System:*

(1) Management should have the flexibility to select the methods which most fairly reflect the firm's financial position and results of operations. A narrowing of acceptable methods may result in some firms showing less fairly their financial position and results of operations.

(2) Investors may see through the effects of using different accounting methods, as suggested by efficient markets theory and as supported by empirical research, which suggests additional disclosures rather than greater uniformity.

(3) Because the specification of accounting principles is a political process, standard-setting bodies would probably encounter difficulties obtaining consensus on which currently acceptable methods to eliminate.

15.17 (Tuck Corporation; comprehensive review problem.)

a.
Balance in Marketable Equity Securities on December 31, Year 1	$ 125,000
Less Cost of Marketable Equity Securities Sold	(35,000)
Plus Decrease in Unrealized Holding Loss on Marketable Securities	4,000
Plus Cost of Marketable Equity Securities Purchased	?
Balance in Marketable Equity Securities on December 31, Year 2	$ 141,000

The cost of marketable equity securities purchased is $47,000.

b.
Cost of Marketable Equity Securities Sold	$ 35,000
Less Loss on Sale of Marketable Equity Securities	(8,000)
Sales Proceeds	$ 27,000

c.
Balance in Allowance Account on December 31, Year 1	$ 128,800
Plus Provision for Estimated Uncollectible Accounts	144,600
Less Write-offs of Specific Customers' Accounts	(63,000)
Balance in Allowance Account on December 31, Year 2	$ 210,400

The provision for estimated uncollectibles is $144,600.

d.
	LIFO	Difference	FIFO
Beginning Inventory	$1,257,261	$ 430,000	$1,687,261
Purchases	2,848,054	--	2,848,054
Available	$4,105,315	$ 430,000	$4,535,315
Less Ending Inventory	(1,525,315)	(410,000)	(1,935,315)
Cost of Goods Sold	$2,580,000	$ 20,000	$2,600,000

e.
Unrealized Holding Loss on Investments in Securities (SE)	5,000	
Investments in Securities		5,000

To recognize unrealized holding loss on investments in securities.

f. Dividend revenue of $8,000. The unrealized loss of $5,000 (see Part *e.*) is not included in the calculation of net income for Year 2.

15.17 continued.

g. Investment in Davis Corporation................... 87,000

     Equity in Earnings of Unconsolidated
          Affiliates..................................... 87,000

To recognize share of Davis Corporation's
earnings in Year 2; .40 × $217,500 = $87,000.

Cash.. 24,000

     Investment in Davis Corporation.............. 24,000

To recognize dividend received from Davis
Corporation; .40 × $60,000 = $24,000.

Investment in Davis Corporation................... 20,000

     Cash... 20,000

To record additional investment in Davis
Corporation.

h. Cash.. 7,000
   Accumulated Depreciation.......................... 19,000

     Equipment.. 23,000
     Gain on Sale of Equipment........................ 3,000

i. Balance in Rental Fees Received in Advance on December 31, Year 1...................................... $ 46,000

   Plus Cash Received for Rentals During Year 2.............. ?

   Less Rental Fees Earned During Year 2....................... (240,000)

   Balance in Rental Fees Received in Advance on December 31, Year 2...................................... $ 58,000

Cash received during Year 2 totaled $252,000.

j. Balance in Estimated Warranty Liability on December 31, Year 1...................................... $ 75,200

   Plus Estimated Warranty Cost Provision for Year 2........ 46,800

   Less Cost of Actual Warranty Services........................ (?)

   Balance in Estimated Warranty Liability on December 31, Year 2...................................... $ 78,600

Warranty costs incurred during Year 2 totaled $43,400.

k. First 6 Months: .025 × $1,104,650.00......................... $ 27,616.25

   Second 6 Months: .025 × $1,102,266.25[a] 27,556.66

   Total Interest Expense...................................... $ 55,172.91

[a]$1,104,650.00 – ($30,000.00 – $27,616.25) = $1,102,266.25.

continued.

l. Interest Expense... 20,996
    Mortgage Payable.. 19,004
        Cash..   40,000
    To record mortgage interest and principal pay-
    ment; $20,996 = .07 × $299,947.

m. Present Value of Payment on January 1, Year 3............. $ 10,000
    Present Value of Remaining Lease Payments ($10,000 ×
        5.20637)..   52,064
            Total... $ 62,064

n. Capitalized Lease Obligation, December 31, Year 1........... $ 62,064
    Lease Payment on January 1, Year 3 ....   (10,000)
    Interest Expense for Year 2 (.08 × $52,064).......................   4,165
        Total.. $ 56,229

o. $$\frac{\text{Deferred Tax Expense Relating to Depreciation}}{\text{Income Tax Rate}} = \frac{\$12,000}{.30} = \$40,000.$$

p. Convertible Preferred Stock (5,000 × $100).........   500,000
        Common Stock (25,000 × $10)......................   250,000
        Additional Paid-in Capital........................   250,000
    To record conversion of preferred into common
    stock.

q. Treasury Stock..   8,800
        Cash...   8,800
    To record purchases of treasury stock.

    Cash...   25,200
        Treasury Stock......................................   21,600a
        Additional Paid-in Capital..........................   3,600b
    To record the sale of treasury stock.

    a1,800 shares × $12 = $21,600.

    bAdditional Paid-in Capital on December 31, Year 1....... $ 130,000
        Plus Amount Arising from Conversion of Preferred
            Stock   250,000
        Plus Amount Arising from Issue of Common Stock......   200,000
        Plus Amount Arising from Sale of Treasury Stock........   ?
        Additional Paid-in Capital on December 31, Year 2....... $ 583,600

    The additional paid-in capital arising from the treasury stock
    sales is $3,600.

                        Solutions

15.17 continued.

r.

Cash

√ 240,000

Operations

(1)	300,000	87,000	(7)
(3)	8,000	15,000	(10)
(8)	24,000	3,000	(11)
(13)	56,000	4,827	(15)
(14)	2,000	78,400	(25)
(17)	2,911	268,054	(26)
(20)	15,000	4,000	(27)
(29)	57,600		
(30)	12,000		
(31)	3,400		
(32)	500		
(34)	20,000		

Investing

(3)	27,000	47,000	(5)
(11)	7,000	20,000	(9)
		1,373,600	(12)

Financing

(16)	828,409	119,500	(2)
(22)	600,000	19,004	(18)
(23)	25,200	5,835	(19)
(28)	100,000	8,800	(24)
(33)	5,000		
√	280,000		

Marketable Securities—Net				Accounts Receivable—Net		
√	125,000			√	1,431,200	
		35,000	(3)	(25)	78,400	
(4)	4,000					
(5)	47,000					
√	141,000			√	1,509,600	

15-17 r. continued.

Inventories			Prepayments		
√	1,257,261		√	28,000	
(26)	268,054		(27)	4,000	
√	1,525,315		√	32,000	

Investment in Thayer—Net			Investment in Hitchcock		
√	92,000		√	120,000	
		5,000 (6)	(10)	15,000	
√	87,000		√	135,000	

Investment in Davis			Land		
√	215,000		√	82,000	
(7)	87,000				
(9)	20,000	24,000 (8)			
√	298,000		√	82,000	

Building			Equipment		
√	843,000		√	497,818	
			(12)	1,373,600	23,000 (11)
√	843,000		√	1,848,418	

Leasehold			Accumulated Depreciation and Amortization		
√	98,182				376,000 √
			(11)	19,000	56,000 (13)
√	98,182				413,000 √

Goodwill—Net			Notes Payable		
√	36,000				100,000 √
		2,000 (14)			100,000 (28)
√	34,000				200,000 √

Accounts Payable			Rental Fees Received in Advance		
		666,100 √			46,000 √
		57,600 (29)			12,000 (30)
		723,700 √			58,000 √

15.17 r. continued.

Estimated Warranty Liability		
	75,200	√
	3,400	(31)
	78,600	√

Interest Payable on Notes		
	1,500	√
	500	(32)
	2,000	√

Dividends Payable		
	25,000	√
	5,000	(33)
	30,000	√

Income Taxes Payable—Current		
	140,000	√
	20,000	(34)
	160,000	√

Bonds Payable				
		1,104,650		√
(15)	4,827	828,409	(16)
		2,911	(17)
		1,931,143		√

Mortgage Payable				
		299,947		√
(18)	19,004		
		280,943		√

Capitalized Lease Obligation				
		62,064		√
(19)	5,835		
		56,229		√

Deferred Tax Liability		
	130,000	√
	15,000	(20)
	145,000	√

Convertible Preferred Stock				
		700,000		√
(21)	500,000		
		200,000		√

Common Stock		
	1,000,000	√
	250,000	(21)
	400,000	(22)
	1,650,000	√

Additional Paid-in Capital		
	130,000	√
	250,000	(21)
	200,000	(22)
	3,600	(23)
	583,600	√

Unrealized Holding Loss on Marketable Securities			
√	25,000		
		4,000	(4)
√	21,000		

15.17 r. continued.

Unrealized Holding Loss on Investment in Securities		
√	16,000	
(6)	5,000	
√	21,000	

Retained Earnings			
		277,000	√
(2)	119,500	300,000	(1)
		457,500	√

Treasury Stock			
√	27,000		
(24)	8,800	21,600	(23)
√	14,200		

References to T-Account Entries

(1) Net Income.
(2) Dividends declared by Tuck Corporation.
(3) Sale of marketable securities.
(4) Recovery of unrealized holding loss on marketable securities.
(5) Purchase of marketable securities.
(6) Write down of investment in Thayer Corporation to market value.
(7) Tuck's share of Davis Corporation's earnings.
(8) Tuck's share of Davis Corporation's dividends.
(9) Additional investment in Davis Corporation.
(10) Tuck's share of Hitchcock's earnings ($102,000 – $87,000).
(11) Sale of equipment at a gain.
(12) Acquisition of equipment.
(13) Depreciation expenses.
(14) Amortization of goodwill.
(15) Interest on 6-percent bonds.
(16) Issue of 8-percent bonds.
(17) Interest on 8-percent bonds.
(18) Payment of principal on mortgage.
(19) Payment of principal on lease obligation ($10,000 – $4,165).
(20) Deferred tax liability.
(21) Conversion of preferred stock.
(22) Issue of common stock.
(23) Sale of treasury stock.
(24) Purchase of treasury stock.
(25) Increase in accounts receivable.
(26) Increase in inventories.
(27) Increase in prepayments.
(28) Increase in notes payable.
(29) Increase in accounts payable.
(30) Increase in rental fees received in advance.
(31) Increase in estimated warranty liability.
(32) Increase in interest payable.
(33) Increase in dividends payable.
(34) Increase in income taxes payable—current.

15-25

15.18   (Champion Clothiers, Inc.; selecting accounting methods.)

The objectives of the case are as follows:

1. To illustrate the impact of alternative accounting methods on the financial statements.

2. To illustrate the wide array of avenues open to a firm to manage reported earnings.

3. To consider the arguments for and against managing earnings.

Techniques for Managing Earnings

The techniques for managing earnings fall into three categories: (1) selection of accounting methods (LIFO versus FIFO, accelerated versus straight-line depreciation, purchase versus pooling of interests), (2) application of accounting methods (nature of LIFO pools, depreciable lives of plant assets, amortization period on pension obligation), and (3) timing of asset acquisitions and dispositions (maintenance and advertising, sale of marketable securities and land).

LIFO versus FIFO. Remaining on LIFO is probably the best choice here because of the potential tax savings. Most firms now use LIFO for financial reporting as well, so that lack of comparability with one's competitors is not an issue. As discussed later, a number of research studies have shown that investors look through the accounting numbers to the underlying economics of accounting choices. Evidence indicates that the stock market penalizes firms that select FIFO in order to report higher earnings (at the expense of paying more taxes). There are sufficient disclosures in the annual report to convert a LIFO firm to a FIFO basis if an analyst feels it is a more appropriate cost flow assumption. Thus, a firm can realize the tax benefits of LIFO and disclose sufficient information so that the analyst can compute FIFO earnings.

Nature of LIFO Pools. It is obvious that broader pools are preferable for tax purposes in order to minimize the probability of dipping into an old, lower priced layer. The consistency requirement between tax and financial reporting for LIFO dictates remaining with broader pools for financial reporting as well. If a firm practices earnings management, it is preferable to use avenues that do not have negative economic consequences.

15.18 continued.

Depreciable Lives and Depreciation Method. Unlike LIFO, there is no consistency requirement between tax and financial reporting with respect to depreciation. Thus, a firm must choose on other grounds. A firm might use economic reality as the criterion. On this basis, the depreciable life would be the economic life of the assets. The depreciation method selected would be one that mirrored the economic decline in the usefulness of the assets. Unfortunately, the firm cannot observe or predict either of these items very accurately. The choice comes down to whether the firm wishes to portray a conservative or a nonconservative image to investors. The vast majority of publicly-held firms take the nonconservative position and write off depreciable assets over their estimated economic lives using the straight-line method. This is the position we would take.

Purchases versus Pooling of Interests. The position we would take here is that the accounting method used should not drive the economics of the transaction or the way the firm structures it. However, if the economics are the same regardless of whether the firm uses purchase or pooling, we opt for pooling because of its positive earnings effects. Without additional information, it is difficult to judge all of the important economic effects in this case. If the firm issues 40 percent of the stock to the public and 10 percent to the shareholders of Green Trucking, the Champion family will have a 50 percent interest in the firm. This should be sufficient to maintain effective control. It is not clear whether the company already has sufficient cash to structure the deal as a cash/purchase method transaction or whether the Champion family will have to inject more cash. Also, the treatment of the transaction for tax purposes is unclear. If one can make the heroic assumption that the economics are the same, we would opt for pooling in this case.

Amortization Period for Pension Obligation. There is no necessity that the firm fund the prior service obligation over the same period that it amortizes it to expense. Assuming that the economics (funding) will not change, we would opt for the longer amortization period to increase earnings.

Delay of Maintenance Expenditures. The firm can take this action to improve earnings in the short run, but it catches up later. Delaying the expenditure until 1998 will depress 1998 earnings. Delaying the maintenance indefinitely could affect the operational efficiency of the assets involved. We would tend not to use this avenue if other options were available to obtain the desired earnings per share.

 Solutions

15.18 continued.

> *Delay of Advertising Expenditures.* The desired timing of the advertising campaign should be the deciding factor here. Because the post-Christmas timing seems set, we would not argue for delaying it. We might approach the firm's auditor about the possibility of capitalizing the advertising expenditure in 1997 and writing it off as an expense in 1998, the year of expected benefit. Auditors are reluctant to do this on intangibles such as advertising, but it is worth a try. The problem with this, however, is that this treatment of the expenditure negatively affects 1998 earnings..

> *Sale of Marketable Securities.* The securities were probably purchased as a temporary investment of excess cash. If the firm could invest the sales proceeds in another investment alternative with equivalent returns and risk after considering transaction costs, we might use this avenue for propping up earnings for 1997. However, if the firm held the marketable securities for longer term purposes and viewed them as a desirable long-term investment, we would not likely sell them.

> *Sale of Land.* As long as the firm still viewed the parcels as attractive locations for future stores, we would not sell them at this time.

The president of Champion is concerned with the *trend* in earnings per share. Several of the choices require retroactive restatements of prior years' earnings per share (LIFO versus FIFO, accelerated versus straight-line depreciation, purchase versus pooling of interests). These restatements affect the trend line of the desired level of earnings per share for 1997.

Assuming that the firm changes its depreciable life, depreciation method, corporate acquisition method, and pension obligation amortization period, earnings per share for 1994 through 1997 would be as follows:

	1994	1995	1996	1997
As Reported or Expected	$ 1.20	$ 1.38	$ 1.60	$ 1.65
Depreciable Lives	--	--	--	+ .04
Depreciation Method	+ .05	+ .06	+ .07	+ .08
Corporate Acquisition Period	+ .02	+ .04	+ .06	+ .10
Pension Amortization Period	--	--	--	+ .05
Revised	$ 1.27	$ 1.48	$ 1.73	$ 1.92

15.18 continued.

Earnings per share increased approximately 16 percent per year between 1994 and 1997. Maintaining this growth rate requires 1994 earnings per share to be approximately $2.02. We would be inclined to get some of the additional ten cents per share needed from the sale of marketable securities as long as there were no negative economic consequences of doing so. We would probably stop at this point and report earnings per share of $1.92. Using other avenues would probably have negative economic consequences.

Arguments For and Against Managing Earnings

The arguments for and against managing earnings vary both as to their underlying logic and to the evidence that is brought to bear in support of the position. The section presents the arguments in as unbiased a manner as possible so that readers can make up their own minds.

Capital Market Efficiency. The major argument against managing earnings is that capital markets are efficient, in the sense that market prices adjust quickly and *in an unbiased manner* to publicly-available information, and that earnings management is therefore a waste of valuable managerial time. An expanding number of theoretical and empirical studies have provided support for the efficiency of capital markets. For example, several studies have examined the effects of changes in accounting methods on stock prices. Researchers have shown that changes in accounting methods that have no real or economic effects (that is, those that do not affect cash flows) have little affect on stock prices. Using information from the financial statements and notes, the stock market at the aggregate level distinguishes changes with real effects from those that do not have real effects and reacts accordingly.

Proponents of earnings management acknowledge this recent work but counter with three observations. First, all of the empirical work on market efficiency has looked at the aggregate market (for example, all stocks traded on the New York Stock Exchange). There are numerous examples of cases where the market priced the securities of particular firms at a particular point in time inefficiently. Proponents of this view point to examples where the market prices of particular firms' shares decreased dramatically after the effects of using specific accounting procedures were carefully analyzed and reported in the financial press.

 Solutions

15.18 continued.

Second, the empirical work on market efficiency has focused for the most part on publicly-available information. There is little or no evidence to suggest that the market is able to access "inside" or nonpublic information. Information about the effects of changes in accounting methods is available in the financial statements and notes and has been studied empirically. However, information about management's efforts to manage the timing of asset acquisitions or dispositions is usually not disclosed separately and consequently has not been adequately studied.

Third, proponents of earnings management note that most of the empirical work on capital market efficiency has focused on equity securities traded on the New York Stock Exchange. Researchers have not tested adequately the efficiency of other capital markets (for example, the over-the-counter-market as well as short-term credit and long-term debt markets).

Proponents of earnings management would conclude that capital markets are not necessarily perfectly efficient in all cases. If by managing earnings the firm can take advantage of these inefficiencies and obtain capital at a lower cost than if earnings management were not practiced, then the shareholders of the firm are better off.

Opponents of earnings management might accept the notion that some degree of inefficiency exists in capital markets. They would then argue, though, that capital resources get allocated in a less than socially-optimal way if, because of earnings management, certain firms receive more resources than would otherwise be the case.

Management Incentives and Survival. Because over long enough time periods net income equals cash inflows minus cash outflows from operating and investing activities, some corporate managers acknowledge that earnings management is not particularly beneficial in the long run. They point out, however, that the long run is made up of a series of short-run periods in which shareholders' make decisions to retain or to fire management. Shareholders, they would argue, do not want to see wide, unexpected fluctuations in earnings from year to year. Earnings management is necessary to smooth out these fluctuations and create the impression that management has operations under control. Corporate managers also observe that all firms practice earnings management and that management's survival dictates that they do so to maintain the firm's position relative to other firms. They further point out that researchers have not yet provided sufficient and convincing evidence for not managing earnings. Opponents of earnings management, primarily academic researchers, point to an expanding number of studies that call into question the perceived benefits of earnings management. Whether the two viewpoints are ultimately reconcilable depends on the results of continuing research on the relation between accounting numbers and stock prices.

CHAPTER 16

INTERNATIONAL FINANCIAL REPORTING

Questions, Exercises, Problems, and Cases: Answers and Solutions

16.1   See the text or the glossary at the end of the book.

16.2   a. Foreign operations self-contained within a particular foreign country need not make foreign currency conversions on an ongoing basis. The only conversion required is the remission of dividends or other distributions to the U.S. parent company. The base for such distributions is total shareholders' equity (or net assets). Exchange rate changes affect the U.S. dollar-equivalent amount of funds the foreign entity might remit to the U.S. parent as either a dividend or a return of its original capital investment.

b. Foreign operations viewed as integrated extensions of the U.S. parent company require currency conversions on an ongoing basis to settle accounts receivable, accounts payable, bonds payable, and similar monetary items. Exchange rate changes affect the U.S. dollar-equivalent amounts of these items. The presence of these items on the parent's books gives rise to exchange rate adjustments. The presence of these items on the books of the foreign entity should also give rise to exchange rate adjustments when the foreign unit is an integrated extension of the U.S. parent company.

16.3   The U.S. parent company uses the all-current translation method for operations self-contained within a particular foreign country. The parent company does not expect regular dividends from such foreign entities. The foreign unit realizes an exchange gain or loss only when it makes a currency conversion at some time in the future to remit dividends or other distributions to the U.S. parent. The extensive delay of such a distribution for self-contained operations suggests that any unrealized, or potential, exchange gain or loss not affect net income each period but accumulate in a separate shareholders' equity account until such distributions occur.

The U.S. parent uses the monetary-nonmonetary translation method for foreign operations closely integrated with the U.S. parent company. Such operations require ongoing currency conversions to settle receivables and payables. Because the U.S. parent recognizes exchange gains and losses arising from such currency conversions in computing net income from its activities, similar recognition is appropriate for operations viewed as integrated extensions of the U.S. parent.

16.4 An increase in the value of the foreign currency relative to the U.S. dollar results in a credit change in the foreign exchange adjustment account. The U.S. parent company is better off from having invested funds in a foreign currency whose value increased relative to the U.S. dollar than from leaving the funds in its U.S. bank account. A decrease in the value of the foreign currency relative to the U.S. dollar results in a debit change in the foreign exchange adjustment account. The U.S. parent is worse off from having invested funds in a foreign unit whose currency decreased in value than if it had left the funds in its U.S. bank account.

16.5 A foreign exchange gain arises when (1) the foreign entity is in a net monetary asset position and the foreign currency increases in value, or (2) the foreign entity is in a net monetary liability position and the foreign currency decreases in value, relative to the U.S. dollar. The gain occurs in the first case because the net monetary asset position converts into more U.S. dollars after the exchange rate change than before the change. The gain occurs in the second case because the net monetary liability position requires fewer U.S. dollars to settle the net obligation after the exchange rate change than before the change.

A foreign exchange loss arises when (1) the foreign entity is in a net monetary asset position and the foreign currency decreases in value, or (2) the foreign entity is in a net monetary liability position and the foreign currency increases in value, relative to the U.S. dollar. The loss occurs in the first case because the net monetary asset position converts into fewer U.S. dollars as a result of the exchange rate change. The loss occurs in the second case because the net monetary liability position requires more U.S. dollars to settle the obligation than before the exchange rate change.

16.6 a. This statement is not correct. Cost of goods sold and depreciation expense translate using the current exchange rate under the all-current method and at the historical exchange rate under the monetary-nonmonetary method. Furthermore, the exchange adjustment under the all-current method uses net assets (= assets minus liabilities = shareholders' equity) as the base, whereas the monetary-nonmonetary method uses the net monetary position as the base. The amount and perhaps even the direction of the adjustment will differ under the two translation method.

b. This statement is incorrect for reasons similar to those in Part *a.* above. The all-current method translates nonmonetary assets and liabilities using the current exchange rate, whereas the monetary-nonmonetary method translates them using the historical exchange rate. Furthermore, the cumulative foreign exchange adjustment under the all-current method will differ from the cumulative foreign exchange gain or loss under the monetary-nonmonetary method because the two translation methods use a different base for computing the exchange adjustment.

16.7   The all-current translation method uses the net assets position (= assets minus liabilities) as the basis when computing the foreign exchange adjustment, whereas the monetary-nonmonetary translation method uses the net monetary asset or net monetary liability position. The foreign unit was probably in a net asset position overall (assets exceeded liabilities) but a net monetary liability position (monetary liabilities exceeded monetary assets) with respect to monetary items. A decrease in the value of the foreign currency relative to the U.S. dollar under these circumstances results in a debit change in the foreign exchange adjustment account under the all-current translation method and a foreign exchange gain under the monetary-nonmonetary translation method.

16.8   The central issue is not which body should set accounting principles but whether the standard-setting body sets accounting principles with a view toward the relevance and reliability of financial statement information versus some other objective, such as raising tax revenues. One might argue that investors' information needs will likely play a more significant role in actions by standard-setting bodies in the private sector than in the public sector, but this is not a necessary result. The public sector sets acceptable accounting standards in Japan yet its accounting principles look increasingly similar to those set in the private sector in the U.S., the U.K., and Canada.

16.9   Achieving uniformity in accounting principles provides similar measurement methods but not necessarily comparable financial statement information. Economic, institutional, and cultural differences exist between countries. Forcing all firms to use the same accounting method for a particular transaction may obscure these differences and detract from the usefulness of the information.

16.10   Achieving uniformity in accounting principles could occur without full delegation of authority and responsibility if each country implemented accounting principles enunciated by an international standard-setting body. The IASC now follows this approach. Individual countries pledge their best efforts in gaining acceptance of IASC pronouncements within their countries. The current arrangement has not yet led to uniform accounting principles because individual countries have not always concurred with IASC standards. Whether full delegation of authority and responsibility to the IASC or some other body is necessary to achieve uniformity remains an open question.

16.11   Requiring foreign firms to follow U.S. accounting principles in their financial statements filed with the SEC probably reduces information processing costs for investors in U.S. markets because the financial statements are similar to those of U.S. firms. This requirement also guards against the use of accounting principles that are widely at variance with U.S. standards. The arrangement could work well for registrants from particular countries if the SEC concluded that such countries' standards were sufficiently similar to those in the U.S. to warrant acceptance of the financial statements as originally prepared in those countries.

16.12   (Selecting the exchange rate for foreign currency translation.)

		(1) All-Current Method	(2) Monetary-Nonmonetary Method
a.	Cash	C-E	C-E
b.	Accounts Receivable	C-E	C-E
c.	Inventories	C-E	H
d.	Prepaid Rent	C-E	H
e.	Investment in Securities (10 Percent Ownership)	C-E	C-E (if Investments Valued at Market Value)
f.	Land	C-E	H
g.	Building	C-E	H
h.	Accumulated Depreciation	C-E	H
i.	Patent	C-E	H
j.	Goodwill	C-E	H
k.	Accounts Payable	C-E	C-E
l.	Bank Loan Payable	C-E	C-E
m.	Bonds Payable	C-E	C-E
n.	Common Stock	H	H
o.	Sales	C-A	H[a]
p.	Cost of Goods Sold	C-A	H
q.	Depreciation Expense	C-A	H
r.	Interest Expense	C-A	H[a]
s.	Income Tax Expense	C-A	H[a]

[a]The historical rate is technically correct; the historical rate in these cases is the average exchange rate during the current period. Thus, we accept either C-A or H as correct answers.

16.13   (Identifying the foreign currency translation method.)

a.	M	f.	C
b.	C	g.	N
c.	M	h.	M
d.	C	i.	N
e.	B	j.	B

16.14   (Identifying the nature of a foreign exchange adjustment.)

a.   Use of the all-current translation method results in a credit change in the foreign exchange adjustment account. The parent company's investment in the net assets (= assets minus liabilities = shareholders' equity) of the subsidiary increases in value as a result of the increased value of the foreign currency, relative to the parent placing its capital in a U.S. investment. Use of the monetary-nonmonetary translation method results in a foreign exchange loss. The net monetary liability position of the subsidiary requires a larger number of U.S. dollars to settle the net obligation as a result of the decreasing value of the U.S. dollar than if no change occurred in the value of the dollar.

b.   Use of the all-current translation method results in a debit change in the foreign exchange adjustment account. The parent's investment in the net assets of the subsidiary decreases in value as a result of the decreased value of the foreign currency, relative to the parent placing its capital in a U.S. investment. Use of the monetary-nonmonetary translation method results in a foreign exchange gain. The net monetary liability position of the subsidiary requires a smaller number of U.S. dollars to settle the net obligation as a result of the increasing value of the U.S. dollar than if no change occurred in the value of the dollar.

16.15   (Interpreting translated financial statements.)

a.   The foreign currency decreased in value relative to the U.S. dollar. Indicators of the decreasing value of the foreign currency (increasing value of the U.S. dollar) include:

(1) The translated U.S. dollar amount for inventories using the end-of-the-period exchange rate is less than the amount using the beginning-of-the-period (historical) exchange rate.

                                Solutions

16.15 a. continued.

      (2) The translated U.S. dollar amount for property, plant and equipment using the end-of-the-period exchange rate is less than the amount using the beginning-of-the-period (historical) exchange rate.

      (3) The net asset position of the foreign entity resulted in a negative foreign exchange adjustment under the all-current method.

      (4) The net monetary liability position of the foreign entity resulted in a foreign exchange gain under the monetary-nonmonetary translation method.

b.   The subsidiary is in a net asset position. A decrease in the value of the foreign currency relative to the U.S. dollar results in a decrease in the value of the parent's investment relative to the parent having invested the funds in a U.S. investment.

c.   The subsidiary is in a net monetary liability position. A decrease in the value of the foreign currency relative to the U.S. dollar results in requiring fewer U.S. dollars to settle the net obligation than if no change in the exchange rate had occurred.

16.16 (U.S. Manufacturing; translating foreign currency financial statements.)

a. **All-Current Translation Method—YEAR 4**

Balance Sheet	Foreign Currency	Exchange Rate	U.S. Dollars
Assets:			
Cash	FC 100	$1.00:FC1	$ 100
Accounts Receivable........	200	$1.00:FC1	200
Inventories	300	$1.00:FC1	300
Fixed Assets (Net)..........	400	$1.00:FC1	400
Total Assets................	FC 1,000		$1,000
Liabilities and Shareholders' Equity:			
Accounts Payable...........	FC 400	$1.00:FC1	$ 400
Bonds Payable	200	$1.00:FC1	200
Total Liabilities...........	FC 600		$ 600
Common Stock	FC 300	$2.00:FC1	$ 600
Foreign Exchange Adjustment.........................	--	See Below	(380)
Retained Earnings..........	100	See Below	180
Total Shareholders' Equity....................	FC 400		$ 400
Total Liabilities and Shareholders' Equity..................	FC 1,000		$1,000

Statement of Income and Retained Earnings			
Sales Revenue...................	FC 2,000	$1.50:FC1	$ 3,000
Cost of Goods Sold	(1,200)	$1.50:FC1	(1,800)
Selling and Administrative Expenses	(400)	$1.50:FC1	(600)
Depreciation Expense.........	(100)	$1.50:FC1	(150)
Interest Expense................	(20)	$1.50:FC1	(30)
Income Tax Expense..........	(120)	$1.50:FC1	(180)
Net Income	FC 160		$ 240
Dividends.........................	(60)	$1.00:FC1	(60)
Retained Earnings, December 31, Year 4	FC 100		$ 180

16.16 a. continued.

Calculation of Foreign Exchange Adjustment for Year 4

	Foreign Currency	Exchange Rate	U.S. Dollars
Net Asset Position, January 1, Year 4.................	FC --		$ --
Increase from Common Stock Issued..................	300	$2.00:FC1	600
Increase from Net Income..	160	See Above	240
Decrease from Dividends	(60)	$1.00:FC1	(60)
Subtotal			$ 780
Net Asset Position, December 31, Year 4	FC 400	$1.00:FC1	400
Foreign Exchange Adjustment for Year 4			$ (380)

b. **Monetary-Nonmonetary Translation Method—Year 4**

Balance Sheet	Foreign Currency	Exchange Rate	U.S. Dollars
Assets:			
Cash	FC 100	$1.00:FC1	$ 100
Accounts Receivable........	200	$1.00:FC1	200
Inventories	300	$1.50:FC1	450
Fixed Assets (Net)..........	400	$2.00:FC1	800
Total Assets................	FC 1,000		$ 1,550
Liabilities and Shareholders' Equity:			
Accounts Payable............	FC 400	$1.00:FC1	$ 400
Bonds Payable	200	$1.00:FC1	200
Total Liabilities...........	FC 600		$ 600
Common Stock	FC 300	$2.00:FC1	$ 600
Retained Earnings..........	100	See Below	350
Total Shareholders' Equity	FC 400		$ 950
Total Liabilities and Shareholders' Equity.................	FC 1,000		$ 1,550

16.16 b. continued.

Statement of Income and Retained Earnings

	Foreign Currency	Exchange Rate	U.S. Dollars
Sales Revenue	FC 2,000	$1.50:FC1	$ 3,000
Cost of Goods Sold	(1,200)	$1.50:FC1	(1,800)
Selling and Administrative Expenses	(400)	$1.50:FC1	(600)
Depreciation Expense	(100)	$2.00:FC1	(200)
Interest Expense	(20)	$1.50:FC1	(30)
Foreign Exchange	--	See Below	220
Income Tax Expense	(120)	$1.50:FC1	(180)
Net Income	FC 160		$ 410
Dividends	(60)	$1.00:FC1	(60)
Retained Earnings, December 31, Year 4	FC 100		$ 350

Calculation of Foreign Exchange Gain for Year 4

	Foreign Currency	Exchange Rate	U.S. Dollars
Net Monetary Position, January 1, Year 4	FC --		$ --
Increases:			
Issue of Common Stock	300	$2.00:FC1	600
Sales	2,000	$1.50:FC1	3,000
Decreases:			
Purchase of Plant and Equipment	(500)	$2.00:FC1	(1,000)
Purchase of Inventories	(1,500)	$1.50:FC1	(2,250)
Acquisition of Selling and Administrative Services	(400)	$1.50:FC1	(600)
Payment of Interest Expense	(20)	$1.50:FC1	(30)
Payment of Income Tax Expense	(120)	$1.50:FC1	(180)
Payment of Dividends	(60)	$1.00:FC1	(60)
Subtotal			$ (520)
Net Monetary Asset (Liability) Position, December 31, Year 4	FC (300)	$1.00:FC1	(300)
Foreign Exchange Gain for Year 4			$ 220

16.16 continued.

c. The foreign currency decreased in value relative to the U.S. dollar during Year 4, resulting in a negative foreign exchange adjustment on the subsidiary's net asset position under the all-current translation method. The subsidiary's net monetary liability position coupled with a declining value of the foreign currency results in a foreign exchange gain under the monetary-nonmonetary translation method.

d. (1) FC160/FC2,000 = 8%.

(2) $240/$3,000 = 8%.

(3) $410/$3,000 = 13.7%.

The ratios in (1) and (2) are the same because the all-current translation method uses the same exchange rate for each revenue and expense and net income excludes any foreign exchange adjustment for the year. The ratios in (2) and (3) are different because (a) the all-current method translates all revenues and expenses using the current exchange rate whereas the monetary-nonmonetary method uses a combination of current and historical exchange rates, and (b) the monetary-nonmonetary method includes the foreign exchange gain or loss in net income.

16.17 (Casey Corporation; translating foreign currency financial statements using the all-current method.)

a.

Translation of Financial Statements of McCann Corporation—Year 1
All-Current Method

Balance Sheet	Irish Pounds	Exchange Rate	U.S. Dollars
Cash	£ 40,000	1.45	$ 58,000
Accounts Receivable	80,000	1.45	116,000
Inventories	90,000	1.45	130,500
Fixed Assets (Net)	125,000	1.45	181,250
	£ 335,000		$ 485,750
Accounts Payable	£ 120,000	1.45	$ 174,000
Common Stock	200,000	1.50	300,000
Foreign Exchange Adjustment	--	See Below	(10,600)
Retained Earnings	15,000	See Below	22,350
	£ 335,000		$ 485,750
Income Statement			
Sales	£ 500,000	1.48	$ 740,000
Cost of Goods Sold	(300,000)	1.48	(444,000)
Depreciation Expense	(25,000)	1.48	(37,000)
Other Expenses	(155,000)	1.48	(229,400)
Net Income	£ 20,000		$ 29,600
Retained Earnings Statement			
Balance, Beginning of Year	£ --		$ --
Net Income	20,000	See Above	29,600
Dividends	(5,000)	1.45	(7,250)
Balance, End of Year	£ 15,000		$ 22,350

Computation of Foreign Exchange Adjustment—Year 1

	Irish Pounds	Exchange Rate	U.S. Dollars
Net Asset Position, January 1, Year 1	£ --		$ --
Plus:			
Capital Contributed by Casey	200,000	1.50	300,000
Net Income, Year 1	20,000	1.48	29,600
Less Dividends, Year 1	(5,000)	1.45	(7,250)
Subtotal			$ 322,350
Net Asset Position, December 31, Year 1	£ 215,000	1.45	311,750
Foreign Exchange Adjustment, Year 1 (Debit)			$ 10,600

16.17 continued.

b.

Translation of Financial Statements of McCann Corporation—Year 2
All-Current Method

Balance Sheet	Irish Pounds	Exchange Rate	U.S. Dollars
Cash..................................	£ 75,000	1.52	$ 114,000
Accounts Receivable...........	110,000	1.52	167,200
Inventories........................	200,000	1.52	304,000
Fixed Assets (Net)..............	100,000	1.52	152,000
	£ 485,000		$ 737,200
Accounts Payable...............	£ 150,000	1.52	$ 228,000
Notes Payable	100,000	1.52	152,000
Common Stock...................	200,000	1.50	300,000
Foreign Exchange Adjustment	--	See Below	5,350
Retained Earnings.............	35,000	See Below	51,850
	£ 485,000		$ 737,200

Income Statement			
Sales.................................	£ 600,000	1.49	$ 894,000
Cost of Goods Sold	(360,000)	1.49	(536,400)
Depreciation Expense	(25,000)	1.49	(37,250)
Other Expenses..................	(155,000)	1.49	(275,650)
Net Income	£ 30,000		$ 44,700

Retained Earnings Statement			
Balance, Beginning of Year..............................	£ 15,000	See Part a.	$ 22,350
Net Income	30,000	See Above	44,700
Dividends..........................	(10,000)	1.52	(15,200)
Balance, End of Year..........	£ 35,000		$ 51,850

16.17 b. continued.

Computation of Translation Adjustment—Year 2

	Irish Pounds	Exchange Rate	U.S. Dollars
Net Asset Position, January 1, Year 2..................	£ 215,000	1.45	$ 311,750
Plus Net Income, Year 2.....	30,000	1.49	44,700
Less Dividends, Year 2	(10,000)	1.52	(15,200)
Subtotal			$ 341,250
Net Asset Position, December 31, Year 2	£ 235,000	1.52	357,200
Foreign Exchange Adjustment, Year 2 (Credit)			$ 15,950
Foreign Exchange Adjustment, January 1, Year 2 (Debit).........................			(10,600)
Foreign Exchange Adjustment, December 31, Year 2 (Credit)......................			$ 5,350

c. The Irish pound decreased in value relative to the U.S. dollar during Year 1. Casey Corporation's investment in the net assets of McCann Corporation decreased in value as a result of the declining value of the Irish pound (but, perhaps, offset by increases in the market values of individual assets and liabilities held by the subsidiary).

d. The Irish pound increased in value relative to the U.S. dollar during Year 2. Casey Corporation's investment in the net assets of McCann Corporation increased in value as a result of the increasing value of the Irish pound.

e. **Year 1**
Irish Pounds: £20,000/£500,000 = 4.0%.
U.S. Dollars: $29,600/$740,000 = 4.0%.

Year 2
Irish Pounds: £20,000/£500,000 = 5.0%.
U.S. Dollars: $44,700/$894,000 = 5.0%.

The all-current translation method translates all revenues and expenses in any particular year using the same exchange rate. Thus, the relations between revenues, expenses, and net income do not change.

16.18 (U.S. Rental Properties; translating foreign currency financial statements.)

a. **All-Current Translation Method—YEAR 1**

Balance Sheet	Canadian Dollars	Exchange Rate	U.S. Dollars
Assets:			
Cash	C$ 77,555	.80	US$ 62,044
Rent Receivable	25,000	.80	20,000
Building (Net)	475,000	.80	380,000
Total Assets	C$ 577,555		US$462,044
Liabilities and Shareholders' Equity:			
Accounts Payable	C$ 6,000	.80	US$ 4,800
Salaries Payable	4,000	.80	3,200
Common Stock	555,555	.90	500,000
Translation Adjustment	--	See Below	(57,656)
Retained Earnings	12,000	See Below	11,700
Total Liabilities and Shareholders' Equity	C$ 577,555		US$462,044
Income Statement			
Rent Revenue	C$ 125,000	.85	US$106,250
Operating Expense	(28,000)	.85	(23,800)
Depreciation Expense	(25,000)	.85	(21,250)
Income Tax Expense	(30,000)	.85	(25,500)
Net Income	C$ 42,000		US$ 35,700
Retained Earnings Statement			
Balance, January 1, Year 1	C$ --		US$ --
Net Income	42,000	See Above	35,700
Dividends	(30,000)	.80	(24,000)
Balance, December 31, Year 1	C$ 12,000		US 11,700

16.18 a. continued.

Computation of Foreign Exchange Adjustment for Year 1

	Canadian Dollars	Exchange Rate	U.S. Dollars
Net Asset Position, January 1, Year 1	C$ --		US$ --
Plus:			
Capital Contributed by P	555,555	.90	500,000
Net Income, Year 1	42,000	See Above	35,700
Less Dividends, Year 1	(30,000)	.80	(24,000)
Subtotal			US$511,700
Net Asset Position, December 31, Year 1	C$ 567,555	.80	454,044
Foreign Exchange Adjustment, Year 1			US$ 57,656

b. **Monetary-Nonmonetary Translation Method—Year 1**

Balance Sheet	Canadian Dollars	Exchange Rate	U.S. Dollars
Assets:			
Cash	C$ 77,555	.80	US$ 62,044
Rent Receivable	25,000	.80	20,000
Building (Net)	475,000	.90	427,500
Total Assets	C$ 577,555		US$509,544
Liabilities and Shareholders' Equity:			
Accounts Payable	C$ 6,000	.80	US$ 4,800
Salaries Payable	4,000	.80	3,200
Common Stock	555,555	.90	500,000
Retained Earnings	12,000	See Below	1,544
Total Liabilities and Shareholders' Equity	C$ 577,555		US$509,544

Income Statement	Canadian Dollars	Exchange Rate	U.S. Dollars
Rent Revenue	C$ 125,000	.85	US$106,250
Operating Expense	(28,000)	.85	(23,800)
Depreciation Expense	(25,000)	.90	(22,500)
Income Tax Expense	(30,000)	.85	(25,500)
Foreign Exchange Loss	--	See Below	(8,906)
Net Income	C$ 42,000		US$ 25,544

Retained Earnings Statement	Canadian Dollars	Exchange Rate	U.S. Dollars
Balance, January 1, Year 1	C$ --		US$ --
Net Income	42,000	See Above	25,544
Dividends	(30,000)	.80	(24,000)
Balance, December 31, Year 1	C$ 12,000		US$ 1,544

 Solutions

16.18 b. continued.

Computation of Foreign Exchange Loss for Year 1

	Canadian Dollars	Exchange Rate	U.S. Dollars
Net Monetary Position, January 1, Year 1..................	C$ --		US$ --
Plus:			
Capital Contributed by Parent........................	555,555	.90	500,000
Cash and Receivables from Rents	125,000	.85	106,250
Less:			
Cash Disbursed for Building............................	(500,000)	.90	(450,000)
Cash Disbursed and Liabilities Incurred for Operating Expenses.....	(28,000)	.85	(23,800)
Cash Disbursed for Income Taxes.................	(30,000)	.85	(25,500)
Cash Disbursed for Dividends.........................	(30,000)	.80	(24,000)
Subtotal			US$ 82,950
Net Monetary Position, December 31, Year 1	C$ 92,555	.80	74,044
Foreign Exchange Loss.......			US$ 8,906

c. **All-Current Translation Method—Year 2**

Balance Sheet	Canadian Dollars	Exchange Rate	U.S. Dollars
Assets:			
Cash	C$ 116,555	.84	US$ 97,906
Rent Receivable	30,000	.84	25,200
Building (Net).................	450,000	.84	378,000
Total Assets...............	C$ 596,555		US$501,106
Liabilities and Shareholders' Equity:			
Accounts Payable............	C$ 7,500	.84	US$ 6,300
Salaries Payable	5,500	.84	4,620
Common Stock	555,555	.90	500,000
Translation Adjustment..	--	See Below	(33,854)
Retained Earnings..........	28,000	See Below	24,040
Total Liabilities and Shareholders' Equity.................	C$ 596,555		US$501,106

16.18 c. continued.

Income Statement

Rent Revenue	C$ 150,000	.82	US$123,000
Operating Expense	(34,000)	.82	(27,880)
Depreciation Expense	(25,000)	.82	(20,500)
Income Tax Expense	(36,000)	.82	(29,520)
Net Income	C$ 55,000		US$ 45,100

Retained Earnings Statement

Balance, January 1, Year 2	C$ 12,000	See Part a.	US$ 11,700
Net Income	55,000	See Above	45,100
Dividends	(39,000)	.84	(32,760)
Balance, December 31, Year 2	C$ 28,000		US$ 24,040

Calculation of Foreign Exchange Adjustment for Year 2

	Canadian Dollars	Exchange Rate	U.S. Dollars
Net Asset Position, January 1, Year 2	C$ 567,555	.80	US$454,044
Plus Net Income	55,000	See Above	45,100
Less Dividends	(39,000)	.84	(32,760)
Subtotal			US$466,384
Net Asset Position, December 31, Year 2	C$ 583,555	.84	490,186
Foreign Exchange Loss			US$ 23,802

Change in Foreign Exchange Adjustment for Year 2

Balance, January 1, Year 2	US$ (57,656)
Plus Foreign Exchange Adjustment for Year 2	23,802
Balance, December 31, Year 2	US$ (33,854)

16.18 continued.

d. **Monetary-Nonmonetary Translation Method—YEAR 2**

Balance Sheet	Canadian Dollars	Exchange Rate	U.S. Dollars
Assets:			
Cash	C$ 116,555	.84	US$ 97,906
Rent Receivable	30,000	.84	25,200
Building (Net)................	450,000	.90	405,000
Total Assets................	C$ 596,555		US$528,106
Liabilities and Share-			
holders' Equity:			
Accounts Payable............	C$ 7,500	.80	US$ 6,300
Salaries Payable	5,500	.80	4,620
Common Stock	555,555	.90	500,000
Retained Earnings..........	28,000	See Below	17,186
Total Liabilities and			
Shareholders'			
Equity..................	C$ 596,555		US$528,106
Income Statement			
Rent Revenue	C$ 150,000	.82	US$123,000
Operating Expense	(34,000)	.82	(27,880)
Depreciation Expense	(25,000)	.90	(22,500)
Income Tax Expense..........	(36,000)	.82	(29,520)
Foreign Exchange Loss.......	--	See Below	5,302
Net Income	C$ 55,000		US$ 48,402
Retained Earnings Statement			
Balance, January 1, Year 1.	C$ 12,000	See Part b,	US$ 1,544
Net Income	55,000	See Above	48,402
Dividends.........................	(39,000)	.84	(32,760)
Balance, December 31,			
Year 1	C$ 28,000		US$ 17,186

16.18 d. continued.

Computation of Foreign Exchange Gain for Year 2

	Canadian Dollars	Exchange Rate	U.S. Dollars
Net Monetary Position, January 1, Year 2..................	C$ 92,555	.80	US$ 74,044
Plus Cash and Receivables from Rents.....................	150,000	.82	123,000
Less:			
Cash Disbursed and Liabilities Assumed for Operating Expenses.....	(34,000)	.82	(27,880)
Cash Disbursed for Income Taxes................	(36,000)	.82	(29,520)
Cash Disbursed for Dividends........................	(39,000)	.84	(32,760)
Subtotal...................			US$106,884
Net Monetary Position, December 31, Year 2	C$ 133,555	.84	112,186
Foreign Exchange Gain......			US$ 5,302

16.19   (Marks and Spencer: balance sheet format, terminology and accounting methods for a U.K. company.)

See the solution to Problem 2.34.

16.20   (United Breweries Group; balance sheet format, terminology and accounting methods for a Danish company.)

See the solution to Problem 2.35.

16.21   (BMW; income statement format and terminology for a German company.)

See the solution to Problem 4.35.

16.22   (Marks and Spencer; income statement format, terminology and accounting methods for a U.K. company.)

See the solution to Problem 4.36.

16.23   (Elf Aquitaine Group; statement of cash flows format and terminology for a French company.)

See the solution to Problem 5.34.

       Solutions

16.24 (Rolls-Royce; statement of cash flows format and terminology for a U.K. company.)

See the solution to Problem 5.35.

16.25 (Glaxo Holdings; adjusting the financial statements of a U.K. company to U.S. accounting principles.)

a.

| | June 30 | |
	Year 7	Year 8
Assets:		
Current Assets	£ 2,864	£ 3,635
Fixed Assets	1,628	2,109
Total Assets	£ 4,492	£ 5,744
Liabilities and Shareholders' Equity:		
Current Liabilities	£ 1,406	£ 2,027
Provision for Liabilities	185	267
Amounts Falling Due within One Year	96	78
Convertible Bonds	--	90
Total Liabilities	£ 1,687	£ 2,462
Shareholders' Equity	2,805	3,282
Total Liabilities and Shareholders' Equity	£ 4,492	£ 5,744

b.

| | June 30 | |
	Year 7	Year 8
Assets:		
Current Assets	£ 2,864	£ 3,635
Fixed Assets	1,628	2,109
Goodwill	11	26
Total Assets	£ 4,503	£ 5,770
Liabilities and Shareholders' Equity:		
Current Liabilities	£ 1,406	£ 2,027
Provision for Liabilities	185	267
Amounts Falling Due after One Year	96	78
Convertible Bonds	--	90
Increase in Deferred Tax Liability	165	199
Total Liabilities	£ 1,852	£ 2,661
Shareholders' Equity	2,651	3,109
Total Liabilities and Shareholders' Equity	£ 4,503	£ 5,770

16.25 continued.

   c. **Rate of Return on Assets**
U.K. Accounting Principles:
$$£912 + (1 - .35)(£75)/.5(£4,492 + £5,744) = 18.8\%.$$
U.S. Accounting Principles:
$$£872 + (1 - .35)(£75)/.5(£4,503 + £5,770) = 17.9\%.$$

Profit Margin for Rate of Return on Assets
U.K. Accounting Principles:
$$£912 + (1 - .35)(£75)/£3,397 = 28.3\%.$$
U.S. Accounting Principles:
$$£872 + (1 - .35)(£75)/£3,397 = 27.1\%.$$

Assets Turnover
U.K. Accounting Principles:
$$£3,397/.5(£4,492 + £5,744) = .66.$$
U.S. Accounting Principles:
$$£3,397/.5(£4,503 + £5,770) = .66.$$

   d. **Rate of Return on Common Shareholders' Equity**
U.K. Accounting Principles:
$$£912/.5(£2,805 + £3,282) = 30.0\%.$$
U.S. Accounting Principles:
$$£872/.5(£2,651 + £3,109) = 30.3\%.$$

Profit Margin for Rate of Return on Common Shareholders' Equity
U.K. Accounting Principles:
$$£912/£3,397 = 26.8\%.$$
U.S. Accounting Principles:
$$£872/£3,397 = 25.7\%.$$

Assets Turnover
U.K. Accounting Principles:
$$£3,397/.5(£4,492 + £5,744) = .66.$$
U.S. Accounting Principles:
$$£3,397/.5(£4,503 + £5,770) = .66.$$

Leverage Ratio
U.K. Accounting Principles:
$$.5(£4,492 + £5,744)/.5(£2,805 + £3,282) = 1.68.$$
U.S. Accounting Principles:
$$.5(£4,503 + £5,770)/.5(£2,651 + £3,109) = 1.78.$$

16.25 continued.

e. The rate of return on assets and its associated profit margin are less under U.S. accounting principles than under U.K. accounting principles because of the amortization of goodwill and additional deferred taxes. The rate of return on common shareholders' equity under U.S. accounting principles exceeds that under U.K. accounting principles because of the reclassification of a portion of retained earnings under U.K. accounting methods to a deferred tax liability under U.S. accounting principles. This reclassification causes the leverage ratio to increase and thereby increase the rate of return on common shareholders' equity. The adjustments for accounting principles for Glaxo do not necessarily extrapolate to other U.K. companies.

f. and g.

GLAXO HOLDINGS
Statement of Cash Flows for the Year Ended June 30, Year 8
(Amounts in Millions of U.K. Pounds)

	f. U.K. Accounting Principles	g. U.S. Accounting Principles
Operations:		
Net Income	£ 912	£ 872
Depreciation	151	151
Increase in Pension and Other Provisions	21	21
Increase in Deferred Taxes	24[a]	59[b]
Goodwill Amortization	--	5
Increase in Accounts Receivable	(135)	(135)
Increase in Inventories	(77)	(77)
Increase in Accounts Payable	77	77
Cash Flow from Operations	£ 973	£ 973
Investing:		
Sale of Tangible Fixed Assets	£ 32	£ 32
Acquisition of Marketable Securities	(527)	(527)
Acquisition of Investments	(45)	(45)
Acquisition of Tangible Fixed Assets	(621)	(621)
Cash Flow from Investing	£(1,161)	£(1,161)
Financing:		
Increase in Short-Term Borrowing	£ 452	£ 452
Increase in Convertible Bonds	90	90
Issue of Common Stock	20	20
Dividends Paid	(364)	(364)
Cash Flow from Financing	£ 198	£ 198
Net Change in Cash	£ 10	£ 10
Cash, Beginning of Year	24	24
Cash, End of Year	£ 34	£ 34

[a]Income tax expense of £371 minus income tax paid of £347 = £24.

[b]Amount based on U.K. GAAP of £24 + Increase to Convert to U.S. GAAP of £35 = £59.

16.25 continued.

h. The cash flows from operating, investing and financing activities are identical under U.K. and U.S. accounting principles. This result generally occurs unless firms change their accounting methods for income tax purposes when they convert accounting principles from one country to another. Although one cannot establish clear links between various cash flows, it appears that Glaxo used the excess cash flow from operations after paying dividends to acquire property, plant and equipment. It placed the proceeds from additional short-term borrowing in marketable securities. Perhaps Glaxo observed an opportunity to invest in marketable securities with an expected yield that exceeded the cost of short-term borrowing.

16.26　(Tanaguchi Corporation; interpreting financial statement ratios of a Japanese company using Japanese and U.S. accounting principles.)

a. The principal adjustments to convert Tanaguchi Corporation from Japanese GAAP to U.S. GAAP relate to intercorporate investments.

	Japanese GAAP	**U.S. GAAP**
Marketable Securities	Acquisition Cost	Market-Value Method
Investment in Tanaka Corp. (25%)	Acquisition Cost	Equity Method
Investment in Taka-hashi Corp. (80%)	Acquisition Cost	Consolidation
Investment in Other Companies (less than 20%)	Acquisition Cost	Market-Value Method

The profit margin, rate of return on assets, and rate of return on common shareholders' equity increase as a result of adjusting the financial statements to U.S. GAAP. The effect of applying the market-value method depends on when Tanaguchi Corporation acquired the securities. Stock market prices increased in Japan throughout the 1980s but exhibited a downward trend in the early 1990s. The effect of applying the market-value method is unclear.

The effect of applying the equity method for the investment in Tanaka Corporation depends on whether this investee operated at a profit or a loss for Year 5 and on its rate of profitability. If Tanaka Corporation operated at a profit, then applying the equity method increases the profit margin of Tanaguchi Corporation (net income increases without a change in sales revenue). Whether the rate of return on assets increases or decreases depends on Tanaka Corporation's rate of profitability, since application of the equity method increases both the numerator and denominator of Tanaguchi Corporation's rate of return on assets. Tanaguchi Corporation's rate of return on shareholders' equity should increase as a result of applying the equity method for a profitable Tanaka Corporation (net income in the numerator increases without a change in the denominator).

　16-23

16.26 a. continued.

      The effect of consolidating Takahashi Corporation on the profitability ratios depends on its profitability in a manner similar to the equity method for Tanaka Corporation discussed above. The effect of consolidation on assets turnover and risk ratios depends on whether the ratios for Takahashi Corporation exceed or are less than those for Tanaguchi Corporation on an unconsolidated basis.

      Another minor adjustment to convert to U.S. GAAP is for bonuses to directors and statutory auditors. U.S. GAAP treats these costs as expenses in calculating net income.

      The ratios in Column (1) and Column (2) of Exhibit 16.33 do not differ materially, suggesting that conversion from Japanese GAAP to U.S. GAAP does not make a major difference.

b. A good way to begin coverage of this part is to place Table 1 from this Teaching Note on an overhead transparency. Ask the students to list examples of economic, strategic, institutional or cultural factors that might affect their interpretation of financial statements. The following list presents several such items.

Economic—extent of competition in the industry; degree of capital versus labor intensity in manufacturing; exposure to foreign exchange rate changes; role of technological change.

Business Strategy—Niche strategy to gain market dominance in a narrow, focused market; low margin strategy to generate high market share; diversification strategy across products and geographical markets to reduce risk.

Institutional Structure—Degree of government regulation in the economy and in the industry; existence of import/export controls; level of taxation; process for setting acceptable accounting standards.

Cultural—Role of religious norms; work/leisure tradeoffs; changing demographics (aging of population, role of women and family).

To emphasize the impact that these factors can have on the interpretation of financial statements, the instructor may wish to ask students in the class from other countries to describe differences in business practices that they observe in their own countries versus the U.S. that relate to the economic, strategic, institutional, or cultural factors listed above. The discussion sets the stage for discussing differences between the U.S. and Japan that might explain differences in the financial ratios in Exhibit 16.33 of the case.

16.26 b. continued.

TABLE 1
Economic, Strategic and Environmental Factors Affecting
Interpretation of Financial Statements

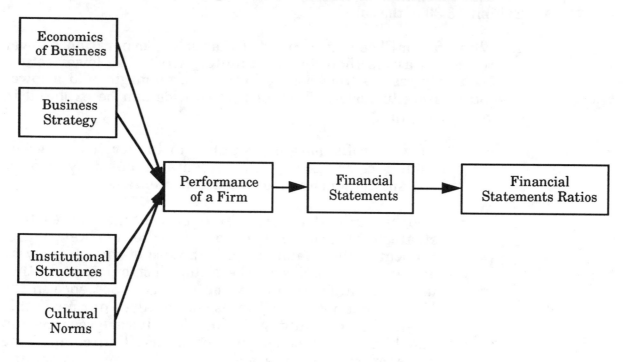

16-25

16.26 b. continued.

Profitability Analysis

Table 2 in this Teaching Note sets out the profitability ratios for Tanaguchi Corporation based on U.S. GAAP and the median ratios for U.S. machine tool companies in a more structured format than Exhibit 16.33 of the case.

1. What factors seem to explain Tanaguchi Corporation's lower return on assets than its U.S. counterparts? The lower return on assets results from both a lower profit margin and a lower total assets turnover. Each of these ratios can be explored in greater depth.

    a. The lower profit margin results from higher cost of goods sold and income tax expense percentages offset by a lower selling and administrative expense percentage.

    • The higher cost of goods sold percentage relates to a strategy of pricing low to generate market share. Students will be familiar with the use of this strategy by Japanese companies in the auto, electronics, and other industries in efforts to develop a market presence in the U.S. Japanese companies have also pursued this strategy successfully in Japan. The lower gross margin and higher market share should result in comparable rates of return on assets to U.S. firms. Although inventory turnover is higher for Tanaguchi Corporation, the overall asset turnover is lower than for U.S. companies (explored more fully below); thus, the return on assets is smaller. The explanation commonly given in Japan is that profitability (measured either by return on assets or earnings per share) is not as important as market share. Higher market share drives out competitors and permits dominance of the market. The result is that most industries in Japan have a relatively small number of large firms, usually one from each *keiretsu*, that each have a significant market share. Note that Tanaguchi Corporation's use of a weighted average cost flow assumption should lower its cost of goods sold percentage, relative to LIFO, while its use of accelerated depreciation will increase its cost of goods sold percentage, relative to straight-line. The net effect of adjusting for these two differences in accounting principles between the U.S. and Japan was to increase the cost of goods sold percentage of Tanaguchi Corporation and does not account for the overall higher percentage in this case.

16.26 b. continued.

TABLE 2

Profitability Analysis of Tanaguchi Corporation

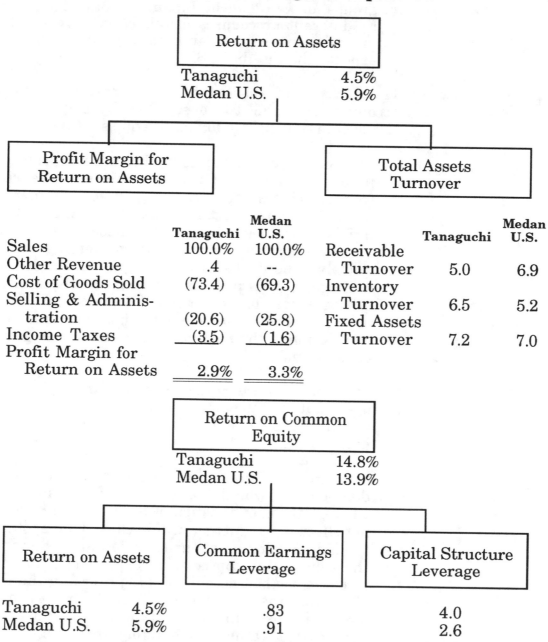

Return on Assets	
Tanaguchi	4.5%
Medan U.S.	5.9%

Profit Margin for Return on Assets

	Tanaguchi	Medan U.S.
Sales	100.0%	100.0%
Other Revenue	.4	--
Cost of Goods Sold	(73.4)	(69.3)
Selling & Administration	(20.6)	(25.8)
Income Taxes	(3.5)	(1.6)
Profit Margin for Return on Assets	2.9%	3.3%

Total Assets Turnover

	Tanaguchi	Medan U.S.
Receivable Turnover	5.0	6.9
Inventory Turnover	6.5	5.2
Fixed Assets Turnover	7.2	7.0

Return on Common Equity	
Tanaguchi	14.8%
Medan U.S.	13.9%

	Return on Assets	Common Earnings Leverage	Capital Structure Leverage
Tanaguchi	4.5%	.83	4.0
Medan U.S.	5.9%	.91	2.6

- The higher income tax percentage results from high statutory tax rates in Japan. The effective tax rates are computed as follows:

Tanaguchi Corporation: 3.5% + (2.9% + 3.5%) = 55%
Median U.S.: 1.6% + (3.3% + 1.6%) = 33%.

 Solutions

16.26 b. continued.

- The lower selling and administrative expense percentage may relate to a leaner sales and administrative organization as a result of operating within corporate groups, or *keiretsu*, in Japan. It may also be explained by different procedures for allocating overhead between manufacturing cost and selling and administrative expense than in the U.S.

b. The lower total assets turnover results from a lower accounts receivable turnover offset by a higher inventory turnover and a slightly higher fixed asset turnover.

- The lower accounts receivable turnover relates to the practice in Japan of taking noninterest-bearing notes from customers and permitting these customers to delay payment for up to six months. The explanation for this practice is partly cultural. Japanese sellers do not wish to embarrass Japanese buyers by forcing them to pay quickly when the buyer is unable to do so. The explanation is in part also economic. Sellers increase the selling price for the interest implicit in the delayed payment. The seller frequently discounts these notes at a bank, usually the bank within its corporate group, when it needs cash.

- The faster inventory turnover for Tanaguchi Corporation may relate to the earlier implementation of a just-in-time inventory system and to the practice of pricing low to gain market share.

- Converting Tanaguchi Corporation to straight-line depreciation would increase the fixed asset turnover, whereas the capitalization of leases would reduce it. The net effect is a reduction in this case. One explanation for the higher fixed asset turnover in Japan might relate to the substantial appreciation experienced in real estate prices in the last decade. Selling prices in the numerator of the fixed asset turnover reflect the opportunity cost of assets in use, including land. Because of land's appreciated value, firms likely increase their selling prices to provide a return commensurate with the economic value, not book value, of the land. The land in the denominator, however, is reported at acquisition cost. This valuation mismatch is probably greater in Japan.

16.26 b. continued.

2. Next, ask why Tanaguchi Corporation's return on common equity is higher than that of U.S. companies, given the significantly lower return on assets. The answer lies in the heavier use of financial leverage by Japanese companies as seen in the higher capital structure leverage ratio. (Note that the common's share of operating earnings ratio is lower in Japan than in the U.S. because of the lower operating profitability and higher level of interest expense of Japanese companies.) The risk ratios indicate that the heavier leverage comes from short-term rather than long-term borrowing. The instructor might raise the question as to why Japanese companies take on such a high level of debt and compound the risk by heavily using short-instead of long-term debt. The balance sheet indicates that most of the short-term debt is bank borrowing. The borrowing is typically through the bank in the borrower's corporate group, Menji Bank in this case. The bank generally rolls over this debt at maturity, so that the analyst might view it as long-term borrowing. (Unlike the U.S., there is no provision in Japanese GAAP for classifying, as long-term debt, short-term debt scheduled to be refinanced with a new maturity date exceeding one year.) It is unlikely that a bank would force a borrower within its corporate group into bankruptcy. Thus, such borrowings do not carry the type of risk that similar short-term bank borrowing in the U.S. carries. Note also that the average interest cost on debt in Japan tends to be less than in the U.S. For Tanaguchi Corporation, the average borrowing cost is 5.6 percent pretax [= ¥13/.5(¥185 + ¥200 + ¥20 + ¥20 + ¥20 + ¥20)] and 2.5 percent after tax [= (1 − .55)(5.6 percent)]. The lower interest rates in Japan occur partly because the Bank of Japan (central bank) lends funds to commercial banks at below market interest rates, with the expectation that the commercial banks will pass along this lower rate to corporate borrowers and thereby stimulate economic activity in Japan. Also, individuals in Japan have few alternatives for their savings other than commercial banks. These banks tend to pay relatively low interest on such savings accounts. With capital markets becoming increasingly global, it is not clear whether these below market rate policies are sustainable. Finally, tax rates are higher in Japan than in the U.S., reducing the after-tax cost of borrowing for Japanese firms.

 Solutions

16.26 b. continued.

Risk Analysis

Next ask whether the level of financial risk of Tanaguchi Corporation is at an intolerable level. The low current and quick ratios, relative to U.S. machine tool companies, suggest high short-term liquidity risk. The ratios for the Japanese company are lower largely because of the inclusion of bank borrowing in current liabilities. Reclassifying the borrowing as long-term debt, as seems appropriate given the discussion above, results in current ratios for Tanaguchi Corporation over 2.0:1 and quick ratios over 1.25:1. The interest coverage ratio is almost twice that of U.S. firms, largely because of a lower borrowing rate (see discussion above) and higher net income before interest and taxes. These comments coupled with the low probability that the lending bank will force the firm into bankruptcy results in a conclusion that the risk level is not at an intolerable level.

Market-Based Ratios

Note that the adjustments for differences in accounting principles significantly reduced the price-earnings and market value of common equity ratios of Tanaguchi Corporation. Several recent studies performed similar adjustments for a larger set of actual Japanese companies [French and Poterba, 1990; Bildersee et al., 1990] and found that approximately one-half of the difference in the price-earnings ratio is due to accounting principles differences.

The remaining differences in these market-based ratios may relate to the significant under valuation of land on the financial statements. As real estate values in Japan have increased in recent years, market equity values have increased as well.

Synthesis

The instructor may wish to place the following on an overhead transparency to summarize the main insights from this case.

A. Analyzing and interpreting financial statements of companies in different countries require an understanding of both (1) differences in accounting principles and (2) differences in economic, strategic, institutional, and cultural factors that affect the way firms conduct their business.

B. Accounting principles used in preparing reports for stockholders in Japan conform closely with those used for tax reporting.

C. Restatements of balance sheet and income statement amounts for differences in the accounting for inventories (weighted average to LIFO) and for depreciable assets (declining balance to straight line) tend to be offsetting.

16.26 b. continued.

D. The most important difference in accounting principles between the U.S. and Japan relates to intercorporate investments. Because information on affiliates and subsidiaries is seldom included in the annual report to stockholders under the Japanese Commercial Code, the analyst should access the supplemental equity/consolidated statements filed with the Securities Division of the Ministry of Finance.

E. Financial ratio analysis suggests that Japanese companies are less profitable and more risky than their U.S. counterparts. Differences in corporate strategies, institutional structures and culture practices in Japan explain much of the differences in the financial ratios.

REFERENCES

Bildersee, John S., John J. Cheh, and Changwoo Lee, "The International Price-Earnings Ratio Phenomenon: A Partial Explanation," *Japan and the World Economy* (1990), pp. 263-282.

Choi, Frederick D. S. and Kazuo Hiramatsu, *Accounting and Financial Reporting in Japan*, Wokingham, Berkshire: Van Nostrand Reinhold (UK) Co., Ltd., 1987.

Freitas, Lewis P., "Views from Abroad: Japan," *Journal of Accounting, Auditing, and Finance* (Fall 1980), pp. 70-76.

French, Kenneth R. and James M. Poterba, "Were Japanese Stock Prices Too High?" *Journal of Financial Economics* (1991), pp. 337-363.

Kester, W. Carl, *Japanese Takeovers*, Boston, Mass.: Harvard Business School Press (1991).

KPMG Peat Marwick, *Comparison of Japanese and U.S. Reporting and Financial Practices* (1989).

Lowe, Howard D., "Shortcomings of Japanese Consolidated Financial Statements," *Accounting Horizons* (September, 1990).

Robert Morris Associates, *Annual Statement Studies* (1990).

Skully, Michael T., "Japanese Corporate Structure: Some Factors in its Development," *The International Journal of Accounting* (Spring, 1981), pp. 67-98.

The Japanese Institute of Certified Public Accountants, *Corporate Disclosure in Japan* (1987).

Solutions

APPENDIX A

COMPOUND INTEREST: CONCEPTS AND APPLICATIONS

Questions, Exercises, Problems, and Cases: Answers and Solutions

A.1   See the text or the glossary at the end of the book.

A.2   Rent paid or received for the use of the asset, cash.

A.3   In simple interest, only the principal sum earns interest. In compound interest, interest is earned on the principal plus amounts of interest not paid or withdrawn.

A.4   There is no difference; these items refer to the same thing.

A.5   The timing of the first payment for an annuity due is *now* (at the beginning of the first period) while that for an ordinary annuity is at the *end* of the first period. The future value of an annuity due is computed as of one year after the final payment, but for an ordinary annuity is computed as of the time of the last payment.

A.6   The discount rate that sets the net present value of a stream of payments equal to zero is the implicit rate for that stream.

     (1) Guess a rate.

     (2) Compute the net present values of the cash flows using the current guess.

     (3) If the net present value in (2) is less than zero, then increase the rate guessed and go to Step (2).

     (4) If the net present value in (2) is greater than zero, then reduce the rate guessed and go to Step (2).

     (5) Otherwise, the current guess is the implicit rate of return.

     The process will converge to the right answer only if one is systematic with the guesses, narrowing the range successively.

A.7   Present values increase when interest rates decrease and present values decrease when interest rates increase.

A.8   6 percent. The present value will be larger the smaller the discount rate.

A.9   (Effective interest rates.)

    a.   12 percent per period; 5 periods.

    b.   6 percent per period; 10 periods.

    c.   3 percent per period; 20 periods.

    d.   1 percent per period; 60 periods.

A.10   a. $100 \times 1.21665 = \$121.67$.

    b. $500 \times 1.34587 = \$672.94$.

    c. $200 \times 1.26899 = \$253.80$.

    d. $\$2,500 \times (1.74102 \times 1.74102) = \$7,577.88$

$$(1.02)^{56} = (1.02)^{28} \times (1.02)^{28}.$$

    e. $600 \times 1.43077 = \$858.46$.

A.11   a. $100 \times .30832 = \$30.83$.

    b. $250 \times .53063 = \$132.66$.

    c. $\$1,000 \times .78757 = \$787.57$.

A.12   a. $100 \times 14.23683 = \$1,423.68$.

    b. $850 \times 9.89747 = \$8,412.85$.

    c. $400 \times 49.96758 = \$19,987.03$.

A.13   a. $\text{DM}5,000 \times 3.20714 \times 1.06 = \text{DM}16,998$.

    b. $\text{DM}5,000 \times 10.06266 \times 1.25971 = \text{DM}63,380$.

A.14   a. $\text{Fr}150,000 \times .62741 = \text{Fr}94,112$.

    b. $\text{Fr}150,000 \times .54027 = \text{Fr}81,041$.

A.15   a. $4,000 × 6.97532 = $27,901.

       b. $4,000 × 7.33593 = $29,344.

A.16   a.   ¥45,000,000/10.63663 = ¥4.23 million.

       b.   ¥45,000,000/12.29969 = ¥3.66 million.

A.17   a.   90,000 lira × 14.20679 × 1.05 = 90,000 × (15.91713 − 1.0) lira = 1,342,542 lira.

       b.   90,000 lira × 18.53117 × 1.10 = 90,000 × (21.38428 − 1.0) lira = 1,834,585 lira.

A.18   a.   £145,000/4.62288 = £31,366.

       b.   £145,000/4.11141 = £35,268.

A.19   a.   (10) $100 × T(1, 5, 4).

            (11) $100 × T(2, 30, 4).

            (12) $100 × T(3, 13, 1.5).

            (13)   DM5,000 × T(1, 20, 6) × T(1, 1, 6) =
                   DM5,000 × T(1, 20, 6) × 1.06 =
                   DM5,000 × T(1, 21, 6)—but this is not in the tables.

            (14)   Fr150,000 × T(2, 8, 6).

       b.   (15) $4,000 × T(3, 5, 8).

            (16)   ¥45,000,000/T(3, 8, 12).

            (17)   90,000 lira × T(3, 11, 10) × 1.10 =
                   90,000 lira × T(3, 11, 10) × T(1, 1, 10).

            (18)   £145,000/T(4, 6, 12).

       c.   Asking questions about compound interest calculations on examinations presents a difficult logistical problem to teachers. They may want the students to use compound interest tables, but not wish to incur the costs of reproducing them in sufficient numbers for each student to have a copy. They may not wish to give an open book test. This device is useful for posing test questions about compound interest. The device is based on the fact that teachers of accounting are not particularly interested in testing their students' ability to do arithmetic. Teachers want to be sure that students know how to use the tables and calculating devices efficiently in combination. Such a combination suggests that the human do the thinking and the calculator do the multiplications and divisions.

   A-3   **Solutions**

A.20 a. $1,000(1.00 + .94340) + $2,000(4.21236 − .94340) + $2,500(6.80169 − 4.21236) = $14,955.

b. $1,000(1.00 + .92593) + $2,000(3.99271 − .92593) + $2,500(6.24689 − 3.99271) = $13,695.

c. $1,000(1.00 + .90909) + $2,000(3.79079 − .90909) + $2,500(5.75902 − 3.79079) = $12,593.

A.21 a. $3,000 + ($3,000/.06) = $53,000.

b. $3,000 + ($3,000/.08) = $40,500.

A.22 a. $3,000/.06 = $50,000.

b. $3,000/.08 = $37,500.

c. ($3,000/.06) × .79209 = $39,604.50.

d. ($3,000/.08) × .73503 = $27,563.63.

A.23 a. $60,000 + ($60,000/.1664) = $420,577. $(1.08)^2 − 1 = .1664$.

b. $60,000 + ($60,000/.2544) = $295,850. $(1.12)^2 − 1 = .2544$.

A.24 7.00 percent. Note that $100,000/$55,307 = 1.80809. See Table 4, 2-period row and observe 1.80809 in the 7-percent column.

A.25 12 percent = $(\$140,493/\$100,000)^{1/3} − 1$.

A.26 a. 16 percent = $(\$67,280/\$50,000)^{1/2} − 1$.

b.

Year (1)	Book Value Start of Year (2)	Interest for Year = (2) × .16 (3)	Amount (Reducing) Increasing Book Value (4)	Book Value End of Year = (2) + (3) + (4) (5)
1	$50,000	$8,000		$ 58,000
2	58,000	9,280	$ (67,280)	-0-

A.27 (Berman Company; find implicit interest rate; construct amortization schedule.)

a. 14.0 percent.

$$\text{Let } x = \frac{\$8,000}{(1+r)} + \frac{\$8,000}{(1+r)^2} + \frac{\$8,000}{(1+r)^3} + \frac{\$100,000}{(1+r)^3} = \$86,000$$

If r = 14.0 percent, then x = $18,573 + $67,497 − $86,000 = $70.

If r = 14.1 percent, then x = $18,542 + $67,320 − $86,000 = $138.

b.

Year (1)	Book Value Start of Year (2)	Interest for Year = (2) X .14 (3)	Payment End of Year (Given) (4)	Amount (Reducing) Increasing Book Value = (3) − (4) (5)	Book Value End of Year = (2) + (5) (6)
1	$ 86,000	$12,040	$ 8,000	$ 4,040	$ 90,040
2	90,040	12,605	8,000	4,605	94,645
3	94,645	13,250*	108,000	(94,750)	(105)
OR 3	94,645	13,355*	108,000	(94,645)	-0-

*Interest would actually be recorded at $13,355 (= $108,000 − $94,645) so that the book value of the note reduces to zero at its maturity.

A.28 a. Terms of sale of 2/10, net/30 on a $100 gross invoice price, for example, mean that the interest rate is 2/98 for a 20-day period, because if the discount is not taken, a charge of $2 is levied for the use of $98. The $98 is used for 20 days (= 30 − 10), so the number of compounding periods in a year is 365/20 = 18.25. The expression for the exact rate of interest implied by 2/10, net 30 is $(1 + 2/98)^{(365/20)} − 1 = 1.020408^{18.25} − 1 = 44.59\%$.

b. Table 1 can be used. Use the 2-percent column and the 18-period row to see that the rate implied by 2/10, net 30 must be at least 42.825 percent (= 1.42825 − 1).

A.29 (Present value of a perpetuity).

$30,000 + ($10,000/.01) = $1,030,000.

A.30 Present value of future proceeds = .72845($35,000) + C = $35,000; where C represents the present value of the foregone interest payments. Table 2, 16-period row, 2-percent column = .72845.

C = $35,000 − $25,495.75 = $9,504.25.

 Solutions

A.31   a. Will: $24,000 + $24,000(3.31213) = $103,488.72 (Preferred).

Dower Option: $300,000/3 = $100,000.

b. Will: $24,000 + $24,000(3.03735) = $96,896.40.

Dower Option: $300,000/3 = $100,000 (Preferred).

A.32   Present value of deposit = $3.00.

Present value of $3.00, recorded 20 periods, have discounted at .50 percent per period = $3.00 × .90506 = $2.72.

Loss of $.28 (= $3.00 − $2.72) in foregone interest vs. Loss of $1.20 in price.

Net advantage of returnables is $.92.

A.33 $1.00(1.00 + .92456 + .85480 + .79051 + .73069) = $1.00 × 4.30036 = $4.30.

$4.30 − $3.50 = $.80.

A.34 $600/12 = $50 saved per month. $2,000/$50 = 40.0.

Present value of annuity of 1 discounted at 1 percent for 50 periods = 39.19612.

The present value of the annuity is $40 when the annuity lasts between 51 and 52 weeks. Dean Foods will recoup its investment in about one year.

A.35   a. $ 3,000,000 × 7.46944 = $22,408,320.

b. $ 3,000,000 × 7.36578 = $22,097,340
             500,000 × 1.69005 =   845,020
                                   $22,942,360

c. $ 2,000,000 × 7.36578 = $14,731,560
          1,000,000 × 2.40183 =   2,401,830
             500,000 × 1.69005 =   845,020
                                   $17,978,410

d. $17,978,410 × .20   = $ 3,595,680.

A.36   (Friendly Loan Company; find implicit interest rate; truth-in lending laws reduce the type of deception suggested by this problem.)

The effective interest rate is 19.86 percent and must be found by trial and error. The time line for this problem is:

which is equivalent, at least in terms of the implied interest rate, to:

Scanning Table 4, 5-period column, one finds the factor 2.99061, which is approximately 3.00, in the 20-percent column, so one can easily see that the implied interest rate is about 20 percent per year.

A.37   (Black & Decker Company; derive net present value/cash flows for decision to dispose of asset.)

$40,698. The $100,000 is gone and an economic loss of $50,000 was suffered because of the bad purchase. The issue now is do we want to swap a larger current tax loss and smaller future depreciation charges for no tax loss now and larger future depreciation charges.

    The new machine will lead to depreciation charges lower by $10,000 per year than the "old" machine and, hence, income taxes larger by $4,000. The present value of the larger taxes is $4,000 × 3.60478 (Table 4, 12 percent, 5 periods). Let S denote the proceeds from selling the old machine. The new current "outlay" to acquire the new machine is $50,000 − S − .40($100,000 − S) or $10,000 − .60S, so that for the new machine to be worthwhile:

$$\$10,000 - .60S < -\$14,419$$

OR

$$.6S > \$24,419$$

OR

$$S > \$40,698.$$

  A-7   **Solutions**

A.38   (Lynch Company/Bages Company; computation of present value of cash flows; untaxed acquisition, no change in tax basis of assets.)

a. $440,000 = $390,000 + $50,000 = $700,000 − $260,000.

b. $3,745,966 = $440,000 × 8.51356; see Table 4, 20-period column, 10-percent row.

A.39   (Lynch Company/Bages Company; computation of present value of cash flows; taxable acquisition, changing tax basis of assets.)

$4,258,199.   If the merger is taxable, then the value of the firm V satisfies:

(1) $$V = 8.51356 \times [\$700,000 − .40 (\$700,000 − V/20)]$$
       $$V = \$5,959,492 − \$2,383,797 + .17027V, \text{ or}$$
       $$.83972V = \$3,575,695, \text{ so}$$
       $$V = \$4,258,199.$$
To understand (1), observe that:

$$V = \text{Value of firm}$$

$$V/20 = \text{New depreciation charge}$$

$$\$700,000 − V/20 = \text{New taxable income}$$

$$.40(\$700,000 − V/20) = \text{New income tax payable, so}$$

$$\$700,000 − .40(\$700,000 − V/20) = \text{New aftertax cash flow to be capitalized at 10 percent for 20 years using present value factor 8.51356.}$$

A.40 (Rigazzi; present value of cash flows for investment project.)

a. $270,561.

Dec. 31	Cash Inflows		Cash Outflows		Total	Present Values at 12%	
	Operating Receipts	Salvage	Maintenance	Test Runs	(1) + (2) − (3) − (4)	Factor	Cash Flow
Year	(1)	(2)	(3)	(4)	(5)	(6)	(7)
0				$20,000	($20,000)	0.89286	($ 17,857)
1	$130,000		$ 60,000		70,000	0.79719	55,804
2	130,000		60,000		70,000	0.71178	49,825
3	130,000		60,000		70,000	0.63552	44,486
4	130,000		60,000		70,000	0.56743	39,720
5	130,000		100,000		30,000	0.50663	15,199
6	130,000		100,000		30,000	0.45235	13,570
7	130,000		100,000		30,000	0.40388	12,116
8	130,000	$30,000			160,000	0.36061	57,968
							$ 270,561

(7) = (5) × (6).

b. $78,868 = $250,000/3.16987.

A-9

Solutions

A.41   (Valuation of intangibles with perpetuity formulas.)

   a. $50 million = $4 million/.08.

   b. Increase.

   c. $66 2/3 million = $4 million/(.08 − .02).

   d. Increase.

   e. Decrease.